SOCIOLOGY

Snapshots and Portraits of Society

PINE FORGE PRESS TITLES OF RELATED INTEREST

Adventures in Social Research: Data Analysis Using SPSS for Windows *by Earl Babbie and Fred Halley*

Race, Ethnicity, Gender, and Class: The Sociology of Group Conflict and Change *by Joseph F. Healey*

Shifts in the Social Contract: Understanding Change in American Society *by Beth Rubin*

Sociological Snapshots: Seeing Social Structure and Change in Everyday Life, 2nd Ed., *by Jack Levin*

Diversity in America *by Vincent N. Parrillo*

The McDonaldization of Society, Rev. Ed., *by George Ritzer*

Expressing America: A Critique of the Global Credit Card Society *by George Ritzer*

Sociology: Exploring the Architecture of Everyday Life *by David M. Newman*

Sociology: Exploring the Architecture of Everyday Life (Readings) *by David M. Newman*

Sociology for a New Century

A Pine Forge Press Series edited by Charles Ragin, Wendy Griswold, and Larry Griffin

Global Inequalities *by York Bradshaw and Michael Wallace*

How Societies Change *by Daniel Chirot*

Cultures and Societies in a Changing World *by Wendy Griswold*

Crime and Disrepute *by John Hagan*

Gods in the Global Village *by Lester R. Kurtz*

Waves of Democracy *by John Markoff*

Development and Social Change: A Global Perspective *by Philip McMichael*

Constructing Social Research *by Charles C. Ragin*

Women and Men at Work *by Barbara Reskin and Irene Padavic*

Cities in a World Economy *by Saskia Sassen*

The Pine Forge Press Series in Crime and Society

Edited by George S. Bridges, Robert D. Crutchfield, Joseph G. Weis

Readings: Crime

Readings: Criminal Justice

Readings: Juvenile Delinquency

SOCIOLOGY

Snapshots and Portraits of Society

Jack Levin and Arnold Arluke

Northeastern University

Pine Forge Press

Thousand Oaks, California ▪ London ▪ New Delhi

For information, address:

Pine Forge Press
A Sage Publications Company
2455 Teller Road
Thousand Oaks, California 91320
(805) 499-4224
E-mail: sales@pfp.sagepub.com

Sage Publications Ltd.
6 Bonhill Street
London EC2A 4PU
United Kingdom

Sage Publications India Pvt. Ltd.
M-32 Market
Greater Kailash I
New Delhi 110 048 India

Production: Scratchgravel Publishing Services
Designer: Lisa S. Mirski
Typesetter: Scratchgravel Publishing Services
Cover: Paula Shuhert and Graham Metcalfe
Production Manager: Rebecca Holland

Printed in the United States of America
96 97 98 99 00 10 9 8 7 6 5 4 3 2 1

Library of Congress Cataloging-in-Publication Data

Levin, Jack, 1941–
Sociology : snapshots and portraits of society / Jack Levin and Arnold Arluke.
p. cm.
Includes bibliographical references and index.
ISBN 0-8039-9084-7 (pbk. : alk. paper)
1. Sociology. I. Arluke, Arnold. II. Title.
HM51.L3588 1996
301—dc20 95-37238
CIP

About the Authors

Jack Levin is Professor of Sociology and Criminology at Northeastern University. He has authored or co-authored a number of books, including *Elementary Statistics in Social Research; The Functions of Discrimination and Prejudice; Gossip: The Inside Scoop; Hate Crimes: The Rising Tide of Bigotry and Bloodshed;* and *Overkill: Mass Murder and Serial Killing Exposed.* His work has appeared in professional journals, including *Youth and Society, Criminology, The Gerontologist,* and *Sex Roles,* as well as in *The New York Times, The Boston Globe,* the *Detroit Free Press,* and *The Chicago Tribune.* Levin received Northeastern University's Excellence in Teaching Award and was recently honored by the Council for Advancement and Support of Education as its Professor of the Year in Massachusetts.

Arnold Arluke is Professor of Sociology and Anthropology at Northeastern University. He has co-authored several books: *The Making of Rehabilitation: A Political Economy of Medical Specialization; Gossip: The Inside Scoop;* and *Regarding Animals: Social Studies of Other Species.* His work has appeared in professional journals, including *The Journal of Contemporary Ethnography, Qualitative Sociology, Sociological Quarterly, Journal of Health and Social Behavior,* and *Human Organization.* He has also received Northeastern University's Excellence in Teaching Award.

About the Publisher

Pine Forge Press is a new educational publisher, dedicated to publishing innovative books and software throughout the social sciences. On this and any other of our publications, we welcome your comments, ideas, and suggestions. Please call or write to:

Pine Forge Press
A Sage Publications Company
2455 Teller Road
Thousand Oaks, California 91320
(805) 499-4224
Fax (805) 499-7881
E-mail: sales@pfp.sagepub.com

CONTENTS

PREFACE

Instructors of introductory sociology usually hope that they will kindle in their students some enthusiasm for the contributions of the field, but the question is always *how.* We wrote this book with two specific outcomes in mind, both of which relate to the general goal of getting students to understand and appreciate the sociological perspective:

1. To serve as a springboard to more abstract thinking about society
2. To encourage students' interest in learning more about the field of sociology

An important function of sociology is to help broaden the educational experience of all college students but especially those in fields of study that may be narrow in scope and purpose. One measure of the effectiveness of an introductory sociology course is the extent to which the students come to view their world with a sociological eye. In this regard, we take the visual metaphor quite literally. In fact, each chapter of this book is introduced by a photographic essay posing a sociological question.

When students truly "see" the sociology in things, they are also developing their abstract thinking skills—the very skills that are of vital importance in any job or career. Unfortunately, students too often receive from their introductory courses little help in cultivating their abilities to think at an abstract level. Instead, they are asked to read and memorize long lists of terms that seem more to obfuscate and complicate rather than to clarify reality.

The "snapshots" in this book are casual and informal, but they are designed to ease students into the formal world of sociological analysis. Each snapshot relates some abstract sociological concepts to the concrete problems confronting ordinary people. Social structure, culture, socialization, the group experience, institutions, deviance, social inequality, collective behavior, and social change are introduced as major variables but almost always in the context of everyday life.

At the same time, the entire book serves as a springboard from the informal, concrete world of the student into the more formal, abstract world of sociological theory and method. In order to accomplish this, each chapter contains a "seeing" essay that introduces, defines, and discusses many of the major sociological ideas. This essay builds the "bridge" between the informal world of the snapshots and the formal world of the "portraits," a selection of research articles taken from the sociological literature. The portraits are either journal articles or chapters from larger studies authored by social scientists, representing the variety of methods and concepts existing in the field. Although they are similar to the selections found in traditional readers, most of the portraits were specifically chosen by us because of their appeal to students. Many deal with problems that students grapple with (for example, drug use, cults, acquaintance rape, AIDS, and cheating on exams) and activities that students engage in (dating and marriage, football, television watching, work, fraternities and sororities, and rock concerts). Other portraits focus on larger social issues that bear indirectly, but significantly, on the lives of students (for example, crime, aging, discrimination, poverty, health, and civil disturbances).

Students also need active ways to develop the ability to see and articulate abstractions and to analyze data about social reality. The physical and biological sciences usually include a lab component in their courses, which gives students opportunities for "hands-on" experiences. Because sociology should attempt to do the same, each chapter of this book concludes with ideas for student writing and research assignments. There is nothing fancy or complicated about the proposed tasks. They are designed to encourage students to *begin* to write from a sociological perspective or to collect data about their everyday lives.

To the extent that the first outcome is realized, students will, we hope, also achieve the second: They will be eager to learn more about the sociological perspective. Some will take more sociology courses or even major in the discipline.

Unlike many other fields, sociology cannot simply depend on students' prior familiarity with the study of behavior to provide a background of information or to enhance their interest. In high school, very few had the opportunity to select a sociology course. Some may have a vague idea that sociologists study human behavior or that sociology is somehow related to social work, but that was probably the extent of their knowledge of the discipline.

Partly as a result of their lack of familiarity, only a small number of students declare a sociology major upon entering college. More typically, students who enroll in introductory sociology courses represent a range of disciplines and interests. It is therefore a major function of the introductory sociology course—for many undergraduates, perhaps their only point of formal contact with sociology—to convince students to take upper-level courses in the field. This places a special burden on instructors to provide a positive learning climate, one in which students' interest is encouraged.

This book has been a joint effort, but it required a division of labor. Jack Levin wrote the snapshots and bridging essays, and Arnold Arluke selected and edited the portraits and, in addition, took the photos and assembled the photo essays.

A number of people were important in making *Sociology: Snapshots and Portraits of Society* a reality. We are grateful to Laura Freid, Keith Botsford, Lori Calabro, and Janice Friedman at *Bostonia.* We also thank David Gibson at *Northeastern University Magazine,* Rachelle Cohen at the *Boston Herald,* and Marjorie Pritchard at *The Boston Globe.*

We depended a great deal on the insightful comments and suggestions of the following reviewers: Paul Baker, Illinois State University, and Mary Rogers, University of West Florida. Jamie Fox, Earl Rubington, Billy Brittingham, and Bill Levin were generous with both their encouragement and their ideas. We thank the following people for their willingness to serve as subjects of the photo essays: Maryanna Antoine, Elvis Cordova, Ron Corona, Christopher Crowell, Emma Faber, Glenn and Daniel Gritzer, Dayna and Paula Hollins, Robert Iorio, Catherine Kasongo, Jennifer Kelley, Alan Klein, Mary Mello and Cody, Jason Legoro, John Lund, Catherine Meyers, Gina Mastromattei, Jane, Pearl, Ruby, and Angelo Nathanson, Laura Rice, Doug Robare, and Julie Worth.

Steve Rutter of Pine Forge Press made all the difference. If he made us slave over a "hot" PC, then it was worth every minute. No editor could have done more.

We are grateful to our families and friends—Flea, Michael, Bonnie, and Andrea Levin, Lauren Rolfe, Nat, Linda, Lisa, Adam, and Seth Arluke, and Lakshma and Julian Chiabella. They have been more than patient, tolerating all of our idiosyncrasies.

We dedicate this book to the thousands of students we have had the pleasure of teaching. They have taught us a great deal about sociology and about life.

Jack Levin
Arnold Arluke

The Sociological Eye

For both of us, photography is a favorite hobby. As amateurs, we've never tried to take formal or posed pictures. We recognize the value of portraits, but neither of us has the expertise or the equipment necessary to create the expensive and carefully crafted family and personal portraits produced by a specialized commercial studio.

Instead, the heart of our shared interest—what we have always found most satisfying—is the art of taking snapshots: informal, often candid photos of everyday life. We particularly enjoy capturing on film the problems experienced by ordinary people as well as the spontaneous, unguarded moments in the lives of loved ones.

Many of the essays in this book are snapshots too, but they are sociological snapshots. Each one depicts a social situation encountered by the people we meet every day—the circumstances of ordinary people caught up in ordinary (and occasionally not so ordinary) social events. Thus, you will find essays about family and class reunions, television soap operas, behavior in elevators, children who have unpopular names, the people who do dirty work in occupations, spectators at football games, bystander apathy, people who act in deviant ways while driving in automobiles, heartburn, fads through the generations, popular rumors about shopping malls, contemporary images of fat people, and so on. At the extreme end, you will also discover a few essays concerning such topics as the death penalty, mass killers, and hate crimes. (Sadly, in today's society, even ordinary people have to be aware of such extraordinary topics.)

The snapshots in this book are informal in another sense as well: Most take a casual approach with respect to the presentation of statistical evidence. A number appeared originally in *Bostonia* (a magazine of "culture and ideas"). Others were opinion pieces that were earlier published in newspapers. Some were written specifically for this book. But all of them were designed to bridge the gap between academic sociology and everyday life. As a result, in every snapshot you will find a mix of both social science and journalism. There are very few references, quantitative data, and formal evidence, the kind that you typically expect to find in an introductory sociology textbook. Sometimes the essays present only anecdotal confirmation—illustrations and examples rather than hard statistical fact. Some are speculative pieces about changes in society or about the future. Others seek to throw new perspective on aspects of society that may have seemed obvious to you before. None is meant to replace the technical journal articles written for professional sociologists. All are meant to help you see the contribution of the sociological approach and to ease you as gently as possible into the more formal world of sociological analysis.

After teaching classes in sociology for a number of years, we have noticed that many of our students are troubled by the abstractness of sociological insight. They often complain about not being able to see how social structure touches their everyday lives or how culture contributes to ordinary events. They are asked to examine not the structure of individuals, but rather the structure of entire groups, organizations, institutions, communities, or societies.

What we believe is missing, from a pedagogical viewpoint, are the snapshots of culture and social structure—society—that bridge the gap existing in many students' minds between what may appear to be vast sociological abstractions, on the one hand, and common experiences, on the other. This book relates abstract sociological concepts to the concrete experiences involving ordinary individuals in our society.

There is one final sense in which the snapshots in this book are informal. They often reflect, frequently in an explicit way, the ideas that the "photographer" considers to be valuable or problematic. In taking pictures of the world around us, we often photograph our families and friends, and occasionally the unusual circumstances of daily life, but always with a point of view implicit in our choice of subject. In other words, our snapshots reflect our values—the things that we appreciate or cherish. They are often intended to preserve and understand the images of the people we love, the problems in everyday life that bother us, or the things we believe need changing.

Like all scientists, sociologists have values. They are human beings too, having grown up in a particular social setting and having been exposed selectively to certain kinds of ideas.

Max Weber, a turn-of-the-century German sociologist who contributed a great deal to our understanding of religion, inequality, and social change, strongly believed that sociology could be value-free. He fully recognized that the subjects sociologists chose to study were frequently influenced by their personal values. For example, it would not be surprising that a sociologist who grew up in extreme poverty might decide to study inequality; a rape victim might research the causes of sexual violence; an African American sociologist might specialize in race relations; and so on.

But when Weber talked about value-free sociology, he really wasn't talking about subject selection. Rather, he meant that sociologists must not permit their values, their biases, or their personal opinions to interfere with their analysis of that subject. They must instead attempt to be objective in collecting and analyzing information; they must seek out and consider *all* the evidence, even that which might contradict their personal opinions. Weber would have advised that we must "let the chips fall where they may." Hopefully, we have not allowed our personal biases to determine the conclusions that we reach in our snapshots—just their subjects.

But please don't be fooled into believing that the snapshots in this book represent the end point for sociological thinking and research. On the contrary, they are only the beginning. Of course, all of them are based on either sociological theorizing, sociological data, or both. But their informality, brevity, and casualness also betray a serious weakness that they share. All of the snapshots lack the methodological rigor and the long-term, painstaking effort that typically characterize the formal, carefully crafted research articles in the field of sociology.

Just so you don't get an unduly narrow notion of what sociology is all about, this book also contains a set of portraits. In each section there are formal articles taken from either professional academic journals or important books in the field. In each portrait you will find a conscientious and detailed study of some important social phenomenon. The portraits differ from the snapshots in their attention to particulars, in their effort to reconstruct every important aspect of their method, and in their attempt to present a systematic and thorough analysis of a sociological issue or problem. The sociologists who created the portraits in this book spent a good deal of their time fidgeting with ideas, retouching words and phrases, and refining their descriptions. On the whole, the portraits are more challenging than the snapshots. But, then, you should also get more out of them. The portraits were written for other professional sociologists to use in their own teaching and research.

Thus, each section of the book contains both snapshots and portraits. To get you from one to the other, we have also included a bridging essay for each section. This essay discusses the snapshots and portraits in the context of the major sociological ideas related to the topic at hand. The bridging essays emphasize the importance of the sociological literature. But they also ease the transition from the brief and informal snapshots to the more challenging and lengthier portraits in each section.

Thus far we have employed the photographic metaphor to distinguish the "snapshots" from the "portraits." Yet, thanks to the photography of Arnie Arluke, we have included photographs in a quite literal manner. In each section you will find a photo essay organized around a particular important question related to the topic.

Each section of *Sociology: Snapshots and Portraits of Society* has been organized in a consistent format. First, there is the photographic essay. Second, there are the snapshots themselves. Third, there is a bridging essay in which the basic sociological concepts are defined, discussed, illustrated, and then linked with the snapshots and portraits for that particular section. Next, there are the portraits. And, finally, there are ideas for student writing and research assignments in "Developing Your Own Snapshots." Most of these assignments require you to apply a sociological eye to your everyday lives or to begin, in a preliminary way, to collect data using a sociological method.

Now that you understand the "snapshots and portraits" part of the title of this book, we ask that you stop a moment longer and consider the "sociological" part as well. As you probably already surmise—even if you have never taken a course in it—psychology deals with the behavior and personality of individual human beings. Thus, psychologists might study a person's attitudes, hostility, attractiveness, moods, helpfulness, learning styles, prejudices, and so on. In contrast, sociologists focus not on any one individual but on what happens between individuals when they interact. Thus, sociologists might study the relationship between husband and wife, interaction in a small task group at work, peer groups in a high school, family relations, prison culture, relations between managers and workers, and so on.

In order to explain the unique and important contribution of sociology, I'd like to separate myself from my co-author and reveal a little bit about my daily routine. Every time I drive from my suburban home to my office in the city, I think about how painfully predictable and orderly my daily commuting routine has become. I live some 25 miles from downtown; so I have plenty of time, while sitting in bumper-to-bumper traffic, to think. In my darker, more impatient moments, I play "what if" games: "What if I had sold my house and moved into the city?" "What if I were teaching in a college located in a remote, rural area?" "What if I had taken the train into work?" "What if I could change my schedule to avoid the rush-hour commute?" Would I still be stuck in traffic? Probably not.

To a sociologist, the interesting thing about my predicament is the fact that it is shared by so many other people. This, of course, explains why traffic jams happen daily. Tens of thousands of residents have similar work schedules, live in the suburbs, and drive their cars to work in the city. They get up at about the same time every morning, take a shower, brush their teeth, and have a cup of coffee. Then they take to the roads—most of them at the same time that I do!

Sociologists seek to understand the predictable and patterned aspects of what happens between people when they get together; sociologists' term for this is *social structure*. And, in the case of sitting in maddening bumper-to-bumper traffic every day, social structure has become my biggest headache.

The negative consequences of social structure can be seen in other ways as well. In the snapshot "Better Late Than Never," we see that college students are usually expected to "bloom" on time. That is, they are supposed to excel academically from an early age and to enter college by the age of 18 or 19. Indeed, if they vary from the expected pattern, students are given a name. They are called "late bloomers."

Of course, whether or not a student is ultimately successful in the classroom (and in a career) is partially a matter of individual effort, talent, and luck. But there is definitely an important sociological side to being successful as well: You probably won't excel academically if you are denied the opportunity to do so.

Traditionally, men were much more likely than women, regardless of grades and test scores, to be given the opportunity for higher education. Similarly, it was far more probable for individuals who were born into wealthy circumstances to attend college than for their economically less fortunate counterparts.

Opportunity also varies by society. In most societies, blooming on time is strictly enforced, no matter how much potential an individual might have. You go to college either at the age of 18 or not at all; you either get As and Bs by the time you're 12 years old or receive a trade school education at best. In American society we still prefer blooming on schedule—most college students fit the mold, but we also allow some flexibility in timing. In fact, 25 percent of all college students are now over 30; and almost 20 percent of college freshmen had Cs and Ds in high school.

Of course, social structure also has desirable aspects. Because social life is somewhat predictable, we are able to count on instructors meeting their classes, doctors making their appointments, final exams beginning and ending pretty much on time, and so on. Because of the strict scheduling of time in an educational context, school administrators definitely benefit: They can predict with some certainty precisely how many textbooks, classrooms, and teachers they will need for an upcoming academic year. In fact, it would not be too much of an exaggeration to suggest that life without some degree of social order—social structure—would be utterly chaotic and therefore impossible over the long term. Perhaps the rush-hour commute is unpleasant, but at least we can be fairly sure that classes will be held when scheduled and that shops, stores, and restaurants will be open when they are expected to be.

In "Heartburn and Modern Times" it is suggested that even basic biological processes (the regurgitation of stomach acid back into the esophagus that causes the burning sensation we call heartburn) may be influenced by a weakening of social structure. French sociologist Emile Durkheim, who lived at the turn of the century, used the term *anomie* to describe a social situation in which the rules of everyday life have broken down and individuals become confused as to how to behave. Because of a sudden and dramatic change in circumstances, their old patterns of social interaction are disturbed and new patterns have not yet been established. Individuals caught in an anomic condition are therefore at a loss to know how they are expected to behave. Social life is, for them, no longer patterned, shared, or predictable.

A state of anomie can be brought on by any of several different circumstances: war, a physical disaster, a dramatic drop in income, or the loss of family and friends. Communities that attract large numbers of transients, drifters, and migrants often experience anomic conditions. For example, many who move great distances from home for the sake of a job have left behind all sources of guidance and support—friends, extended kin, church, fraternal organizations, and so on. After arriving in Los Angeles or Miami or Houston, they may have no place to turn for counsel or advice.

In his classic work, Durkheim discovered that anomie actually provokes some individuals to commit suicide. More precisely, he found that the rate of suicide in an area increases during periods of rapid social or economic change and also among those who are recently divorced or widowed. If anomie affects the rate of suicide, it should be less than shocking to discover that anomie produces high rates of antacid use as well. Indeed, anomic circumstances seem to be associated with all forms of pathology including crime, suicide, and even heartburn. Notice, by the way, that we address the *rate* of pathology, including antacid use, rather than whether any individual experiences heartburn. Thus, we are not suggesting that the newcomers in any metropolitan area necessarily suffer heartburn (though this is possible)—only that their presence in large numbers will increase the likelihood that the heartburn rate is generally high. Maybe it's the transients and drifters who have heartburn; or perhaps they give it to more stable members of the population. As sociologists, we are characterizing the metropolitan area as a whole, even if we never look at an individual case. In sum, the *state* of some characteristic of the area (its degree of migration) may have some influence on its *rate* of acid indigestion, not to mention its rate of suicide, homicide, and divorce.

By the way, the two essays in this introductory section are snapshots. You won't find any portraits until you get to the first substantive section, in which we discuss the concept of culture.

SNAPSHOT

Better Late Than Never

Individual Success Doesn't Always Follow a Strict Schedule

Dr. William Levin is professor of sociology at Bridgewater State College, an award-winning teacher and the prolific author of a number of respected books in his field. He also flunked the eighth grade.

I met Bill Levin almost 20 years ago as his master's thesis adviser in what was then the School of Public Communication at Boston University. We hit it off almost immediately. Not only did we share the same last name (though not the same parents), but we also discovered we were both educational late bloomers—mediocre high school students who later developed into serious-minded, dedicated college students. (I can't say that I flunked the eighth grade, but I can still "brag" about being on academic probation during my first year as an undergraduate at American International College.)

Bill Levin's escape from educational mediocrity is far from unique. In fact, there are thousands of educational late bloomers who go on to become brilliant college students. Thousands more interrupt their collegiate pursuits, only to return years later. In fact, we live in a society where second chances are fast becoming a way of life, especially in the educational field.

We tolerate late blooming, but do we know why? Trying to answer just that question, Bill and I recently talked with a number of college students. And in interviews with both late and early bloomers, we were able to identify four important factors: ability, opportunity, some triggering event, and a period of readiness to accept change in which social support is present.

Ability is a prerequisite for almost any success, whenever it occurs in the life cycle. But for late bloomers, ability or talent has an important emotional component. Those who lack intellectual capacity more than make up for it with commitment and involvement. Many of the late bloomers we interviewed were, as high school students, almost fanatically devoted to a cause, a hobby, a job, a sport, or an idea. For example, while in high school, one late bloomer became committed to physical exercise. Hard-pressed to find the time to study, he still managed to jog, run, lift weights, bike, and swim on a regular basis. Another student was heavily involved with illicit drugs. He spent hours in the library, but not doing his homework. Instead, he read and researched articles related to his addiction. Then there was the mechanical engineering major who now has a 3.6 grade point average but had only a 2.5 average in high school. However, he was a member of his school's debating team and chorus in addition to working more than 20 hours per week.

In a sense, the presence of emotional commitment in high school may indicate later academic potential. The question is, how do we transfer that commitment from an extracurricular activity, athletics, or a cause to the college classroom?

Part of the answer involves the second factor in late blooming: the presence of opportunity. Almost everywhere outside the United States, the timing of academic success is inflexible. Students must achieve high grades and achievement test scores early in their academic careers; they must also enter college by a specified age. Thus, in England, India, and Japan, students who have not excelled by the time they reach high school are effectively disqualified as college material. What is more, students are expected to enroll in college by their late teens and are not given opportunities to do so later in life, regardless of their potential. Even after the educational reforms of the post–World War II era, highly structured lines of study separating high school attendance from access to college remain the modal pattern around the rest of the world. In most countries, students not enrolled in an appropriate high school or curriculum are ineligible to attend college.

In sharp contrast, the American educational system gives students a second, third, and even a fourth chance for a college education. If they or their parents are able to pay the bills, even students who have low grades in high school are granted an opportunity to enroll in higher education. One-third of all colleges have open admission policies. Moreover, hundreds of thousands of students who begin at community and junior colleges later transfer into four-year institutions. The increasing number of women who return to college after raising children provides a significant new pool of potential late bloomers. Similarly, the increasing acceptance of midlife career changes has created an entirely new category of late bloomers who continue their education after spending decades in the workforce.

But capacity and opportunity are not always enough for late blooming to occur. Bill Levin, for example, had the opportunity to attend college because his parents saved the money to send him. And like millions of other middle-class students, he went to college primarily because that's what was expected of him. But for Levin and others like him, the commitment to education materialized only because of a triggering event—a reward, a punishment, or both that provided a rationale for making a profound change in lifestyle.

For some of the late bloomers we studied, that triggering event was a work experience during college. Some suggested that a job showed them, perhaps for the first time, the strong connection between grades and the kind of work they were likely to do after they graduated. Even an unpleasant job during college was motivating; it forced them to deal with the likelihood that, unless things changed drastically, this was the kind of boring, monotonous work they might expect to be doing for the rest of their lives.

Other late bloomers pointed to more positive events. Some, such as Bill Levin, gave credit to a great teacher who had inspired them to study or a course that was new and exciting to them. Others were a few years older than their classmates because they had dropped out to work for a year or two, transferred from another college, or spent a few years in the military. Peers also made a difference. For example, one late-blooming college senior reported that a bright, achievement-oriented girlfriend had motivated him by threatening to end their relationship if he didn't "buckle down."

If the series of triggering events is effective, a student enters a period of readiness to change in which social support and encouragement become extremely important. During this stage, the academic community gradually becomes an important reference group, a source of norms and values as well as guidance. The student frequently changes his or her major based on personal interest rather than practicality or parental guidance. For the first time, grades are used as markers of personal worth and school takes on primary importance.

The individual is ready to bloom. He talks informally with instructors during their office hours and after classes; she discusses a lecture with her friends. He spends more time in the library; she writes for the campus newspaper and runs for student government. In this stage, instructors, advisers, and friends can make a huge difference. The student is ready to bloom, but he or she still looks for and needs the help of others on campus.

The time I first met Bill Levin, he had recently discovered the social sciences. Within a year he had become totally immersed in graduate student culture. Like so many of his early-blooming classmates, he read, talked, and slept sociology; it became the focal point of his life.

It is legitimate to ask whether it is worth focusing so much attention on late bloomers. After all, aren't they less successful than their counterparts who achieve "on time"? Actually, one of the few studies to compare late and early bloomers concludes just the opposite: Scientists whose educational achievements came relatively late were more productive than scientists who achieved early. Educational burnout may be less severe for late bloomers not only because they begin later to achieve in earnest, but also because they are more likely to achieve for their own sake rather than for the sake of a parent. The success of a late bloomer may be particularly sweet. You've heard the expression "Better late than never." Have you ever considered the possibility "Better late than early," at least where education is concerned?

Given our present state of knowledge, we are not able to predict who will and will not turn out to be a late bloomer. Until our theories and methods permit such accurate predictions, we must treat every student as a potential late bloomer. This means that we must never give up on anyone. Bill Levin is living proof, and he has plenty of company.

SNAPSHOT Heartburn and Modern Times

Don't Blame the Tex-Mex

According to a Gallup survey conducted several years ago, the ailment known as heartburn is a chronic source of pain and suffering for almost 62 million American adults. Fifty-four percent of them pin the blame on spicy foods; others single out overeating, indigestion, gas, or poor diet. Many regularly take an antacid in pill or liquid form.

For the sufferer, heartburn clearly has a biological basis. It frequently occurs after a meal when acid backs up from the stomach into the esophagus, causing a burning sensation in the chest or throat. From a sociological point of view, however, there may be a good deal more to heartburn than just the discomfort of spicy foods and excessive acidity. Like many other physical ailments, the symptoms of heartburn may be influenced by the stresses and strains frequently associated with residential mobility undertaken to enhance a career or supposedly improve the quality of life.

I ranked 197 metropolitan areas of the United States on the "National Rolaids Heartburn Index," a measure based on an area's per capita sales of all brands of over-the-counter antacids, and then compared these metropolitan areas on a grid of important social, economic, and demographic characteristics. I found striking regional differences in heartburn rates. For example, despite their reputation for having a "laid-back" pace of life, most major cities located in the Far West—for example, San Francisco, Sacramento, Fresno, Seattle, Los Angeles, and Phoenix—had particularly high rates of antacid use. Indeed, 40 percent of all high-heartburn metropolitan areas were located in western states. Also having particularly high rates were such southern cities as Charlotte, North Carolina; Richmond, Virginia; and New Orleans, Louisiana.

By contrast, midwestern cities had extremely low rates of heartburn. Green Bay, Wisconsin; Sioux City, Iowa; Columbia, Missouri; and Fort Smith, Arkansas, all placed close to the bottom. In fact, almost half of the 40 metropolitan areas with the lowest rates of heartburn were located in midwestern states. But the lowest heartburn rate of any city in the United States was found in El Paso, Texas, despite that city's penchant for spicy Tex-Mex cuisine.

Data on northeastern cities were also surprising. Overall, those cities seldom exhibited either high or low heartburn levels. Only 11 percent of both the highest-heartburn metropolitan areas and the lowest-heartburn areas were located in the Northeast. New York City, for example, registered only a moderate rate of heartburn, though it is well known for its fast-paced, hectic way of life.

How can these regional variations in rates of antacid use be explained? Differences in diet and physical environment might contribute to the overall level of heartburn. Over-the-counter antacid use may not be an accurate measure of heartburn (a few people without heartburn take these antacids, and many with heartburn do not).

Despite such methodological problems, a major contributing factor to the rate of heartburn in an area can be found in what might be called "gold rush fever." All of the cities with a high incidence of heartburn have recently experienced tremendous population growth as a result of migration from other cities and regions of the country. For the sake of a job or a better way of life, former midwesterners and easterners have "gone west." They have packed their bags, left behind family and friends, and traveled thousands of miles to cities on the West Coast. This may explain why the most attractive and appealing metropolitan areas also have the highest rates of heartburn. They attract individuals who are dissatisfied with their present lives and are willing to move in order to enhance them.

Cities with stable populations are more likely to have a low incidence of heartburn. These cities appeal less to individuals who want to increase their economic opportunities. In such cities, construction comes to a standstill as the demand for real estate remains constant. Of the top 15 housing markets, not one is located in a low-heartburn metropolitan area, but five are in the high-heartburn group. The city of El Paso never experienced the oil-based boom-and-bust cycle of heartburn-plagued Texas cities such as Dallas or Houston.

Wherever there are large numbers of transient, rootless people, there are also likely to be anxiety, stress, frustration . . . and high levels of heartburn. Sociologists call this state of affairs *anomie,* a social condition that prevails where newcomers to an area are confused about the rules of living. When things are anomic, there is widespread disorganization and isolation, a breakdown in the shared expectations governing social life.

One indicator of anomie is the presence of social pathology. Thus, high-heartburn areas were more likely than their low-heartburn counterparts to also have high rates of violent crime, divorce, and alcohol consumption. Heartburn may be another, albeit more subtle, indicator that something is wrong.

Other researchers have noticed that pathology varies by specific metropolitan area. Social psychologist Robert Levine of California State University recently compared cities in terms of their level of psychological stress. He found that 6 of his 10 cities with the highest stress were located in the Far West. He determined that stress was especially high in metropolitan areas that contained large numbers of migrants, residents who were born out of state. Not coincidentally, the western states had the greatest percentage of migrants; gold rush fever strikes again!

Census Bureau data suggest that the population flow to the Far West may be on the verge of reversing itself. In the future, easterners and midwesterners may cease exporting their heartburn to other areas of the country. Who knows? New York, Philadelphia, or Boston might even become the next heartburn capital of the United States.

DEVELOPING YOUR OWN SNAPSHOTS *About Social Structure*

1. *Writing topic:* In the essay about educational late bloomers, we presented several factors that seem to contribute to succeeding behind schedule, including ability, opportunity, a precipitating incident, and social support. Think of someone you know (perhaps a friend or a relative) who possessed the talent to bloom educationally, but never did. In a short essay, explain how his or her position in the social structure (gender identity, age, socioeconomic status, sexual orientation, religion) may have helped prevent his or her educational success.
2. *Writing topic:* In the essay about heartburn, I focused on per capita antacid use by metropolitan area. How do you think a psychologist who was interested in the causes of heartburn would conduct this study? Would he or she examine a number of metropolitan areas? What do you think he or she would look for in individuals who suffer from heartburn? What conclusions might a psychologist draw, and how might they differ from those derived by a sociologist?
3. *Research topic:* One measure of the importance of being on time is just how precisely individuals keep their clocks and watches set. The importance of precise time varies from society to society, so the precision of watches and clocks may also vary from place to place. Because it is unreasonable to ask you to travel to another society, instead compare the clocks and watches in your own home, apartment, or dormitory floor with those in someone else's home, apartment, or dormitory floor. (You might, for example, compare men's and women's floors to determine the influence of gender on the importance of time. Or you might compare different kinds of office buildings.) In writing, record the error (from actual time) on each clock or watch and then take an average for each place. Also include the number of watches and clocks in a state of disrepair. Now identify the winner!

4. *Writing topic:* Instant millionaires—those who win the lottery—aren't always as happy as you might believe. Many of them experience tremendous anomie. In a short essay, speculate as to exactly how the lives of instant millionaires might abruptly change . . . for the worse. Also indicate what you think they might do to minimize the "pain" of suddenly being wealthy.
5. *Research topic:* Interview someone who has recently experienced a dramatic change in lifestyle: an individual who has moved thousands of miles, has been recently widowed or divorced, or has just married. (It would be great, but very difficult, to interview an instant millionaire.) Try to determine whether the abrupt change in this person's way of life has had any negative effects of which he or she is aware. Where does he go for help and guidance? Is she more anxious about the future? How does he fill the hours of the day with meaningful activities? If the person has had little or no trouble adjusting, you might want to determine why. Through friendships, religion, community organizations, or a commitment to work, has the person found a new source of structure in his or her life?

CHAPTER 1

Culture

WIN EVERYTIME YOU PLAY
STOP & SHOP
TRIPLE WINNER GAME
AT STOP & SHOP!
The
Jimmy Fund
9
4
1
8
380
115

SNAPSHOT

The Immaculate Americans

Being Cleaner Doesn't Mean We're Better

Body odor is big business. Every year we immaculate Americans spend more money on deodorants and mouthwashes than we contribute to the United Way. In addition, we probably pass more time scrubbing, washing, spraying, bathing, squirting, and gargling than any other people in the history of the world. Americans, in fact, learn from an early age that cleanliness is considered next to godliness—a sign that an individual is morally pure and sinless. No wonder Americans spend more than $1 billion annually on soap; it's part of our culture.

In other parts of the world, however, we are regarded as neurotically concerned with our personal cleanliness. In some European countries, for example, American tourists are easily identified by their demands for a room with a private bath. Meanwhile, their European counterparts more often stay in rooms where they wash up daily in a small sink and take their baths down the hall. In many countries anyone caught showering twice a day would probably be regarded as either eccentric or ill.

Notwithstanding our present-day preoccupation, Americans can hardly take credit (or blame) for inventing a concern for cleanliness. Arab intermediaries, in arranging a marriage, sometimes rejected a prospective bride who didn't "smell nice." Sniffing and nose kissing have long been practiced by Eskimos, Philippine Islanders, and Samoans who recognized the desire for a pleasant odor. And bathing for purification is an ancient custom practiced by the early Hebrews, Muslims, and Hindus.

Medieval royalty took baths, but only on occasion. In England, for example, King John bathed three times a year, always before a major religious festival. But church authorities and medical practitioners in the Middle Ages generally frowned on bathing, denying the general population access to the few existing baths. Instead, medieval people used strong perfumes in order to disinfect the air and reduce the onslaught of black plague. Even after the Middle Ages, Queen Elizabeth I of England bathed only monthly (whether she needed it or not). Major efforts to enhance personal cleanliness for the masses really weren't made until the mid-19th century. During the Industrial Revolution, the British were the plumbing pioneers. For those who lacked private facilities, the state built public bathhouses consisting of individual bathrooms with centrally controlled plumbing. By the early part of the 20th century, however, cultural diffusion had taken effect, and America had taken the lead in developing private bathrooms for most citizens. For the first time in history, the home bathroom was no longer viewed as a status symbol but instead was regarded as a middle-class necessity.

Of course, everything is relative when it comes to culture, and some Americans have acquired such lofty cultural standards today that they think foreigners smell. Perhaps they are right, at least when judged by a national norm that refuses to tolerate any body odor at all. The odorous outsiders (who probably smell pretty much as human beings are intended to) are then regarded by some Americans as dirty, slovenly, or perhaps even morally impure.

The bias is not new. Odor has often been used to discredit entire groups of people. During the Middle Ages, for example, European Jews were widely believed to have drunk the blood of Christian children as part of the Passover ritual in order to rid themselves of an "odor of evil." It was also rumored that upon their conversion to Christianity, the Jewish malodor miraculously disappeared.

Closer to home, African Americans, Latinos, Hawaiians, and Native Americans have all been stereotyped in cultural images at one time or another as smelling different. And one of the most offensive olfactory stereotypes is that of elderly citizens—especially nursing home residents—who are too often portrayed as reeking from incontinence, indifference, and the ravages of age.

Just how accurate are such cultural images of group differences in odor? Is it possible that the members of different ethnic and racial groups really do have distinctive smells? Consider, for example, the possible effect on the quality and quantity of perspiration of dietary differences or of jobs requiring strenuous physical activity. Such factors do vary by group; they might even differ by ethnicity or social class. Yet the perception of such group differences in odor seems out of proportion to their actual occurrence, if they happen at all.

More likely, the charge of minority malodor is perpetuated by bigots who are eager to justify discriminatory treatment against a group of people by dehumanizing them. The reasoning is simple enough: Animals, not human beings, give off a stench. Human beings must be treated according to the rules of civilized society; but animals can be mistreated, even slaughtered, at will. The members of group X give off a stench (they don't bathe and live like pigs); therefore, they can be mistreated.

The sociological question is answered best through a recognition that perception of odor is only one component in the much larger repertoire of cultural racism. Our beliefs about various groups are often supported by deeply rooted emotions that are acquired early and can linger throughout life. In the Jim Crow South, white southerners had an intense emotional reaction to the possibility of desegregating their public facilities. Black skin was regarded almost as a contagious physical condition, something dirty that might rub off and contaminate individuals who were fortunate enough to be white. Hence, norms required separation of public conveniences that imply close contact such as restaurants, theaters, buses, water fountains, and restrooms.

In his analysis of race relations in the United States, Dr. James Comer, himself a black American who overcame poverty and discrimination to become a well-known psychiatrist and author, recounts the story of a white teenaged girl who was scolded by her father for having put a coin in her mouth. He yelled, "Get that money out of your mouth—it might have been in a nigger's hand!" His reaction reminds us of an important principle of human behavior: You really don't have to smell like a skunk to be treated like one.

SNAPSHOT

Hate Crimes Against Women

Being as Nasty as They Want to Be

Bigotry is making a comeback. Americans now tolerate forms of prejudice and discrimination that a decade ago would have been unthinkable. What in 1969 or 1974 might have been whispered behind closed doors is today more readily expressed in public; what was once considered taboo is now more socially acceptable to say even among total strangers. During the past few years, we have generated a culture of hate in which bigotry finds legitimacy.

Women have often been a target of that hate. Andrew Dice Clay has made the art of slurring women a specialty. When Clay hosted "Saturday Night Live," a cast member and a popular singer—both women—refused to perform on that show, claiming that the comic's appearance would legitimize the ravings of "a hatemonger."

At the same time, rock idol Madonna, who brought us such controversial classics as "Like A Virgin" and "Like A Prayer," has more recently extolled the pleasures of being spanked by men in a song titled "Hanky Panky." Popular rappers such as Ice-T and N.W.A. ("Niggas with Attitude") express a violent sexual theme based on the view that "women are only asking for it anyway."

At Syracuse University, sociologist Gary Spencer recently studied the growth of JAP ("Jewish American Princess") jokes on campuses around the country. He concluded that these jokes undoubtedly contain an element of sexism. In their more benign form, JAP jokes depict Jewish women as greedy and materialistic. But even more sinister versions suggest that the world would be better off if all Jewish females were eliminated: "A Solution to the JAP Problem: When they go to get nose jobs, tie their tubes as well" (cited in Anti-Defamation League, 1988).

A part of the culture of hate is the portrayal of women as victims of grotesque forms of violence in motion pictures that are ostensibly meant for an adult audience but that appeal to teenagers. The R-rated "slasher" films depict the torture, assault, and murder of women, with obvious sexual significance. In *Tool Box Murders,* for example, a "glassy-eyed lunatic" is shown in a grotesque act of violence against a young woman while romantic music plays softly in the background. Such films undoubtedly lead some to believe that sex and violence are inseparable, that you cannot or should not have one without the other. Edward Donnerstein and his colleagues have concluded that a heavy diet of slasher movies can make some men more accepting of sexual violence against women. The danger of imminent violence might allow censorship of such movies without violating First Amendment freedoms, but few now contemplate this.

The FBI is keeping track of a growing phenomenon that it calls *hate crimes*. These are criminal acts (against either property or people) that are aimed at individuals because they are members of a particular group. Those directed against women because they are women are on the rise.

Of course, not all attacks against females can be regarded as hate crimes. Many are motivated by the relationship of the individuals involved. The murder of Boston suburbanite Carol Stuart allegedly by her husband Charles in October 1989 was apparently motivated by greed and/or the hatred of one individual for another. After shooting his wife in the head, Charles Stuart shot himself in the abdomen and called 911. He blamed his wife's murder on a "black stranger." It cannot be argued that Carol Stuart was an interchangeable victim; she was chosen apparently because of her relationship with her assailant.

Hate crimes are usually perpetrated against total strangers. Therefore, everyone in a particular group is a potential target. Moreover, when an assault is involved, it is usually a brutal attack carried out by several offenders who frequently injure their victim sufficiently to require hospitalization.

The case of the "Central Park Jogger" has all of these elements. In April 1989 a gang of teenaged thugs, allegedly shouting, "Let's get a woman jogger," ambushed, beat, and then raped a 28-year-old woman as she ran through Central Park after dark. Her attackers pelted her with rocks, smashed her with their fists and a metal pipe, and then left her for dead. For 13 days she lay hospitalized in a comatose state suffering from a fractured skull, brain injury, and disfiguring cuts and bruises. The Central Park jogger just happened to be in the wrong place at the wrong time. Any other female jogger would have been similarly at risk.

Clearly, antifemale attitudes did not develop overnight. Just like other aspects of culture, prejudice against women has been around for many generations—actually, for centuries. And like other cultural phenomena, antifemale attitudes are learned early in life—transmitted through the teachings of parents, siblings, friends, teachers, children's books, and television programs. By the time children are five years old, they already know the "proper" behavior in the gender roles they are expected to play. Recognizing their advantaged position, young boys often refuse to cross the gender lines and play with their sisters' dolls. By contrast, girls are more willing to take the leap across gender roles—they frequently see their predicament and are less averse to playing with their brothers' trucks and guns.

The culture of hate is not confined to music, humor, and motion pictures. Many men hold women responsible for eroding their economic position in society. Most are able to express their hatred vicariously in a manner that, however disgusting, is not illegal—by telling a JAP joke at a party, laughing at an Andrew Dice Clay performance, enjoying an R-rated slasher film, or parroting the lyrics of a misogynist hit record.

But some men become violent. Serial killers such as Ted Bundy, Son of Sam, the Hillside Strangler, and the Green River Killer all targeted women as their primary victims. In December 1989 a resentful young man took his semiautomatic rifle into the engineering college at the University of Montreal to get even with the "feminists" he claimed were responsible for his failures in life. In slaughtering 14 female engineering students, Marc Lepine blamed women for his failed relationships, low-paying jobs, and lack of education. Engineering, he reasoned, was a masculine occupation from which women must be excluded. Instead, the director of admissions at the University of Montreal had denied him admission to its engineering program, and that was "the last straw."

If we are serious about reducing violence against women, we must be willing to mount an assault against those aspects of our culture that legitimize the expression of anger and resentment against an entire group or category of people. In short, we should try to transform the culture of hate into a culture of compassion and tolerance.

SNAPSHOT

The Demise of Bystander Apathy

We Admire Idols of Activism

In 1964, in a now-classic case, Kitty Genovese was stabbed to death in the middle of the night while 38 of her neighbors listened from the safety of their apartments. Though the victim screamed for help and her assailant took almost 30 minutes to kill her, no one even reported the incident to the police, never mind fighting off Genovese's killer.

Social scientists of the day argued that this apparent indifference was a result of what they called "diffusion of responsibility." That is, although they may have been concerned for the victim, Genovese's neighbors also felt a lack of personal responsibility to intervene. They reasoned, "Why should I risk my neck when there are other witnesses who will surely come to the rescue?"

However it was explained at the time, the Genovese case was the first nationally recognized episode of bystander apathy—one of the most distasteful byproducts of the American preoccupation with spectatorship. Although it was first acknowledged then, bystander apathy is not a phenomenon peculiar to the 1960s; nor is it exclusive to any one generation of people.

Recent newspaper stories also support the belief that people still do not help one another. Take the Manchester, New Hampshire, woman who was brutally raped in a yard just steps away from her apartment. She was apparently in full view of several of her neighbors, but they ignored her pleas for help. In Raleigh, North Carolina, a motorcyclist injured in an accident lay face down on a crowded highway and counted 900 cars over a three-hour period before anyone stopped to assist him. In Boston, a third-year medical student was jumped by four teenagers while riding his bicycle home from the hospital. Many people watched, but none of them intervened. In New York City, a group of jeering and joking youths watched while a 30-year-old man was electrocuted on the third rail of the subway station at Times Square . . . and so on.

Observers of the social scene have used such cases in arguing for the existence of a destructive and callous side of human nature. Based in part on the writings of Freud and, more recently, of ethologists such as Konrad Lorenz, who emphasize the evolutionary basis for aggressive behavior, they have focused on bystander apathy to illustrate how people are moving away from one another. This point of view is sometimes so thoroughly one-sided, however, that it ignores the fact that altruism is a value in virtually all human societies and forms the basis for most of the world's religions. Americans have long celebrated altruism by awarding medals for outstanding acts of selfless heroism, such as the medals awarded by the Carnegie Hero Fund Commission or, during wartime, the Congressional Medal of Honor.

While some observers dwell on the seedier side of human nature, hundreds of others donate one of their kidneys for transplantation into another human being. Thousands more donate their blood at some personal expense and inconvenience. And millions regularly donate money to their favorite charities.

Today, more than 30 years after the Genovese case, these acts of generosity and selflessness seem more abundant than ever. In addition, there seems to be less tolerance for individuals who respond to others with indifference or selfishness. Bystander apathy seems fast becoming the exception to what may be a new norm of social life: being willing to risk inconvenience, embarrassment, and even personal safety to assist victims of crimes and accidents. The evidence at this point is anecdotal and informal, but it is nonetheless highly suggestive. Numerous recent reports cite acts of great heroism and courage performed by average citizens who haven't otherwise stood apart. These good samaritans are serious about taking personal responsibility for the plight of others, refusing to take refuge in the anonymity of the crowd.

We used to hear about airliners being hijacked; now we also hear about passengers on a flight who overpower and subdue a potential hijacker. We used to see purse snatchers and muggers; now we also see bystanders who chase and catch the mugger. We used to read about physicians who drive past automobile accidents because of the fear of a lawsuit; now we also read about doctors who rescue accident victims and, in the process, may suffer injuries of their own. We used to see corruption in government and industry; now we also see whistleblowers who risk being fired in order to expose practices that they believe to be dangerous to the public.

One example of personal altruism can be found in the behavior of Lennie Skutnik, the young man who was honored by ex-President Reagan in 1982 for his heroic rescue of a survivor of an Air Florida crash in the icy waters of the Potomac River.

In 1986 Richard Young, a New York City firefighter, risked serious injury to rescue a total stranger—a truck driver who hung by his arms from the steering wheel of the cab of his truck as it dangled over the edge of a bridge. Arriving on the scene, Young threw himself under the truck driver's body to break his fall. In saving the man's life, Young broke a leg and ankle and severely injured his back.

In 1987 a 23-year-old Vietnamese immigrant went on a shooting spree through the streets of a major city, killing five people and wounding two others before ending his own life. More of the wounded might have succumbed to their injuries if it hadn't been for the selfless efforts of two young people who came forward under gunfire to move victims from the street to an ambulance.

In 1991 two armed robbers on the run from the police were followed by John Amato, an alert ex-cop who was listening to a description of their getaway car on his police scanner. At great personal risk, Amato tailed the two suspects—even though they had spotted him—and kept the police informed over his cellular phone. Thanks to him the two robbers were eventually arrested and charged.

In 1992 a small plane crashed into a small, ice-covered pond, injuring its student pilot and his flight instructor. The duo might have died were it not for the heroic efforts of two passersby who rushed out to the sinking plane and rescued them with a ladder they laid on the ice. One of the rescuers, David Leal, suffered a dislocated shoulder and hypothermia in the process.

In 1994 Jennifer Harbury, a young woman who was educated in the United States, staged a 32-day hunger strike in Guatemala City to dramatize the absence of human rights there and to demand information about her missing husband. As a result, the Guatemalan government immediately charged Harbury with making false accusations against the Guatemalan army. On Human Rights Day in Boston, Rigoberta Menshu, herself a winner of the Nobel Prize for Peace, defended and praised Harbury for her humanitarian efforts on behalf of the people of Guatemala.

In 1994 15-year-old Razeena Sadiq was on her way to school when she spotted an apartment building in flames. Without regard for her own safety, Sadiq raced into the burning building four times—at one point crawling on her hands and knees through the smoke-filled corridors—to guide 13 residents to safety. Afterward, she gave her coat to a half-naked man whom she had rescued and then pounded on doors until she found him a place to escape the early-morning cold.

What characteristics distinguish these samaritans from the rest of humanity? Social scientists have discovered that individuals who intervene in a dangerous situation are likely to have had training in first aid, lifesaving, or police work. In addition, they tend to be exceptionally tall and heavy. These attributes give them the sense of competence or efficiency—through training and strength—necessary for assisting others in potentially hazardous situations. Good samaritans also tend to be adventurous types who have taken other risks with their personal safety.

The most important conditions accounting for the rise of the good samaritan may be found in the types of heroes they choose to emulate. Researchers have discovered a common factor among German Christians who, during World War II, helped rescue the victims of Nazi persecutors; civil rights activists of the 1950s and 1960s (called Freedom Riders); and altruistic children. That factor is the presence of a model of altruism. In the case of a child, the model is likely to be an intensely moralistic parent with whom the young samaritan can closely identify. In adults, models for appropriate behavior are also found in national heroes.

On the national level we continue to have our idols of consumption: those bigger-than-life images on the screen, television, or playing field, whose accomplishments fill our leisure hours with music, comedy, and drama. But there is now a new breed of national hero as well. Today we have idols of activism—individuals who are admired and revered not for their ability to keep us entertained but for their courage to take active charge of their own lives and the lives of others. In the face of overwhelming and impersonal social, political, and economic forces such as the threat of nuclear war, big government, and corporate mergers, we increasingly admire those who come forward from their place among the spectators. This change in our culture may have made heroes out of the likes of Oliver North, Bernard Goetz, the Guardian Angels, Sylvester Stallone as Rambo and Rocky, Dustin Hoffman in the film *Hero,* Charles Bronson in *Death Wish,* and Jeff Bridges in *Fearless;* it has also made us admire the courage of Lennie Skutnick and Razeena Sadiq.

SNAPSHOT

Elevator Culture

You Really Can't Do Anything Else but Stare at the Door

Social psychologists have conducted an experiment in which they gave elevator riders at Ohio State University an opportunity to help themselves to a coupon good for a free Quarter Pounder with cheese. Upon entering the elevator, riders saw a poster reading "Free McDonald's Burger" and a pocket underneath it containing coupons for one Quarter Pounder. All they had to do was take one.

Fifty-six people entered the elevator alone. Of this number, 26 were randomly permitted to ride without other passengers, while 16 rode with one other passenger and 14 rode with two other passengers. (All of the other passengers were really confederates of the experimenters, who randomly decided whether subjects rode with two, one, or no other riders.)

This experiment's results showed that people riding alone were much more likely to help themselves to a cheeseburger than were riders accompanied by other passengers. In fact, of the individuals riding by themselves, 81 percent took a free coupon. With one other passenger present, however, only 38 percent took a coupon; and with two other passengers present, only 14 percent helped themselves to a coupon.

Why would elevator passengers avoid doing something to their advantage—taking a free cheeseburger—just because other riders were present? The answer seems to involve the influence of *elevator culture:* a set of unspoken, unwritten rules of behavior that are widely shared and generally observed by people who ride in elevators with other passengers. The riders in this experiment avoided doing something that might call attention to themselves in the public setting of the elevator, even if it meant sacrificing a free lunch. They didn't want to look different.

Actually, there isn't much you can do that is right in an elevator, especially if you are among strangers. Almost all of the rules of elevator riding seem to be *proscriptive*—things you are definitely not supposed to do. The only prescriptive (positive) rule dictates standing quietly while facing the elevator door, and that is precisely what most passengers do. Unless they want to be regarded as weird, most riders avoid talking to anyone they don't know, staring at anyone, touching anyone, or even breathing on anyone. They don't want to violate the personal space of other riders, even in a crowded elevator.

One interesting thing about elevator culture is that it extends far beyond the elevator walls. Actually, almost any public setting—walking on the streets of a city, eating in a restaurant, or sitting in the park—carries a set of rules that severely limit the quality and quantity of social interaction. In all of these places there is little, if any, talking to, touching, or looking directly at strangers. As a result, strangers in a big city who are physically close might as well be miles apart, as far as interaction is concerned.

Of course, individuals also have some control over their culture; they don't have to passively conform to it. In an early study of conformity, Solomon Asch studied a group of eight people in a classroom, who were asked to match the length of a line drawn on the blackboard with one of three comparison lines drawn on an index card. All judgments were made out loud and in the order of the room's seating. Only one participant in the Asch study was actually a naive subject; and he voiced his judgment after hearing several other "students" state theirs first. (These others were confederates of Asch who had been instructed to respond incorrectly when asked to match the length of the lines.)

Over a number of trials with different groups, approximately one-third of the naive subjects made incorrect estimates in the direction of the inaccurate majority; in other words, about one in three conformed. But when a lone dissenter supported the naive subject by going against the majority judgment, the rate of conformity dropped dramatically to less than 6 percent.

Thus, if even one person waiting in line for a table in a restaurant starts talking to other customers, he or she might serve as a role model for other customers to imitate. Who knows? Maybe lots of people will get involved in the conversation. And if one rider in a crowded elevator has the courage to take a coupon for a free cheeseburger, everybody might conceivably end up having lunch on McDonald's.

SNAPSHOT

Baby Boomers

A Generation without a Gap

Rock music has long been a symbol of adolescent rebellion. The greasers of the 1950s wouldn't have been caught dead listening to recordings of Glenn Miller, Woody Herman, or any other musician reminiscent of their parents' day. Similarly, members of the 1960s hip generation were too intent on distancing themselves from what they saw as oppressive traditional authority to regard tunes by Fats Domino and Chuck Berry with more than historical curiosity.

That's why it is so intriguing that today's high school and college students don't reject—and, in fact, embrace—older popular music. Of course, they still identify with the new superstar songsters—Boyz II Men, Pearl Jam, Alice in Chains, and the like. But, amazingly, they also admire longtime rock idols of the 1960s and early 1970s who are now well into middle age. During the past few years, such oldsters as Pink Floyd, Fleetwood Mac, Aerosmith, Carly Simon, The Grateful Dead, Mick Jagger, Van Morrison, Bonnie Raitt, George Harrison, and Paul Simon have all had top-selling albums. Simon's Grammy-winning album *Graceland* was the top-ranked compact disc just a few years ago. And, according to *Billboard Magazine,* among the top concert moneymakers of 1992 were middle-agers Billy Joel, Bob Seger, and David Bowie. During the same period, concerts by 1960s oldies legends like 51-year-old Gene Pitney and Shirley Alston Reeves, former lead singer of the Shirelles, attracted sell-out crowds. In 1994 the top concert draws continued to include many middle-agers like The Rolling Stones, Pink Floyd, Billy Joel, Barbra Streisand, Elton John, Phil Collins, and the Grateful Dead.

Part of the continuing popularity of the 1960s rock stars is their nostalgic appeal to the moving human population explosion we call the baby boomers: 76 million American men and women who were born between 1946 and 1964. Many of them were just coming of age during the 1960s as the Beatles, Rolling Stones, and Bob Dylan entered the music scene or later as Woodstock launched their generation into the 1970s. As their oldest members now approach their 50s, the baby boomers are becoming nostalgic. They have glowing memories of the formative period in their lives and the music that it spawned.

Across the country, popular radio stations have capitalized on this wave of nostalgia by airing 1960s music or by sprinkling hits of that era throughout their otherwise contemporary format. But it isn't only nostalgic baby boomers who crave the sounds of the 1960s; their younger brothers and sisters and in some cases their children also do. Recently, for example, *Teen Magazine* reported the results of a survey of its readers' favorite entertainers. Among the names of current idols in the entertainment world were names associated with a previous generation, many of whom are 20, even 30 years older than their teenaged fans. Similarly, a 1992 poll of the youthful audience for a popular MTV all-request music program named "Heart and Soul" by the Monkees as its top video of the year and 42-year-old Davy Jones as its choice for "cutest guy." Even senior citizen singers Frank Sinatra and Tony Bennett have made spectacular comebacks, enjoying popularity even in the teenage music market.

Music is only one example of the baby boomers' immense and continuing cultural clout. During the 1960s, long before they were given a label, today's baby boomers had not only large numbers (half the population of the United States was under 25) but also plenty of disposable income. And they often spent it on 35mm single-lens reflex cameras, stereo components, bell-bottom jeans, miniskirts, hula hoops, and so on. Business interests were, of course, thoroughly pleased with such free-spending habits. So pleased, in fact, that commercials such as Oil of Olay ads promised that you wouldn't look "over 25!" And in his best-selling work *The Greening of America,* law professor Charles Reich discussed the possibility that our entire society would soon be transformed in the image of youthful hippies of the day.

During the closing years of the 1960s there was reason to make such a prediction. The baby boomers were role models for many adults who emulated their teenaged children's appearance. Thus, middle-aged women donned bell-bottom jeans, tie-dyed shirts, sandals, and peace beads, while their husbands wore their hair shoulder-length, their ties psychedelic, and their sideburns to the end of their ear lobes. Many also grew beards and mustaches to lengths that today would be regarded as thoroughly outrageous. The style of the day was that of the baby-boomer generation: It seemed as if everybody was either young or wanted to be.

Although in the 1990s the baby boomers have reached midlife, they have lost none of their cultural clout. Just as they set trends as youths, so they are now setting trends as adults. The baby boomers still boast large numbers and spend lots of money. Of course, their consumer habits have changed with age and the times; they now buy VCRs, microwave ovens, compact disc players, and personal computers. But the fact that they continue to consume is enough to explain why so many midlife models are appearing in ads and commercials.

Moreover, notwithstanding the efforts of fashion designers, few women today actually feel obligated to wear the miniskirts of a younger generation. Instead, high school and college students often follow their parents' lead by adding to their form-fitting wardrobe the loose styles formerly associated with middle age. The more youthful punk movement may have affected trends in new-wave fashion, art, and music; but their small numbers and limited purchasing power pretty much ensured that punk style would not influence older generations.

Will the cultural clout of baby boomers persist into old age? Will they continue to set trends in music, art, and fashion in their sixties and seventies? They will, of course, still have large numbers on their side. By the year 2025, when the baby boomers achieve senior citizenship, more than 20 percent of the population will be over 65. Yet, it is a sad truth that numbers alone are as likely to assure poverty as power. Elder Americans living 200 years ago commanded much greater respect and privilege than they do today, despite (or perhaps because of) the fact that only 10 percent of the population lived to celebrate their 60th birthday. Granted, this figure is skewed somewhat by high rates of infant mortality. Nonetheless, under Puritanism, old age was regarded as a sign of election and a special gift from God. But when longevity increased and more people survived to old age, the cultural clout of elders declined. Specifically, preferential seating arrangements in public vehicles for older people vanished; mandatory retirement laws appeared; youthful fashions were preferred; and eldest children lost their inheritance advantages.

Besides sheer numbers, then, graying baby boomers of the future will need to maintain the free-spending habits that endeared them to commercial interests if they are to maintain their cultural clout. Not only will they need plenty of money, but they must be willing to spend it as they did in the past. If they are anything like previous generations of older Americans, however, this may not be realistic. Senior citizens tend to become "economy conscious" by reducing their use of credit and by shopping for price. Even if many baby boomers refuse to or cannot afford to retire at 65 or 70, they will likely temper their consumerism in favor of preparing for an uncertain future in terms of health care, economic depression, inflation, and the like. Depending on the course of public policy over the next few decades, even financially secure individuals may become quite conservative in their spending habits. This does not mean that aging baby boomers will be asked to live in poverty, only that they may be forced to give up their place as the cultural kingpins of American society.

SEEING CULTURE THROUGH SNAPSHOTS AND PORTRAITS

Several students in the course I teach on the sociology of violence have come from other countries to attend school in Boston. Two were from Asia, one from Europe, one from South America, and one from an island in the Caribbean. About 15 minutes into our first meeting, I realized that their presence in the classroom would change how I approached the course. It didn't take a psychic to figure out that communication would be more difficult: From the first day there were lots of bewildered looks and blank stares to remind me. Then there were the questions.

At first I considered the problem to be only one of language. In plain English, I believed that my plain English was, to them, not so plain. By the end of our first session together, however, I recognized that the problem was more profound than just misunderstood words and phrases. Indeed, from the types of questions they were asking, I concluded that some of the international students in my class also lacked familiarity with the practices, objects, and ideas that most Americans learn and share every day and therefore take for granted as the "American way of life." My foreign students were unfamiliar with American culture.

In ordinary conversation the term *culture* might refer to opera, classical music, and ballet. In the language of sociology, however, *culture* encompasses these forms of art, but it also includes much more. It embraces the entire way of life in a society: all of the practices, objects, and ideas that are learned and shared by its members. The American way of life, for example, is distinguishable, first of all, by cultural objects and activities—items of *material culture* such as rock music, rap, lipstick, Superman comics, color TVs, large automobiles, fast food, videogames, and personal computers. Second, American culture includes a set of *values* toward which many Americans strive—ideas about what is desirable. Specifically, these values include making lots of money and becoming wealthy and powerful. Third, American culture contains *norms,* a set of rules or guidelines for behavior that tell Americans the right and proper way to behave in a particular social situation.

Even the smallest social settings can develop a shared set of norms. In "Elevator Culture" I discussed the "proper" way to behave when riding in an elevator with other passengers. Surprisingly, perhaps, it turns out that elevator culture permits very little positive guidance for behavior; in fact, there may be only one socially correct way to stand in an elevator. No wonder some people prefer to take the stairs!

At the turn of the 20th century, American sociologist William Graham Sumner distinguished between two types of norms. He called the important norms *mores;* these are the rules of behavior to which the members of a group demand compliance. In American society mores include prohibitions against murder, rape, cannibalism, and terrorism. Sumner also identified *folkways,* the small norms of behavior for conducting routine affairs. Thus, folkways include rules for shaking hands with people you meet, eating with a knife and fork, wearing dress clothes to a job interview, taking a shower regularly, listening to an instructor give a lecture, merging two lanes of traffic (every other car), asking someone for a date, sending a birthday card to a loved one, and even standing in a crowded elevator.

Returning to my class, consider an example in which unfamiliarity with a particular item of material culture hampered communication. In our discussion of the manner in which mass killings are reported by the media, I introduced James Huberty's 1984 rampage through a McDonald's restaurant located in a San Diego suburb. I noted that several newspapers around the country had referred to Huberty's killing spree (he killed 21 people) as "Mass McMurder" and "The Big Mac Attack." The American students immediately understood the glib, possibly offensive, aspects of these newspaper headlines, but three of the international students had only questions: "What is a Big Mac?" one asked. Not knowing the logo of this famous hamburger chain, another wanted to know why the paper called Huberty's attack "McMurder." Before continuing our discussion of mass killings, therefore, we spent several minutes talking about fast food.

Now, familiarity with American culture varies quite a bit around the world. And among my international students I noticed immense variation in this respect. A young woman from Western Europe was quite familiar with American customs and practices, at least much more so than her counterparts from Asia and South America. Though she had been in the United States only a few days before the course began, she had eaten many times in American fast-food restaurants (McDonald's has locations throughout Western Europe), had watched American television (possibly our most successful export), and was also better acquainted with the American brand of humor. That's because the cultural objects and customs in her own country are similar to ours. They are likely to be, of course, because we Americans have had frequent contact with Europe and have derived much of our culture from it. The process whereby cultural traits spread from one society to another (for example, from England to the United States) is known as *cultural diffusion.*

Clearly we can thank (or blame) cultural diffusion for giving us many important ideas and objects that originated in or at least passed first through Europe. In "The Immaculate Americans" we saw that it was the British who, during the Industrial Revolution, were plumbing pioneers. But many aspects of our culture outside of the bathroom were borrowed elsewhere. In 1936 anthropologist Ralph Linton dramatically emphasized just how much the "100 percent American" is indebted to discoveries and inventions from societies around the globe. He noted, for example, that we have borrowed

Beds from the Near East
Pajamas from India
Moccasins from Native Americans of the eastern woodlands
Shaving from ancient Egypt or Sumer
Neckties from Croatia
Glass from Egypt
Umbrellas from southeast Asia
Rubber from the Natives of Central America
Forks and spoons from Italy
Watermelon from Africa
Oranges from the Eastern Mediterranean
Cantaloupe from Persia
Sugar from India
Cigarettes from Mexico
Paper from China
Tobacco from Brazil
Maple syrup from the Native Americans of the eastern woodlands

Ideas that we often take for granted or believe to be constants in nature—for example, our ideas about cleanliness, economic success, and marriage—may actually originate in the culture that we learn. But what is the origin of culture? We know that people aren't born with it, although they are born with the *capacity* for culture. Only humans seem to have this full capability; other animals often share a way of life but not one that is learned and passed along to the next generation. For the most part, animals are programmed from birth to act and react in social situations. (For example, birds don't learn to fly by watching other birds do it first; nor do parent birds teach them. The ability to fly comes from instinct alone.) The central importance of the *culture* concept is its ability to explain how patterns of social behavior—social structure—develop in human beings even though they lack the inborn programmed instincts so common in other animals. Anyone who has ever observed a colony of ants knows that this insect develops intricate patterns of social behavior. Yet ants don't sit in classrooms or receive lessons in life from their parents. They don't, in a word, learn.

The origin of a particular type of cultural content—whether one or another thing is regarded as proper and right—is also a fascinating question. Many sociologists believe that economics may play a major role in determining the particular character of a culture. The important 19th-century theorist Karl Marx argued, in writing about what he saw as the inevitable rise of communism, that the economic system of a society determines almost everything about other social institutions. He believed that religion, family life, and the press were all handmaidens of the prevailing economic system; that is, they existed essentially to support and maintain the economic status quo, to make sure that it survived. From a Marxian point of view, therefore, the Protestant cultural belief about work (the religious conviction that hard work is a sign of self-worth and personal salvation) exists largely because capitalism needs a way to dupe or mislead workers. The work ethic is a way of motivating workers to tolerate their terrible working conditions, accept their exploitation by the owners of production, and be achievement-oriented in the interest of maximizing corporate profits. According to Marx, cultural expressions such as religious beliefs develop and change mostly to serve the needs of the prevailing economic system—whether feudalism, capitalism, or socialism. In his view, culture has no independent impact on the social structure. A particular economic system develops first; it then determines the shape of the culture that follows, including the shape of religious ideas.

You don't have to accept Marx's view of the origin of religion to agree that mass culture—popular art and music—in a capitalistic society like ours is rooted in the demands of the economic system. Middle-aged rock musicians such as Van Morrison, Paul Simon, Tom Petty, and Billy Joel may not help to preserve capitalism, but their continuing popularity is probably a result of their appeal to huge numbers of people who grew up in the 1960s and 1970s and who are willing to spend their hard-earned money on nostalgia. In "Baby Boomers: A Generation without a Gap" it was suggested that the so-called baby boomers continue to have plenty of cultural clout, but only as long as they spend money. How will they be treated if they give up their credit cards? Only time will tell.

In his materialist view of the origins of culture, anthropologist Marvin Harris has similarly suggested that the variety of cultural behavior around the world is a result of living in the material world—that is, of the adaptations that individuals in a society make to their particular environment. Like Marx, Harris writes that the evolution of societies is not caused by the operation of any major cultural ideas (for example, by religion) but by changing economic circumstances. In 1487, for example, the Aztecs suffered a profound shortage of animal protein in their diet; they were not able to raise cattle, sheep, goats, horses, pigs, or llamas. In response, they incorporated cannibalism into their warfare. After a battle they would eat their enemies—thousands of them—as an alternative source of animal protein. Cannibalism became ritualized and took on religious significance, but only because it first satisfied an important material need.

However, culture isn't always a result of shared economic exigencies or material problems of survival. Rejecting this view, many sociologists have provided evidence that culture—in the form of widely shared, profound religious values—can also help determine patterns of social relationships and social structure in a group of people.

In a classic account of the influence of Protestantism on capitalism, Max Weber's *The Protestant Ethic and the Spirit of Capitalism* uncovered compelling evidence for a position that is at odds with that of Karl Marx or Marvin Harris. Rather than seeing the economy as determining Western religious cultural values, Weber instead showed that capitalism would never have become the primary means of Western economic activity without the foundation laid by the widespread acceptance of Protestant values. He argued that Protestantism came first, setting the stage for capitalism to emerge.

Weber's view can be summarized as follows. Until the spread of Protestantism in the 16th century, economic activity was considered a necessary evil, something that an individual did in order to survive. During the middle ages, in fact, any Christian who loaned someone money and charged interest would have been regarded as having committed a mortal sin requiring eternal damnation.

The goal of capitalism is to make a profit. Before Protestantism, capitalists were seen as immoral, mercenary, and disreputable. But under the Protestant ethic, just the opposite became true: Not only was profit making tolerated, it was viewed as a sign of salvation. The more money individuals accumulated and the greater their success in the economic sphere, the more secure they could be about achieving election in the hereafter. Making money suddenly took on profound religious significance.

As was illustrated in "Hate Crimes against Women," sociologists have long recognized that sexism (like racism) has a cultural basis. Just like the profit motive in Western societies, sexism has become conventional and socially approved; it often originates in the mainstream, rather than at the margins, of a society. And as with any other aspect of culture, sexism is expected to be widely shared, enduring, and learned. This is an important, if subtle, point; it means that we shouldn't necessarily look for sexism in only the most pathological, most deviant members of our society.

In her portrait ("The Rape Culture") Dianne Herman takes the idea of an antifemale cultural bias into the area of sexual assault. She presents a good deal of evidence that rape is probably more widespread in the United States than in any other developed country. Not coincidentally, she also emphasizes that Americans consider sex to be dirty and violent. In fact, the inspiration for rape can often be located in a "normal" need, learned early in life by American males, to feel they must prove their masculinity by being dominant over females. Herman indicates that rapists often differ very little, if at all, in terms of important personality characteristics from American men who are normal and well-adjusted and do not sexually assault women. The answer to the problem of rape seems, therefore, to lie not so much in the individual makeup of a few deranged American males as in their access to and immersion in American culture.

Culture has thus far been associated with an entire society. Clearly, within any large and diverse social system, there may be a *dominant culture*—ideas and actions that come to be shared by the majority of people or at least by the society's most powerful members. The dominant culture in American society, for example, has traditionally included a belief in the work ethic, according to which doing the best job possible is widely regarded as a means to achieve self-esteem and religious salvation. Education is also believed to provide a legitimate opportunity structure for achieving the so-called American Dream.

At the same time, we should acknowledge that American society is a complex mixture of peoples, histories, and cultural ideas. In the broad cultural expanse known as America, it would be a mistake to portray any individual as a cultural copy of every other individual. In reality, many Americans are located in a *subculture*—a distinctive set of practices, objects, and ideas not widely shared throughout the dominant culture. Thus, the members of a subculture accept only some of the aspects of the dominant culture while also sharing their own set of values. To illustrate an important subculture, consider the behavior of first- and second-generation Italian Americans who have settled together in large metropolitan areas of the United States. They may have adopted the American work ethic as well as other American ideas, but they may still cling to a cultural heritage that affects the way they gesture when speaking as well as their speech, clothing, diet, and family celebrations.

If we are to portray the cultural diversity of a large society, it is important to emphasize that culture often varies within an entire society. This can be seen in Daniel Monti's portrait of gangs ("The Culture of Gangs in the Culture of the School"). In his study Monti shows that gangs can be considered subcultures within the dominant culture represented by American school systems. Rather than remain in conflict with school officials, however, gangs are often accommodated within a school's officially endorsed culture. It becomes possible, as a result, for the subculture of gangs and school officials to coexist—and sometimes quite nicely—on a continuing basis.

As members of a society we become so familiar with our own culture that we tend to regard it as part of the natural order—the best or perhaps the only way for conducting the affairs of a society. American sociologist William Sumner was early to recognize the ease with which one's own culture is used as a standard against which all other cultures are judged and seen as inferior. He coined the term *ethnocentrism* to refer to the common tendency for individuals to see their own group as "the center of everything."

Sometimes, therefore, the most effective strategy for learning about our own culture is to reverse the ethnocentric bias and focus on the ways in which our society differs from other peoples of the world. In other words, use them as a yardstick for evaluating us. David Bayley's portrait, "Forces of Order," examines the relationship of the Japanese criminal justice system to suspects and defendants, but it is actually meant to explore important aspects of American cultural values. By investigating how criminals are treated by Japanese police and prosecutors, we can recognize the assumptions that Americans collectively make about prospects for changing criminal behavior and, indirectly, their cultural assumptions about human nature.

Ethnocentric Americans might tend to see the Japanese system of criminal justice as repressive, harsh, and cruel and our own system as kind, gentle, and eager to forgive (perhaps too eager to forgive in the case of rapists and murderers). It turns out, however, that just the opposite may be true. If the analysis in Bayley's portrait is correct, it is Americans, not the Japanese, who tend to be punitive and unforgiving. The rhetoric of rehabilitation notwithstanding, Americans remain skeptical that the lives of criminals can ever be turned around, even when they are given a helping hand out of trouble.

PORTRAIT

Forces of Order

David H. Bayley

Americans are often urged to study foreign countries and cultures, the usual reason given being the need to overcome parochialism and to broaden intellectual horizons. These are valuable purposes, to be sure, but they obscure another one, which is equally important and often overlooked. Foreign travel is a means of learning about oneself and one's society. What is distinctive in one's own world, too familiar usually to be recognized, becomes obvious by comparison with the lives of others. It is important to discover what differences there are among the peoples of the world; it is no less important to discover what makes these differences alien.

This [article] is an attempt to learn about the police problems of the United States by studying Japanese police institutions. Japan is a particularly apt comparison with the United States. It is modern and affluent, congested and urbanized. It belongs to the world's "developed" nations. Comparisons between the United States and Japan are not vitiated by disparities in technical capacity, educational levels, wealth, or dominant modes of production. What stands out between the two is culture, not modernity. The thrust of the analysis will be to note differences in institutional practices between the nations' police, then to explain why the practices diverge in characteristic ways. In this way, it should be possible to highlight what in American history, culture, and character shapes police performance today.

A study of the police also provides a new vantage point for viewing contemporary Japanese society. Police penetrate society more completely than any other governmental agency, and police officers see things that most private citizens do not. Their perspective, though not representative, is not less authentic than any other. And it may have the advantage of being more extensive. The police are also a part of society. Because society works in them one can learn something about the society by observing them. Borrowing from the anthropologists, the police may be regarded as a village—not the only one but a real one nonetheless. . . .

The study is based on about two years of intensive field research in Japan distributed over twenty years and many visits. The research in Japan involved observation of police operations and interviews with hundreds of officers. Because operations are organized for the most

From *Forces of Order: Policing Modern Japan* (pp. ix–xii, 126–137, 149–150) by David Bayley, 1991, Berkeley, CA: University of California Press. Reprinted by permission of the author.

part in terms of police stations, I made a selection of police stations located in a variety of socioeconomic areas—urban, rural, heavy industrial, upper-class residential, university, commercial, entertainment, and so forth. The sample was drawn from five prefectures—Tokyo, Aomori, Osaka, Kochi, and Fukuoka. Generally about five days were spent studying each station. Observation of police operations was carried out mostly at night—the busiest hours for the police. I would accompany officers working in patrol cars or in Japan's unique police boxes (*koban*). Formal interviews were held with the chief of each police station (or his deputy) and with the heads of each major section—patrol, criminal investigation, crime prevention, and administration. Because I was particularly interested in contact-behavior, interviews were held with at least one officer at every rank level within the patrol section of each station. Interviews were also conducted with all ranks of detectives but not necessarily in each station. The police are organized into prefectural commands, so it was important to talk to senior officers at prefectural headquarters. This meant the chief of the prefecture and the heads of each functional section. Some specialized operations are organized on a prefectural, as opposed to a station, basis, and they required additional study—riot control, traffic regulation, vice surveillance, and some criminal investigation. . . .

The Individual and Authority

One Sunday afternoon a man of about forty years old, dressed in a neat suit and tie, was brought to a koban by two patrol officers. He had parked illegally on a narrow residential street. He was thoroughly chastened, and the officers, after talking to him for several minutes, decided that instead of issuing a parking ticket, which would require payment of a fine, they would have him send a formal letter of apology to the chief of the local police station. So the man sat down at a koban desk and wrote out a letter in longhand. After giving his name, address, age, occupation, and nature and date of the offense, he wrote as follows: "I am very sorry for the trouble caused by illegal parking. I will be very careful in the future that I will never repeat the same violation. For this time only please I beseech your generosity." After signing his name and adding his seal,[1] he was allowed to go on his way, justice having been done in the minds of all concerned.

Variations of this quaint little drama occur frequently in relations between the Japanese police and public. Police officers freely adapt their responses to misconduct according to the personal background and demeanor of offenders. The most important basis for doing so is a display of contrition by the offender. Apology is one form repentance takes. Written apologies, as in this case, are widely used by police officers in connection with relatively minor offenses where an automatic fine is levied. The letter written by this man was copied from a form kept in the koban under a clear plastic cover. Some offenders, knowing about the procedure, ask to be allowed to give an apology in lieu of the fine. The decision depends totally on the judgment of the officers involved. Unless they believe that an offender is truly contrite and will not offend again, they insist on due punishment. To Americans, giving an apology would seem a minor price to pay. One can imagine them being irate at not being allowed to apologize, and wondering about what kind of favoritism was involved. To the Japanese, however, apologizing can be acutely embarrassing—so much so in fact that often the police simply warn the offender rather than demanding a formal apology.

Late one night koban officers were summoned by a young woman to save her from a man who, she said, had tried to force her to come to a hotel. It turned out that they had had an affair some time before and he, meeting her by accident, wanted to resume it on the spur of the moment. The woman was both furious and scared. The man, flashily dressed in a pink shirt and white slacks, was very embarrassed and steadfastly maintained that he had only asked her to come for a cup of tea. Discounting his denials, they lectured him sternly about using threats. Then the officers arranged that if he apologized to the woman and wrote a letter saying he would not do this again, the woman would sign an undertaking that she would not press charges. Taken into the room where the woman was, he shuffled his feet reluctantly and with bad grace mumbled "Sumimasen ne"—"I'm really sorry." Drunken men who relieve themselves outdoors are often let go if they are cooperative and apologetic; if they try to run away, they are fined. Youths under twenty found smoking in public may have their parents or teachers notified, but not if they voluntarily destroy their cigarettes on the spot and apologize.

Late one evening two patrol officers on bicycles stopped a man for drunken driving; he tried to escape by reversing his car, which narrowly missed one officer and punched a hole in the side of a small wooden house. A breath test showed he was drunk and he was marched on foot to a koban. The police wrote up the incident in detail and asked the man extensive questions about himself. As the interrogation dragged on, the driver became progressively more clear-eyed, subdued, and finally penitent. One of the young bike officers and the senior patrol officer of the koban disagreed sharply about the appropriate penalty to assess. The patrol officer wanted as severe a punishment as the law allowed—after all, it was he who had almost been run over—and the senior patrol officer wanted leniency, arguing that the man was a respectable businessman from out of town, that he could make amends to the homeowner directly because he owned a construction company, that he had a good driving record, and that he was very sorry for what he had done. Two full hours after the accident, the officers agreed that the case would not go to court but that the man would have to repair the damage under police supervision and would be given a ticket for drunken driving. The exact charge would be determined by traffic specialists at police headquarters.

The police, who are seldom surprised about human behavior, are well aware that contrition can be feigned and their goodwill abused. The police response is suitably cynical. Some kinds of chronic offenders—such as streetwalkers, bar owners who do not close on time, and women who solicit for striptease shows—are allowed to sign formal apologies precisely in order to create a file of admitted offenses. When the police then do decide to prosecute, the collection of apologies clearly demonstrates that they are habitual offenders and deserve no leniency.

The Japanese recognize that it is difficult in practice to separate discretionary treatment based on a calculation of the genuineness of contrition from treatment based on pure sympathy. But this possibility does not disturb them as it would Americans. With disarming candor Japanese police officers explain the importance of showing sympathy for people enmeshed in the law. Only by letting the "warm blood flow," as they say, will offenders eventually learn to respect both the law and its agents. There are many instances of this. The police discovered that a bicycle being ridden without a light had been stolen. The owner of the cycle, who lived near where the young thief worked, refused to prosecute a "child," though the thief was sixteen years old. Because the boy was very contrite, the police too refused to press the matter. Charges were dropped by the police against a university student caught shoplifting 9,000 yen worth of phonograph records, because he had no previous criminal record, and was very repentant. A taxi driver parked illegally in front of a small store. The police discovered that because he had many previous violations, notification of this offense would cause his license to be suspended. Already bearing heavy expenses from a recent divorce, the taxi driver was on the brink of financial ruin. The police prevailed on the store owner to write a letter saying he had given permission for the taxi to park there, thus shifting the blame for the offense. Knowing that their sympathetic impulses may get in the way of performing their duties, officers sometimes take steps to protect themselves. For example, chauffeured limousines habitually double-park outside cabarets, waiting for their owners to finish the night's carouse. Near one koban, chauffeurs were usually given a fifteen-minute grace period before the police ordered them to move on. Orders were given through a loudspeaker because, said the officers, if they went in person, they would have trouble being stern with the drivers, who were only following orders. Though police officers acknowledge that sympathy occasionally causes them to forget duty, they consider the risk worth running in order to establish a personal bond between citizens and the police, subject to the qualification that serious or chronic misconduct is not to be forgiven.

The Japanese language reflects the acceptability of molding law enforcement to individual characteristics. *Giri* and *ninjo* are the significant words for explaining the moral obligations of life. *Giri* refers to duty, the obligations of conscience. *Ninjo*—sometimes translated "fellow-feeling"—refers to sympathy felt by one person for another; it connotes empathetic sensitivity to the needs of the other. A moral person embodies both *giri* and *ninjo*. *Giri* without *ninjo* lacks warmth; *ninjo* without *giri* lacks principle. An exquisite dilemma is created—one repeatedly treated in Japanese literature, drama, and cinema—when *giri* and *ninjo* conflict. In Japan, as in the United States, *ninjo* prompts an individuating response, but unlike the United States, duty—*giri*—does so as well. Though the Japanese acknowledge universalistic standards, *giri* is not a matter of abstract principle. At its core are considerations of dyadic human relationship; that is, reciprocal obligations between specific people or between an individual and a specific group. The importance of this for the police is that by knowing the personal circumstances of an offender, they can draw conclusions about the network of personal obligations in which the individual is lodged. They can judge whether *giri* is likely to constrain the individual, whether, therefore, he is likely to do what he says. *Giri* provides a basis for intellectually individuating, since it provides a way of discussing the sanctioning power of social bonds. This is similar to an American police officer deciding that because an offender is a respectable doctor and dutiful father, he can be excused for a violation because he would not want to jeopardize his reputation. Americans know that personal relationships can create constraining obligations, but their moral vocabulary does not recognize it explicitly. Japanese police consider personal circumstances openly because their morality—and their language—stresses the primacy of such networks, thereby making the assessment of the consequences of individuation more predictable.

Police officers in the United States also exercise discretion on the basis of demeanor and background of offenders. The difference is that they deny that they do. They pretend that they mechanically apply the law to all offenders, regardless of personal characteristics, leaving punishment entirely up to the courts. To Americans, unequal enforcement on the basis of individual attributes smacks of favoritism, prejudice, or corruption. Though the police do it, recognizing that offenders vary as to the chances of again committing the same offense, they know they run a substantial risk of public censure. The use of discretion has not been legitimated in the United States as it has in Japan. And because its use is hidden, there are few opportunities for police officers to work out, even among themselves, appropriate grounds for its use.

When the Japanese adapt their behavior to the attitude of an offender, they are reinforcing strong ethical norms that require people to acknowledge guilt. This includes acknowledging responsibility for duties unfulfilled. The great injunction erring Japanese must obey is to say publicly, "I'm sorry." A patient in a hospital died three weeks after being transfused mistakenly with blood of the wrong type. While the doctor in charge was absolved of legal responsibility, the incident was not considered settled until the doctor agreed, prompted by a senior official in the public prosecutor's office, to send a letter of apology to the parents. When a military plane was involved in a crash with a commercial aircraft, the director-general of the Defense Agency resigned after apologizing publicly for failing in supervision. Hikers in the mountains of northern Japan were asked to write out formal apologies if they were caught taking rare alpine plants. An aliens registration office refused to process a renewal application for an American professor until the professor had apologized in writing for appearing after the expiration date. Another professor, who could not produce his passport when asked by the police, had to write a letter of apology to the local police station. Three men got caught in an elevator that stopped between floors in a multistoried bar. The police were called when the men created a scene, shouting and arguing, because the management refused to accept responsibility and apologize. After the massacre of passengers at Lod Airport in Israel in 1972 by radical Japanese youths, the Japanese government published a formal letter of apology to Israel and to the relatives of the victims. To Americans this act appears to be similar to expressions of condolence American presidents automatically send when there has been a natural disaster abroad or a foreign statesman has died. To the Japanese, however, it had a more profound meaning. It was a symbolic act of national atonement. The burden of responsibility may sometimes be too great to be met through apology, as when the father of a radical terrorist hanged himself after seeing his son in police custody on television.

An apology is more than an acceptance of personal guilt; it is an undertaking not to offend again. This theme is strikingly confirmed in Japanese folktales, which are an important though little-used indicator of cultural values. Professor Betty Lanham surveyed a selection of popular folktales from the United States and Japan.[2] She found that half the Japanese stories stressed forgiveness for evil behavior acknowledged. In only one popular American folktale was forgiveness asked and given—Cinderella. Even more revealing were the changes that the Japanese wrought in Western folktales when they were translated into Japanese. In a Japanese version of "Goldilocks and the Three Bears" the story ends with Goldilocks apologizing for her rude behavior and the bears forgiving her and inviting her back. In the American version, Goldilocks runs away, relieved at the narrowness of her escape. In one version of "Little Red Riding Hood" the Japanese have made a change that is almost too good to be true. The wicked wolf captures Little Red Riding Hood and her grandmother, puts them in a sack, and carries them off. Confronted by a hunter responding to their calls for help, the wolf falls on his knees and tearfully asks forgiveness, saying "I won't ever do anything bad again. Please forgive me."

These stories suggest that Japanese and Americans differ profoundly in their views about the mutability of character. The Japanese believe that behavior patterns can be permanently remolded. An act of contrition is not a hollow ritual but an undertaking with respect to the future that can succeed. When police officers accept written apologies—except in the special case of habitual offenders—they do so in order to constrain subsequent behavior. In the United States contrition is not so strongly linked to reform; Americans are skeptical that the past can easily be transcended. It is instructive that in the American version Goldilocks runs away; she never admits her thoughtlessness. Maybe this is why there are so many stories in the United States of offenders who outdistance their past by moving to new communities. They do not apologize and remain; they pay a formal penalty and "start again" by physically going someplace else. The Japanese believe that the network of human obligations within which individuals live will produce reformed behavior. The society, in its constituent groups, supports the erring individual in forming new behavior patterns. Apology is the sign that obligations are accepted; forgiveness is the sign that the promise is accepted. Unless character is considered mutable, neither act is meaningful.

If the web of informal human relations is more constraining in Japan than in the United States, more effective in producing reformed behavior, it would be reasonable to expect that recidivism rates would be lower in Japan than in the United States. This is probably the case among offenders as a whole—that is, all who have been discovered committing a criminal offense—but it is not true for persons imprisoned and then released—the usual basis for computing recidivism in the United States. In Japan 47 percent of all persons released from prison at the end of their sentences were reimprisoned for further offenses within three years and 57 percent within five years.[3] In the United States 41 percent of prisoners released from state prisons were imprisoned again within three years.[4] The great majority of American prisoners (92 percent) were held in state facilities in 1987.[5] About 61 percent of persons sentenced to Japanese prisons have been there before, while in U.S. state prisons only 37 percent of adults and 6.5 percent of juveniles have had a prior commitment.[6] According to American criteria for judging the effectiveness of a criminal justice system, the Japanese system is less effective than the American.

The explanation for the paradoxical relation between recidivism and beliefs about the mutability of character—changeable in Japan, unchangeable in the United States—is that formal sanctions against criminal behavior, especially imprisonment, are used more sparingly in Japan than in the United States. Japan appears to divert a larger proportion of offenders away from court adjudication, where they might be sentenced to prison, than is the case in the United States. For example, 32 percent of Penal Code defendants in 1987 were sent to summary courts where the maximum penalty could be a fine; 28.5 percent had their prosecution suspended; 26 percent were referred to family courts; and only 8.5 percent were formally tried.[7] Although hard data are lacking in the United States, there is general agreement that prosecutors file charges before courts in about 50 percent of cases submitted to them. Furthermore, once defendants get to courts, Japanese defendants are less likely than American to be imprisoned, at least for serious offenses. For example, 44 percent of people tried for Penal Code offenses in 1986 were given prison sentences.[8] In county courts in the United States, which handle the bulk of all criminal convictions, 71 percent of serious felony offenders were sentenced to prison.[9] Because Penal Code offenses cover more than the serious felony offenses examined in the United States, it is important to examine sentences for comparable offenses. Seventy-eight percent of convicted Japanese murderers were sentenced to prison, compared with 95 percent of the American; 66 percent of Japanese rapists, 86 percent of American; 86 percent of Japanese robbers, 87 percent of American; 73 percent of Japanese thieves, 65 percent of American; and 50 percent of Japanese who committed bodily injury versus 74 percent of Americans who committed aggravated assault. With the exception of larceny, American courts are more likely than the Japanese to send people to prison. The supposition that a larger proportion of offenders goes to prison in the United States than in Japan is further supported by the fact that a much larger proportion of the total population is in prison in the United States than in Japan, even allowing for differences in crime rates. The incarceration rate for Americans is 5 times greater than for Japanese (228 vs. 44.2 per 100,000), despite the fact that the serious crime rate is only 3.2 times as high.[10]

Recidivism is higher, therefore, in Japan, not because the criminal justice system is not effective, but because it is primarily the more serious offender who is sent to jail. Jails are a last resort in Japan; in the United States they are a generalized response.

Shaping official response in accordance with the background and demeanor of offenders, especially sincere repentance, is not unique to the police; it is a characteristic of the Japanese criminal justice system as a whole. Prosecutors, for instance, have almost unlimited discretion with respect to decisions to prosecute. The Code of Criminal Procedure states that prosecutors are to consider "character, age, and situation of the offender," as well as "conditions subsequent to the commission of the offense." In the past few years, prosecutors have chosen not to prosecute about 36 percent of the suspects submitted to them for commission of serious Penal Code offenses. In about 81 percent of these cases, the decision was based on criminological reasons, not insufficiency of evidence. The more serious the offense, of course, the more likely it is that prosecution will take place. In murder cases, prosecution is more or less mandatory. Appeals against a prosecutor's decision not to prosecute are possible but rarely made.

Criminological considerations affect prosecution in the United States as well, but it is impossible to tell how much. By and large, American prosecutors are not required to prosecute, even when evidence is sufficient for conviction. Estimates of how many cases are actually dismissed are very impressionistic. A common figure is 50 percent.[11] If the proportion is so high, and therefore larger than in Japan (50 percent as opposed to 35 percent), it is possible that relative to all offenders the proportion in which criminological considerations play a role in determining prosecution is as great as in Japan.

In both countries the behavior of the offender also influences the severity of the sentences handed down by the courts. Whether there is a significant difference in the operation of this factor between the two countries cannot be determined without comparing statutory provisions against actual sentences and without knowing what was going on in the minds of the judges. It is clear, however, that sentences in general are lighter in Japan than in the United States. Not only are fines awarded more commonly but prison sentences are significantly shorter. In 1987, 40 percent of Japanese prison sentences for Penal Code offenses were for less than one year. Ninety-six percent were for three years or less.[12] In the United States in 1987, the average prison sentence for felony convictions in state courts was over six years.[13] Like many states in the United States, Japan has a death penalty. It is imposed exclusively for murder.[14] In both countries defendants who cooperate and confess their guilt are treated more leniently than those who demand trial and are then convicted.[15] Similarly, prior criminal record also influences sentences.

In both Japan and the United States, therefore, prospects for rehabilitation are assessed and allowed to affect the response of the criminal justice system. What is striking about Japan is the extent to which individuation has been accepted explicitly, certainly much more than in the United States where the word "rehabilitation" has a bad odor among the general populace. In Japan, police officers, prosecutors, and judges openly discuss whether the attitude of an offender and his personal social environment are conducive to improved behavior. The norms governing differential responses, whether by police officers or others, are matters of explicit consideration, thereby ensuring that actions of the system are consistent with the public's view of justice.

The legitimation of discretionary uses of authority by police officers enhances their identification with the rest of the criminal justice system. Appropriate to their tasks, they make choices in terms of the same goals and values that shape decisions at higher levels. The police are not aware of being subprofessionals to the extent that police officers are in the United States. This is an important reason why relations between police and courts, as well as police and prosecutors, are less hostile in Japan. American police officers bitterly and publicly assail prosecutors and courts for failing to support their efforts to curb crime. In a favorite word, they complain of being "handcuffed." Japanese detectives display less of this. The major impediments to criminal investigations which detectives cite are lack of resources and declining public cooperation. Though they can be pressed into discussing changes of legal procedure since World War II that have limited investigatory authority, there is no emotional intensity to the discussion. Criminal investigations have been made more difficult, but manageably so. Even though Japanese courts have authority to determine the proper application of police powers, acting in accordance with procedural safeguards very much like those in the United States, the police feel part of the same community of justice.

The Japanese police officer can devote so much more time to considering appropriate treatment because he need devote less time, compared with American police, to determining guilt. The reason for this is that the characteristic stance of a Japanese confronting the police is submissiveness. More than simply being polite or deferential, Japanese are willing to admit guilt and to accept the consequences of their actions. The approved reaction of a suspect in the face of authority is compliance; he must not feign innocence or seek to avoid punishment. In an apt phrase, the suspect is not to act "like a carp on the cutting board." The offender places his fate in the hands of society's authoritative agents, cooperating with them in setting the terms of his reconciliation with the community. Japanese police officers who have dealt with American suspects—mostly around military bases—are shocked at their combativeness. Even when Americans are caught redhanded, say police officers, they deny their guilt. They display no contrition and immediately begin constructing a legal defense. They insist on talking to lawyers, remain uncommunicative, and act as if being accused is an infringement of their civil rights. Japanese suspects readily sign interrogation records; Americans never do. From the Japanese viewpoint, Americans are unwilling to accept responsibility for wrongful actions. . . .

The cooperativeness of the Japanese people with the police and prosecutors is indicated by one stunning fact: Four-fifth of suspects are prosecuted without arrest. The great majority of suspects cooperate voluntarily in their own prosecution. In 1987, for example, 78 percent of all suspects for Penal Code and other serious crimes were examined by officials without being arrested. Only 19 percent were held for longer than three days. In the United States, on the other hand, arrest is the beginning of a criminal case; it is the way in which prosecution is instigated. And arrest is tantamount to detention in jail, at least until a judge has heard the charge. . . .

The primary purpose of Japanese criminal justice, unlike American, is not to exact punishment. Its actions are symbolic, indicating social exclusion. In psychological terms, the system relies on positive as well as negative reinforcement, emphasizing loving acceptance in

Chart 1

Variables	*Japan*	*United States*
I. Police		
1. Discretion	Legitimated	Suspect
2. Authority	Moral	Legal
3. Enforcement	Individuated	Categorized
4. Relations with rest of criminal justice system	Collegial	Antagonistic
II. Sanctioning Process		
1. Sanctions	Informal, not explicit	Formal, explicit
2. Outcomes	Repentance	Punishment
3. Approved behavior	Confession	Plea-bargaining
4. Agency	Community	Government
III. The Individual		
1. Stance before authority	Submissive	Combative
2. Demeanor	Embarrassment	Anger
3. Character	Mutable	Immutable
IV. Political Culture		
View of government	Organic	Artifactual

exchange for genuine repentance.[16] An analogue of what Japanese police want the offender to feel is the tearful relief of a child when confession of wrongdoing to parents results in an understanding laugh and a warm hug. Japanese officers want to be known for the warmth of their care rather than the strictness of their enforcement. As one perceptive observer has written, "the Japanese law-enforcement system does not apply punishment to fit the crime, but rather to fit the demeanor of the culprit after the crime."[17]

The discussion . . . has shown that the behavior of the police is related in subtle ways to general patterns of value and behavior. . . . Police behavior meshes in particular with views about the mutability of character, the nature of government, the utility of various kinds of sanctions, and the role of authority. The aspects of police behavior and culture that have been discussed are listed in Chart 1.

NOTES

1. A seal (*hanko*) is a small wooden stylus imprinted with a Japanese character. It is legal authentication of a signature.
2. Betty Lanham and Masao Shimura, "Folktales Commonly Told American and Japanese Children: Ethical Themes of Omission and Commission," *Journal of American Folklore* (January–March 1967), pp. 33–48.
3. Study by the Ministry of Justice, 1982.
4. *Sourcebook of Criminal Justice Statistics, 1988,* p. 658. This figure is based on an eleven-state study in 1983.
5. Ibid., p. 619.
6. Ministry of Justice, 1989, and *Sourcebook of Criminal Justice Statistics, 1988,* p. 622.
7. *White Paper on Crime, 1988,* p. 14.

8. Ibid., p. 17. These figures are for prison sentences that were not suspended. They are for 1986.
9. Bureau of Justice Statistics, *Bulletin: Felony Sentences in State Courts, 1986,* p. 2.
10. *White Paper on Crime, 1988,* p. 108, and *Sourcebook of Criminal Justice Statistics, 1988,* p. 613. Figures for 1987. For the calculation on respective serious crimes rates, see chapter 1.
11. Frank W. Miller, *Prosecution* (Boston: Little, Brown, 1969), chap. 8. Donald M. McIntyre and David Lippman, "Prosecutors and Early Disposition of Felony Cases," *American Bar Association Journal* (December 1970), pp. 1154–59.
12. *Summary of the White Paper on Crime, 1988,* p. 99.
13. *Sourcebook of Criminal Justice Statistics, 1988,* p. 562. The average sentence imposed by U.S. district courts in 1987 was five years and three months. *Sourcebook,* p. 558.
14. Penal Code, Articles 199–200.
15. Japanese evidence comes from the testimony of prosecutors. U.S. data are very clear on this point. Mark Cunniff, *Sentencing Outcomes in 28 Felony Courts, 1985* (Washington, D.C.: Bureau of Justice Statistics, 1987), p. 26; Alfred Blumstein, et al., *Research on Sentencing: The Search for Reform* (Washington, D.C.: National Academy Press, 1983), vol. 1, p. 18.
16. John Braithwaite, *Crime, Shame and Reintegration* (Cambridge: Cambridge University Press, 1989).
17. Karel van Wolferin, *The Enigma of Japanese Power* (New York: Alfred A. Knopf, 1989), p. 88.

PORTRAIT

The Rape Culture

Dianne F. Herman

When Susan Griffin wrote, "I have never been free of the fear of rape," she touched a responsive chord in most women.[1] Every woman knows the fear of being alone at home late at night or the terror that strikes her when she receives an obscene telephone call. She knows also of the "minirapes"—the pinch in the crowded bus, the wolf whistle from a passing car, the stare of a man looking at her bust during a conversation. Griffin has argued, "Rape is a kind of terrorism which severely limits the freedom of women and makes women dependent on men."[2] . . .

From *Women, A Feminist Perspective,* edited by Jo Freeman, 3rd Edition, 1984, Mountain View, CA: Mayfield Publishing Company. Reprinted with permission of Dianne F. Herman.

Rape Is Not Natural

Because of the aggressive–passive, dominant–submissive, me-Tarzan–you-Jane nature of the relationship between the sexes in our culture, there is a close association between violence and sexuality. Words that are slang sexual terms, for example, frequently accompany assaultive behavior or gestures. "Fuck you" is meant as a brutal attack in verbal terms. In the popular culture, "James Bond alternatively whips out his revolver and his cock, and though there is no known connection between the skills of a gun-fighter and love-making, pacificism seems suspiciously effeminate."[3] The imagery of sexual relations between males and females in books, songs, advertising, and films is frequently that of a sadomasochistic relationship thinly veiled by a romantic facade. Thus, it is very difficult in our society to differentiate rape from "normal" heterosexual relations. Indeed, our culture can be characterized as a rape culture because the image of heterosexual intercourse is based on a rape model of sexuality.

Legal Definitions of Rape

If healthy heterosexuality were characterized by loving, warm, and reciprocally satisfying actions, then rape could be defined as sex without consent, therefore involving either domination or violence. Instead, rape is legally defined as sexual intercourse by a male with a female, *other than his wife,* without the consent of the woman and effected by force, duress, intimidation, or deception as to the nature of the act. The spousal exemption in the law, which still remains in effect in most states, means that a husband cannot be guilty of raping his wife, even if he forces intercourse against her will. The implication of this loophole is that *violent, unwanted* sex does not necessarily define rape. Instead, rape is *illegal* sex—that is, sexual assault by a man who has no legal rights over the woman. In other words, in the law's eyes, violence in legal sexual intercourse is permissible, but sexual relations with a woman who is not one's property are not.

From their inception, rape laws have been established not to protect women, but to protect women's property value for men.

Society's view of rape was purely a matter of economics—-of assets and liabilities. When a married woman was raped, her husband was wronged, not her. If she was unmarried, her father suffered since his investment depreciated. It was the monetary value of a woman which determined the gravity of the crime. Because she had no personal rights under the law, her own emotions simply didn't matter.[4] Because rape meant that precious merchandise was irreparably damaged, the severity of the punishment was dependent on whether the victim was a virgin. In some virgin rapes, biblical law ordered that the rapist marry the victim, since she was now devalued property.[5] The social status of the victim was also important, as a woman of higher social status was more valuable.

Until the feminist movement compelled a change in the 1970s, special circumstances surrounded the legal definition of rape.[6] Rape complaints were assumed to be charges easily proved, often falsely made, and very difficult to defend against. To establish that the woman had not consented to intercourse, some states required proof of injury or resistance sufficient to show that the victim preferred death to rape. A victim's prior sexual history was allowed as evidence, based on the assumption that a general propensity to consent to sexual intercourse would make it more likely that a woman would consent on any given occasion. Some states required corroboration rules, or evidence other than the victim's testimony, to substantiate a charge of rape. (In 1971, before New York amended its corroboration statute, New York City had 2,415 prosecutable rape complaints but only 18 convictions.)[7] It was also formerly common practice for judges to instruct juries to evaluate the victim's testimony with caution, a procedure not common in other types of criminal trials. Provisions for psychiatric examinations of complaining witnesses also were common in many states. Polygraph, or lie-detector, tests are still widely used by prosecuting attorneys as screening devices for false rape complaints.

Due to pressure from feminist groups, the legal definition of rape has been broadened in many states over the last decade.[8] Evidentiary rules requiring corroboration, cautionary instruction, psychiatric examinations, and prior sexual history have been eliminated or revised in most states. A survey of 151 criminal-justice professionals in Florida, Michigan, and Georgia found that these types of reforms in rape-law legislation have received widespread acceptance and approval. "Further, the findings suggest that law reform need not generate the confusion, uncertainty, or antagonism predicted by some early analysts."[9]

Some jurisdictions have established categories of sexual offenses that allow for sex-neutral assaults, taking into account that men and children, as well as women, can be victims. Others have allowed prosecution when sexual assaults include acts other than penetration of the vagina by the penis, such as sodomy or oral copulation. The latest struggle has been to remove the spousal exemption in the laws, so that husbands are not immune to prosecution for rape by their wives. Each of these changes reflects an evolving understanding that rape laws should not be in existence to regulate control of virginal female bodies for sole ownership by one man; rather, rape should be defined as a sexual assault and crime of violence by one person against another.[10]

How Common Is Rape?

There was a steady increase in the rape rate between the mid-sixties and 1980, when it leveled off. In 1964, 11.2 rapes and attempted rapes were reported nationally per 100,000 inhabitants. That figure climbed to 26.2 reports per 100,000 by 1974, and, in the 1980s, has fluctuated between 33.5 and 37.9.[11] Since male victims rarely report rape, this means that, in 1987, 73 of every 100,000 females in the United States reported that they were victims of rape or attempted rape.[12]

These statistics are based on *reported* rapes. Victimization surveys indicate that for every reported rape, an additional one to three rapes have occurred but have not been reported.[13] Diana E. H. Russell's 1978 study of 930 San Francisco women found that 44 percent reported at least one completed or attempted rape.[14] Only 8 percent, or fewer than one in twelve, of the total number of incidents were ever reported to the police. Using Russell's findings, the actual incidence of rape is 24 times higher than F.B.I. statistics indicate.

In addition, a woman is probably less safe from rape in this country than she is in any other developed nation. The United States has one of the highest rape rates in the world.[15] In 1984, the United States had 35.7 rapes per 100,000. The Bureau of Justice Statistics found European nations had an average of 5.4 rapes per 100,000 inhabitants in that same year.[16]

Victims of Rape

Many myths surround the crime of rape, but perhaps most common are those that imply that the victim was responsible for her own victimization. Projecting the blame on the woman is accomplished by portraying her as a seductress. The conventional scenario is one of a man who is sexually aroused by an attractive, flirtatious woman. But the image of the rape victim as seductive and enticing is at odds with reality. Rapes have been committed on females as young as six months and as old as ninety-three years. Most victims tend to be very young. In one study in Philadelphia of reported rapes in 1958 and 1960, 20 percent of the victims were between ten and fourteen years of age; another 25 percent were between fifteen and nineteen.[17] According to data compiled in 1974 by Women Organized Against Rape, 41 percent of rape victims seen in hospital emergency rooms in Philadelphia were sixteen or younger. The category with the highest frequency of victims was the range between thirteen and sixteen years of age.[18] A comprehensive review of the literature on rape victimization published in 1979 noted that the high-risk ages are adolescents (aged thirteen to seventeen) and young adults (aged eighteen to twenty-four).[19] In 1985, The National Crime Survey, based on findings from a continuous survey of a representative sample of housing units across the United States, reported that the rape rate is highest for those white women between ages sixteen and nineteen, and for those black women between ages twenty-five and thirty-four.[20] . . .

. . . Rape is a crime commonly committed by an assailant who is known to the victim. Even in cases where women do report to the police, victim and offender are frequently acquainted. In a study of 146 persons admitted to the emergency room of Boston City Hospital during a one-year period from 1972 to 1973 with a complaint of rape, 102 of these rapes were reported to police. Forty of these victims who reported the assault knew their assailant.[21] Burgess and Holmstrom believe that victims who know their rapists are less apt to report the crime. Their study found that victims who reported rapes by assailants known to them had more difficulty establishing their credibility than did victims raped by strangers, and these cases had a higher likelihood of dropping out of the criminal-justice system.[22] . . .

In 1982, *Ms.* Magazine reported a series of studies on college campuses confirming that, even given new and more liberal attitudes about premarital sex and women's liberation, date rape and other forms of acquaintance rape may be reaching epidemic proportions in higher education. In some cases, women have even been assaulted by men ostensibly acting as protective escorts to prevent rape.[23] A 1985 study of over 600 college students found that three-quarters of the women and more than one-half of the men disclosed an experience of sexual aggression on a date. Nearly 15 percent of the women and 7 percent of the men said that intercourse had taken place against the woman's will.[24] The victim and offender had most likely known each other almost one year before the sexual assault. Date rape occurred most frequently when the man initiated the date, when he drove to and from and paid for the date, when drinking took place, and when the couple found themselves alone either in a car or indoors. In these instances, it appears that college men may feel they have license to rape.

In explaining date rape, one set of authors have stated,

> Women are often seen as legitimate objects of sexual aggression. Rape can be viewed as the logical extension of a cultural perspective that defines men as possessors of women. The American dating system, in particular, places females in the position of sexual objects purchased by men. Women are groomed to compete for men who will shower them with attention and favors, men are socialized to expect sexual reward (or at least to try for that reward) for their attention to women. This perspective presents the woman as a legitimate object of victimization: If a man is unable to seduce a woman, and yet has provided her with certain attention and gifts, then he has a right to expect sexual payment. Only the situation of rape by a total stranger escapes the influence of this reasoning. In any other case, if a woman knows her attacker even slightly, she is likely to be perceived as a legitimate victim of a justified aggressor.[25]

The tendency to dismiss rape allegations when victim and offender know each other has contributed to the silence that surrounds marital rape. Finkelhor and Yllo in their study of marital rape found that only one textbook on marriage and the family of the thirty-one they surveyed mentioned rape or anything related to sexual assault in marriage.[26] These authors cite studies that indicate that at least 10 percent of all married women questioned on this topic report that their husbands have used physical force or threats to have sex with them.[27] Marital rape may be the most common form of sexual assault: More than two times as many of the women interviewed had been raped by husbands as had been raped by strangers.[28] . . .

. . . Husbands' desires to frighten, humiliate, punish, degrade, dominate, and control their spouses were found to be the most common motivations for the sexual assaults. In their 1980–1981 study of Boston area mothers, Finkelhor and Yllo found that about half of the marital rape victims were also battered.[29] Many cases were uncovered in which wives were tortured through sadistic sexual assaults involving objects. Many more were humiliated by being forced to engage in distasteful or unusual sexual practices. One-quarter of the victims in their survey were sexually attacked in the presence of others—usually their children.[30] Many times, the rape was the final violent act in a series of physical and emotional abuses or the payback when a woman filed for separation or divorce. Sadly, many woman suffer years of abuse thinking that the assaults are caused by their failure to be good wives or feeling that they have no way out and that this is the lot of the married woman. Too often, their husbands justify their attacks on their wives by blaming the wives for causing their loss of control, or by saying that they are entitled to treat their spouses any way they choose.

Because rape so frequently involves people who know each other, most rapists and their victims are of the same race and age group. In 1985, approximately 80 percent of all rapes and attempted rapes were intraracial.[31] One reason that the myth that rapes are interracial dies hard is that cases of this type frequently receive the most publicity. In a study of rape in Philadelphia, researchers discovered that the two major newspapers, when they reported on rape cases, mentioned mainly interracial offenses. Intraracial rapes were only occasionally mentioned.[32] Gary LaFree examined the effect of race in the handling of 881 sexual assaults in a large midwestern city. He found that black males who assaulted white women received more serious charges, longer sentences, and more severe punishment in terms of executed sentences and incarceration in the state penitentiary.[33] Although black women are three times more likely to be raped than are white women, rape is least prosecuted if the victim is black.[34] The rape of poor, black women is not an offense against men of power. . . .

Why Men Rape

. . . One of the most surprising findings of studies on rape is that the rapist is normal in personality, appearance, intelligence, behavior, and sexual drive.[35] Empirical research has repeatedly failed to find a consistent pattern of personality type or character disorder that reliably discriminates the rapist from the nonrapist. According to Amir, the only significant psychological difference between the rapist and the normal, well-adjusted male appears to be the greater tendency of the former to express rage and violence. But this finding probably tends to overemphasize the aggressive personality characteristics of rapists, since generally only imprisoned rapists have been studied. Those few rapists who are sentenced to prison tend to be the more obviously violent offenders. In fact, studies by some researchers have found one type of rapist who is fairly meek and mild-mannered.[36] What is clear is the rapist is not an exotic freak. Rather, rape evolves out of a situation in which "normal" males feel a need to prove themselves to be "men" by displaying dominance over females.

In our society, men demonstrate their competence as people by being "masculine." Part of this definition of masculinity involves a contempt for anything feminine or for females in general. Reported rapes, in fact, are frequently associated with some form of ridicule and sexual humiliation, such as urination on the victim, anal intercourse, fellatio, and ejaculation in the victim's face and hair. Insertion into the woman's vagina of broomsticks, bottles, and other phallic objects is not an uncommon coup de grace.[37] The overvaluing of toughness expresses itself in a disregard for anything associated with fragility. In the rapist's view, his assertion of maleness is automatically tied to a violent repudiation of anything feminine.

Most rapes are not spontaneous acts in which the rapist had no prior intent to commit rape but was overcome by the sexual provocations of his victim. Statistics compiled from reported rapes show that the overwhelming majority are planned. In one study, 71 percent of all reported rapes were prearranged, and another 11 percent were partially planned. Only 18 percent were impulsive acts.[38] Planning is most common in cases of group rape. Even when the rapist is acting alone, a majority of the rapes involves some manipulations on the part of the offender to place his victim in a vulnerable situation that he can exploit. . . .

Most convicted rapists tend to project the blame on others, particularly the victim. Schultz found that the sex offender is twice as likely to insist on his innocence as is the general offender.[39] "In two-thirds of the cases one hears, 'I'm here on a phony beef,' or 'I might have been a little rough with her but she was asking for it,' or 'I might have done it but I was too drunk to remember.'"[40] They also rationalize the act by labeling their victims "bad" women. Some rapists excuse and deny their crime by portraying the victim as a woman of questionable sexual reputation or as a person who has placed herself in a compromising position, thus "getting what she deserved."[41] . . .

American culture produces rapists when it encourages the socialization of men to subscribe to values of control and dominance, callousness and competitiveness, and anger and aggression, and when it discourages the expression by men of vulnerability, sharing, and cooperation. In the end, it is not only women who become the victims of these men, but also the offenders themselves, who suffer. These men lose the ability to satisfy needs for nurturance, love, and belonging, and their anger and frustration from this loss expresses itself in acts of violence and abuse against others. The tragedy for our society is that we produce so many of these hardened men. . . .

Society's Response to Rape

. . . The police have considerable discretion in determining whether a crime has been committed. In 1976, according to a study by the F.B.I., 19 percent of all forcible rapes reported to the police were unfounded.[42] *Unfounding* simply means that the police decide there is no basis for prosecution. . . .

According to many studies, one of the most frequent causes of unfounding rape is a prior relationship between the participants. In the Philadelphia study, 43 percent of all date rapes were unfounded. The police, according to the researcher, seemed to be more concerned that the victim had "assumed the risk" than they were with the fact that she had not given consent to intercourse.[43]

Another common reason police unfound cases is the apparent lack of force in the rape situation. The extent of injuries seems to be even more important in the decision to unfound than is whether the offender had a weapon.[44] There is no requirement that a male businessperson must either forcibly resist when mugged or forfeit protection under the law. But proof of rape, both to the police and in court, is often required to take the form of proof of resistance, substantiated by the extent of the injuries suffered by the victim. Yet local police departments frequently advise women not to resist if faced with the possibility of rape.

> In a confusion partially of their own making, local police precincts point out contradictory messages: They "unfound" a rape case because, by the rule of their own male logic, the woman did not show normal resistance; they report on an especially brutal

> rape case and announce to the press that the multiple stab wounds were the work of an assailant who was enraged because the woman resisted.[45]

The victim is told that if she was raped it was because she did not resist enough. But if she fights back and is raped and otherwise assaulted, police blame her again for bringing about her own injuring because of her resistance. . . .

One reason physicians are reluctant to diagnose injuries caused by a sexual assault is due to their reluctance to have to give up their valuable time to testify on behalf of the prosecution. In the early seventies, the District of Columbia newspapers reported that doctors at D.C. General Hospital were intentionally giving negative medical reports of rape victims so they would not be called to court. In one case that reached the appeals court, the doctor had reported absolutely no injuries even though police photographs showed bruises and scratches on the victim's face. As a result, the trial court dismissed the rape charges and the defendants were only found guilty of assault with intent to commit rape.[46]

For many women, the experience of having their account of events scrutinized, mocked, or discounted continues in the courtroom. Women have often said that they felt as though they, not the defendants, were the persons on trial. According to Burgess and Holmstrom, "Going to court, for the victim, is as much of a crisis as the actual rape itself."[47] They quote one victim shortly after she appeared in the district court: "I felt like crying. I felt abused. I didn't like the questions the defense was asking. I felt accused—guilty 'til proven innocent. I thought the defense lawyer made it a big joke."[48] They relate how one twelve-year old girl had a psychotic breakdown during the preliminary court process.[49]

The victim, by taking the case to court, incurs extensive costs, both psychological and financial. Expecting to testify just once, she is likely to have to repeat her story at the hearing for probable cause, to the grand jury, and in superior-court sessions. To convey the discomfort of such a process, feminists have recommended that individuals imagine having to tell an audience all the details of their last sexual experience. In addition to exposing themselves to public scrutiny, rape victims may be subject to harassment from the friends or family of the perpetrator.

Financially, the time away from work nearly always stretches beyond expectations. According to Burgess and Holmstrom, the victims they accompanied to court were often forced to sit three to four hours in the courthouse, only to be told that the case had been continued. After they and their witnesses had taken time off from work and, in some cases, traveled great distances, they were less than enthusiastic about the idea of seeing justice done.[50] Wood has said, "Due to the traumatic experience which a victim must go through in order to attempt to secure the attacker's successful prosecution, it is amazing any rape cases come to trial."[51]

Even if the victim is resilient enough to pursue her case, she may encounter prejudicial attitudes from judges and juries. . . .

. . . Shirley Feldman-Summers and Karen Lindner investigated the perceptions of victims by juries and found that, as the respectability of the victim decreased, the jury's belief that the victim was responsible for the rape increased.[52] In a sense, juries have created an extralegal defense. If the complainant somehow "assumed the risk" of rape, juries will commonly find the defendant guilty of some lesser crime or will acquit him altogether.[53] A seventeen-year-old girl was raped during a beer-drinking party. The jury probably acquitted, according to the judge, because they thought the girl asked for what she got."[54] In one case, according to Medea and Thompson, "a woman who responded with 'fuck off' when approached lost her case because 'fuck' is a sexually exciting word."[55] If the victim knew the offender previously, especially as an intimate, juries will be reluctant to convict.

> In one case of "savage rape," the victim's jaw was fractured in two places. The jury nevertheless acquitted because it found that there may have been sexual relations on previous occasions, and the parties had been drinking on the night of the incident.[56]

. . . Despite attempts to educate the public about the dynamics of rape, myths still persist. Martha Burt, in a study of almost 600 Minnesota residents, found that most believed that "Any healthy woman can resist a rapist"; "In the majority of rapes, the victim was promiscuous or had a bad reputation"; "If a girl engages in necking or petting and she lets things get out of hand, it is her fault if her partner forces sex on her"; "One reason that women falsely report a rape is that they frequently have need to call attention to themselves." Burt found that rapists also subscribed to these myths in attempts to excuse and rationalize their behavior.[57] The implications of her study is that the general population's attitudes toward women who are raped is very similar to the rapist's view of his victim.

During the 1986–1987 school year, a survey was taken of over 1500 sixth to ninth graders who attended the Rhode Island Rape Crisis Center's assault-awareness program in schools across the state. The results of the survey strongly indicated that even the next generation of Americans tends to blame the victim of sexual assault. For example, 50 percent of the students said a woman who walks alone at night and dresses seductively is asking to be raped. In addition, most of the students surveyed accepted sexually assaultive behavior as normal. Fifty-one percent of the boys and 41 percent of the girls stated that a man has a right to force a woman to kiss him if he has spent "a lot of money" on her. Sixty-five percent of the boys and 57 percent of the girls in junior high schools said it is acceptable for a man to force a woman to have sex if they have been dating for more than six months. Eighty-seven percent of the boys and 79 percent of the girls approved of rape if the couple were married. Interestingly, 20 percent of the girls and 6 percent of the boys taking the survey disclosed that they had been sexually abused."[58]

In cases of rape, judges, juries, police, prosecutors, and the general public frequently attribute blame and responsibility to the victim for her own victimization. Unfortunately, these negative responses are often compounded by reactions from family and friends. Encounters with parents, relatives, friends, and spouses many times involve either anger at the victim for being foolish enough to get raped or expressions of embarrassment and shame that family members will suffer as a result of the attack. . . .

The Rape Culture

. . . As long as sex in our society is construed as a dirty, low, and violent act involving domination of a male over a female, rape will remain a common occurrence. The erotization of male dominance means that whenever women are in a subordinate position to men, the likelihood for sexual assault is great. We are beginning to see that rape is not the only way in which women are sexually victimized, and that other forms of sexual exploitation of women are rampant in our society.[59] Feminists have raised our consciousness about rape by developing rape crisis centers and other programs to assist victims and their families, by reforming laws and challenging politicians, by training professionals in medicine and in the criminal-justice system, and by educating women and the general public on the subject. They are also enlightening us about pornography; sexual harassment on the job and in higher education; sexual exploitation in doctor, dentist, and therapist relations with patients; and sexual assault in the family, such as incest and rape in marriage.

Rape is the logical outcome if men act according to the "masculine mystique" and women act according to the "feminine mystique." But rape does not have to occur. Its presence is an indication of how widely held are traditional views of appropriate male and female behavior, and of how strongly enforced these views are. Our society is a rape culture because it fosters and encourages rape by teaching males and females that it is natural and normal for sexual relations to involve aggressive behavior on the part of males. To end rape, people must be able to envision a relationship between the sexes that involves sharing, warmth, and equality, and to bring about a social system in which those values are fostered.

NOTES

1. Susan Griffin, "Rape: The All-American Crime," *Ramparts*, 10 (Sept. 1971), 26.
2. Ibid., 35.
3. Griffin, 27.
4. Carol V. Horos, *Rape* (New Canaan, Conn.: Tobey Publishing Co., 1974), 4.
5. Ibid., 5.
6. National Institute of Law Enforcement and Criminal Justice, *Forcible Rape: An Analysis of Legal Issues* (Wash. D.C.: U.S. Government Printing Office, 1978), 5–33.
7. Pamela Lakes Wood, "The Victim in a Forcible Rape Case: A Feminist View," *American Criminal Law Review*, 7 (1973), 372.
8. Rosemarie Tong, *Women, Sex and the Law* (Totowa, N.J.: 1984), 90–123.
9. Barbara E. Smith and Jane Roberts Chapman, "Rape Law Reform Legislation: Practitioner's Perceptions of the Effectiveness of Specific Provisions," *Response*, 10 (1987), 8.
10. Tong, *Women, Sex and the Law*, 90–123.
11. *Forcible Rape: An Analysis of Legal Issues*, 2. Table 1 reports the rape rate for each year from 1960 to 1975. Figures for subsequent years can be found in *Uniform Crime Reports: Crime in the United States* (Federal Bureau of Investigation, U.S. Department of Justice, Washington, D.C.) for each year.
12. *1987 Uniform Crime Reports for the United States* (Wash. D.C.: U.S. Department of Justice, 1987), 14.
13. Duncan Chappell, "Forcible Rape and the Criminal Justice System: Surveying Present Practices and Reporting Future Trends," in Marcia J. Walker and Stanley L. Brodsky, eds., *Sexual Assault* (Lexington, Ma.: Lexington Books, 1976), 22. Annual Surveys by the federal government report that from 1973 to 1986, between 41 and 61 percent of all rapes and attempted rapes were reported to the police. Bureau of Criminal Justice Statistics Bulletin, *Criminal Victimization 1986,* Table 5, p. 4. However, the National Institute of Law Enforcement and Criminal Justice reported in *Forcible Rape: Final Project Report*, March 1978, that "the *actual* number of rapes in the United States is approximately four times the reported number" (p. 15).
14. Diana E. H. Russell, *Sexual Exploitation* (Beverly Hills, Calif.: Sage Publications, 1984), 35–36.
15. Diana Scully and Joseph Marolla, "'Riding the Bull at Gilleys': Convicted Rapists Described the Rewards of Rape," *Social Problems*, 32 (Feb. 1985), 252.
16. *International Crime Rates*, NCJ-110776 (Special Report by the Bureau of Justice Statistics), May 1988, Table 1, p. 2.
17. Menachem Amir, *Patterns in Forcible Rape* (Chicago: University of Chicago Press, 1971), 341.
18. Women Organized Against Rape, *W. O. A. R. Data* (Philadelphia: mimeo., 1975), 1.
19. Russell, *Sexual Exploitation*, 79.
20. U.S. Department of Justice, Bureau of Justice Statistics, *Criminal Victimization in the United States, 1985,* NCJ-104273, May 1987, Table 9, p. 18.
21. Lynda Lytle Holmstrom and Ann Wolbert Burgess. *The Victim of Rape* (New Brunswick, N.J.: Transaction, 1983), xxi.
22. Ibid.
23. Karen Barrett, "Date Rape, a Campus Epidemic?" *Ms.*, 11 (Sept. 1982), 130.
24. "Date Rape: Familiar Strangers," *Psychology Today* (July 1987), 10.

25. Susan H. Klemmack and David L. Klemmack, "The Social Definition of Rape," in Marcia J. Walker and Stanley L. Brodsky, eds., *Sexual Assault* (Lexington, Mass.: Lexington Books, 1976), 136.
26. David Finkelhor and Kersti Yllo, *License to Rape, Sexual Abuse of Wives* (New York: Holt, Rinehart and Winston, 1985), 6.
27. Ibid., 6–7.
28. Ibid., 8.
29. Ibid., 22, 113.
30. Ibid., 133.
31. *Criminal Victimization—1985*, Table 37, p. 39.
32. Comment, "Police Discretion and the Judgment That a Crime Has been Committed—Rape in Philadelphia," *University of Pennsylvania Law Review,* 117 (1968), 318.
33. Gary D. LaFree, "The Effect of Sexual Stratification by Race on Official Reactions to Rape," *American Sociological Review*, 45 (1980), 842.
34. *Criminal Victimization—1985*, Table 7, p. 17.
35. Menachem Amir, *Patterns in Forcible Rape* (Chicago: University of Chicago Press, 1971), 314. See Also Benjamin Karpman, *The Sexual Offender and His Offenses* (New York: Julian Press, 1954), 38–39.
36. See, for example, Camille E. LeGrand, "Rape and Rape Laws: Sexism in Society and Law," *California Law Review*, 61 (1973), 922; and Marray L. Cohen, Ralph Garofalo, Richard Boucher, and Theoharis Seghorn, "The Psychology of Rapists," *Seminars in Psychiatry,* 3 (Aug. 1971), 317.
37. Susan Brownmiller, *Against Our Will: Men, Women, and Rape* (New York: Simon and Schuster, 1975) 195.
38. Amir, *Patterns in Forcible Rape*, 334.
39. Leroy Schultz, "Interviewing the Sex Offender's Victim," *Journal of Criminal Law, Criminology and Police Science*, 50 (Jan./Feb. 1960), 451.
40. R. J. McCaldon, "Rape," *Canadian Journal of Corrections,* 9 (Jan. 1967), 47.
41. Diana Scully and Joseph Marolla, "Convicted Rapists' Vocabulary of Motive: Excuses and Justifications," Social Problems, 31 (1984), 542.
42. *1976 Uniform Crime Reports,* 16.
43. Comment, "Police Discretion," 304.
44. See, for example, Duncan Chappell et al., "Forcible Rape: A Comparative Study of Offenses Known to the Police in Boston and Los Angeles," in James M. Henslin, ed., *Studies in the Sociology of Sex* (New York: Appleton-Century-Crofts, 1971), 180.
45. Ibid., 291.
46. Janet Bode, *Fighting Back* (New York: Macmillan Publishing Co., 1978), 130–131: *United States v. Benn* 476 F. 2d. 1127, 1133 (1973).
47. Ann Wolbert Burgess and Lynda Lytle Holmstrom, *Rape, Victims of Crisis* (Bowie, Md.: Robert Brady Co., 1974), 197.
48. Ibid.
49. Ibid., 211.
50. Ibid., 200.
51. Wood, "The Victim in a Rape Case," 335.
52. Shirley Feldman-Summers and Karen Lindner, "Perceptions of Victims and Defendants in Criminal Assault Cases," *Criminal Justice Behavior*, 3 (1976), 327.
53. Note, "The Rape Corroboration Requirement: Repeal Not Reform," *Yale Law Journal,* 81 (1972), 1379).
54. Wood, "The Victim in a Rape Case," 341–342.
55. Andrea Medea and Kathleen Thompson, *Against Rape* (New York: Farrar, Straus and Giroux, 1974), 121.
56. Wood, "The Victim in a Rape Case," 344–345.
57. Martha R. Burt, "Cultural Myths and Supports for Rape," *Journal of Personality and Social Psychology*, 38 (1980), 855.
58. Jacqueline J. Kikuchi, "What Do Adolescents Know and Think about Sexual Abuse?" (Paper presented at the National Symposium on Child Victimization, Anaheim, Calif., April 27–30, 1988.)
59. See, for example, Lin Farley, *Sexual Shakedown* (New York: Warner Books, 1978); Kathleen Barry, *Female Sexual Slavery* (New York: Avon Books, 1979); Andrea Dworkin, *Pornography: Men Possessing Women* (New York: Putnam, 1981).

PORTRAIT

The Culture of Gangs in the Culture of the School

Daniel J. Monti

The picture of tough young men swaggering down school corridors, intimidating their teachers and fellow students, fighting with dangerous weapons, and selling drugs is compelling and scary stuff. It has spilled across the airways and through the print media and arises frequently in discussions about the sorry state of public education. Notwithstanding the publicity and furor over gangs in schools, we do not know much about the subject beyond the mounds of frightening testimony built by school teachers, administrators, and students. We do not know how far gangs have spread throughout public school systems. Nor are we at all clear on how big a problem they really pose in the schools where they appear. . . .

Much heated discussion about gangs revolves around the issue of how well or poorly these groups are integrated into the conventional world (Horowitz, 1990). The position taken here is that gangs and their members do not stand apart from the larger culture but are trying to find a way to fit in it (Katz, 1988). Who they are and what they do complements what is going on in the larger society, even though it may not flatter that society. The culture of the school, marked as it is by bureaucratic procedures and meritocratic principles, has become more susceptible to challenges from gangs, communal groups whose members draw on the strength of their ascribed status as part of a fictive brotherhood. How representative of these different, yet complementary, cultures manage to coexist is the subject of this paper. . . .

The present study was conducted during 1989 and 1990 in a school district outside a major United States city. Several administrators from the Fairview School District were certain that there was some gang activity in their schools, but they had no idea how much. They asked the author to conduct a study of gangs in the district's schools in order to determine the nature and extent of gang activity. The present paper is derived from that study.

The research was based on observations and interviews conducted at nine elementary schools and the district's sole junior and senior high school. Approximately 200 students from the elementary schools were interviewed. Another 100 students were interviewed at each of the other schools. Several teachers, counselors, and principals were interviewed more informally at each site. . . .

The Subculture of Gangs in the Culture of the School

Gangs create a subculture in schools that parallels the culture endorsed by adults who are supposed to operate the site. The two cultures do not clash so much as bump; and the bumping occurs in ways that allow adults to carry on many of their routines and to ignore the influence that gangs have acquired. The gang subculture is an exaggerated and better-organized version of the "peer culture" that operates in all schools to varying degrees. It serves as a powerful device for socializing youngsters and is every bit a part of the school's "hidden curriculum" as are the racial, class, and gender biases that some observers find lurking in most every school routine (Anyon, 1989; Lubeck, 1989). The gang subculture has another source of strength and legitimacy. It is an expression of the tension that frequently exists between the school and the community in which it is embedded.

The "peer culture" in schools is noteworthy because it can be simultaneously maddening and silly and because it ordinarily can be accommodated within the officially endorsed culture of the school. Indeed, the adults who operate schools often try to capture that peer culture and channel its energy into age- and sex-segregated clubs or teams that somehow complement the school culture. The gang subculture is far more intrusive and disruptive than the broader peer culture of which it is part. The gang culture is remarkable for the degree to which it is organized and sets itself up as a challenge to the official culture administered by adults.

The subculture of gangs is not expressed in a single way, however. It can very from one to another school setting. It even can be accommodated within the school's officially endorsed culture under many circumstances. There are occasions when gangs and school officials coexist quite nicely and find ingenious, if somewhat tortured, ways to ignore or avoid offending the other party. This ability and wish not to offend the other party too openly is the key to understanding how the subculture of gangs existed so well in the Fairview School District.

. . . School staff [are willing] to transfer gang members to other buildings, an action that both "protects" the students and rids the school of a troublemaker. School personnel also offer outright denials about the presence of gangs and often fail to report incidents involving gang members for fear that they will reflect badly on their management skills. Such actions, however, are not reserved only for gang members. These are rather standard administrative practices. Their application in matters involving gangs becomes altogether too common to avoid detection and throws both the receiving schools and bureaucratic machinery used to process transfer students into an overheated mess.

Gang members, for their part, also can work to soften their appearance at school without jeopardizing their effectiveness outside of school. They can refrain, at least at the high school level, from provocative displays of intimidation and violence. Gang members attending Fairview High School certainly did this. They also offered school personnel satisfactory explanations for those fights that could not be avoided. The confrontations, it was suggested, were just about "he say-she say" stuff (i.e., rumors or unkind comments about persons) or disagreements between students from different towns. Students first used this explanation in the junior high school and found that it worked rather well. School officials readily accepted and/or passed along such explanations in reports about even substantial fights among numerous students. There was a measure of truth to both explanations; but carefully overlooked was the fact that these exchanges ordinarily involved persons associated with different gangs.

Gang members also masked their involvement in such "illegitimate groups" by participating in regular school activities and by doing at least passable academic work. Some gang members at Fairview High School did considerably better than that. They avoided more overt forms of drug dealing and wore clothing that did not immediately identify them as gang members. Finally, they acquired the grudging admiration of a sizable portion of the non-gang student body by purchasing items that others could not afford and by providing a measure of protection for youngsters from their respective municipalities.

In these and other ways, then, gangs and school staff were able to find a basis for mutual tolerance, if not respect. The culture of the gang could be accommodated in the culture of the school by defining and treating it as similar to the broader peer or "teen culture." In its more exaggerated and intimidating forms, the gang culture rendered the officially endorsed school culture ineffective and toothless. It did so while allowing most of the school's bureaucratic routines to stand, if only as a feeble memorial to the vacant claims of a more conventional world on the lives of many youths.

It is in this latter way that most persons see the gang culture affecting schools; and there are many instances when this view is warranted. On such occasions, gangs might be seen as establishing a "counterculture" that lays out codes of conduct, beliefs, and routines that compete with those promoted by school staff (Yinger, 1960). However, gangs ordinarily do not supplant the regular school culture. They merely nudge it aside.

The gang culture is reactionary in that local customs are extolled and defended against the encroachment of persons and ways of behaving considered to be alien (Tilly, 1979). In its most extreme forms, the gang culture actively resists conventional models and myths of success and discourages many students from endorsing them. It also promotes the introduction of illegal activities into school routines. Its support for these acts transforms the school from a haven into a sanctuary, from a place of safety into a place immune to the law.

This view of the gang culture is appealing on several levels. It is consistent with much popular and scientific speculation about gangs and it feeds commonly held prejudices about the public schools. Were schools more effective, one would expect less gang activity to take place there. Gangs also might be seen, therefore as doing little more than filling a vacuum created by the absence or ineffectiveness of a more conventional culture in the schools. Gangs may not present the best face that a local community can offer, but they do represent a parochial alternative to the more cosmopolitan world view offered in the school. They implicitly challenge the values and work of more conventional community groups and reject as unrealistic the idea that youngsters like themselves might grow into more conventional adult roles. Schools are seen and are treated as being largely irrelevant and not worthy of respect. Gang members act out against the school instead of passively accepting what it has to offer.

The idea that gangs fill a big social and moral hole in school implies that they perform an important service. It would be inaccurate to portray this service as benefiting only the members of gangs. Historically, gangs have given expression to feelings held by many community residents toward outsiders (Thrasher, 1927). Within the culture of the school, then, gangs might be viewed as reinforcing or laying the groundwork for some important, perhaps even conventional, values. Among the strongest of these values would be loyalty to real and fictive kin, attachment to a place, and collaborative economic ventures.

Many observers have commented on the family-like quality of life within gangs and ties among gang members (Horowitz, 1990; Vigil and Yun, 1990). The notion of gangs as a "substitute family" speaks to the continuing importance of the family as an institution and the impoverished state of that institution in communities where gangs are found. It is important to bear in mind, however, that the uprooted members of many immigrant populations often created families for themselves from persons in the same rooming house, fraternal lodge, or church (Hohenberg and Lees, 1985). This helped them to survive in an otherwise ill-defined and sometimes hostile urban setting.

Gang members have accomplished this to varying degrees, but school officials are understandably reluctant to encourage them to build on that success within the school building. Some merely spend a great deal of their spare time together, but others have been known to share a common dwelling. Included in this second category would be youngsters, interviewed by the author, who sold drugs in order to pay rent on a house they shared because living at home had become too painful.

The place to which most gang member show loyalty and for which they express warm feelings is their territory or "turf." Not all gangs exhibit the same degree of attachment to a territory (Monti, 1993). No matter how thin that attachment might be, however, it is nonetheless critical to any effort to build a permanent community. Observers have noted that some gangs are enmeshed in a stable community and some gangs exist almost as a tiny island, free from much contact with many other persons or groups that might be near them. In either case, it is the fact of being rooted to a place that makes more credible any group's claim to being part of a community with its own routines, rituals, and folklore. Theorists have long held that such ties are vital to any group's successful integration in an unsettled urban world (Wirth, 1938; Suttles, 1968).

Another prominent feature of successful group and community life, of course, is the ability to earn a living. The degree to which gangs or gang members engage in ventures to acquire money varies quite substantially. Individual gang members sometimes hold marginal jobs in the regular economy even as they are involved in illicit enterprises. Most of the moneymaking opportunities pursued by gangs as groups are fixed firmly on the illegal margins of the irregular economy (Monti, 1993; Skolnick, 1993; Padilla, 1993). This is not surprising, given the history of entrepreneurial activities inside some minority communities and the African American community in particular (Lane, 1986). Nevertheless, contemporary youth gangs have reproduced some collaborative techniques for making and investing money that have served different ethnic groups for generations.

Foremost among these strategies are rotating credit associations and mutual trade associations (Cummings, 1980; Velez-Ibanez, 1983; Light, 1972). The former requires persons, usually of modest means, to commit a portion of their disposable income to a common fund whose proceeds are given to a single contributor for some useful purpose. The fund is replenished and reallocated to other contributors until it has been "rotated" through the entire group. In essence, members of the group advance credit to each other under the assumption that persons will contribute to the fund even after they have enjoyed their turn at the trough. Mutual trade associations require the collaboration of individual entrepreneurs who compete fiercely but share some expenses and preserve the integrity of their market against would-be rivals. They are intended to restrain both the number of traders or producers in an area and the tactics that members use to capture clients.

The illicit ventures engaged in by gangs combine important features of rotating credit associations and mutual trade associations. Gang leaders often extend other members credit to buy their first supplies of drugs and assign them sales territories. Better-established groups also create a common "defense fund" that is intended to be used by members who are arrested or need legal assistance. Gang members who become more deeply involved in the drug trade frequently reduce their expenses by using the same wholesale distributor. They also go to great lengths to protect each other when competitors attempt to encroach upon their trading territory. The collaborative strategies attached to the drug trade also find expression in other illegal ventures such as extortion, burglary, and car stealing. Furthermore, older gang members take seriously their roles as teachers and patrons of younger members. In this way, the social and economic benefits of gang membership come to reinforce each other.

The youngsters who sell drugs on a retail basis do not earn a great deal and move in and out of the trade as their need for spending money rises and falls. They may even come to view themselves as being exploited (Padilla, 1992). Nevertheless, they establish a precedent for successful retail trades that capture a healthy share of a white middle-class market.

This is an achievement for any ethnic enterprise, and it has historical roots in illicit businesses created by earlier generations of minorities with few conventional alternatives available to them (Lane, 1986).

However valid and real the parallel between organized drug dealing by gangs and more conventional ethnic enterprises may be, there are practical barriers to realizing the full benefits of such enterprises for youth gangs that sell drugs. First, the purveyors work exceedingly hard to conjure up dreadful adult images for themselves, but they are unmistakably children and cannot participate more fully or effectively in a conventional adult world (Katz, 1988, p. 129). Second, most pass in and out of the trade (Padilla, 1992, 1993) and, more generally, drift in and out of delinquency until they become adults (Matza, 1964). Third, and finally, their work and violence are confined exclusively to the fringes of the irregular economy. They cannot easily translate their successful work into more conventional activities leading to other careers, or at least they have not shown much inclination to do so, in part because so much of their energy is spent on activities that stand in opposition to conventional standards (Katz, 1988, pp. 145–147). That is why the presence and impact of gangs in schools is so troubling.

It was known well before the present study that much of what gangs do in and out of schools is destructive and cannot be dismissed casually. The fact that gang activity often is tolerated in schools speaks to the ineffectiveness of school personnel, the irrelevance of the standards they support, and the persistent tension between the school and the community in which gangs are found. It is equally apparent that the relation between the culture of the gang and the culture of schools is far more complex than is commonly supposed. Educational routines and administrative practices in some schools encourage more severe gang activity or can discourage it. The object of the author in this paper has been to describe and to account for some of the complexity in the relation between gang activity and the culture of schools.

REFERENCES

Anyon, J. (1989). "Social Class and the Hidden Curriculum of Work." In *Schools and Society*, edited by J. H. Ballantine, pp. 257–279. Mountain View, CA: Mayfield Publishing Company.

Cummings, S. ed. (1980). *Self-Help in Urban America*. Port Washington, NY: Kennikat Press Corporation.

Hohenberg, P. M., and Lees, L. H. (1985). *The Making of Urban Europe 1000–1950*. Cambridge: Harvard University Press.

Horowitz, R. (1990). "Sociological Perspectives on Gangs: Conflicting Definitions and Concepts." In *Gangs in America*, edited by C. R. Huff, pp. 37–54. Newbury Park, CA: Sage Publications.

Katz, J. (1988). *Seductions of Crime*. New York: Basic Books.

Lane, R. (1986) *Roots of Violence in Black Philadelphia 1860–1900*. Cambridge: Harvard University Press.

Light, I. (1972). *Ethnic Enterprise in America*. Berkeley: University of California Press.

Lubeck, S. (1989). "Sandbox Society: Summary Analysis." In *Schools and Society*, edited by J. H. Ballantine, pp. 280–292. Mountain View, CA: Mayfield Publishing Company.

Matza, D. (1964). *Delinquency and Drift*. New York: John Wiley & Sons, Inc.

Monti, D. (1993). "Gangs in More- and Less-Settled Communities." In *Gangs: The Origins and Impact of Contemporary Youth Gangs in the United States*, edited by S. Cummings and D. Monti, pp. 219–256. Albany: State University of New York Press.

Padilla, F. (1992). *The Gangs as an American Enterprise*. New Brunswick: Rutgers University Press.

Padilla, F. (1993). "The Working Gang." In *Gangs: The Origins and Impact of Contemporary Youth Gangs in the United States*, edited by S. Cummings and D. Monti, pp. 173–192. Albany: State University of New York Press.

Skolnick, J. H., Blumenthal, R., and Correl, T. (1993). "Gang Organization and Migration." In *Gangs: The Origins and Impact of Contempo-*

rary Youth Gangs in the United States, edited by S. Cummings and D. Monti, pp. 193–218. Albany: State University of New York Press.

Suttles, G. (1968). *The Social Order of the Slum.* Chicago: University of Chicago Press.

Thrasher, F. M. (1927). *The Gang: A Study of 1,313 Gangs in Chicago.* Chicago: University of Chicago Press.

Tilly, C. (1979). "Collective Violence in European Perspective." In *Violence in America,* edited by H. D. Graham and T. R. Gurr, pp. 83–118. Beverly Hills: Sage Publications.

Velez-Ibanez, C. G. (1983). *Bonds of Mutual Trust.* New Brunswick: Rutgers University Press.

Vigil, J. D., and Yun, S. C. (1990). "Vietnamese Youth Gangs in Southern California." In *Gangs in America,* edited by C. R. Huff, pp. 146–162. Newbury Park: Sage Publications.

Wirth, L. (1938). "Urbanism as a Way of Life." *American Journal of Sociology* 44: 1–24.

Yinger, J. M. (1960). "Contraculture and Subculture." *American Sociological Review* October: 625–635.

DEVELOPING YOUR OWN SNAPSHOTS *About Culture*

1. *Writing topic:* Name five of your heroes from such fields as business, sports, entertainment, religion, and politics, or from everyday life. Then write an essay in which you identify the particular cultural values reflected in their heroic accomplishments. To start, consider whether they are idols of production, consumption, or activism.
2. *Writing topic:* We have seen how much cultural clout the baby boomers have had in American society. Thinking about music, art, comedy, and television, identify some of the contributions that your generation has made to American popular culture.
3. *Research topic:* Analyze the lyrics to three top-40 songs in which an angry message is expressed. Can you identify these lyrics with a culture of hate? Could anyone possibly use these lyrics to justify sexual assault against women? Do you believe that song lyrics reflect or affect the values of audience members?
4. *Research topic:* Let's say you were a sociologist who was studying the culture of your campus. Construct a one-page questionnaire to identify some of the values and practices that are widely shared among the students at your college. Then give the questionnaire to a sample of students. (To get at how values operate in everyday life, you might want to ask such questions as how many hours a week your respondents spend doing things like studying, partying, watching TV, and so on. You might also ask them to rank-order certain activities—getting good grades, having a date, being well liked, making lots of money—in terms of how important they are.)

5. *Research topic:* Pick up a recent issue of a supermarket tabloid—preferably *The National Enquirer* or *The Star*. Analyze all the profiles in that issue with respect to the human qualities and problems that they emphasize. First determine how many profiles feature celebrities. How many of these are entertainers, business leaders, or politicians? How many would you regard as idols of consumption? Next find out how many profiles feature ordinary people who do extraordinary things. How many were good samaritans? How many performed miracles or great acts of courage? How many would you regard as idols of activism?
6. *Research topic:* Just as gangs may constitute subcultures within a high school, so certain groups of students (for example, those in particular organizations and clubs) on campus may be viewed as subcultures in the context of the larger college or university community. Interview some members of such a campus group to discover to what extent they accept the values of the dominant culture (for example, success through hard work). In what respects are they subcultural—that is, what values, norms, and customs do they share that differ from those of most other students?
7. *Writing topic:* Following David Bayley's ("Forces of Order") comparative analysis as a guide, write a brief essay in which you examine a particular cultural practice or activity (for example, family life, education, voting, economic inequality, and so on) that seems to differ sharply from what we do in American society. Can you identify the underlying values that might be responsible for the difference between societies? Does ethnocentrism get in the way of examining objectively the cultural practice or activity you have identified?
8. *Writing topic:* In the photo essay "The American Dream?" visual images are presented of what might widely be associated with happiness and success in America. Thinking of your own future, write a brief essay in which you describe one of your long-term dreams. Also indicate the values you personally hold that seem to be motivating your hopes for the future. Finally, how does your personal dream differ, if at all, from "The American Dream"?

CHAPTER 2

Socialization

SCHOOL BUS

SNAPSHOT

Mapping Social Geography

Why We Create the World in Our Own Image

Ask Johnny to locate the United States on a world map and he might very well point to the continent of Africa or South America. According to a recent Gallup survey, 20 percent of Americans aged 18 to 24 can't identify their own country. When it comes to geographic knowledge, America's young people place last behind their counterparts from Mexico, Britain, France, Italy, Canada, Japan, West Germany, and Sweden.

To many, this lack of geographic knowledge is shocking. Just as startling, however, is our ignorance of *social* geography. Many Americans have grown up with a distorted view of social reality. Even if they are able to distinguish the United States from Mexico or Canada, they don't realize, for example, that Caucasians are a minority among the world's racial groupings, or that Christianity is a minority religion worldwide.

One can easily demonstrate American parochialism by questioning even the most sophisticated individuals about elementary social facts. For example, what percentage of the population of the United States is Jewish? Black? Catholic? Or what percentage of our population will be over 65 years of age by the year 2000?

I am always somewhat surprised when college students estimate that 30 percent of the population of the United States is Jewish (actually, the figure is close to 1.9 percent); that 40 percent of all Americans are black (actually, the figure for those who regard themselves as African American is more like 12 percent); that 60 percent of our population is Catholic (actually the figure is 20 percent at most); or that 40 percent of our elders are in nursing homes (the figure is more like 4 percent).

Where does misinformation about our society come from? Why can't Americans seem to get their social facts straight? Part of the answer is that all of us are socialized with an unrepresentative sample of social reality. Inevitably, we learn to view the world from our own biased and limited slice of experience. We tend to apply what we see every day to what we don't see.

Consequently, given our tendency to separate our schools and neighborhoods by race, social class, religion, and age, it is not surprising that our generalizations are often inaccurate. A person growing up in Boston may come to believe that 60 percent of the population of the United States is Catholic because that is what he or she sees in the neighborhood or at work. If the same person had grown up in Waco, Texas, he or she might instead believe that there were only two or three Catholics in the United States. Similarly, people living in Washington, D.C., may be convinced that 70 percent of all Americans are African American; growing up in Vermont, they might answer zero.

A second reason for our distorted view of social reality is that we usually don't validate or test our beliefs about society in any systematic way. Thus we can go through a lifetime unknowingly clinging to old false stereotypes.

If Ivan Boesky is implicated in an insider trading scandal, some individuals will conclude that Boesky engaged in shady business practices because he is Jewish. If an Italian American makes headlines because he is a member of organized crime, many will remember that he is of Italian descent. If someone French does the same thing, we don't remember an ethnic identity at all because it seems irrelevant. Or we treat the French criminal as an exception that proves the rule.

A third reason for our misinformation about social reality is our infatuation with television. Communication research conducted for more than a decade indicates that frequent television viewers tend to overestimate the percentage of the world population that is white and male; underestimate the amount of poverty in our country; and exaggerate the amount of violence they are likely to encounter. Frequent viewers also overestimate the proportion of jury trials in our courts and the number of miracle cures performed by doctors. They are socialized to accept a false view of social reality because this is precisely what they see on TV. The world of prime-time television is overpopulated by white males who possess more than their share of wealth and power. On dramatic series, defendants typically receive a jury trial and doctors routinely cure their patients. As noted in the snapshot "Confessions of a Soap Opera Addict," many viewers do not distinguish the fantasy that they see portrayed on television from the real world. For them, television is the real world.

What difference does it make that so many Americans are socialized to accept a distorted view of social reality? That they operate on the basis of false stereotypes of what our society is like? That they are misinformed about other people and maybe about themselves? The answer lies in the relationship between the way we define the world and the decisions we make about it.

For example, if we are mistakenly convinced that a majority of our citizens will be over 65 by the year 2020, we might decide to avoid national bankruptcy by reducing our commitment to social security for the elderly.

If Jews are mistakenly believed to make up 30 percent of our population, then the myth of a dominant Jewish presence in banking or the press sounds more plausible.

If we underestimate the amount of poverty in our country, then we might also vote down social programs for the poor and the homeless.

And if we exaggerate the amount of violence we are likely to encounter in everyday life, then we are also more likely to double-lock our doors, buy a handgun, and support the death penalty. That is exactly what is happening right now: Firearms are increasingly available, and a majority of Americans favor the death penalty.

We can assume, I believe, that most children will continue to watch four or five hours of television daily and therefore continue to be socialized to the same unrealities depicted on the tube. In all probability, they will also maintain segregated relationships in daily life. What can we do, then, to assure that Americans' perception of reality is not so far off the mark? The burden of responsibility, I believe, can be placed on our nation's classrooms.

One of the important functions of formal education is to broaden our personal experience, to serve as an agent of socialization with aspects of life that we might otherwise never experience firsthand—in short, to clarify social reality. In our efforts to improve basic skills in English, mathematics, and geography, we must not forget to place equal emphasis on the skills necessary to good citizenship and humanitarianism. Thus, young people need to be made aware of the existence of poverty and homelessness, flaws in the criminal justice system, prejudice and discrimination, and their own mortality. If our schools can teach Johnny to identify the United States on a world map, they can also teach Johnny that he is not at the center of the universe.

SNAPSHOT

Confessions of a Soap Opera Addict

The Daytime Serials Are More Than I Bargained For

I've been watching *Days of Our Lives* each day of my life for the past 22 years. It all started in 1968 when I took a year off to finish my doctoral dissertation. Each afternoon my wife and I sat together in the living room of our small apartment: She watched soap operas; I wrote my thesis. Working at home was tough enough, and eavesdropping on midday melodrama didn't help. In fact, it only reinforced my long-held impression that soaps were at about the same intellectual level as Saturday morning cartoons—but these, at least, had action. Did anyone really care whether Julie and David got together again, when Marie would discover that her fiancé was actually her long-lost brother, or whether Missy was pregnant with "another man's" child?

I didn't think so. Soap operas were television's "opiate of the masses," I had decided—the medium through which too many Americans vicariously escaped their dreary existence into the make-believe world of the rich and beautiful. While the pressing economic and social problems of our society went ignored, millions of *General Hospital* groupies became Luke and Laura, if only for a few minutes a day. They needed that soap opera fix to make their lives seem exciting and worthwhile. America's daytime serial fanatics were being distracted from improving their own lives by an insidious form of fantasy and escapism.

I was especially annoyed by the depiction of women. They seemed always to be getting pregnant, not for the purpose of having children but to manipulate and control the men in their lives. They used pregnancy to trap boyfriends into unwanted marriages or husbands into maintaining unwanted marriages. In addition, any woman who dared have a career in a field traditionally dominated by men—medicine, law, business—was either mentally ill or evil. The sex role socialization was unmistakable: Women were to stay out of the boardrooms and executive offices and stay in the kitchens and bedrooms.

It occurred to me that in some perverse way soap operas were a mass form of socializing young people to accept the status quo. Even while college students of the 1980s were scheduling or skipping courses to accommodate *General Hospital*, the majority of daytime serial watchers were high school graduates who had never attended college, mostly middle-aged women. Many used the characters on soaps as role models for how to handle their spouses. But what they learned frightened me: first, that infidelity and promiscuity were acceptable, even desirable, modes of sexual behavior; second, that divorce was the answer to any difference, no matter how trivial. If your marriage wasn't smooth as glass, get a divorce or a lover. Better yet, get a lover and then a divorce.

By the third or fourth week of watching out of the corner of my eye, I noticed something peculiar was happening to me. If I had to be away during a weekday afternoon, I'd call home for a rundown of that day's episodes. I scheduled meetings with colleagues so I wouldn't miss a particular serial. It got to the point where my wife would have to tear me away from a show to take a phone call or answer the door. It was painful to admit, but I was hooked; I was brainwashed; I had become a socialized "soapie."

Perhaps as a sort of therapy, I spent a good part of the next few years immersed in the study of soap operas. It was legitimate: I was teaching a course in mass communication, and my students were discussing the impact of television on society. I read what the experts—psychologists, sociologists, and assorted communications specialists—had to say. I even assigned student projects to analyze the characters on daytime serials.

Surprisingly, to me at least, they concluded that soap operas were much better than prime-time dramatic series in representing women, minorities, and older people in central roles. While young and middle-aged males were vastly overrepresented on prime-time television, in soap operas one-half of the characters were women. Even more to their credit, soap operas featured actors and actresses who remained on the show for decades. Many of them aged gracefully and remained attractive while they continued to play roles central to the plot. Indeed, older people were treated much better on soap operas than on most other television fare. And the daytime serials frequently focused on a range of social problems: intergroup conflict, juvenile delinquency, alcoholism, organized crime—issues that were all but ignored by the soaps' prime-time counterparts.

It was soon clear to me why soaps are so appealing. For one, they provide the things we find lacking in modern life. Monday through Friday, without fail (barring an occasional hijacking or presidential news conference), we follow our "good friends" into their offices, living rooms, and bedrooms. We attend their weddings and funerals and visit them in the hospital after surgery or childbirth. We watch them argue with their spouses, make love with other people's spouses, and punish their children. We often learn more about the personal lives of our favorite soap opera characters than we know about our real neighbors. In an era of anonymity, soap operas give us intimacy. Sadly, for those who are socially isolated, this may be the only source of intimacy in their lives, but perhaps this is better than nothing.

Soap operas make us feel good about ourselves. Misery loves miserable company, and our own problems are somehow less painful when we're able to compare them with the troubles of those we admire. The world of the daytime serial is the world of the wealthy, beautiful, and powerful—our cultural heroes, the people we aspire to become. Yet these characters have problems with their families and friends, maybe worse problems than ours. So we feel better—at their expense, of course.

Soap opera intimacy often takes the form of snooping, but only in the most positive sense. By eavesdropping, we're given the opportunity to rehearse our own emotional reactions to problems that may confront us. Observing untimely deaths, kidnappings, divorces, and mental illness on television, we learn something about the manner in which we might handle similar problems in our own lives.

At least part of the influence of daytime serials can be attributed to the credibility of television as a form of mass communication. Study after study shows Americans trust the authenticity of the images they see on the tube. In the process, however, frequent viewers often develop a distorted view of social reality. They tend to exaggerate, for example, the amount of violence they are likely to encounter in everyday life, the proportion of criminal cases that end in a jury trial, and the likelihood that physicians will perform miracle cures. For these viewers, the fantasy world on television becomes the reality. During the five years that Robert Young played Dr. Marcus Welby, the actor received more than 250,000 letters asking him for medical advice. Admiring fans were apparently unable to distinguish actor Young from character Welby.

This incredible power of soap operas as an agent of socialization was brought home to me when I met two longtime stars of *Days of Our Lives,* Susan and Bill Hayes (Doug and Julie). As an interested observer, I couldn't resist asking them the questions that might confirm what I always suspected: Do soap opera addicts confuse the fantasy world of the daytime serials with the real world in which they live? Yes, and often. Whenever a *Days of Our Lives* star gives birth (it's only a pillow), gets married (a rhinestone wedding ring), or dies (usually a failure to renegotiate the actor's contract), cards and gifts appear at the studio, they said.

For me soaps have a special appeal. As a sociologist, I investigate problems that have no easy solutions. I spend years studying serial killers, for example, and am troubled that we can't predict from childhood experience who will eventually commit hideous crimes. I research the causes of prejudice and discrimination and still see the number of racist acts of vandalism and desecration increasing. And like others, I see criminals too often get suspended sentences while their victims suffer; the rich get richer as homelessness grows; and the questionable ethics of politicians go unpunished.

And that's where soaps are different. Warm, friendly, and predictable, they make sure people get what they deserve.

SNAPSHOT

Foul Play in the Stands

A Look at Sports Fan Aggression

I have always regarded my annual visit to Foxboro Stadium to see the New England Patriots as a form of recreation—in the same league as an evening at a comedy club or an afternoon dip in the pool. Apparently, however, not all football fans agree with me.

On a recent visit, in fact, I overheard two men extolling the virtues of professional football and boxing. In an increasingly loud and obnoxious conversation, they argued that football was important, if not essential. In their view, it serves as a safety valve, an outlet for relieving our feelings of anger and hostility that might otherwise swell up inside and eventually burst in a bloody explosion of aggression and violence. According to these men, without combative contact sports, we would surely be at the mercy of our primal instincts, engaging in war with one another if not with most of the nations in the world.

If you've ever been to a professional football game, you might well agree that it provides an arena for the fans to let off steam. Spectators shout obscenities and racial slurs, scream at officials, and follow the cheerleaders in their ritualistic exhortation to "push em back, push em back . . . way back." During a lull in the action, fans sometimes display their crazy mascots (for example, a bird, a bear, or a lion) or hold up aggressively worded signs ("Cream the Colts," "Destroy the Dolphins," "Liquidate the Lions"). It is obvious that at least some of the fans vicariously participate in the game. Maybe they even believe they are part of the football team.

Psychologists call this phenomenon "catharsis of aggression." They argue that by letting off steam at a hockey or football game, spectators become less hostile, less angry, and less likely to be aggressive in the future. From this point of view, football followers are also less apt to punch another person in the nose or go after someone with a knife. In societal terms, they may be less prone to attack the shoreline of a neighboring state, to drop bombs on civilians in other countries, or to otherwise go to war. And you thought that football was mere sport.

Catharsis of aggression may sound reasonable, but so did the Edsel until Ford Motor Company examined its sales figures. If fans really get mellower and calmer as a result of attending a combative contact sporting event, why do we read so much about violent outbursts or riots among spectators at boxing matches, soccer contests, and football games? In case you missed the headlines during the past few years, fans have been beaten, trampled, and even hacked to death with machetes at these events. Most of these brutal events in the stands followed outbursts of violence among the players. Apparently the spectators imitated their heroes on the field of play.

Jeff Goldstein and Robert Arms, while professors at Temple University, studied the level of hostility among spectators at an Army–Navy football game in Philadelphia. In interviews with fans before and after the contest, these two social psychologists discovered that spectators' anger increased after they watched the game, whereas the level of hostility among spectators attending a "control" gymnastic meet did not differ before and after the competition.

Maybe it's the beer. Perhaps spectators at football games would benefit from catharsis if only they didn't drink so much during the game. After all, alcohol does tend to weaken our inhibitions against expressing aggression. Or perhaps it's the kind of people who attend combative sporting events. Maybe football and hockey attract individuals who are by nature vicious and violent.

Robert Arms and his associates wondered the same thing, so they brought their own subjects—college students enrolled in a psychology course—to a sporting event. On a random basis, one-third of their students attended a professional hockey contest, one-third attended professional wrestling, and one-third attended a swimming competition. All of them arrived together and were escorted to a spare dressing room. None was allowed to have any alcohol. They were assigned to one or another of the sporting events regardless of whether they liked the particular sport.

So in this study there was no beer and as much chance of attending swimming as wrestling. Yet significant increases in hostility were registered among students who attended hockey and wrestling, but not among spectators assigned to observe swimming. Apparently spectators become more hostile after observing an aggressive sporting contest whether that aggression is realistic, as in football and hockey, or a spoof, as in professional wrestling.

I suppose it still could be argued, regardless of the influence of contact sports on fans, that these sports have a more general effect of draining off the aggression that would otherwise end in war and murder. If catharsis of aggression works in this way, however, wouldn't you think the murder rate would drop after a well-publicized boxing match? But when sociologist David Phillips examined the homicide rates in America immediately following televised heavyweight prize fights, he found a brief but sharp increase in homicides of 13 percent. This effect seemed to peak on the third day after the prize fights.

Years ago anthropologist Richard Sipes examined another version of this argument by comparing societies classified as either warlike or peaceful. Now, if those in favor of football are correct that the sport really does drain hostility, then we would expect combative contact sports to be common in peaceful societies but relatively scarce in warlike societies. Instead, Sipes found exactly the opposite. Members of warlike societies loved football; members of peaceful societies weren't interested in it. Sipes concluded that combative sports could not be regarded as an alternative to war for the reduction of pent-up aggression. Rather, societies whose members are aggressive in one area of life tend to be aggressive in other areas of life as well. Indeed, football and hockey may actually socialize youngsters to express aggressive behavior later in life, including preparing them for warfare. What better way for children to develop affection for winning than to incorporate competitive teamwork into their play?

I don't recall television, bowling, or bingo fanatics arguing that their favorite pastime saves us from ourselves. Can't lovers of football and hockey just admit that the violence on the field of play is exciting, entertaining, perhaps a diversion from their otherwise mundane lives, or even an excuse to get together with the boys? Surely these are reasons enough to see professional athletes beat one another to a pulp.

SNAPSHOT

Sticks and Stones May Break . . .

In Reality, Names May Indeed Hurt You

What's in a name? Plenty if you happen to be political spokesperson Larry Speakes, Professor Robert Smart, psychiatrist Ronald Bliss, or District Court Judge Darrell Outlaw. Whether or not such names inspired career choices, they undoubtedly have provided material for countless after-dinner conversations. Can't you imagine Dr. Bliss being ribbed about teaming with Dr. Ruth for a late-night advice show?

According to psychologist Ron Harre and his associates at SUNY at Binghamton, and as confirmed in countless other studies, the influence of names begins in childhood. Names that we are familiar with—common names such as John and Michael—are associated with images of strength and competence; whereas unusual names like Ivan and Horace conjure up weakness and passivity. Consequently, children who are unfortunate enough to have been given bizarre or unpopular names are sometimes poorly adjusted and pessimistic about their prospects of being successful in the future; they tend to score lower on achievement tests and get lower grades in school.

This phenomenon extends into adulthood. People who have strange or unusual names are more likely to suffer from mental illness or to have criminal records. In many cases a self-fulfilling prophecy may operate during the socialization process. A child is ridiculed because of his name. As a result, he develops a negative attitude toward himself that influences his behavior in the classroom and on the playground. And teachers and peers notice this poor behavior. They assume that kids with unusual names aren't very competent or skillful. So little is seen, little is expected, and little is obtained.

The importance of names is nowhere more important than in Hollywood. Consider all the celebrities who weren't born with the right name for the image they want to portray. The former Elliot Goldstein is now Elliot Gould; Alphonso D'Abrusso is Alan Alda; Robert Zimmerman calls himself Bob Dylan; Frances Gumm's stage name was Judy Garland; and Patricia Andrzejewski is better known as rock singer Pat Benetar.

The flip side of this is that uncommon names sometimes imply uniqueness. Thus one might speculate that Zsa Zsa Gabor, Ya Hoo Serious, River Phoenix, Moon Zappa, Pee Wee Herman, Yakov Smirnoff, Rip Torn, Mister T, Whoopie Goldberg, and Minnie Pearl owe at least part of their celebrity status to their names.

Minority groups are also painfully aware of the power of a name to socialize its members to failure and negative self-esteem. People of color prefer to be called *black* or *African American*. They reject labels such as *colored* and *Negro,* contending that they were long ago assigned to them by outsiders. Jesse Jackson recently called for the elimination of the *black* label in favor of a group identity such as *Afro-American* that would emphasize an African cultural heritage in the same way that white ethnic groups—Irish Americans, Polish Americans, and Italian Americans—choose to stress their European ancestry. Even the term *minority* may be falling out of favor as more and more people of color refuse to see themselves as playing a minor role in American society. Similarly, many women now resent being labeled *girls, babes,* and *chicks* because of the infantilized image. And older Americans tell survey researchers that they prefer being called *senior citizens* rather than *aged* or *elderly,* indicating that old age continues to be a difficult situation for millions.

People who have a physical disability have often been victimized by harmful and misleading names. Given the negative connotations of the word *cripple,* it is clear why people seek to avoid being referred to in this way. But even the word *handicapped* is not always appropriate; this word derives its meaning from an earlier period in which individuals with physical disabilities were forced to the streets, to beg literally cap in hand. Numerous individuals today—blind, hearing-impaired, in wheelchairs, and on crutches—actively seek to maximize their independence and prefer not being labeled as handicapped.

By characterizing the entire person, the word *disabled* ignores the possibility that an individual possesses strengths as well as weaknesses. Very few persons are actually disabled in the absolute sense; most possess certain disabilities—some more severe than others—but they also have abilities that can be nurtured and developed if they are not overlooked. A paraplegic may never be able to run in the New York Marathon without the help of her wheelchair, but she may still become a brilliant lawyer or physician.

The symbolism in name-calling makes it just as dangerous as sticks and stones. Thousands change the name that appears on their birth certificate; thousands more drop an offensive middle name or use a nickname to avoid the negative attention provided by the formal version of their name. For minority groups, the painful history represented by a label often becomes part of the consciousness-raising rhetoric of their causes. Socialization counts a great deal: To accept the name is regarded as accepting the stereotyped image group members have worked so hard to modify or overcome. Under such circumstances the word may not be the thing, but it certainly has an effect; it means an individual or group's identity.

Whoever suggested that names will never hurt you must have been named John or Judy or maybe even Robert. It is doubtful that Horace or Hortense would have agreed.

SNAPSHOT Adult Socialization Can Be Murder

Development Continues Throughout Life

Everything we have learned about the process of socialization suggests that what happens to us while we are very young is extremely important for shaping the rest of our lives. Suffering a horrible experience at the tender age of 2 can leave us with a lifelong phobia. Losing a loved one at 4 or 5 can contribute to making an individual an emotionally needy adult. Failing the sixth grade can affect our self-image, even many years later.

Yet, although early childhood may be critical, we must not forget that socialization continues throughout life. To focus on only the first few years in the biography of an individual may be to ignore some of the most influential aspects of his or her development.

Erik Erikson, for example, who was a student of Sigmund Freud and a famous theorist in his own right, proposed that the close personal relationships that are formed by an individual during young adulthood help determine a sense of intimacy. According to Erikson, if such relationships are not successfully established, the individual will suffer a profound sense of isolation. In midlife (between the ages of 30 and 50), a failure to master the challenges of work and raising a family can result in a nonproductive, egocentric sense of self.

In order to understand what can happen when adult socialization fails, we might examine its most extreme, most deadly consequences. It is interesting to note that most mass murderers—those who massacre large numbers of people—don't kill until they are middle-aged men in their thirties, forties, or even fifties. James Huberty, for example, who massacred 21 people, mostly Hispanic children, at a San Ysidro McDonald's, was 41; George Hennard, who opened fire in a Killeen, Texas, cafeteria, killing 23, was 35; and R. Gene Simmons, who exterminated 14 members of his family in Russellville, Arkansas, was 46. If early childhood had been the critical factor, these killers would probably have expressed their murderous impulses much earlier in life—say, by the time they were in their teens or early twenties.

Many mass killers do have profound problems growing up. They may have been abused, neglected, or even abandoned. But so have hundreds of thousands—perhaps even millions—of people who never kill anyone and who never will. The determining factor in the process of creating a mass murderer seems to reside in what happens to a killer when he attempts to make the transition into adulthood or even later. Does he have adequate support systems—family, friends, and neighbors—to get him through the tough times, to encourage and support him when he loses a job or an important relationship? Or is he set adrift to fend for himself in an unfamiliar and unfriendly world of anomie? In Erik Erikson's terms, does he suffer isolation at the very time in his life that he needs social support?

Also relevant is whether mass killers are successful at home and at work. Most of them have suffered a number of losses in important areas of life—for example, the loss of a close relationship by separation or divorce or a profound financial loss through being fired or laid off. In Erikson's terms, having failed to master the challenges of work and raising a family, they feel a sense of stagnation. James Huberty, after losing his job, moved from a small town in Ohio to a suburb of San Diego. After settling in California, he again became unemployed. This time, however, his family and friends were back home in Ohio. He didn't have anyone to give him the psychological boost that he needed.

What happens (or fails to happen) in the biography of a mass murderer may give us clues as to what can be done to prevent violence in general, even that committed by otherwise unremarkable members of society. Of course, it would be wonderful if we were able to intervene in the early childhood of every individual who is in trouble. But we must also not ignore troubled young people who are already in their teen years and beyond early intervention.

Most adult offenders do have a juvenile record, but the majority of teenagers with a juvenile record do not later become criminals. Many adolescents who commit deviant acts when they are 14 wouldn't dream of committing the same crimes when they reach 24 or 25. Just because we cannot reach troubled youngsters during the first few years doesn't mean that we should give up on them later. On the contrary, if Erikson is right, we should be doing everything possible to help such teenagers over the obstacles of developing into adults so that they can become productive citizens. In the process, we might even prevent a mass murder.

SEEING SOCIALIZATION THROUGH SNAPSHOTS AND PORTRAITS

It was a disquieting scene: three African Americans waiting for a bus, and, across the road, a young white child—he couldn't have been more than 2 or 3 years old—shouting racial slurs at the top of his lungs as he took bites from a candy bar. Just as the trio got aboard the bus, the boy's mother rushed over, picked him up, and carried him away. At first she was furious . . . that he had left her side without asking permission. But then she smiled as he continued to yell, "Nigger!" and point in the direction of the bus as it sped away.

Just like the child at the bus stop, we aren't born knowing the content of our culture; we get it from other people. We absorb our culture—we learn love of country, motherhood, apple pie, and racism—through a process of interacting with others—parents, teachers, friends, television characters—that we call *socialization.*

Understanding socialization tells us how culture becomes part of individual personality—why so many members of a society accept various aspects of the way of life to which they are exposed, even if they are not coerced to do so. For example, the American cultural value associated with the success ethic might be incorporated into the personality of a workaholic who spends every spare moment at the office and has little energy left over to meet the emotional needs of family members. At a less extreme level, countless Americans stay in school, secure a college diploma, and climb the company ladder—rung by difficult rung—because they aspire to become wealthy and powerful corporate executives. On the other end of the continuum, anyone who refuses to accept the success ethic, who gives up on climbing the ladder of success and decides instead to work as little as possible, may be regarded as weird or lacking in moral fiber or even worthy of contempt. In a similar way, racism has a cultural component that is too frequently expressed in the behavior and attitudes of individuals who have been socialized from an early age into prejudice and hatred.

As suggested in our earlier discussion of the concept of culture, if we were explaining the patterns of behavior found in other animals, we might suggest that they know how to respond to various situations instinctively. That is, birds know how to leave the nest, dogs know how to nurse, and rats know how to attack when cornered because all of them possess a built-in, programmed, automatic mechanism (that is, an *instinct*). In sharp contrast, human beings must be taught to nurse, leave the nest, and attack when cornered. In the absence of socialization, human beings would have difficulty with the basic elements of survival.

In "Mapping Social Geography" we examined the sources of the cognitive elements in our culture—those aspects that give us basic information about reality. We also discovered that our shared knowledge of what the world around us is like isn't always accurate. In fact, many of us have a distorted view of social reality. The impact of such distortions in our perception may be profound: Many of our everyday decisions are in part a result of what we believe the world to be like. If, for example, we exaggerate the likelihood of being a victim of violence, we might decide to carry a handgun. If we underestimate the extent of poverty in our nation, we may oppose programs that aid the homeless.

"Mapping Social Geography" reminds us that much of what we consider part of the natural order may actually be socially constructed—that is, part of a process whereby individuals create a shared understanding of reality. Consider a phenomenon that is apparently found in nature: the stage of life known as old age. Actually, old age is a social construction—a stage of life that we, as members of society, have created. Of course, aging is a biological process—a gradual progression that begins with birth and ends with death. But we have decided to have a separate category known as elders or senior citizens. In American society this stage of life has begun at the age of 65 because this is the age at which Americans have been eligible to receive social security, have retired, and have received their senior-citizen discounts from pharmacies, cinemas, and airlines. In other societies, however, old age has begun at 50 or 55 or 60. People have created old age; they can make it begin whenever they want!

Socialization is absolutely essential for individuals to become humanized and humane members of their society. Without internalizing culture, we might all turn out to be sociopaths—essentially unsocialized individuals who lack conscience, human warmth, and empathy for the problems of other people. Yet just because individuals accept the values and norms of their group doesn't necessary mean that they will automatically reject immorality or violence. Even the most brutal, most repulsive behaviors have been taught during the normal course of socialization. In Gary Alan Fine's "The Dirty Play of Little Boys" it becomes clear that aggressive pranks, sexual talk, and racist invective are part of preadolescent peer culture, at least for boys. Adult sex roles are shaped in sports and informal male activities by the shared expectations of childhood peer groups.

Gary Fine's study indicates clearly that the peer group is important during the period of preadolescence, just as it is during the teenage years. According to sociologist David Riesman, the peer group has become so important in American society that he sees it as a major agent of socialization. Even with the passage of decades, Riesman's classic work, *The Lonely Crowd,* continues to teach us about American social character. Riesman sees the major source of socialization as having recently changed with larger shifts in social character from inner-directed to other-directed types. Until the mid-20th century, parents continued to be the primary agents of socialization for their youngsters. *Inner-directed* children internalized a set of normative criteria during their early years that remained with them for life to guide their behavior and attitudes. More recently, however, parents have been challenged by the peer group as the major source of values and norms. Many youngsters become motivated not to please their parents but to gain the approval of their friends, associates, or contemporaries. They act not so much out of an internal sense of what is right and wrong but more out of a desire to do what the peer group believes to be right and wrong. In Riesman's terms, Americans have become *other-directed.*

"Foul Play in the Stands" suggested that, through their choice of games, some cultures actually promote the expression of aggressive behavior. Rather than acting as a safety valve for pent-up hostility, watching players block, tackle, or punch each other actually teaches spectators to become more, not less, aggressive. In some societies, where aggressive behavior is virtually absent from everyday interaction, combative sports simply do not exist. Such games have little appeal in a society that socializes youngsters to be cooperative and peaceful. But in warlike societies, combative contact sports such as boxing and football predominate—and for good reason: They socialize individuals to accept the legitimacy of violence. So much for the catharsis theory of aggression.

Any discussion of the way in which values are transmitted in American society would be incomplete if it failed to include a discussion of the mass media. In particular, television has an immense influence as an agent of socialization; the average child spends 4 to 5 hours daily in front of the tube. I often hear concerned Americans criticize television for what it supposedly does to children. And much of this criticism is well-deserved. But let's put the effect of television in perspective: There is far less street crime in Japan, yet Japanese television is even more violent than ours. Why? Perhaps because few Japanese parents use television as a baby-sitter. Instead, they sit with their children while they watch the tube, ready to monitor, interpret, and discuss. It isn't that American television is so strong, but that our other institutions—family, business, religion, and schools—aren't doing their part, that may be at the heart of the problems we now face.

Socialization does not come to an abrupt end just because someone grows up. Terenzini et al. ("The Transition to College") suggest that the transition from work or high school to college can be extremely troublesome. For nontraditional, first-generation college students, in particular, going to college may represent a major break in the life course and in family tradition.

To some degree, adults continue to change throughout life; and they too are much influenced by what they watch on the tube. "Confessions of a Soap Opera Addict" suggested that the fantasy on TV is often seen as reality. In the extreme case, soap opera characters become our "good friends." We may even send them gifts. In "Adult Socialization Can Be Murder" I examined an extreme example of adult development gone awry—the case of murderers who don't start killing until they reach their thirties, forties, or even fifties. If early childhood were really the critical factor, why didn't these killers begin their murder sprees when they were 12 or 18 or 24? Why did they wait until they were middle-aged?

As we have seen, many Americans share an overall way of life. They accept at least some values and practices from the dominant culture as their own. At the same time, just as they share in the dominant culture, many Americans' worldviews are also colored by membership in a subculture—a group whose members have their own peculiar set of values, objects, and practices. In "Sticks and Stones May Break . . . " we saw the importance of subculture membership in establishing an individual's personal identity. The question "Who am I?" is often answered in subcultural terms: "I am Irish American," "I am Latin American," and so forth. These subcultural names are important in symbolic terms for their ability to express the shared consciousness and pride of a group in society whose members may struggle with their subcultural identity.

Charles Horton Cooley, writing at the turn of the century, suggested that our self—our conscious awareness that we are separate and distinct from other people and objects—is developed through social interaction. That is, we form a sense of who we are by interacting with other people. In this process, we come to judge our self—that we are smart or stupid, attractive or ugly, a good or bad person, and so forth—based on the judgments that others make about us. Thus, the people in our lives are, in a sense, a mirror in which we see our own reflection. Cooley called the result of this process the *looking-glass self*.

Depending on how we believe that significant others—our parents, teachers, and friends—see us, we respond to ourselves as we might respond to others. That is, we become proud of ourselves, ashamed of ourselves, happy about ourselves, and so on.

The work of George Herbert Mead, a University of Chicago social philosopher who wrote at about the same time as Cooley, provides insights into the development of the self that continue to give major direction for research. Particularly germane is his discussion of *role-taking*—the process whereby an individual puts him- or herself in someone else's shoes, even if only through imaginary game-playing in childhood, and comes to take their point of view. Five-year-old Mary plays with her doll. She scolds her doll in the way that her own mother scolds her. Assuming a stern expression on her face, the young girl points a finger at her doll and says, "Mary, you shouldn't have eaten those cookies without my permission. You should be ashamed of yourself. You are a bad, bad girl." If role-taking is successful, Mary eventually learns to take another person's point of view regarding the world around her as well as herself (for example, her mother's view that Mary is a bad girl if Mary is constantly scolded). In this case, role-taking has an unfortunate outcome.

In the early stages of role-taking, children define themselves in the way that particular significant others (for example, mother or father) view them. If parents see a child as stupid, the child will come to see herself as stupid; if parents see a child as lazy, then he will develop a self-image as someone who is lazy. During the early years, then, a child's self-image may change dramatically at any given time, depending on the particular others whose viewpoints are temporarily adopted. As the child grows older, however, he or she develops a capacity to take the role of the generalized other. Rather than take one role at a time, a child is able to take the viewpoint of an entire community, the whole society. In the process, an individual has internalized the culture and possesses a more or less coherent self that transcends the particular others with whom he or she happens to be interacting at any given time.

The importance of the concept of self can hardly be exaggerated. According to the California Task Force to Promote Self-Esteem and Personal and Social Responsibility, self-esteem is a primary factor affecting how well an individual functions in society. Many, if not most, of our major social problems, the California Task Force contends, originate in low self-esteem. The chain of cause and effect runs both ways—self-esteem itself is affected by an individual's involvement in such social problems as poverty, domestic violence, and educational inequality.

If self-esteem develops in social interaction, then names can hurt you as much as sticks and stones. In "Sticks and Stones May Break . . . " we saw that children who are given unpopular or unusual names may be treated negatively. In response, they develop poor self-esteem and actually behave badly as predicted. Thus, labeling children with an unpopular name can sometimes become the basis for a self-fulfilling prophecy: They are expected to perform poorly, are treated accordingly, and eventually perform as expected.

To see what labeling can do to students' performance, social psychologists Robert Rosenthal and Lenore Jacobson told teachers that certain of their students were "bloomers" based on their high IQs. Actually, the so-called bloomers had been chosen at random, and their IQs were no higher than those of students not labeled as bloomers—at least at the beginning of the study. By the end of the year, however, the IQ scores of the bloomers were significantly higher than they had been when they entered the class. Apparently, the expectation given to teachers was enough to make the labeled children perform at a higher level.

When applied to a group of people, names often contain a cultural stereotype—an unflattering image that the members of a society learn from their parents, teachers, friends, and the mass media. The racial slur "nigger," shouted by the toddler in the bus stop scene that opened this section, is only a name. But it contains one of the nastiest cultural stereotypes ever taught to our children.

In general, socialization ensures at least a minimal level of conformity to cultural norms and values. To suggest, however, that all or even most Americans are perfectly socialized members of society would be a tremendous exaggeration—one that sociologist Dennis Wrong captured in 1961 in what he called an "oversocialized conception" of human beings. Americans are not rubber stamps of one another when it comes to accepting either the dominant culture or any particular subculture. Each individual is a unique product of both nature and nurture. In addition, many people conform not because they want to do so but because they feel coerced or threatened with punishment. If socialization were perfect, we probably wouldn't need so many police officers, courts, jails, and prisons. If socialization were complete, it would be impossible for cults to break through the barriers to change imposed by the development of a stable self in childhood. However, as suggested by Christopher Edwards in "The Dynamics of Mass Conversion," cults are indeed able to resocialize their recruits into a way of life that may be profoundly at odds with the dominant culture.

PORTRAIT

The Dirty Play of Little Boys

Gary Alan Fine

The tormented Earl of Gloster moaned in *King Lear*, "As flies to wanton boys, are we to the gods; they kill us for their sport." These mordant lines may tell us more about the interests of boys than gods. Why do boys kill flies for their sport? Why, as Plutarch noted, do they throw stones at frogs; or why, as Swift depicted, do they pour salt on sparrows' tails? What are boys like, or more to the point, what do boys do? While mountains of tomes have been devoted to scientific, development studies of boys, few researchers have spent time with them on their own turf.

My chosen site was around the world of sport. For three years I spent springs and summers observing ten Little League baseball teams in Minnesota, Rhode Island, and Massachusetts as they went through their seasons. I observed at practice fields and in dugouts, remaining with the boys after games and arriving early to learn what they did when adults were not present. As I came to know these boys better, I hung out with them when they were "doing nothing."

My goal was to elucidate the process by which the rich veins of preadolescent male cultures are developed—particularly those areas considered morally unacceptable by adults. In sport and in informal male activity, sex role development and display is crucial—certainly in the view of the participants. If we hope to understand how adult sex roles are shaped, we must observe the blossoming of these roles in childhood peer groups. . . .

In examining the social lives of these middle-class, suburban white preadolescent baseball players, I focused on their friendships. For these boys, as for most of us, friendship constitutes a staging area in which activities improper elsewhere can be tested in a supportive environment. The moral choices children are experimenting with are played out with their chums. Boys are "boys" only when they are with their peers. . . .

. . . I begin my analysis by describing some forms that this preadolescent dirty play takes. Specifically I focus on: aggressive pranks, sexual talk and activity, and racist remarks. . . .

Aggressive Pranks

. . . [A]ccounts [of pranks] suggest that children are continually engaging in troublesome behavior. However, we need to be careful not to overgeneralize this behavior. Talk about these legendary pranks is far more common than their doing. After their original occurrence, the story is told and retold. Talking about the prank conveys the meaning of the event with

---

From *Society, 24*, p. 63.

far less danger to the participants. Pranks represent an attempt by preadolescents to explore the boundaries of moral propriety. In their talk, preadolescents place a premium on daring behavior as expressed through what they term "mischief."

Pulling a prank is a form of social behavior, both in that pranks vary from community to community and because preadolescents who play these pranks invariably do them with those closest to them. In one suburb, "mooning" cars (pulling down one's trousers while facing away from the traffic) was the most common prank; in another "egging" cars and houses was most common, and in the others the most frequent prank was to ring doorbells and run away. Virtually all of the boys who play these pranks do so in the company of their best friends. In one community, of the forty-eight boys who named their prank partners, 89 percent of these were described as "best" or "close" friends. Friendship, therefore, serves as the staging area in which this type of ritualized dirty play occurs. Given the value placed on taking chances, the copresence of friends is likely to promote the performance of aggressive pranks in defining the action as legitimate, providing status for the boy if he succeeds, and goading him if his fear of adults threatens to stand in his way.

Rather than defining pranks as expressions of an aggressive instinct directed at those who control them—the traditional psychiatric approach—I see pranks as social action designed to shape a boy's public identity. The dirty play has something of a status contest about it, where the goal is not to do harm, but to gain renown for being daring. The prank is but the set-piece that provides the basis of identity attributions—not an aggressive end in itself.

Sexual Talk

Whatever latency might have been during Freud's childhood, in contemporary America preadolescence is a period of much sexual talk and some sexual behavior. This sexual talk, among boys in particular, with its aggressive overtones is worrying to parents who are unable to understand how their sons could possibly talk that way about each other and about girls. Yet, however much we might object, boys strive to be "masculine" and they talk about girls in terms both unflattering and too explicit for what their parents expect them to know.

Males maturing in our sexualized society quickly recognize the value of being able to talk about sexual topics in ways that bring them credit. As with pranks, sexual talk is a social activity and is a form of presenting oneself in desirable ways. In fact, given the reality that many of the talkers have not reached puberty, we can assume that their sexual interests are more social than physiological. Boys wish to convince their peers that they are sexually mature, active, and knowledgeable.

One means by which a person can convince others that he has an appropriate sexualized self is through sexualized behavior. This can include behavior among same-sex peers (mutual masturbation, homosexual experimentation, or autosexual activities such as measuring the length of one's penis) or behavior with girls. These behaviors, like pranks, although not frequent for any one child, may be notable and remembered. One public kiss, if done well, can serve for a thousand private caresses. The second "proof" of sexuality is talk—both talk that has a behavioral referent and talk that is in itself an indication of a sexualized self. In the first instance, the talk presents behavior that should, by rights, remain private ("kiss and tell"), and must be convincing as narrative; the latter serves as an end in itself—such as sexualized insults and talk about biological and physiological processes. This indicates that the child knows, in the words of one preadolescent, "What's a poppin.'" These expectations are primarily social, and are based on the desire to reveal what preadolescents consider adult competences, although adults will consider these same things to be dirty when performed by preadolescents.

A boy must walk a narrow line between not showing enough involvement with girls, in which case he may be labeled effeminate, immature, or gay, and showing too much serious, tender attention, in which case he may be labeled "girl crazy." For these reasons, much talk indicates that boys are interested in girls sexually, but they are not so interested that they find any to their liking. While preadolescent boys have girlfriends, they must be careful about what they say about them to other boys. Girls can easily break the bonds of brotherhood among boys.

A related fear among boys is that of being tarred as homosexual or gay. During my research (in the late 1970s) boys attempted to define their sexualized selves in contrast to "improper" sexual activity. To be sure, most of these boys have never met anyone whom they believe really is a homosexual, and they have, at best, a foggy vision of gay sexual behaviors. Despite this, it is common to hear boys saying things like "You're a faggot," "What a queer," and "Kiss my ass."

Being gay has little to do with homosexual behavior; rather it suggests that the target is immature. Indeed, some homosexual behavior (for example, mutual masturbation) occurs among high-status boys who would never be labeled gay. Being gay is synonymous with being a baby and a girl. In each instance the target has not comported himself in accord with the traditional male sex role. Homosexual rhetoric has an additional benefit for the speaker in that its use suggests that the speaker is mature himself, and can be differentiated from the boy who is scorned.

Racist Invective

When I inform white audiences that I found considerable racial invective in the middle-class suburban communities I studied, many are surprised; most of the blacks I tell are not. These boys had little direct contact with blacks, but as they lived near major metropolitan areas, they were well aware of racial tensions.

One of the Little League teams, a team in southern Rhode Island, was particularly notable for the racial epithets uttered by players. The team was lily-white, but there were four black children on other teams in the league and this team had a black coach two seasons before. The talk by one of the star players was particularly virulent, and his hatred was particularly reserved for two of the black children in the league, Roger and Bill Mott: "I was talking with some players about the best home-run hitters in the League, and I mentioned that Billy Mott was pretty good. Justin replies with disgust: 'That dumb nigger.' He immediately described how 'two niggers tried to jump me.'" Most racial talk was not serious in intent, but was joking. In driving some boys home one day in a Massachusetts suburb we passed two black youths walking quietly through town. One boy leaned out of my car window and yelled "Get out of here, you jungle bunnies." The other boys broke up in gales of laughter. Or: "One of the groundskeeper's helpers is a swarthy adolescent. Justin playfully tells his friends Harry and Whitney that the boy is a Puerto Rican and, therefore, is 'half nigger and half white.' Justin calls him a 'punk' and Justin and Whitney both call him 'half and half.' The boy, within earshot, is becoming angry; Justin, Harry, and Whitney run away laughing."

Remember that most times this rhetoric occurs it is not spoken in anger, but in play—although play of a rather nasty disposition. Preadolescents, emphasizing status and position among peers, are very concerned about group boundaries. It should be no surprise that they draw lines between those who are part of the group and those who must remain outsiders. This explains some of the concerns about sexuality and gender at this period and also explains the concern with race, class, nationality, and geographical affiliation (school, town, etc.). Further, during preadolescence children learn the adult significance of these boundary issues. Even if parents do not tell white children that blacks are inferior, the children still learn that race is a crucial division in our society, and preadolescents will assume that those who are not "us" are suitable subjects for attack. Although such an analysis does not work equally well for all children with regard to each demographic or social category, it is fair to emphasize that social differentiation is common to the period and is reflected in remarks adults find disquieting and offensive.

Why Dirty Play?

. . . Dirty play can be seen as a claim-making behavior. Each instance attempts implicitly to make a statement about the rights of preadolescents to engage in a set of activities and have a set of opinions in the face of adult counterpressures. When children behave in accord with adult prescriptions, which they often do, their play causes little comment, but when a preadolescent chooses to play in a way contrary to adult authority the play becomes an issue. Preadolescents recognize this problem and are typically sophisticated enough to engage in their dirty play out of the eyesight and earshot of their adult guardians. They are claiming for themselves the right to make public statements about race, sex, or authority. This play is remarkably sophisticated in that it deals with those areas of adult social structure adults typically wish to preserve for themselves.

These acts are sociopolitical, although playful. While the content of this dirty play is troubling to many, it is also troubling that our children feel competent to make judgments and act on them. They reflect a judgment on adult social order and, typically, one different from that which adults officially put forward, although one that (especially in the case of racial and sexual remarks) they may privately believe. . . .

It may be apt to speak of these examples of dirty play that question the adult authority structure through the metaphor of playful terrorism. Ultimately such "terrorism" is politically impotent because of the lack of organization of the "terrorist groups," their lack of commitment and uniformity of beliefs, the tight control adults have over them, and the rewards that can be offered to those who conform. Still, it is hard to miss the potential threat to the authority structure inherent in some of this play which tests boundaries and legitimacy.

The dirty play I have described is important in shaping relationships within the group, as well as outside. Its performance is a technique for gaining status within a peer group. Preadolescent interaction can be seen, in part, as a status contest at an age at which status really matters. Status matters at all ages, but during preadolescence, with its change in orientation toward adult status symbols and a social world outside of the eyes of adults, the evaluation of peer position is of particular importance.

Boys gain renown from participating in these actions. There is a premium on being willing to do things that other boys wish to do but are afraid to. If there is some consensus that the prank is desirable, the boy who performs it or leads the group gains status for breaking through the barrier of fear in which others are enveloped. There is risk involved in throwing eggs at houses or at moving cars; one could get caught, beaten, grounded, or even arrested.

The costs, coupled with the lack of status rewards, suggest why it is apparently so rare for preadolescents to engage in these behaviors when alone. It is not that they have a personal, destructive impulse but, rather, they want to show off in the presence of friends. To think of these children as bad misses the point; they are, more or less, amoral—in that enforcing the dictates of morality is not one of their primary goals; rather, their aim is to get by with as much interpersonal smoothness as possible. The concern with those wonderful Goffmanlike images of "presentation of self," "teamwork," and "impression management" is omnipresent.

One of the collective tasks of preadolescents is to define themselves in contrast to other groups that share some characteristics. In my empirical discussion of dirty play among white middle-class boys I focused on racial and sexual differentiation. Whites are not blacks, and boys are not girls. Also, there is the belief held to fiercely by many of those whom I have studied that whites are better than blacks, and that boys are better than girls. Given the stance of today's tolerant, egalitarian society and particularly those social scientists who choose to write about it, such beliefs are heresy, morally repugnant, and represent a social problem. Yet, from the standpoint of the preadolescent white boy they seem perfectly natural. Ethnocentrism always does. Indeed, when we look over the lengthy landscape of human history we see that social differentiation has been more the rule than the exception. People always wish to make their own group special and distinct. This basic need of humanity is sometimes (partially) overcome, but surely the desire for differentiation is not a mark of Cain.

When boys torment girls or jeer at blacks, we may see this as a kind of dirty play that does not necessarily adhere to the moral selves of these social actors. The positive side of such group actions is that the preadolescents are learning some measure of communal feeling, even though it is directed at another group. It is significant that much of what we consider to be dirty or cruel play is at the expense of some other group or members of another group. Even disagreeable play that is internally directed typically is focused on a boy who is to be differentiated from the group in some significant way: such as because of some physical handicap or because of the belief that he can be morally differentiated (for example, as "gay").

Preadolescent dirty play does not simply appear from nowhere. It is a transformation of things that boys see enacted by older boys or by adults, or learn about through the media. The content does matter. Yet, this is often material that many adults sincerely wish they had not communicated. Unfortunately we cannot shield preadolescents from that which we do not want them to learn. They are information vacuum cleaners and, of the information gained, will selectively use that which fits their purposes.

The themes of preadolescent dirty play are far from unrecognizable. Aggression, sexism, and racism are found in adult activity. These themes are also indicated in dramatic media representations, even when the themes are ostensibly being disparaged. Still, audiences can choose to select whatever information they wish from a media production, even if this material is incompatible with the official morality of the society. The best example of this during the research project was the reaction to the film, *The Bad News Bears*. Although the film ostensibly warned against the dangers of overcompetition and excessive adult involvement in youth sports, the images that preadolescents took from the film were techniques of talking dirty and acting grossly ("stick this where the sun never shines").

We all know that often a moral message is but the sugar coating for sexual or aggressive doings that the producers use to capture an audience. This technique is as applicable to media productions aimed at adults as those aimed at children. In the case of children this may be compounded by the fact that preadolescents often attempt to act mature. Maturity does not have a clearly defined meaning; however, maturity as a concept implies a change in behavior. To validate that we are acting maturely, we need to act differently from the ways we have acted before. This typically takes the form of doing those things we had not known about or had not been allowed to do under the watchful eyes of adults. As a consequence, many of these markers of maturity will be precisely those things that adults see as dirty play. It is not that the children are being childish or immature in their view, but the contrary. They are attempting to live up to adult standards of behavior, and address adult issues from which they had previously been excluded.

Socialization to society's expectations has been well established as one important feature of children's play; yet, what is learned through play is diverse and some of what is learned may be formally offensive to those given the task of guiding children's development. The agenda for children's development is not always set by adults, although it typically is based on a reflection of what they do.

Taming Dirty Play?

. . . The connection of a boy's dirty play with his moral self is a matter of negotiation, with different ideologies prevailing at different times, places, among different groups, and depending on the relationship of the judger to the person judged. The likely intention of the actor, the presence of others supporting the action, the social supports for the action, and the actual expected outcome influence the way in which children's dirty play will be evaluated.

Children's dirty play is virtually inevitable. There are so many needs and traditions connected with the doing of these actions that we would be hard pressed to visualize a serious program that would eradicate these behaviors. These are play forms we must live with. We do have one weapon—a long-term weapon, but a dramatically effective one as many of us can testify: guilt. In planting the seeds that this type of behavior is morally objectionable, we may recognize that these teachings will not work when given. Yet, often they will eventually be effective when reward structures change and when social needs alter. The seed of morality will (imperfectly) bloom at some later date and in some other place. As children grow older, and their needs for presentation of self change, they come to believe that such behaviors they used to delight in are morally offensive. While we object to children playing concentration camp guards, holding mock lynchings, or simply torturing their peers in the name of fun, we should recognize that this too may pass. Although sometimes morality does not change, if the new "improved" morality is supported by the subtle reward structures of adult society, we can say with a fair measure of confidence that dirty players emerge into saintly adults—at least adequately saintly adults. Children, in dealing with a transformed version of the raw, emotional issues of life, distress adults but they need not permanently smudge the very core of their angelic souls.

PORTRAIT

The Transition to College

Patrick T. Terenzini, Laura I. Rendon, M. Lee Upcraft, Susan B. Millar, Kevin W. Allison, Patricia L. Gregg, and Romero Jalomo

. . . This paper sought at least preliminary answers to the following questions:

1. Through what social, academic, and administrative mechanisms do students new to a campus become involved in the academic and social systems of their institutions?
2. What processes are involved in the transition from high school or work to college?
3. Who are the important people who facilitate or impede that process?
4. What experiences play a major positive or negative role in the success or failure of that transition?
5. Is the nature of the transition process different for different kinds of students? For similar students entering different kinds of institutions? . . .

Four institutions were selected that promised to afford considerable variation on both student characteristics (e.g., race/ethnicity, gender, age, socioeconomic class) and institutional traits (e.g., mission, size, curricular emphasis, type, and the presence/absence of residential facilities). (All institutional names are fictitious.)

> *Southwest Community College* (SCC): A relatively new community college in a major southwestern metropolitan area. One-third of the students are Hispanic and about 18 percent are African-Americans; about 3 percent are Native Americans. Enrollment: 3,200.
>
> *Bayfield College* (BC): A predominantly white, residential, liberal arts college in a Middle Atlantic state. Enrollment: 4,300.
>
> *Urban State University* (USU): A predominantly black, urban, commuter, comprehensive state university in a major midwestern city. Enrollment: 7,100.
>
> *Reallybig University* (RBU): A large, eastern, predominantly white, residential research university. Enrollment: 36,000. . . .

The Place of College in the Life Passage

College as Continuation: Traditional Students. The educational portion of the American Dream is a story of uninterrupted study and progressively greater academic accomplishment, beginning in kindergarten and culminating in college or graduate or professional school. For many Americans (primarily, but not exclusively, white), this passage is completed as expected. At Reallybig University and Bayfield College, for example, when asked what had gone into their decision to attend college, virtually all students were surprised by the question, indicating that they had never considered *not* going to college. For example, two traditional-age, white students at Reallybig University explained their "decision" to go to college:

> Going to college . . . was never even, like, a question! Um, both my parents went to college and I guess they figured that all their kids would go to college. I mean . . . it was never even too much a question. Um, both my sister and I did pretty well in school and so college was just like the definite thing to follow high school.

From *Research in Higher Education, 35,* pp. 57–73.

Another student chimed in:

> Yeah, I agree. Uh, going to college was never a question. You know, that's never something I thought about, whether I'm gonna go to college or not, that was kind of a given.

These students (and many others like them) and their parents have assumed all along that going to college is what one does after completion of high school. College was simply the next, logical, expected, and desired stage in the passage toward personal and occupational achievement. The passage actually originated in the educational attainment of parents, older siblings, or close relatives who have at least attended, and frequently completed, college (Pascarella and Terenzini, 1991). The new student from such a background, entering a college like Bayfield or a university like Reallybig, had accepted and was simply extending an established set of family and sociocultural values and tradition. For most of these students, the very fact that they had been admitted to a moderately selective college or university was evidence that academically they "belong" at their institution.

While these students occasionally expressed some concern about their ability to meet the academic competition, making new friends dominated their conversation. For them, the most threatening disjunction was interpersonal, not academic. A new student at Reallybig University described his experience:

> I hated it. [Another student: "So did I. I cried."] Like, for the first couple of . . . I, I hated it, 'cause I was like, here I am in a situation where I know absolutely nobody. I mean, it's like, it's like you're just dropped in, it's like here you go! And you know no one. You know, you had all these close friends and good friends, and you're always having a good time. And I had a great time in high school, and I, you know, a really great time. And I got here and I knew nobody. And it was just like, it was terrifying. . . . When I first got here, I wanted to transfer. I was like, "That's it! Send me to a branch campus! I'll commute from home." . . . Then I started thinking of it, like, "Okay. It has to get better." And like, it's great. I love it now.

College as Disjunction: First-Generation Students. On the surface, the educational transition for first-generation students may seem much like that of traditional students entering "traditional schools" like Bayfield or Reallybig. For all students, the transition involves adaptation to a new set of academic and social systems. Among nontraditional, primarily first-generation, college students, however, the adaptation to college was far more difficult. Indeed, for many, going to college constituted a major *disjunction* in their life course. For these students, college-going was not part of their family's tradition or expectations. On the contrary. Those who were the first in their immediate family to attend college were *breaking*, not continuing, family tradition. For these students, college attendance often involved multiple transitions—academic, social, and cultural. A young Native American student explained her motivation for attending Southwest Community College.

> Right before [my mother] died, she took me out to the reservation, and when we were outside the reservation, and she pointed it out to me and said, "Do you want to be like this? Sitting around and doing nothing? Or do you want to go on?" So it was probably the reason why I went to college. Because they really have no life out there. She goes, she goes, "The majority," she told me that the majority of the Indians that, that don't, don't, that don't go to college or don't finish high school just move back to the reservation and just sit there.

A young African-American student at Urban State described being beaten up in high school by classmates who disapproved of his interest in ideas and his attention to his schoolwork. Later in the interview, when asked what was special about USU, he replied without hesitation: "Well, like I said before. It's very open-minded here. . . . You can read in the hall or on the steps, and nobody will throw a brick at you." A classmate (in another interview) described his reason for going to college:

> I have a lot of reasons, but I guess, basically, because of where I live, a lot of kids are killed often, and, you know, I decided to further my education just to get away from it. I, I don't like the fact that people are, you know, constantly shooting at you. It, it's, uh, it's bothersome. You don't want to be bothered with these gang bangers gettin' you, rising up, so I said, "Either I make a difference or I get out of here." And I said, "I'll do both."

Because of their family and educational backgrounds, going to college often constituted a significant and intimidating cultural transition for the first-generation students in our study. Attending and completing college carried the potential for radical changes in these students and the lives they led. Indeed, for many (such as the two young people quoted above) the decision to go to college was a conscious decision to escape the occupational dead-ends and hopelessness their life courses otherwise promised.

Several cautions are warranted here. Further research is needed about the subtle and complex ways first-generation students negotiate separation. Cultural disjunction does not necessarily imply that all students need or want to separate totally from the culture to attain success (Rendon, 1992), and further research should probe how nontraditional students maintain or reject their personal cultural integrity and succeed or fail in college as a result of this process. Not all students are like Richard Rodriguez (1982), who attributes his academic success to shedding his Mexican-American identity. In fact, many college students maintain strong ethnic affiliation values and achieve a moderate to excellent level of academic success (Gurin and Epps, 1975; Rendon, 1992).

For many of these nontraditional students, the academic transition to college was the most challenging. When asked what they expected to find in college and what they actually found, most spoke of the anticipated academic rigors of college in comparison with high school. Most came expecting to have to study hard. Most found what they had expected, but others (a relatively small minority) commented that college was not all that much more difficult than high school had been. The majority, however, appeared to be deferring involvement in the nonacademic activities and life of the campus until they felt they had their academic lives under control.

In contrast, traditional students spoke more frequently of worrying about making new friends, or (at Reallybig) of becoming lost in the crowd. But if the academic transition was of greater concern, making friends was commonly cited as being the key to "feeling connected" or "a part" of their institution. Several students spoke of looking forward to the time when, once they were on their feet academically, they could devote more time to out-of-class activities and people. For a number of Southwest Community College students, the academic and interpersonal activities often overlapped, easing the transition in both spheres. These students spoke positively of meeting other students in their classes or on the student union's patio, and engaging in both social conversation and group discussion of what was going on in their classes. Several identified these sorts of sessions as among the most effective learning experiences they had (along with in-class discussions of course material).

High School Friends: Assets and Liabilities

The interviews also made clear that high school friends were instrumental in how successfully these new students made the transition to college. When a student knew high school friends who were also new students (or friends or siblings already enrolled) at the same institution, these precollege friends functioned during the early weeks or months of college as a bridge from one academic and interpersonal environment to the next. Such earlier acquaintances provided (and may themselves have received) important support during the transition. Friends performed this "bridge function," however, for a limited period of time. As a student's friendship network began to extend beyond the set of high school acquaintances, the student developed closer relationships with students not known before college, and high school friends slowly faded in importance.

While high school friends who went to the same college appeared to serve a similar "bridging" function for new students at schools like Southwest Community College and Urban State University, high school friends who did *not* go on to college may have served to complicate and hinder the transition. Such high school friends may have functioned as interpersonal anchors, tending to hold the student in the network of friends and pattern of activities and interests of the precollege years. A commuting student at Bayfield (quoted earlier) alluded to the interpersonal pull of high school friends who did not go on to college. A recent high school graduate attending Urban State described an encounter with a high school friend:

> Well, after we graduated, I seen him last week, matter of fact, and, um, he was just hanging on the mailbox, just, just, telling me, "What's up man? What you doin'?" And, you know, he seen the bookbag on my shoulder. "Aw, man! You goin' to school? Aw, man, that ain't nothin', man." You know, I just looked at him and hugged my shoulder bag, and left. You know, 'cause, um, see, he, he's not going to succeed in life. He's gonna be the one that's on the corner with the wine bottle, or he gonna end up dead. See, me, I'm gonna end up in school, you know, probably with a high-paying job, doin' what I like. [Another student comments: "Or at least a job."]

A young woman at Southwest Community College experienced similar pressures:

> My friend . . . plays basketball. But she, like, goes out partying and things like that. But she's after me. She [says]: "You're getting boring. You just stay home and study." I [say]: "No, I'm going [to college]. . . . It's something I'm paying for. And . . . I wanna learn something. . . . I'm gonna be needing [it] . . . in the future."

Thus, it would appear that one's high school friends were not unalloyed assets to students trying to make connections with a new college or university. Depending on the individuals involved and the circumstances, they could be assets or liabilities.

The Family: Asset and Liability

There can be little doubt about the important role new students' families played in providing encouragement to attend college and to persist and succeed while there. With very few exceptions, when asked, "Who are the most important people in your life right now?" students unhesitatingly named one or more members of their immediate family. The sense of debt to parents for their support was greater among students at SCC and USU, but it was also apparent at BC and RBU. Among students at the latter two institutions, the more muted response seemed to reflect more their taking parental support for granted rather than an indication that they enjoyed any less parental support than their commuting peers. Residential students appeared to be developing greater personal independence and autonomy from family and, thereby, to be redefining the nature of the relationship they had with parents to be more one based on the equality of adults rather than on any superordinate–subordinate, parent–child relationship.

For some students, however, particularly those from black, Hispanic, or Native American families, some parents may have tried to maintain a relationship they recognized may be changing. This dimension of the transition process for these students, of course, was intimately related to the cultural disjunctions described above. Some parents may well have recognized that their college-going children—as proud of them as they were—might, metaphorically, never return home. For example, a Southwest Community College student described this loving tension. Asked who the most important people in his life were, he replied:

> My grandmother. Even though she is a big inspiration to me, uh, she has this way of clinging. She hates to let go of things. And I can understand. I think that's why she takes in a lot of us, as we're going along. She hates to let go. And my cousin and I have told her that we're going off, goin' to college. She goes, "I can't believe you're gonna leave." You know, "I need you here with me to do this or that." "Listen, Grandma, life goes on. This may sound cold, but when you're gone, we're still here. And, uh, we need to do some things to prepare for our future." And she's startin' to understand that.

Sensing such fears, some of the students of these parents appeared to find their anxiety levels rising in ways and to degrees probably unimagined by most middle-class white students, faculty members, and administrators.

The Importance of "Validating" Experiences

A number of the nontraditional students who had entered Southwest Community College and Urban State were experiencing serious self-doubts and indicated an array of needs that we came to describe generically as the need for "validation." By that term we refer to a process similar to that described by Belenky, Clinchy, Goldberger, and Tarule (1986). Validation is empowering, confirming, and supportive. It is a series of in- and out-of-class experiences with family, peers, faculty members, and staff through which students come to feel accepted in their new community, receive confirming signals that they can be successful in college and are worthy of a place there, have their previous work and life experiences recognized as legitimate forms of knowledge and learning, have their contributions in class recognized as valuable, and so on. Validation can be something that is done for and in conjunction with the student, but for some students it may also be a self-affirming process as the student discovers new competencies or reaches levels of achievement previously thought unattainable.

In many cases, these students' high school experiences had signaled to them in various ways that they were not seen as serious or competent learners and, thus, were expected to fail. For example, one returning woman reported: "I expected to fail. Two weeks and I was out. I didn't think I could study. I didn't think I could learn." Another student felt she would be "just a number." Yet another student reported she had chosen to attend a community college "because I saw my brother go to a four-year college and he barely made it. He said it's hard. His advice was to go to a community college." Such experiences failed to confirm or validate the student as one capable of learning and deserving of a place in a college classroom.

Some students described invalidating experiences with their college instructors. An African-American woman who held a General Education Degree (GED) and attended Southwest Community College described such an experience:

> I went to secretarial school and I started working on Wall Street for an investment firm. I went in as a file clerk. . . . And within about two or three years, I was making my $35,000–$40,000 a year. . . . But

> when I came to [the campus where she was enrolled] I was made to realize that I was a young black woman with hardly any education. . . . To come [here] and have someone speak to me as if I had the education of a five-year-old . . . that was a real bummer.

Other students talked about invalidating classroom experiences. Said one community college student:

> My math teacher . . . he has a number [for me] . . . I was a number, you know, instead of calling us by name, he would call us by our social security number. There aren't many people in class for him to go through all that and it's quicker for him to say my name than my number.

An RBU student described an encounter in an elevator with one of her large-class instructors. When she commented that she was in the instructor's class, he replied: "So what?"

Some students, however, had enjoyed highly validating, even transforming, college experiences. They spoke of teachers who communicated to them that they were capable of learning, who brought schoolwork to the home of a student who was ill, and who instructed learning activities that allowed students to experience themselves as successful learners. Some students spoke of instructors, who, through the time, energy, and interest they invested in their students, had instilled a sense of obligation to succeed. These students felt they could not let these instructors down. Out-of-class validation was equally important and came from the support of family and peers, who (as noted earlier) were often the most important people in the students' lives.

In contrast, students attending the two predominantly white, residential institutions had already experienced academic encouragement and success in elementary and secondary school and were further validated academically simply by being accepted by their institutions. For these students, the importance of the validation process was more social (being accepted by their peers) than academic.

The Transition and the "Real Learning"

When asked, "Where does the *real* learning occur around here?" a number of students, as might be expected, spoke of the classroom and various formal instructional activities, or of the preparations made for class. When encouraged to define "learning" broadly, however, it was clear that for a substantial number "real learning" meant learning about oneself, discovering abilities or personal sources of strength, developing pride in one's ability to survive, and becoming more independent and self-reliant. Such learning included developing "survival" skills (e.g., money and time management skills, personal goal setting); developing the self-discipline to "just do it" when a task or obligation was recognized; taking responsibility for one's physical, financial, and academic well-being; and developing a clearer understanding of oneself and one's goals through interactions with faculty and peers who held goals, attitudes, or values different from the student's. For some residential students, the transition represented an opportunity to explore a "new self," to try on a different "persona," to redesign one's self in ways that were impossible for students living at home. For some nontraditional students, as described above, the transition *required* a redefinition of self and values.

The most consistent element of this theme, however, was the pride students took in their achievement. Students who had made the transition were very proud of what they had accomplished. New vistas had opened up, new abilities were discovered, and new goals were considered, giving these students deep personal satisfaction.

The Transition as a Cooperative Activity

For residential students, the transition was an ordeal to be shared and experienced together.

There was strength in numbers and some solace in the thought that, "We're all in this together." It appeared to be seen as the process (if not rite) of passage that one must make on the road to "a good job." What they were going through was to be expected and part of the process of beginning "the college experience." For most (but by no means all), even if a bit intimidating, it was a time of exploration, wonder, discovery, and fun. The cooperative character of the process meant helping one another meet and make new friends, establish one's social network, and become established in those of others.

In the voices of many nontraditional students, while many of these same elements were apparent, their volume was more muted. There was also the sense, emanating from the dual nature of the transition as both an educational and cultural passage, that these were serious, potentially dangerous waters. These students supported one another by consciously avoiding criticism of one another's work or performance. The cooperative nature of the passage was evident in students' discussing classwork together outside class, learning from the comments others made in class, making sure too much fun did not interfere with getting schoolwork done, reminding each other in subtle ways that academics were the first priority. In some instances, the cooperative nature of the transition was brought directly into the classroom, as instructors required students to learn about, and then introduce, a classmate; constructed group assignments that required students to get to know each other and to work together on a common project; or invested so much of their own energy and time in helping students that the students came to feel a positive obligation to work hard to succeed. . . .

Conclusion

If involvement is a central mechanism by which students maximize the range and extent of their learning opportunities, the route to involvement remains a circuitous and as-yet poorly mapped one. This research project has identified a number of the dimensions of the transition individuals make from high school or work to college and suggested places where institutions and policymakers might intervene to facilitate the successful passage for most new students. Its purpose has been to shed some light on the nature of the process for different kinds of students attending different kinds of institutions and to identify some of the elements and dynamics of that process for additional examination.

REFERENCES

Belenky, J., B. Clinchy, N. Goldberger, and J. Tarule (1986). *Women's Ways of Knowing*. New York: Basic Books.

Gurin, P., and E. Epps (1975). *Black Consciousness, Identity, and Achievement: A Study of Students in Historically Black Colleges*. New York: Wiley.

Pascarella, E. T., and P. T. Terenzini (1991). *How College Affects Students: Findings and Insights from Twenty Years of Research*. San Francisco: Jossey-Bass.

Rendon, L. I. (1992). From the barrio to the academy: Revelations of a Mexican American scholarship girl. In L. S. Zwerling and H. B. London (eds.), *First-Generation Students: Confronting the Cultural Issues* (pp. 55–64). New Directions for Community Colleges, No. 80. San Francisco: Jossey-Bass.

Rodriguez, R. (1982). *Hunger of Memory: The Education of Richard Rodriguez*. Boston: Godine.

PORTRAIT

The Dynamics of Mass Conversion

Christopher Edwards

New religions occupy an important place in modern American life. The social scientist who wishes to understand or counsel a devotee or his family will find it useful to explore both the individual's relationship to his family and the technology of conversion and faith maintenance by the group. My own experience as a former cult member, acquaintance of hundreds of members and lay counselor to ex-cultists has taught me that each person's family and group experience must be considered in great detail. Nevertheless, striking similarities can be found in the family histories, conversion technologies, and de-conversion technologies among devotees of a number of popular groups. I would like to explore some of these parallels by examining the experience most familiar to me, membership in the Unification Church.

A number of preliminary studies have shown that the population of Unification Church members, or Moonies, comes from middle class and upper middle class homes (Levine, 1978; Galanter et al., 1979; Eden, 1979). In the Eden study of 145 ex-Moonies, 98 percent were in this category. Fifty-four percent of all fathers and 32 percent of all mothers were professionals, 36 percent of all fathers were businessmen, 42 percent of all mothers were housewives, and only five percent of all parents were blue collar workers. Seventy-eight percent of these cult members were partially or fully dependent upon their families for financial help at the time of conversion.

"The Dynamics of Mass Conversion," by Christopher Edwards, from *Cults and the Family,* edited by Florence Kaslow and Marvin B. Sussman, pp. 31–40.

The Eden study revealed that 91 percent of the population came from two-parent homes. This study concluded that no single family or other social factor seemed to account for predisposition to cult membership. The Eden study did show that 88 percent of all joiners were facing three or more major life crises simultaneously, including change in job plans, school plans, job/school situations, change in love relationships, uncertainty about future directions, or commencement of career. Forty-seven percent of the population were facing five or more of these crises at the time of joining. The population is clearly an unstable one at the point of contact with recruiters. This does not, however, account for how and why these people joined this group instead of seeking other opportunities to resolve their conflicts. To begin to answer these questions, we must turn to the nature of group conversion into the Moonies.

The Unification Church practices a technology of conversion. I will outline aspects of this technology so the reader can understand how proselytizers play upon the initiate's family conflicts to effect conversion. A technology of conversion can be defined as an applied method for changing values which encompasses some or all of the following characteristics: careful selection of conversion-prone individuals for indoctrination; the use of interactive techniques designed to rapidly elicit from an initiate his life history information, including goals, fears, basic life conflicts, and emotional needs; the use of a "false" presentation of self or persona accomplished through the control of gesture and speech to facilitate the gaining of trust; the exercise of control over interactions between proselytizer and initiate.

This may be accomplished by varying both the type and amount of information which is exchanged between parties; the presentation of a "group persona" and use of a group persona to create an appealing view of both the group and the individual's relationship to the group. The group persona is a well-established set of interactions between group members which functions to help achieve conversion. It is an advertisement for the group which involves the initiate's participation, an ideal portrayal of the life he could lead with the group; the conversion of the initiate by controlling most or all environmental inputs to the initiate's body, including all inputs for communication of information. This involves control over general level of body activity through alteration of sleep and exercise patterns. It also includes regulation of diet, sexual activity, conversations, books, music, media, telephone use, and location of activities. Recruiters achieve control over perception of time and order by organizing the schedule and rate of activity for each pre-determined activity.

The Unification Church conversion which I experienced in Berkeley and Booneville, California, included all of these elements in the order mentioned above. This technology has not changed essentially in the past five years. It is effective to the extent that it can reveal and symbolically resolve early family and peer conflicts. Unification Church members, like new and established religious believers, seek people in crisis during the times and at the places where such a population is likely to be available. First encounters are often made on campuses or youth hostels where college-age travelers congregate, such as college dormitories or student centers. Examination and graduation periods are critical events for an approach or in lecture halls with a higher degree of success than at other times. Attractive advertisements are used to stimulate the potential novitiate's interest.

Reflecting upon my experiences as a potential member, recruiter, and observer of many attempts at recruitment, I believe that recruiters follow a rigid order of rules for role-playing which increases the recruiter's allegiance while attracting the initiate to the group. A typical pattern would begin with an aggressively friendly greeting, quickly followed by a series of questions which evoke pleasant experiences in the initiate's mind. These are expressed and informed to both initiate and recruiter simultaneously. Recruiters usually reply with distinctly similar stories of their own pleasant experiences. For example, after persuading the initiate to tell him about a favorite subject of study or sport, he will quickly mention a similar life experience in an enthusiastic manner. This is a first step in a group recruiting strategy called "Finding a Common Base," a way for both strangers to perceive each other within a common identity.

When the initiate perceives the recruiter as a peer in an adolescent or young adult group, the recruiter simultaneously perceives the initiate as a person like himself who is about to enter a Unification Church conversion center. This double-mirroring effect is maintained under the control of the recruiter through conversations and friendly non-verbal gestures which elicit a series of pleasant experiences in the mind of the initiate.

In my experience this technique proved most effective when the recruiter could enter a state of ecstasy which he believed to be the result of an externally directed force. This becomes possible for recruiters after it is learned when numerous ecstatic experiences with other members have recurred. Repeated experiences of this sort which have been made meaningful by lectures on God can be drawn upon by recruiters as a strategy for modifying one's own state to enhance recruitment. This self-stimulation and active retrieval of mental experience is constantly reinforced by daily group experience. From the inside—as a member—it is the power of God.

If the recruiter can induce such a state of mild ecstasy in the initiate and both individuals can deepen a state of ecstasy together, this is labeled a spiritual experience or spiritual relationship by the recruiter. The recruiter begins to perceive the initiate as a different person—as a child who is not yet aware of his desire to be led into Heavenly Father's kingdom by his spiritual parent, the recruiter.

Unification Church recruiters frequently give a selective view of their lives and a limited or deceptive view of their current religious affiliation to initiates, a faithful practice of an informal group doctrine called "Heavenly Deception." If the recruiter can paint a selective portrait of himself (based on information given to him by the initiate) which appeals to early childhood experience of the initiate, the recruiter can exert control over the interaction in a pattern similar to the initiate's early relationship to a parent or older sibling.

This practice of appealing to early childhood experience in a deliberate manner can achieve remarkable effects. After a weekend with the group, for example, I experienced a visual resemblance between my recruiter and my father. Different members of the group looked and acted like significant people from my childhood—my mother, grandmother and brother. As a movement recruiter I noticed that my practice of these strategies could rapidly bring initiates to a similar state of mind. Group members tacitly acknowledge and reinforce these tactics at group meetings where discussions about various new spiritual children are held.

An effective recruiting strategy requires that the group continually strengthen emotional bonds between recruiter and initiate by using powerful but relatively disorganized relationships stored in the minds of the believer. In the Unification Church this begins with the introduction of the initiate to a group of smiling peers over a hot meal in a pleasant, noncombative atmosphere. The initiate is seated with people whom the recruiter believes to share a similar background. Recruiters seated around the initiate will individually ask personal questions about his background before repeating the same process of gaining trust with their pleasing gestures and conversations.

Over the course of the evening, a "group persona" will be presented to the initiate, often based upon routines which several recruiters have used together many times with initiates. The intended message throughout the evening is: we are like brothers and sisters living together and enjoying our life as never before. We want you to get to know us better and let us love you.

The evening is filled with singing, a lighthearted talk by a professorial man who heads the American branch of the group, and a slide presentation of a beautiful farm where happy young men and women are pictured arm-in-arm.

The exchange of information throughout this evening is controlled through the hierarchical structure of the group. No information about the religious nature of the group or their daily practices of proselytizing or money-making is given. All information about the ideals of the group, personal histories of members, or actual relationships established between group members is given only when this matches information which has been volunteered by the initiate about his desires and history. This is in accordance with the information that "no negativity," no negative information, can be expressed during the evening.

If members of higher group status detect negativity, they may communicate this to leaders who will eventually lower the status of the recruiter or punish him with difficult and unrewarding tasks.

The recruiter and other members make a concerted effort at the end of the evening to persuade the initiate to join the group for a "fun weekend." In my case, I was promised the opportunity of a beautiful three days of fellowship, games and discussions about human relationships in the countryside with individuals who want to "build a better world."

If the initiate accepts an invitation for the weekend, he is usually brought to the nearest of a series of camps situated in remote regions of the country. In this camp, the group exercises control of essential environmental inputs including all social data. The camps are usually located in areas too remote to be identifiable to recruits. In my experience in Booneville, California, telephones were locked, no electronic media were allowed, and no time was available during the initiates' days to read any hidden printed matter.

During the weekend, the exchange of social data is strictly controlled by the assignment of initiates to one or more veteran members ideally the recruiter of the initiate. The daily activities take place in a group of ten or twelve led by an experienced member. The leader firmly but enthusiastically tells guests that in order to enjoy warm fellowship and fully participate in the group, the leader will guide all relationships by calling on people who have questions and by making all group decisions. He or she usually asks for "no negativity," explaining that this harmony will make the group more intimate. The leader may state that since the weekend is filled with activity to give a new loving experience to guests, there will be no time for discussion between new initiates. This is firmly enforced by aggressive recruiters who remain with each initiate on a 24-hour basis.

Over the course of the weekend, the group leader directs childlike behavior encouraging initiates to sing children's songs, play children's games, eat children's snacks and voice simplistic statements about peace and love. A group leader might be heard encouraging her members to "melt together like peanut butter and jelly" to be closer together. Childlike behavior is lavishly rewarded with praise, applause, smiles and intense looks of approval directed toward the initiate. Characteristics of adult behavior including detachment, establishment of context, individual decision-making, or individual interpretation are discouraged by group leaders who cheerfully postpone unanswered questions with the promise that they will be eventually answered.

Lectures, games, farm work and other group behavior all take place with familial undertones (Edwards, 1979). The entire weekend is highly ordered, geared toward creating as pleasant a group experience as possible as the initiate is instructed to participate completely under the group's direction.

I feel that my own conversion to the group took place with the acceptance and practice of a group dynamic which allowed me to receive parental and sibling affection from these strangers. Work on the farm, known to the group as "practicing the Principle," reinforced this dynamic and relieved the anxiety I was experiencing in facing adult crises about sexual and family relationships, and future vocational plans.

Religious beliefs of the group are introduced following the weekend, after the initiates have received three full days of close attention with emphasis upon childhood play. The beliefs make the practices of the group intelligible and give guidelines for gaining further acceptance from the group.

As I assumed a more dependent, childlike role in the group, I began to trust the group's perceptions more than my own. The beliefs justified this by teaching that new members of the group become more open to God's truth by trusting like children and leaving fallen thinking behind. The appeal to me was an experimental one, a way of testing this group by accepting their beliefs on an as-if basis. My doubts were resolved by confessing to a woman who resembled my grandmother during my childhood. I accepted some of her interpretations as I once trusted my grandmother and her religious interpretations of life. This began after the love-in weekend, despite my lack of religious belief after early adolescence.

Group life reflects the religious belief that individuals enter a spiritual hierarchy by becoming children, siblings, and eventually parents to other spiritual children as they reach a state of perfect identity with Reverend Moon and God. These roles are constantly opposed to the roles converts have experienced during their "fallen" lives. Physical parents, siblings, and their previous childhood roles are disparagingly compared to the simple, perfect spiritual order. Group members learn to idealize their new spiritual family members, expecting the fulfillment of childhood desires for affection without the pain of separation. Older members of the group fulfill the expected parental roles by taking their cues from the initiates. They give gifts of chocolate bars, greeting cards, baubles, or other items in exchange for expressions of loyalty and devotion by new members.

Competition for sexual relationships which would hamper sibling harmony is eliminated by the belief and practice of chastity. Since members believe that sexual relations in the Biblical Garden of Eden are the cause of all man's crimes and misfortune, they wait until Reverend Moon appoints a mate after three years of membership. Three more years of chastity must follow before sexual relations can begin.

Role changes frequently take place in the movement, but only within the unambiguous parent/child/sib triad. The assumption of a group persona and individual persona for witnessing and fund-raising allows Moonies to feel a part of the larger society. As cult businesses have expanded, members have assumed roles as small business executives, public relations people, and salesmen—all within the confines of the group's goals.

Personal goals center upon a simple transformation of the child's desire to grow up and be like his parents, in this case the embodiment of God through the True Parents, Moon and his wife. Nobody has ever been acknowledged by the leader to be a complete adult, a person who would be perfect and on an equal footing with Reverend Moon. A faithful follower, therefore, lives to be a good boy or girl in daily life with the hope that by believing the parents and following their rules, they will learn to completely internalize their perfect parent and become an adult.

Discussion

Conversion is successful to the degree that recruiters can control the interaction between the individual and the group. They manage to do this by controlling the information in the relationship, particularly by retrieving and exploiting the information stored in the convert's mind about his family relationships.

Purely physiological means can be used to increase control over the relationship. For example, food and sleep deprivation can increase stress reactions, requiring initiates to take anxiety-relieving measures such as confession or commitment to the group (Sargent, 1971; Selye, 1976). This was indicated in my Moonie experience and confirmed by one study reporting an average of 4.9 hours of sleep in the group (Eden, 1979). Conversion occurs more rapidly and completely along with control of this physical environment if the recruit is given limited or false information. This creates confusion of context in the mind of the initiate.

Bateson views cognitive development as the product of a series of experiences which cause the brain to select, sort, and discriminate according to logical hierarchies. Three orders of learning within this hierarchical model would include: receipt of a signal or stimulus, classification of the signal within a meaningful or stable context (arrangement of signals), and classification of this context in relation to other experiences. In a situation where a mother calls her daughter to dinner, the sound of the call would be a signal, the perception that it is time to eat would be the context, and the tone of voice as interpreted by the child would indicate the context of context, i.e., the change in the overall relationship between mother and child. The mother's tone comments upon the relationship as a metacommunicative statement above and beyond the immediate circumstances.

The conversion I experienced seems to fit within Bateson's double-bind theory in a very specific way. Bateson's communication theory accounting for schizophrenic and other behavior differences posits three elements: the individual must be involved in an intense relationship requiring accurate discrimination for an immediate response; the individual is involved in a situation where the other person is communicating two orders or logical types of message, one of which denies the other; and the individual is unable to comment on the messages being expressed to correct the discrimination of what order to respond to, i.e., he cannot make a metacommunicative statement (Bateson, 1956).

Initial encounters with group members play upon identity problems by continually shifting the interaction away from examining context and toward "feeling good." By tailoring the presentation to the cues of the initiate about problems in family, peer, and adult relationships, the recruiters can temporarily resolve these problems at a number of levels.

The Eden study revealed the three greatest attractions for initiates in the group were: getting "loved up" or receiving attention; the group's desire to change the world; and the need to find purpose and meaning in life. A common metacommunicative message from the first group weekend could encompass all three of these responses by stating: I am performing well and gaining the approval of these people, and I can make plans to increase this (as peer, child, friend, student and other roles) with them.

Since group members control the interactions, they can confuse context perception while providing clear signals of acceptance of the initiate as child. For example, during the weekend the trainers talk about growing up and forming adult love relationships while they sing children's songs, hold hands by the campfire, speak in stern parental tones to guests, and quickly discourage any attempts at sexual communication. "You must be a child to grow up" is only one of many contradictory messages which exist on both verbal and nonverbal levels. One leader told me sternly: "If you want unconditional love, you have to obey the rules." Another repeatedly stated: "Here you have free will, but once you have heard the Principle, you have no choice."

Bateson (1956) states that double binds exist when both conflicting orders of communication are enforced by punishment. Although the first weekend in the Moonies is primarily oriented toward establishing a positive identity as a child in the group, the indoctrination of the following week focuses on prohibition against any thoughts, feelings, or actions dissonant to the life of the group.

The first weekend redefines the signals into the context: you must be the heavenly child, your true self. The following week's activities emphasize: you must not be a child of fallen parents, a student with individual goals, or a friend of people outside the group who lead you away from God, and you must not play any roles in society which you personally desire. This message is established with a communication context in which the initiate is responding to a "parent" who helps by scolding, encouraging painful confessions about the evils of sex, and counseling to help him overcome the "selfish ways" of extra-cult life. If initiates object, recruiters withdraw their affection, communicate both verbal and nonverbal gestures of intense disapproval, and accuse the initiate of not loving them and not loving the Father in Heaven. The initiate may come to believe that they are being helped and loved by this context and that they can only be helped and loved by this context.

The logic of the group message to converts, as explained above, would be:

1. You must be who you really are (Heavenly Child) through group participation. (Primarily nonverbal)
2. You must not be who you are (Fallen Child of God) through group confession. (Primarily verbal)
3. You must be who we tell you to be (to become your true self).

Individuals are not free to comment on this interaction because of the rigorous schedule, lack of privacy, and silencing of all communication between new initiates. Such an inability to comment is characteristic according to Bateson, of double-bind interactions. In fulfillment of Bateson's final requirement for the double bind to be effective, there is no perceived opportunity to escape. The gates are simply locked for the week.

All of the double-bind behavior is repeated on a daily and weekly basis, ensuring that people begin to adapt to the double-bind conflicts and accept those behaviors which are highly rewarded before they are allowed to leave the farm and work in the city.

If the Moonie indoctrination does create double-bind situations which return people to childhood experience, it would be reasonable to expect that this would have temporary positive effects upon individuals raised in this atmosphere. Several psychiatrists who have treated patients from these training centers (Clark, 1980; Sukhdeo, 1979) have found that their patient diagnosed schizophrenic often improved temporarily during their group membership while other young adults seemed to function poorly in cult life.

Treatment of the Moonie experience as a double bind may hold promise for further study. It may also aid in the development of therapies which can help the ex-member understand this confusing experience. The value of the double-bind model can be assessed if researchers are willing to gather data through extensive interviews with present and former members and begin to map the cult's communication system. The model and the methodology developed in this research could aid in understanding the structure and function of involvement in a number of other new religious movements.

REFERENCES

Bateson, Gregory; Jackson, Don; Haley, Jay; and Weakland, John. Toward a theory of Schizophrenia. *Behavioral Science,* 1 (4), 1956. Rep. in *Steps to an Ecology of Mind.* New York: Chandler, 1972.

Clark, John. Personal communication, 1980.

Eden, Eve. The Unification Church: A study of structure and conversion. Unpublished thesis, University of Michigan, 1979.

Edwards, Christopher. *Crazy for God: The Nightmare of Cult Life.* Englewood Cliffs, NJ: Prentice-Hall, 1979.

Galanter, Marc, et al. The Moonies: a psychological study of conversion and membership in a contemporary religious sect. *American Journal of Psychiatry,* 136 (2), 1979, 165–170.

Levine, Saul. Alternative life styles: the dilemmas of contemporary religious movements. *Adolescent Psychiatry,* 6, 1978.

Sargent, William. *Battle for the Mind.* New York: Harper and Row, 1971.

Selye, Hans, *The Stress of Life.* New York: McGraw Hill, 1976, 405–426.

Sukhdeo, Hardat. Personal communication, 1979.

DEVELOPING YOUR OWN SNAPSHOTS *About Socialization*

1. *Research topic:* Test your own knowledge of social geography. In writing, estimate the percentage of students at your college (or your city who are from foreign countries, who are African American, Asian American, and Latin American, and who are female. Find a source that can give you an accurate count—the library, the registrar's office, city hall, and so on. How close were your estimates to the actual percentages?
2. *Research topic:* Communication researchers suggest that television is fixated on appealing to young, affluent American men, those who buy sponsors' products. As a result, commercial TV does not portray the elderly, minorities, and women as they really are. In fact, many of these groups are virtually absent from the tube.

   Analyze one episode of any prime-time dramatic series. In writing, identify the race, ethnic identity, gender, and approximate age (child, teenager, young adult, middle-aged, or old) of each major character. If possible, also find each major character's occupation and social class (from their job, house, car, and so on). If an alien from Mars knew nothing about American society except for what she learned from this one episode, what would she likely conclude about the makeup of the United States?
3. *Research topic:* Most sociologists believe that the self arises out of social interaction. Cooley's looking-glass self includes this idea, and so does Mead's concept of role-taking. To apply this notion on a personal level, try the following experiment suggested by Manford Kuhn's measure of self-concept, his Twenty-Statements Test. Ask a friend to answer the question "Who am I?" with 20 different responses (on paper). In analyzing your friend's answers, consider how many relate the self to other people: group memberships (for example, fraternity member, sister, son, and so on) or categories (for example, Catholic, Protestant, American, female, and so on). Kuhn says that children tend to define themselves in very specific terms. For example, they might say they are "nice to a sister" or "good at playing cards." Adults tend to define themselves in much more abstract terms—groups or categories of human beings. If you want to learn more about Kuhn's Twenty-Statements Test, see his 1960 article, "Self-Attitudes by Age, Sex, and Professional Training," *Sociological Quarterly* 1:39–55.

4. *Writing topic:* According to Patrick Terenzini and his colleagues ("The Transition to College") there is a good deal of evidence that socialization continues into adulthood. Young adults often make profound changes in their values and goals depending on the social situations they encounter. Sociologists have found, for example, that students become less idealistic as they are trained formally for a career in either law or medicine. Thinking about this finding as it might apply to your own behavior and attitudes, write an essay in which you play the role of participant-observer to discuss how your personal values and aspirations might have changed as a result of your classroom experiences. Since you began taking courses at the college level, have you become more or less idealistic in terms of your career objectives? If you have changed, exactly what do you believe to be responsible for that change? Does your major have something to do with it? Do you ever feel that your instructors are giving you a subtle, perhaps implicit, message about what is important and what is not important in a career or in life? What have you learned from your classmates in this regard? Finally, how do the ideas you have recently acquired differ from those you earlier learned from the members of your family?
5. *Research topic:* Arrange with a teacher or principal to spend one hour observing elementary school children as they play during recess. Keep a written count of the number of aggressive acts (hitting, punching, biting, kicking, or shoving) of boys versus girls. Do your results indicate any gender differences in aggressive behavior? If so, how would you relate your findings to Gary Fine's study of "The Dirty Play of Little Boys"?
6. *Writing topic:* The photo essay "How Do We Become Human?" suggests several different agents of socialization that operate early in life. Write a brief essay that describes an important socialization agent during your own childhood. Make sure that you explain how this influence occurred and what effect it had on you.

CHAPTER 3

The Group Experience

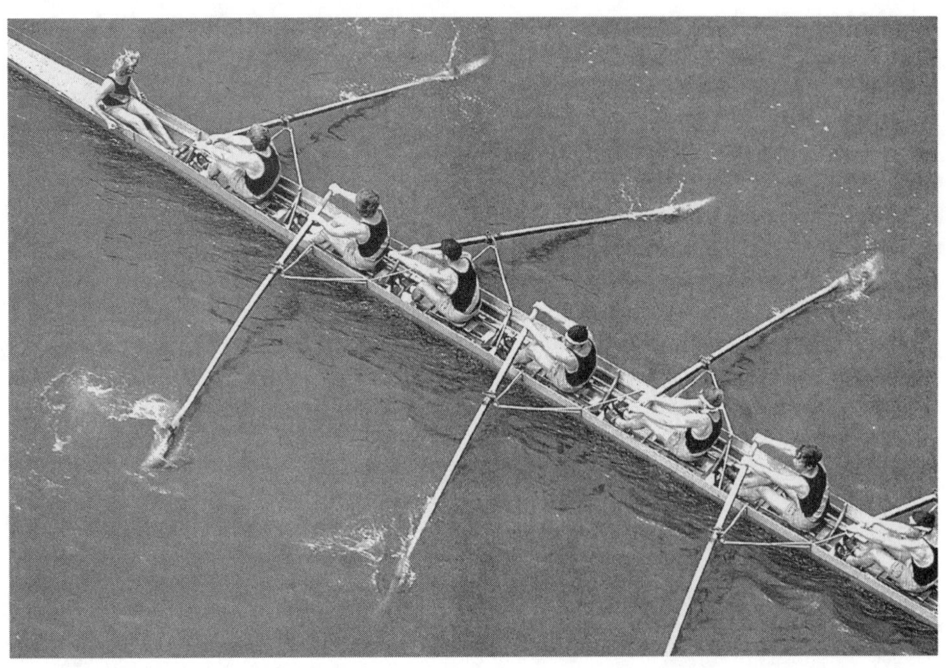

Premium Taste
Low Calorie
BON SANTE
ICE CREAM
ICE CREAM

SNAPSHOT

Just How Powerful Is a Role?

Ask the Prisoners and Guards on Campus

Is it possible for people who are ordinarily decent, caring, and kind to behave as though they are sadistic and cruel—just because we expect them to be? Can the structure of social situations make normal people do crazy, sickening, immoral things?

At the Nuremberg trials for "crimes against humanity" perpetrated in the concentration camps during World War II, Nazi leaders typically looked so normal, so ordinary, so much like the rest of us. Yet they were eventually found guilty of organizing and carrying out mass executions. In addition, thousands of German citizens went along and obeyed orders, even if it meant committing atrocities.

A study by Philip Zimbardo and his associates at Stanford University may help shed light on the phenomenon of normal people doing abnormal, even horrific, things to others. Zimbardo and his colleagues turned the basement of a building on campus into a mock prison. They created a number of "cells" by installing bars and locks on each room and then placing a cot in each one.

Twenty student volunteers—all chosen for their mature and stable personalities—were selected to participate in the study. On a purely random basis (the flip of a coin) half of the students were assigned to play the role of "guards," and the other half were assigned to play the role of "prisoners."

The experiment actually started at the homes of the 10 student prisoners. To increase the realism of the study, all of them were "arrested," put in handcuffs, read their rights, and then driven to "jail" in police cars. They were then completely stripped, sprayed with disinfectants, issued prison uniforms, and placed into the locked "cells."

Everyone knew that the experiment was artificial and that it was supposed to end in two weeks. Nobody was really a prisoner; nobody was really a guard. It was pure make-believe, having been decided by the flip of a coin. Yet, after only a few days, both the prisoners and the guards were playing their roles with frightening determination. Guards were told only to keep order. Instead, they began to humiliate and embarrass the prisoners, coercing them to remain silent on command, to sing or laugh in front of the other inmates, and to clean up messes made by the guards. In some cases, the guards would verbally and physically threaten and intimidate the prisoners—apparently for the purpose of asserting their authority.

For their part, the prisoners became more and more passive and compliant. In accord with the roles to which they had been assigned, the prisoners obeyed orders and accepted commands, no matter how unreasonable. They began to feel totally powerless to fight back. After only six days, four of the prisoners had to be excused from the study, having suffered serious episodes of anxiety, anger, or depression. In fact, the entire experiment was ended in less than one week when it became clear that the guards had become abusive and the prisoners were emotionally at risk.

Interviews conducted after the experiment ended were revealing. Both the prisoners and the guards told Zimbardo and his associates that they were both shocked and ashamed at how they had behaved. None of them would have predicted that they were capable of such cruelty, in the case of the guards, or obedience to authority, in the case of the prisoners. Remember that all of the student volunteers had been selected for their mature, stable personalities. Yet they all acted according to the roles created by the structure of prison life.

How powerful is a role? Just ask the students who volunteered to participate in Zimbardo's study. Then think of the atrocities committed in Nazi Germany.

SNAPSHOT

College Fraternities—A Counteracting Force on Campus

Where Else Would Students Get to Know One Another?

Those who long for a return to a time of strong family ties, neighborliness, and a simpler life often invoke the term *mass society* to characterize a long-standing trend in American society that they deplore. The image of mass society is all too familiar to millions of Americans in the 1990s—people who feel very much alone, city dwellers and suburbanites living in "boxes," dissatisfied customers who talk on the phone to automated voices, rush-hour traffic that won't quit, and long waiting lines.

All these forms of mass society are, indeed, a painful fact of life for millions of Americans. Yet, at the same time that older types of social relations have diminished, they have been replaced by new, and sometimes deceptively effective, forms of intimacy and informality that compensate for the loss of traditional primary ties and counteract feelings of loneliness and isolation.

Technology has provided some degree of compensation. Even when friends and relatives are physically separated, they can still sustain primary contacts by telephone. Or, as a postmodern form of social interaction, they can keep in touch by means of personal computer (the Internet, E-mail, and electronic bulletin boards) even if they are thousands of miles apart.

Of course, technological devices such as long-distance telephones and computers hardly make up for the eclipse of community in America. Their essentially superficial forms of interaction cannot totally compensate for the loss of profound friendship and family networks found in the neighborhoods or communities of another era.

This can be seen clearly in the case of millions of college students around the country who leave their families—perhaps for the first time—to take residence on a campus, sometimes located thousands of miles from home. It should come as no surprise that these students, especially if they are on large and diverse campuses, often search for opportunities for intimacy and friendship. Some find the primary contacts they need in fraternities and sororities.

Membership in college fraternities and sororities seems to ebb and flow, depending on the social circumstances surrounding campus life at a particular time. In 1966 some 30 percent of all college students belonged to Greek-letter societies; by 1976, however, this figure had dropped to only 19 percent nationally. In fact, fully two-thirds of colleges had experienced declining fraternity enrollments. During the 1970s, on some campuses across the country fraternities completely disappeared.

Apparently the fraternity's ability to counteract mass society on campus was overruled, at least during this time, by a more powerful theme among the college-bound baby boomer generation. Many college students of the early seventies regarded fraternity membership as thoroughly inconsistent with their interests in civil rights, student rights, antiwar activism, feminism, racial equality, and independence from institutional constraints.

James A. Fox and I conducted a study showing that the disappearance of college fraternities and sororities was short-lived. By examining fraternity and sorority membership figures around the country, we discovered a major resurgence of interest in campus fraternities. By 1981 almost one-half of all colleges and universities reported growth in fraternity enrollments. As more and more students sought structured opportunities to meet other students, date, and develop friendships, fraternities and sororities began to make a big comeback. Especially on campuses where most of the students came from outside the immediate area, where there were few commuters, and where there was little else to attract students in the wider community, fraternity and sorority membership thrived and prospered. In some southern schools Greek-letter organization membership reached 80 percent.

In a mass society independence can be very lonely. For college students who miss the intimacy of family life, fraternities and sororities provide a new set of "brothers" and "sisters"—and a home away from home.

SNAPSHOT Reunion, American Style

The Ritual of Recommuning

In her novel *Class Reunion,* Rona Jaffe suggests that a class reunion "is more than a sentimental journey. It is also a way of answering the question that lies at the back of nearly all our minds. Did they do better than I?"

Jaffe's observation may be misplaced but is not completely lost. According to a study conducted by social psychologist Jack Sparacino, the overwhelming majority who attend reunions aren't there to invidiously compare their recent accomplishments with those of their former classmates. Instead, they hope primarily to relive their earlier successes.

Certainly, a few return in order to show their former classmates how well they have done; others enjoy observing the changes that have occurred in their classmates (but not always in themselves, of course). But most people who attend their class reunions do so in order to relive the good times they remember having when they were younger. In his study, Sparacino found that, as high school students, attendees had been more popular, more often regarded as attractive, and more involved in extracurricular activities than classmates who chose not to attend. For those who turned up at their reunions, then, the old times were also the good times!

It would appear that Americans have a special fondness for reunions, judging by their prevalence. Major league baseball players, fraternity members, veterans' groups, high school and college graduates, and former Boy Scouts all hold regular reunions. In addition, family reunions frequently attract relatives from faraway places who spend considerable money and time to reunite.

Actually, in their affection for reuniting with friends, family, or colleagues, Americans are probably no different than any other people, except that Americans have created a mind-boggling number and variety of institutionalized gatherings to facilitate the satisfaction of this desire. Indeed, reunions have increasingly become formal events that are organized regularly, and in the process they have also become big business.

Shell Norris of Class Reunion, Inc., says that Chicago alone has 1,500 high school reunions each year. A conservative estimate on the national level would be 10,000 annually. At one time, all high school reunions were organized by volunteers, usually female homemakers. In the last few years, however, as more and more women have entered the labor force, alumni reunions are increasingly being planned by specialized companies rather than by part-time volunteers.

The first college reunion was held by the alumni of Yale University in 1792. Graduates of Pennsylvania, Princeton, Stanford, and Brown followed suit. And by the end of the 19th century, most four-year educational institutions were holding alumni reunions.

According to Paul Chewning, Vice President for Alumni Administration at the Council for Advancement and Support of Education (CASE), the variety of college reunions is impressive. At Princeton, alumni parade through the town wearing their class uniforms and singing their alma mater. At Marietta College, they gather for a dinner dance on a steamship cruising the Ohio River. At Dartmouth, alumni act as lecturers and panelists in continuing education courses for their former classmates.

Clearly, the thought of cruising on a steamship or marching through the streets is usually not, by itself, sufficient reason for large numbers of alumni to return to campus. Chewning contends that alumni who decide to attend their reunions share a common identity based on the years they spent together as undergraduates. For this reason, universities that somehow establish a common bond—for example, because they are relatively small or especially prestigious—tend to draw substantial numbers of their alumni to reunions. In an effort to enhance this common identity, larger colleges and universities frequently build their class reunions on participation in smaller units such as departments or schools. Or they encourage "affinity reunions" for groups of former cheerleaders, editors, fraternity members, musicians, members of military organizations on campus, and the like.

Of course, not every alumnus is fond of his or her alma mater. Michelle Favreault, Associate Director of Alumni Affairs at Brandeis University, suggests that students who graduated during the late 1960s may be especially reluctant to get involved in alumni events. They were part of the generation that conducted sit-ins and teach-ins directed at university administrators, protested ROTC and military recruitment on campus, and marched against "establishment politics." If the sixties generation has a common identity, it may fall outside of university ties or even be hostile to them. Even as they enter their middle years, alumni who hold unpleasant memories of college during this period may not wish to attend class reunions.

Not all reunions are school affairs. People also reunite as an unintended consequence, a latent function of gatherings designed for other reasons. Hundreds of professional associations hold annual conferences or conventions in order to keep their members up-to-date with developments in their fields. Yet many of the professionals who attend pass up the formal sessions—the speeches and seminars—in favor of meeting informally in bars and hotel lobbies with colleagues from other cities and states. Thus attendees are given an excuse to swap experiences with friends they haven't seen since the last meeting. Similarly, the manifest function—the intended and recognized purpose—of wedding ceremonies is to unite the bride and groom in matrimony. Yet weddings (as well as funerals, confirmations, and bar mitzvahs) also serve an important latent function: They provide occasions for scattered families and friends to reunite.

The poignancy of these meetings suggests a more general principle: If reunions make people cry, it is not, as Rona Jaffe proposes, because they have come out on the short end of things *now*. It is because they measured up so well 20 years ago, and they want to relive the good old days with tears of joy.

SNAPSHOT Children of the Organization Men

The New Individualists

For more than 30 years, William H. Whyte's *The Organization Man* was the most widely read book about organizational life. Focusing on middle-class Americans at the mid-20th century, Whyte argued that bureaucratic organizations actually shaped almost every aspect of our lives. They dictated that employees be "groupminded." That is, they were expected to be flexible to the demands of others, to be deeply loyal to the corporation, and to remain committed to a set of careerist values. In this view, organizations rewarded only individuals who were "good team players." Nothing else really counted from the corporate point of view.

In collecting data for his book, Whyte followed his organization men (there weren't any organization women at that time) into their offices, but he also visited their suburban homes, schools, and neighborhoods. He interviewed their wives and observed their children.

Whyte's description of the social role of the corporate wife is particularly telling. Any employee who aspired to be promoted to an executive position needed a wife who obeyed the corporate rules. She had to be willing to make frequent moves from city to city for the sake of her husband's job, to assume exclusive responsibility for household chores and child-rearing, and to stay away from her husband's workplace. She must never gossip about the office with other corporate wives, never get drunk at a company party, never be too friendly with the wives of other employees whom her husband might pass on his way up the corporate ladder, and never show up her husband by being superior to him in any way.

Whyte observed the rise of a pervasive *social ethic*—a widely held belief that the group was the essential source of creativity and that "belongingness" was the basic human need. From this social ethic came the demand for "yes-men," "happy homemakers," "family togetherness," and "team players"—in other words, the worship of the organization.

For their book, *The New Individualists: The Generation after the Organization Man,* Paul Leinberger (whose father was an organization man interviewed 30 years earlier by William Whyte) and Bruce Tucker recently interviewed the sons and daughters of the original organization men as well as hundreds of other "organizational offspring." They focused on baby boomer Americans—men and women born between 1946 and 1964 whose fathers had worked for most of their careers in large organizations. Included in their study were " . . . the middle manager chafing at the slow progress up the promotional ladder, the forest ranger dreaming of writing novels, the aging hippie getting by on marginal jobs, the gypsy scholar in today's brutal academic job market, the entrepreneur starting a software company, the corporate star rising rapidly, and the freelance consultant seeking autonomy."

Leinberger and Tucker found that the organizational offspring were very different from their fathers in terms of outlook, values, and motives. Children of organization men resembled one another with respect to attitude toward organizations, style of interpersonal relations, and patterns of consumption. But unlike their fathers, all of them were strong individualists. Organization men admired the salesman, but their offspring admire the artist. Organization men were conspicuous consumers, but their children cherish creativity. And while organization men were dominated by sociability, their offspring pursue self-fulfillment.

Leinberger and Tucker suggest that social change is partially responsible for the new norms embraced by organizational offspring. During the past 30 years we have seen major changes in the conditions of work, leisure, economics, family life, and politics. The huge number of acquisitions and mergers in the late 1980s made a lie of the concept of corporate loyalty; many long-time executives were summarily dismissed without any cause other than a need to reduce corporate expenses. The dual-career family introduced competing sources of allegiance between work and home. Foreign competition and reduced profits put new strains on American business.

The resulting generational differences have often been profound. As soon as they finished school, organization men married, went to work, and began having children. By their mid-thirties, they had produced the last of their two or three children. By contrast, children of the organization men often remained in school through their twenties, married even later, and were in their thirties when they had their average of 1.8 children.

An obsession with the self can be observed in the individualism of the organizational offspring. At home, in schools, and through the mass media the members of this generation were urged to enhance self-expression, self-fulfillment, self-actualization, self-assertion, self-understanding, and self-acceptance. Just as surely as their parents accepted a social ethic, the children of the organization men developed a *self ethic*.

The organization men were severely criticized for their almost robotlike obedience to corporate aspirations. But their children's individualistic ideal has also come under attack. According to Leinberger and Tucker, the offspring have created the most radical version of the individual in American history—a fundamentally isolated individual who can't make commitments, can't communicate, and can't achieve community. The exclusive emphasis on the self has left many people feeling alone and anxious.

To the extent that organizational offspring remain committed to the self ethic, they are unlikely to provide the human resources for a competitive American workforce—not unless the corporation adjusts to them. This is no small problem. There are approximately 19 million adult children of the organization men. What is more, as the offspring of the managerial class, they represent the middle and upper-middle classes—the very people who have historically dominated American business.

The management philosophy of the organization-man generation survives. In the 1990s corporate managers continue to revere professionalism, control, teamwork, and order. At the same time they have little patience with the ideas of leadership, substance, or vision. At mid-century, when American companies had no real competition, the organization man's view of corporate reality was viable enough. In the contemporary world of global competition and economic uncertainty, however, vision and leadership may be essential for survival. In the long haul, quality becomes more important than quantity.

Leinberger and Tucker present the grounds for believing that the future holds a better fit for children of the organization men between their personal style and structural demands. If they are to succeed in the long run, organizations will be required to adapt themselves to a new generation of individualists—men and women who will soon be replacing their fathers in leadership positions. But just in case they don't adapt, perhaps it is time that we study the next generation—the grandchildren of the organization men.

SEEING THE GROUP EXPERIENCE THROUGH SNAPSHOTS AND PORTRAITS

I've lived in the same house since 1976, and I don't even know my next-door neighbor. It's not that I can't remember his name (though I can't). It's that I don't even know what he looks like. Well, I *didn't* know, until the other day. I was standing alone in a train station in Boston when a complete stranger walked up to me and said, "Aren't you Jack Levin?"

I, of course, nodded my head and asked him politely how he knew me. He told me his name and then informed me that he was my next-door neighbor. When I asked him how long he had lived next door, he responded, "For five years." Shocked and embarrassed, I welcomed him to the neighborhood. Well, what else was I to do?

The amazing thing is that I live in a middle-class suburb—not in a city apartment, but in a single-family house on a quiet residential street with other single-family houses. In addition, I really like people—including my neighbors. But most of my friends and group memberships are somehow associated either with my job or with my family. There seems to be little room left over for interaction with the people on my block.

And, then, there is the assumption—probably unwarranted—that most of my neighbors are no different than I am. They have their own lives too: They are away during the day, probably belong to various organizations at work, and probably have a circle of friends and family with whom they share their leisure hours. What kind of an effort have *they* made to get to know me, I ask? (Boy, am I defensive!)

This section is about the experience of being in groups—ranging from informal groups like families, roommates, neighbors, and peers to the largest formal organizations, such as companies, universities, and government agencies. A group provides the social context for interaction between people—two or more individuals who are aware of one another's presence and who adjust their behavior toward one another. They may talk, laugh, cry, work, play, scream, fight, debate, struggle, or cooperate—but always together. This *interaction* is the essence of the group experience. It is also the essence of what sociologists study.

In 1936 anthropologist Ralph Linton borrowed directly from the theater to analyze the smallest units of group experience: *status,* the social position that an individual occupies at any given time, and *role,* the behavior expected of anyone who occupies that status. Thus, like the actors on a stage, every member of a group is expected to behave in a certain way, depending on the particular social status or "part" that he or she "plays." Of course, the particular bundle of expected behaviors—the role—varies from status to status: from giving lectures and grading exams, when you are occupying the status of teacher, to conversing informally and being supportive, when you are occupying the status of friend. In the status of physician, an individual's role might be to give physical exams and treat illnesses, whereas in the status of homemaker, an individual is expected to feed children and provide shelter. Dentists can stick their fingers in your mouth—but only during working hours. Shoe salespeople can measure your foot size as long as they are in their store. And judges can hold you in contempt of court except when they are eating in a restaurant or mowing the lawn at home. In truth, everybody occupies a number of different statuses and plays a number of different roles each day. The dentist may also be a parent, someone's child, a member of the PTA at school, a part-time student at night, a member of a religious congregation, a vice president of a professional organization, a patient, a customer in stores and restaurants, a good friend, a brother or sister, a spouse, and so on. Each and every status has its own set of expected behaviors.

In "Just How Powerful Is a Role?" we learned that many people will go to great lengths—acting in uncharacteristic and bizarre ways—simply to behave as is socially expected. The experiment described in this essay suggests that roles can powerfully determine how we behave and may also help us understand how atrocities are sometimes committed by normal, even apparently healthy and stable, individuals.

To some extent, the situations we enter are structured by society's expectations for our behavior. Yet roles aren't always set in social cement. In an elaborate process of give and take, action and reaction, we also help to construct and shape the roles we come to play. According to Elyce Milano and Stephen Hall in "College Dating: Psychological Games, Strategies, and Peeves," the norms governing first dates between college students are often unclear. As a result, college students on a first date play "games" with one another as they attempt to define their situation together and arrive at some shared understanding of how to act toward one another.

One of the most important classifications of groups was suggested in 1909 by Charles H. Cooley, the same sociologist who introduced the concept of the looking-glass self discussed in the preceding section. Cooley distinguished between *primary groups* characterized by small size, cohesion, intimacy, and informal interaction and *secondary groups* characterized by formal relationships, distance, and specialized interaction.

According to Cooley, primary groups are "fundamental in forming the social nature and ideals of the individual." They provide the individual with a profound sense of belonging and serve as a major agent of socialization. Primary groups include the family, friends, neighborhoods, and children's play groups; secondary groups include trade unions, church congregations, schools, and football teams.

In our mass society there are actually people who have little more than superficial—that is, secondary—contact with other human beings. Some have no informal or intimate contact at all. Fortunately, while the old, traditional forms of social interaction represented by family and neighborhood may have weakened, they have been replaced by new patterns of interaction. As suggested in "College Fraternities—A Counteracting Force on Campus," students may depend a good deal on fraternities and sororities in order to date and develop lasting friendships.

In fact, some people now need an excuse just to gather together with others. In "Reunion, American Style," we discovered the meaning of sociologist Robert Merton's term *latent function*. He recognized that many of our social arrangements have not only a formal purpose but also an unintended and unrecognized consequence. Thus professional conferences, frequently held annually, provide an opportunity for practitioners to exchange information in formal sessions. But the latent and therefore unintended, unrecognized effect may be even more important. In bars, restaurants, and hotel lobbies, participants from around the country reunite to chat. Their informal conversations often include exchanging ideas, networking, and collaborating on projects.

Still, some groups of Americans continue to suffer an eclipse of community in their everyday lives. Paul Rollinson's research ("The Story of Edward") suggests that elderly tenants living alone in single-room occupancy hotels are left to fend for themselves in almost total isolation.

Secondary groups with a formal structure established to serve a specialized set of objectives are known as *formal organizations*. The formal organization is distinguished by its formal structure: a written set of norms and objectives that define the roles and procedures with which members are officially expected to comply. In American society we have created a broad range of special-purpose formal organizations, including schools, unions, corporations, prisons, hospitals, churches, and synagogues. In each of these organizations the formal structure includes a set of specialized roles in a division of labor. In a university, for example, such roles might include instructors, an ombudsperson, nurses, counselors and tutors, janitors, trustees, cooks, campus security guards, department chairs, secretaries and administrative assistants, students, deans, associate deans, a provost, and a president.

Notice that the specialized roles in a formal organization are interdependent. Instructors and deans send sick students to nurses; cooks in the cafeteria prepare meals for students, faculty, and staff; and students with special needs may see a tutor. In a formal organization the roles also form a hierarchy of authority. In a university, for example, the chain of command runs downward from trustees and the president to the provost, to deans, to departmental chairs, and to instructors and students.

In "The Active Worker" Randy Hodson discovers a surprisingly active and creative role for those who work in a range of organizations. Where a workplace permits flexibility in the execution of tasks, employees respond with enthusiastic compliance. But where the work is alienating, boring, and too much constrained by bureaucratic control, workers may procrastinate, withdraw, and even sabotage the organization.

Also in relation to big business and big organizations, "Children of the Organization Men" took a look at two generations: first the men (very few women did this) who came of age in the 1950s and worked for most of their careers in large formal organizations. What happened to their children? A recent study of organizational offspring indicates that their fathers' loyalty to corporations and conformity to social order were not passed on to the next generation. Instead, the sons and daughters of organization men turned their attention to themselves and cherished raw individualism.

PORTRAIT

College Dating: Psychological Games, Strategies, and Peeves

Elyce Milano and Stephen Hall

Introduction

The authors have been teaching marriage and the family classes for a number of years and have become aware of the fact that the contradictions and dynamics of dating norms intrigue university students. Few other topics provoke as much interest. From class discussions it became apparent that norm conflicts exist in the dating process, and that these conflicts appear to be out of step with current beliefs that suggest that males and females are relating to one another more equally than in the past.

In this paper we will explore the possibility that dating relationships, particularly "first dates," are still based on an "exchange system" and not an equalitarian relationship. Within this context, we will consider the following questions: (1) Do males still expect a return for paying (i.e., that females "put-out") or has this type of dating norm faded away in light of the women's movement? (2) Do males and females still try to live up to traditional norms (i.e.,

From *Readings for Introductory Sociology* (pp. 251–255), R. Larson and R. Knapp, editors, 1982, New York: Oxford Press.

gentlemanly versus ladylike behavior) or has there been a breakdown in such norms making them irrelevant? and (3) What are the implications of strategies or game-playing behavior in dating for interpersonal relationships?

Methodology

Since the present study was exploratory in nature, responses to open-ended questions were synthesized from among 130 male and female freshmen and sophomore students at a southern state university. The data were examined for dominant themes in dating norms. The following kinds of questions were asked: (1) What do you dislike about your dates (e.g., bad experiences you have had on dates, including problems with parents, curfews, money, sex, or any other barriers)? (2) What would you say you most resent about the dates you have had? (3) Is there anything you can think of that you particularly resent being expected to do on a date?

While respondents were asked to evaluate their dating behavior, questions were limited to "first dates" only. Consequently, conclusions drawn about dating norms from the present study cannot be generalized to continuous dating with the same person.

Results: "Paying versus Putting-Out"

Males and females differed in their response patterns. It appears from the data that both the women's movement and economic inflation have combined to affect dating norms. For example, when asked what they resent most about their dates, males most often said they resent having to "pay." The following comment reflects this sentiment:

> I hate having to blow my entire paycheck on my date just because girls think we can't have fun by doing something that doesn't cost a whole lot of money.

The anguish males mentioned in having to wine and dine often (what they perceive to be) ungrateful females, in order not to be thought of as cheap, suggests that the male sex-role is straining under the effects of economic inflation. Males resent it, but continue to try and be good providers early in a dating relationship, much like they do later in marriage. However, there was evidence in the data that though males are still doing this, they do not enjoy it. Consequently, males who may not agree with the principles of the women's movement (e.g., women should pay their own way) find themselves strangely aligned with its ideology, again, as a consequence of economic inflation.

It may or may not be true that females actually expect males to take them to expensive places. It may or may not, in fact, be true that males expect females to "put-out" for either a good or bad date. Nevertheless, the data reflect acceptance of each of these themes. A typical female comment suggests that females often feel men expect them to "pay" socially (i.e., in terms of social prostitution; hence, putting-out):

> I resent being expected to go to bed with my date, especially after somewhere like Hardee's, and always feel like kissing him even when I don't.

Perhaps it is the nature of our buying and selling behavior in the market place that we extend such behavior to the dating relationship. Males seem to support females' suggestions that they are expected to reward their buyers. One male simply said: "It's still true that most guys, *me* included, still expect girls to 'put-out or get-out.' " One can only speculate as to how dating norms would change if both parties were expected to pay their own way. Would the rewards of the date become "just having a good time?" Would going "dutch treat" increase the couple's enjoyment of each other, relieved of the emphasis on the "free meal" or the "easy lay" of the traditional date?

Immediate versus Delayed Gratification

The paying versus putting-out behavior superficially suggests that females are holding-out and males will have sex with anyone for whom they can buy a dinner. However, our data suggest that there is more to it than this. Females are not simply holding-out for the sake of holding-out. Sex to females, before marriage in particular, still means sex with someone for whom one cares—perhaps even someone one might consider as a marital partner. Consequently, having sex before marriage for women has to be meaningful. It is not the meal per se but the meaning of the date, the total situation. If a female does not have much to go on (or has to wonder: Does he like me? Is he just using me?) she will use external criteria (e.g., the date, the meal, the male's behavior) to determine if in fact he is sincere or an exploiter. Some males interpret such scrutiny as cruel and unusual punishment given today's inflationary situation. They cannot relate to women's fears of exploitation or the feeling of being sexually vulnerable. The inability to relate to the female's dilemma may be a result of the males' being exempt from labels such as "slut," "nympho," or "whore" (ever hear of a male slut?). It appears from the data that if females do not like putting-out it is because they are dealing with the knowledge of these negative stigmas.

In addition to stigmas, females still feel they have to "save" themselves for the last buyer, the last sale. However, there is no way of telling if the first date is leading to the last sale or if both parties are just browsing. Consequently, the data indicate that compounding the fears experienced by both males and females of being "ripped-off," and cheated, is the fact that first dates are not based on feelings of trust.

Gentlemanly versus Ladylike Behavior

The data also suggest that if males and females do not like paying and putting-out, they like some of the traditional male-female sex-role behaviors even less. Consider for instance comments by the following male respondents as to what they resent most:

> Having to open doors.
>
> Having to go all the way around to the other side of the car just because she's too helpless to do it herself and if she's not because she'll think I don't like her.
>
> Always expecting me to pull her chair out, light her cigarette, decide where we should go, what we should do.

By contrast, women reflected resentment but in terms of "waiting." Women resent:

> Waiting for males to open doors for me. Knowing that my date will think I am a women's libber if I want to open my own door. I usually have to wait for him to pull my chair out. Why should I have to do that? Why should *he* have to do that?

It is perhaps a function of the first date being such a market-type arrangement that males and females engage in expected behavior rather than in behaviors they simply might want to do out of courtesy for their dating partner. Also, males were understandably confused in these times when they are not certain if they are being "male chauvinist pigs" by opening doors, lighting cigarettes, or pulling out chairs for their dates. Males wonder: Does she expect me to open the door? What will she think if I *don't* open her door? It would appear, therefore, that because first dates are often ambiguous in terms of expectations, males and females do not draw on more relaxed norms that might apply later if a couple continues to date. Rather, on first dates, males and females draw upon what is familiar: traditional norms

The authors do not feel that there is anything inherently wrong with tradition. However, the data reflect that out of the awkwardness of relying on tradition, males and females engage in a great deal of "pretending" behavior. For instance, females mentioned that they *resent:* "pretending they were having a good time," "always having to build up a guy's ego—especially when he may not have one to begin with," "making certain not to disagree too much," "having to ask him *in* even if you've had a rotten time," and finally "being certain not to drink too much, or eat too much, so as to avoid appearing unladylike."

Males, on the other hand, pointed out that they resent having to compliment their dates "even when they look lousy," or having to say "it was fun—when it wasn't." Neither males nor females in our study liked engaging in the psychological game of stroking versus being stroked. Although male and female respondents mentioned that they engaged in such games, very few mentioned that they enjoyed playing. The obvious question then becomes: "Why do something you hate and that you know is, after all, only a game?" Apparently, even if one does not want to "win" the game or play more than one game with the same dating partner, it is far worse to feel that one has totally lost the game. This feeling of not wanting to be a "loser" may be a function of trying to get some "return" (psychological or otherwise) back for one's "investment" of time.

Techniques and Strategies

In order to deal with the ambiguity of expectations and norms of the first date, males and females pointed out that they developed certain "strategies" and/or "techniques" to handle the situation. Consider, for instance, the following comments by one female respondent.

> It always helps a woman to get what she wants if she lets the man feel (think) he dominates. Another way to achieve your goal is for a woman to boost the male ego. Tell him he is handsome, he is sexy, etc. Try not to use crying too much, it works best when not overdone. Maybe it isn't right, but if a woman is really being taken for granted, the best strategy is to make the man jealous. If done properly, this works very well. It never hurts to flirt with your boyfriend or husband. This is not the same as teasing. Dress up, roll your eyes at him, roll your hair, but just do *something to* make yourself more attractive. If you are just going to be at home alone this is even more special. Have a good fight when it's necessary, and then be sure to spend more time making up than you did fighting. You should always take the advantage in making up right after a fight.

It may be a function of the initial game played on the first dates that fosters the development of such strategies. Although many of the respondents pointed out that games broke down with continuous dating, the existence of strategies suggests that games continue to be played.

One of the games females played, for which males developed a strategy, was: "Wanting the male to make a pass, but resenting it when the male *did* make a pass." Apparently, "timing" is the key to understanding this approach-avoidance behavior. For example, if a "pass" was made, or interpreted by the female as being "too fast" (e.g., on the first date), no matter how much she "wanted it," she still resented it and felt uncomfortable about it. Some might ask: "Isn't it rather shallow to feel that one set of behaviors is appropriate on the third date and not on the first?" Such behavior could be interpreted as superficial if one did not understand that females do not resent "the pass" itself, so much as what it means symbolically. Being too hasty is likely to be interpreted by females as: "not caring about them as individuals," "no desire to establish a relationship," "a desire for only a sexual relationship rather than a person-oriented one." Apparently females associate continuous dating with the feeling that one is being asked out because the other person is interested in them as whole persons rather than only as sexual partners. Hence, a pass on a third or fourth date would be interpreted differently from a pass on the first date, as a function of the definition of the dating situation changing over time.

The opposite of this type of behavior is feeling bad that the male does not make a pass after a prolonged dating period. Females worry that such "waiting" is reflective of the fact that they might not be attractive or that the male does not like them. We are not going to second guess the motives of males who do not make advances on subsequent dates. However, one strategy that has been known to pertain to such behavior is the "ripe-fruit" strategy. Here, the male simply waits out the female until he knows definitely she is ready (i.e., "over-ready") in his estimation. Thus in her eagerness to accept his pass and her consequent boosted ego he may "get more" than he would have otherwise.

Discussion and Conclusion

The present paper has attempted to examine the status of dating norms as they apply to first dates. It was discovered from analyzing the responses of 130 male and female college students that (1) first dates resemble buying and selling relationships in that males still pay for their dates but also expect females to "put-out"; (2) females do not hold-out simply for the sake of holding-out. Their motives appear to be related to the fact that they still perceive sex as being permissible before marriage only with those for whom they care. Nevertheless, first dates are replete with distrust, often because each is not certain of the other's motives; (3) because first dates are often ambiguous in terms of norms, males and females still draw on traditional norms (e.g., gentlemanly versus ladylike behavior) to guide them. Pretending behavior (i.e., lying about having a good time, the appearance of one's date, and so on) appears to develop out of the use of traditional norms; and (4) both males and females develop strategies and techniques in order to combat the "games" that each plays in dating relationships.

The literature on dating behavior has not taken the "game-playing" aspect into account. Much of what has been written tends to focus on the dating process in terms of long-term relationships. There is no way of telling from the present data what the implications of this first-date type of behavior are for subsequent dates. Hence, we cannot make definite statements as to long-term effects. However, we suspect that this buying and selling relationship does have effects for the dating relationship that evolves into courtship behavior. Although some of the games may break down, it is important to remember that males and females initially "relate" to one another as if in a market place. Much of what is written about power relationships in marriage and the family may be nothing more than extensions of different aspects of the buying and selling techniques on the "exchange" relationship that exists at all stages of dating and courtship between males and females. Perhaps such effort would better explain how it is that males and females appear to have so little understanding of what the other's perspective is in a variety of relationships.

It should be remembered that while the data on this article might well be interpreted as too negative to some people, it reflects only the *complaints* about dating. "Complaint analysis," while it neglects the positive side of dating, reveals very well many of the social psychological stresses underlying the dating process. The data in this paper should not be interpreted as revealing the total picture of dating relationships.

PORTRAIT

The Active Worker: Compliance and Autonomy at the Workplace

Randy Hodson

Workers do not leave creative activity behind when they enter the workplace. A . . . behind-the-scenes look at any workplace reveals an intricate world of creative, purposive activity, some of it related to the ongoing tasks of the organization and some of it not (Homans 1950; Mars and Nicod 1984; Van Maanen 1977). Indeed, workers' . . . creative abilities are being called on today to rescue American productivity from its pattern of secular decline (Parker 1985; Rothschild and Russell 1986). Workers' creativity is being solicited under such banners as Quality of Work Life Programs, Group Centered Responsibility, and Participative Management.

. . . Most theories . . . anesthetize workers, considering them merely as objects of manipulation . . . (Braverman 1974; Edwards 1979; Poulantzas 1975). Those theories that do include a role for workers' autonomous actions typically place workers' behaviors in theoretical straitjackets. From the management side, workers are seen as engaged in output restriction and foot-dragging (Crozier 1964; Etzioni 1971; Organ 1988). . . . From a radical perspective, workers' behaviors are forced into a theoretical straitjacket of acquiescence ("false consciousness") or resistance to capitalist control of the workplace (Edwards and Scullion 1982; Shaiken 1984; Wood 1982). . . .

Some contemporary researchers argue for a more active view of the worker. . . . For example, Burawoy (1979) argued that workers are . . . concerned with "making out"—devising a way to meet production goals without completely exhausting themselves. . . . [But from this perspective,] workers' creative efforts make little or no difference. Thus even the small range of creative activity allowed workers . . . is rendered . . . inconsequential. . . .

. . . I anticipated that I would find that workers were neither passive objects of manipulation nor intrasigent resisters of every management and organizational goal. . . . What sorts of resistance do workers engage in, under what conditions, and toward what ends? . . .

Method

. . . I started by interviewing clerical workers and then moved to the paraprofessions and semiprofessions and finally to service and manual workers. . . . My initial contacts for securing interviews were mainly through students who had been in continuing studies classes that I have taught on the sociology of work. Although none of these students were themselves included in the study, they provided access to networks that enabled me to select respondents from a wide range of occupations. . . .

My goal throughout the research was to understand the nature of effort at the workplace and the ways it is elicited and stymied. The interviews were largely unstructured and took place in a variety of settings chosen by respondents. These settings included respondents' workplaces, restaurants, parks, and homes. I established a basis for conversation by asking about what motivated them to work hard and what caused them to feel unmotivated. The interviews typically lasted for 1.5 to 2.5 hours.

From *Journal of Contemporary Ethnography, 20,* pp. 47–78.

Besides talking with workers, in most cases, I also visited their workplaces, some repeatedly. I thus had the opportunity to observe most of the workplaces directly and to talk further with the workers and sometimes with their co-workers. The respondents ranged in age from 19 to 54 years. They were employed in jobs arrayed across the major occupational categories and made salaries ranging from poverty-level earnings to earnings about two times the national average. . . .

I called this process to a halt when I felt that additional interviews were yielding little new information. Because of my relatively focused topic, only 17 workers were interviewed. However, these interviews yielded 178 single-spaced pages of transcribed material. When put in paragraph form and cross-filed, this material yielded approximately 2,094 paragraph-length statements by workers.

Compliance and Autonomy

Enthusiastic Compliance

. . . Workers often evaluated the quality of their jobs in terms of the degree of flexibility allowed. Jobs that were flexible enough so that workers could exercise creativity in their work provided the structural preconditions for the emergence of pride, enthusiasm, and extra effort. The worker I interviewed who had the least job flexibility was a long-distance telephone operator. The work involved was too repetitive and too closely supervised, both electronically and by direct supervision, to have a significant sphere of autonomy and flexibility; hence this was one of the most alienated and cynical workers I interviewed. Other jobs had greater spheres of flexibility, and gradations in the autonomy that this allowed provided one of the most important determinants of differential enthusiasm and extra effort. For example, a metal fabrications worker reported that

> free rein implies responsibility and people excel if they think they have responsibility. I know I do. My boss said at the beginning that "I'm not going to stand over you and there are no set breaks, but as long as you get the job done, you'll find time to rest or talk to somebody." So he put the responsibility of knowing what to do and when to do it to me, and I thought it was good.

. . . Worker control over pace and work rules is increased where workers are expected to devise the details of their own procedures as a matter of standard practice. Having responsibility for devising their own work procedures gives workers immense power (see Lipsky 1981). Often, workers have to figure out how to do required tasks with little or no instruction from management. Workers' most frequent source of information is other workers who are currently doing the job or who have done similar work in the past. Hughes (1958) noted that the right to make judgments about the details of work practices is "most jealously guarded" by workers (p. 94).

Having a job that enables one to construct a positive personal identity is also important in motivating extra effort. An administrative secretary reported: "I like to solve problems and in this job you can do a lot of that. And I like working with people. I like meeting people. I wouldn't ever like to work by myself. If I opened my own business, I would want something where the public was involved. I'm just that kind of person." Some work settings facilitate the development of a positive personal identity. Other settings make the development of a viable identity extremely difficult. For example, Snow and Anderson (1987) discussed the problems of establishing viable personal identities among the homeless whose occupational roles are largely restricted to jobs contracted on a day-labor basis. . . .

Making Out. . . . Workers are immensely creative in devising strategies that preserve their autonomy and dignity in the face of excessive or inappropriate demands. Probably the most common behavioral strategy is to withhold enthusiasm and become detached from work. Depending on the nature of the work and the degree of the perceived managerial offenses, this detachment may mean that workers take an extra 10 minutes on breaks or that they avoid work 80% of the time. Along with giving only partial effort comes the creation of smoke screens to obscure this strategy. A worker at a sewage treatment plant reported that many workers neglect to take readings in the tanks at regular intervals and have learned to predict these readings reasonably well by taking recent rainfall amounts into account: "There is no way anyone can tell definitely whether or not we have actually taken the readings." Sometimes managers are fooled by such stratagems. More often, they are not, but the cost of challenging the scam is prohibitively large or the rewards for overturning it are too low. Thus many situations in which workers limit their efforts involve some degree of complicity or least acquiescence by supervisors and management.

Appearances are key to successfully making out. A teacher reported the following practices at his school:

> The principal can in some schools ask to see the lesson plans every week. What you do is make lesson plans but just don't do them. So if they ask you what you did that week, you show them lesson plans that you never used. And have a whole bunch of grades. It looks like you did all the grading, but these can be based on attendance or on oral quizzes. Come up with some flashy thing once a month so everybody thinks something is going on. Open your curtains and then the principal walks by and sees this wonderful things going on this 1 week out of the month that you do it and then the rest of the time actually close your curtains. Really advertise when you're doing something good and when you're not, close up shop. . . .

Brownnosing. Brownnosing is being ingratiating toward one's supervisors and receiving favors or privileges in return. Brownnosing is something other people do: Reports of brownnosing are always in the third person. When a worker has engaged in a behavior that someone else might call brownnosing, they will tend to interpret their behavior as "making out" or as successfully manipulating management. Brownnosing *is* akin to making out in that it rests on an overlap between managerial and worker interests. However, brownnosing is a tainted behavior because it violates the workplace norm of solidarity with other workers and opposition to management.

The attribution of brownnosing to others is not an everyday occurrence. Only about a third of the respondents made any mention of such issues, and none dwelt on this as a major concern. More complaints are made against coworkers for slackness than for brownnosing. While brownnosing itself was not frequently noted, what was commonly condemned was managers treating workers differently. Thus the blame was placed on management for treating workers differently rather than on workers for seeking to brownnose management. A kitchen worker in a nursing home reported that

> if the boss catches someone slacking off, he gets really upset, really. He expects you to have a rag in your hand and be wiping some grease up or he will bite your ear off. You have to look busy. Unless you are one of his favorites—he has a couple of those. If he likes an individual employee, they get better treatment. It's perfectly obvious. They get more free rein. They don't have to look so busy all the time. You will see them in the break room smoking a cigarette a little bit more often. . . .

Conditional Effort

Infringements on autonomy and flexibility were the most common basis for workers saying that they were not enthusiastic about their work. These infringements could take the form of bureaucratic rules or overly strict supervision. Workers seemed much less concerned with machine pacing and instead took it as part of the invisible background against which their roles at the workplace were played out. Human infringements on autonomy were experienced with considerably less tolerance. A waitress whose boss started holding time cards until the waitresses rolled the mandatory two trays of silverware and napkins before checking out at night identified this experience as a pivotal one in coming to dislike her job: "I felt like Larry was trying to babysit or something. A lot of people don't think it should even be our job. That's another reason we're really reluctant to do it. It's like holding our time cards to make us do something we shouldn't have to do in the first place." The reason this episode so irritated the waitress was that it undermined the dignity and honor of her position. . . . Where opportunities for . . . honor in work are perceived as absent, withdrawal of effort is likely to follow (Becker, Geer, and Hughes 1968, 102).

A significant share of behaviors at the workplace . . . [deviate] from . . . the formal organizational agenda. . . . Delay is a particularly common strategy. The . . . theory behind delay is that work delayed is work avoided. Someone else may do the work or the work may not get done, and the consequences may be within the range of management tolerance. A clerical worker reported the following responses to work she dislikes:

> Find something else to do. Some other kind of work that you like better. Goof off. Do my checkbook, play computer games, take a walk with somebody else in the building. I'd rather goof off and do it right later at the last minute if it still has to be done than do a poor job on it now.

Doing poor-quality work appears to be distasteful in most circumstances; it violates the principle of taking pride in one's own work. Delaying unnecessary or undesirable work, however, not only avoids such work but simultaneously realizes the principle of autonomy and creativity in arranging one's schedule, even if one must do so through subterfuge (Fine 1984; Roy 1960).

There are often some things about work that directly anger workers. Frequently, these relate to management. . . .

Managers are condemned for such faults as inability to provide needed materials, laziness, stupidity, lack of leadership in crisis situations ("management by drift"), and destructive infighting with other managers. A waitress reported the following evaluation of her supervisor: "I'm not even sure what he does but give you a bad time. Sometimes, we sit around and wonder how this restaurant ever goes anywhere. I think the managers have no idea what is really going on." . . . A telephone worker complained about the continuing disruptions and deteriorating conditions caused by divestiture in the telephone industry:

> We don't take as much pride in our work in that we don't ever know what is going on. It is chaotic since 1983. Nobody knows what is going on. If you have any experience getting your phone fixed since divestiture, you call, and nobody knows what's going on. Sometimes you can talk to as many as 20 people. The right hand doesn't know what the left is doing. If they can't get their own act together and give decent service, why should *you* try?

. . . A female operator at a chemical plant condemned managers for laziness:

> The lower managers tend to drive around the plant—they'll spend the whole day driving around the plant, listening to the radio or park somewhere. They'll say they're doing an inspection of the plant and walk around the plant for 2 hours and not do anything. The higher management tends to disappear into their offices all day.

> They essentially do nothing, or they say they're going to lunch and to a meeting and then they are gone for 6 hours and don't come back. They pretty much do what they want because there's no one to see what they're doing.

. . . Fears associated with job insecurity also figured heavily into complaints against management. A retail store worker employed in a company in the midst of a union busting drive (which included the company filing Chapter 11 bankruptcy papers) said: "If you are worried about whether or not you are going to have a job next week, it's hard to keep a smile on your face for customers. . . . I have a wife and a son and for me to just be out of a job, it's going to be tough. . . . I'm scared."

Managers were also condemned for being abusive, for not valuing and respecting workers and their contributions, for favoritism, and for being paid so much when workers are paid so little. An administrative secretary in a not-for-profit organization reported painful experiences of status degradation:

> In many instances the whole tag of being a secretary is degrading. I think people don't look at you with the respect you deserve. They think that you are some kind of clerical person that can perform miracles but that you don't have any brains in your head. I think a lot of the lack of motivation here comes from being made fun of for grammar being corrected; there are a lot of cracks in this office about being [local bumpkins], and there are some of us who may be. But after a while it gets old.

Given the apparently light duties of management and the onerousness of their own duties, many workers also experienced steep pay differentials in favor of management as a direct slap in the face.

Along with learning the organizational rules about their jobs, workers simultaneously learn how to bend these rules to maintain their own autonomy and dignity (Willis 1977). Even the experience of learning rules whose main purpose is to limit the autonomy of workers thus becomes an opportunity to exercise creativity through the development of counter-strategies of productivity that create spheres of autonomous activity. . . .

Workers report that managers' responses to restricted effort vary dramatically. Some managers try to run a tighter ship. Sometimes, this eliminates a sphere of restricted activity, but it can also provoke additional restrictions on activity as a response to perceived managerial abuse. Some managers implement new rules or accounting systems, but often these are ineffective in the face of workers applying their full creative efforts to restricting their output and not getting caught or sanctioned (see Ditton 1976). Sometimes, managers are simply unaware of restricted output because they do not care enough to find out about it. They have their hands full with problems with customers, suppliers, or superiors and have simply delegated so much authority and autonomy that workers are pretty much able to write their own rules. Managers may also be limited in their ability to respond to restricted activity by the possibility that workers will retaliate if management seeks to discipline workers. A public school teacher reported that

> it's much easier for the principal to look the other way than to confront a teacher with a disciplinary issue. If they confront the teacher, they are going to be unpopular. Then, they are not going to have the support of the teachers, and their job is going to be made miserable. Teachers have a lot of power over administrators.

. . . Administrators are often limited in their ability to crack down on workers by the fact that they never had control over the details of the work process in the first place. The idea that managers are in control of the production process is a fiction in many settings (Juravich

1985). Whatever degree of input they have into work procedures is frequently contingent on interpretation and compliance by those who are actually doing the work. A laborer in a metal molding shop, who would certainly not be considered a traditionally skilled worker or autonomous professional, reported that "when they give me specific instructions, I just nod my head and say 'yea, sure.' Deep down I'm still gonna do it the way I want because I know it's better." . . .

It would be a mistake to reduce all deviations from management-specified agendas to examples of resistance. . . . Non-task-related behaviors are an important way [to construct] a livable working environment . . . and are often a major part of the daily round of activities for workers. A night shift worker at an automated chemical plant reported a great deal of autonomy in how excess time can be used once one has figured out how to do the required chores in less than the available time:

> You can disappear in that plant and never be seen, especially if you are on night shift where there aren't many people. There are three people in the plant during the night. You could disappear and never be seen. We have intercoms, but you don't have to answer the intercom if you don't want to. Some sleep, some rest. Some of the supervisors don't mind because it's hard to stay up all night, and you might take an hour's nap here and there. They won't really bother you. People will sleep, talk on the phone; some have girlfriends or boyfriends come down and they'll disappear with them out in the plant somewhere, or sit out in the parking lot. . . .

Foot-Dragging. Foot-dragging is differentiated from other types of conditional effort by its heavy reliance on delay, playing dumb, and sometimes rudeness. A waitress reported that if customers were rude or she did not anticipate a good tip, she would not bother to take their dirty plates away but would relax instead:

> If they're nasty, you leave things and don't take them away early. Also, if you're in a bad section and people aren't tipping, you tend not to do any of your other duties either. You keep saying to yourself: "I am only getting paid $2.01 an hour, that's not enough to deal with this."

Selective foot-dragging can also be used to manipulate the work environment so that it more closely matches the workers' preferences. For instance, the waitress just quoted routinely failed to bus tables that had less desirable locations so that the hostess would be forced to seat new customers in more favorable locations (typically window seats), thus increasing the likelihood of good tips. . . .

Playing dumb is one of the most frequently used strategies to avoid unpleasant tasks in preference for other tasks or for non-work-related activities. A teacher reported it as a favored strategy in the school setting:

> Certain teachers would act like they can't run the audio-visual equipment so they get somebody else to do it 'cuz they are just too lazy to do it. . . . Nobody wants to give a presentation in the faculty meetings about whatever is going on in their department or in their classroom—so they just act like they don't know about anything to get out of making a presentation. . . .

Withdrawal. Absenting oneself from work is the most drastic form of limiting work effort. It is, however, a common response, though generally in measured doses. In describing how his colleagues dealt with work they wanted to avoid, a public school teacher made the following observations: "They drink and they do drugs, including on the job. They rush home and turn on the TV at night and they play like they are not at work when they are actually here, busying themselves with gossip or sneaking magazines into the classroom and reading them." Active hiding is also a commonly used option, according to a nursing home worker who spoke somewhat "tongue in cheek": "We've got people who will actually bring their sleeping bag and camp out in the restroom, I think. Sometimes, it is hard to figure out a bathroom to go to. Some places out there they should almost charge rent." Finally, a chemical plant worker reported that workers intentionally hurt themselves to draw sick leave, including inflicting cuts on their hands and reporting back injuries that are hard to disprove. Avoidance of work appears to be most common where there is a breakdown in the normative social order. Such a breakdown is likely to occur where the "individual's anticipated future in the organization looks empty or grim" (Van Maanen 1977, 163). . . .

Absenting oneself from work is also associated with poor wages and/or limited flexibility on the job. As a production worker in a metal-fabricating plant reported, "They don't give me the money or the security or benefits or any of the things other jobs have. So I don't feel I owe them anything."

Sabotage. Machine wrecking is a heady experience, chiefly reserved for those who have both limited attachment to the job and a great deal of resentment against the organization or their immediate boss (Genovese 1974; Scott 1985). Other types of conditional effort are more common on a daily basis because correctly functioning equipment is necessary for the efficient performance of required tasks. Workers therefore have an interest in protecting machinery and maintaining its performance. Defective machinery may limit workers' latitude to do those parts of the job that they enjoy doing or may otherwise limit their ability to control the conditions of their work. Breaking machinery is simply too abrupt and total an interruption for most situations. Where it does occur, it generally involves tension-reducing destruction of peripheral equipment. For instance, at a chemical plant, golf carts were used to access some of the outlying buildings. The plant had four of these carts, so if one was damaged there would generally be another one available. As a result, workers drove them hard, laid skid marks, and banged the carts into each other. This is intentional destruction of equipment, but it does not interfere with other options the worker may want to pursue in negotiating the details of the level and direction of their effort. Such seemingly pointless activities can have significant social and symbolic payoffs for workers as they engage in playful collective activity at the expense of management. Sabotage is fun. Sabotage of all types, including the relatively playful type just discussed, occurs most frequently where, as a hospital orderly stated simply but eloquently, "workers disrespect the job because the job disrespects them." In such settings, being destructive is one of the few ways in which one can find genuine pleasure in work.

Petty theft is also a common response to felt grievances. Theft of small items occurs at most workplaces and is an important mechanism through which grievances are vented. Some degree of retribution and equity can be achieved through a small theft. At a nursing home, this involved stealing serving-size boxes of breakfast cereal. In white-collar settings, it involved stealing paper, pencils, and envelopes for home use. In situations involving food preparation or serving, it involved eating food on the job beyond what was allowed. These activities are not identified as theft by their practitioners (Mars 1982). Rather, they are the particular fringe benefits offered by the job or they are faint and often symbolic compensation for inadequate salary or excessive work demands (Hollinger and Clark 1983). Such activities often involve a certain degree of collaborative effort with other workers, or, at a minimum, an implicit agreement to look the other way. As a result, petty theft can be an important mechanism through which group solidarity is heightened and management is defined as the out-group. Mars and Nicod (1984) reported that maitre'ds in expensive restaurants differentiate between customers whose bills can be padded and those who cannot be so bilked and seat customers that can be cheated in a specific waiter's section as a reward for services rendered or in exchange for complimentary favors. . . . Larger thefts occur, too, but here the motivations, while building on the issue of retribution, also include illicit gain on a more substantial scale. For example, an expensive generator was taken from a chemical plant. Here, the motivation included the desire to have the generator itself as well as a desire for retribution arising from workplace grievances. . . .

Gossip and Infighting. Group mechanisms . . . play a central role in developing norms about appropriate levels of effort. It was noted above that gossip about bosses is a key mechanism for defining the nature of the effort bargain. Such gossip operates through defining bosses as part of the out-group and, conversely, workers as members of the in-group whose definitions of the effort bargain are given greater credibility (Hughes 1974).

Gossip is also commonly used within work groups to create ongoing interpretations of appropriate levels of effort for the members of the group. One particularly common line of discussion among respondents focused on the problem of lazy co-workers and the upholding of group standards. In settings with task interdependence, workers who dragged their feet caused other workers extra effort and were ostracized for their laziness. A computer accounts clerk reported that "people who do not do their share find that they have fewer friends at break time."

In settings with less task interdependence, poor workers are condemned not because they cause others extra effort but because they are getting paid the same but are putting in less effort than other workers. . . . An interview with an operator at a waste water treatment plant involved discussions of workers who abused sick leave policies by declaring fictitious injuries or exaggerating minor ones:

> We earn 8 hours of sick leave per month. Some people use up all their sick time and you wonder about the motivation involved. You never see anyone with 100 hours of sick time on the books get hurt. You always see the people who use all their vacation time, and now they're hurt. That happens time and time again. It seems like you can predict who is going to be hurt and when. For example, tomorrow is the first day of the month and we earn 8 hours. Tomorrow, there will be a tremendous number of sick people. It will be the people who have zero now and will have 8 tomorrow. You won't have a person who has 100 hours today be sick tomorrow.

Workers indicated that management often appeared to be aware of conflict among workers and relied on pressure from co-workers as the first line of control. . . .

Gossip is pervasive at the workplace because it serves so many functions. These include providing an outlet for boredom and stress, social control and boundary maintenance, bragging and self-glorification, and disseminating information. Gossip is most pervasive in settings where there is strong competition between workers and in settings with a lack of leadership or with strong organizational ambiguities. . . .

The social control functions of gossip are evidenced in the following comments by a teacher:

> I guess some teachers who just did everything were seen as brownnosers and as goody-two-shoes and they were often the victim or the butt of a lot of the social gossip. So, in a sense, they pay socially for being good 'cuz everybody is jealous, and so

> anytime there was any scuttlebutt possible to spread about them, it was out in force.

. . . The social outlet functions of gossip were also evidenced by a teacher's comments:

> People are so bored and burnt out by these kids that they have to do something to just kill the time, so they'll go to the teachers' lounge during their planning period instead of doing lessons and get caught up on the latest and who hates who. Getting embroiled in conflicts somehow makes it more bearable because you have some sort of social agenda that you are working as opposed to just your damn work.

Gossip is also an important mechanism whereby workers can learn about working conditions and wages for other workers. A waitress reports that "I heard that people at [another restaurant] can make their whole rent in one weekend." . . . Gossip is not all fun, however. For many workers, it can also be a source of stress and is something to be avoided. A night shift worker reported that being out of the gossip circuit was one of the things he appreciated most about the night shift. . . .

Gossip and character assassination are the primary weapons in interpersonal conflicts at the workplace. Character assassination is popular because it inflicts damage on the target with minimal risk to the attacker. Taking more concrete actions to antagonize co-workers or disrupt their work runs the risk of being called to task by other workers or by management for intentionally disrupting production.

Beside character assassination, the most common tactic in infighting is to intentionally shift work to another person. A food service worker at a nursing home reported chronic attempts by the nursing and food service staffs to shift responsibilities to each other:

> Nursing doesn't like dietary. Dietary doesn't like nursing. Neither one likes housekeeping. Because there is a grey area of responsibility between them. Nursing doesn't want to bother feeding a particularly nasty resident, even though the person should be in their room because they are a distraction and a nuisance and a burden on other people in the dining room—other residents and their families. They will continually try to pawn off that person on the dining room staff. It's not good for the business to have someone who is extremely aggressive, is vulgar, has no control over their bowels or bladder in the dining room.

Outright interference with others' work is rare but not unknown. A waitress reported the following skirmish: "Sometimes other waitresses have even been known to take their tip from the table and then they'll just leave, and, when the customers leave, you're left with clearing off their tables. You don't mind helping but you don't like being taken advantage of."

Infighting may also involve snitching on co-workers to management. A telephone operator reported that "a certain group of employees think they can get ahead by reporting other employees." It is ugly, but it happens. Workers also sometimes try to make other workers appear as fools by pointing out their weaknesses in awkward situations.

Discussion and Conclusions

. . . To understand workplace behaviors, we need a theoretical model of the worker that is neither anesthetized nor limited to resisting management strategies of control. . . .

Our theories need to give greater weight to the ability of workers to create their own environments. Workers' power rests on their "practical autonomy"—the necessity that workers' creative and autonomous activity be solicited if the business of ongoing enterprises is to be achieved (Wardell forthcoming). The analysis of workers' practical autonomy, its varieties, and its antecedents and consequences is a vast, little explored, and terribly important area in the sociology of work. . . .

The typology of worker behaviors suggested here is based on an active view of the worker who is seen as constantly engaged in the social construction of the setting in which productive activity takes place. I have tried to give some suggestions about the settings that give rise to particular behaviors and to suggest avenues for further investigation. Under what conditions do different forms of worker activity emerge? What is the logic of these behavioral options? Enthusiastic compliance appears most likely to emerge where a considerable degree of flexibility is allowed in the execution of organizational tasks. Making out appears to occur where rewards are minimal and where alienation is high because of limited advancement possibilities. Foot-dragging and withdrawal appear most likely to occur where the work is boring or stressful, where it is overly constrained by technical and bureaucratic forms of control, and, again, where future possibilities look grim. Sabotage appears to occur primarily where there is active resentment against a specific boss or some specific aspect of organizational policy. Gossip and infighting appear most likely to occur where there is strong competition between workers resulting from organizational ambiguities about responsibilities and duties. Finally, brownnosing appears to occur where there is competition between workers and where there is extreme inequality in rewards or an ambiguous system for distributing these rewards. . . .

REFERENCES

Becker, H. S., B. Geer, and E. C. Hughes. 1968. *Making the grade: The academic side of college life*. New York: Wiley.

Braverman, H. 1974. *Labor and monopoly capital*. New York: Monthly Review Press.

Burawoy, M. 1979. *Manufacturing consent*. Chicago: University of Chicago Press.

Crozier, M. 1964. *The bureaucratic phenomena*. Chicago: University of Chicago Press.

Ditton, J. 1976. Moral horror versus folk terror: Output restriction, class, and the social organization of exploitation. *Sociological Review* 24:519–44.

Edwards, P. K., and H. Scullion. 1982. *The social organization of industrial conflict*. Oxford: Basil Blackwell.

Edwards, R. C. 1979. *Contested terrain*. New York: Basic Books.

Etzioni, A. 1971. *A comparative analysis of complex organizations*. New York: Free Press.

Fine, G. A. 1984. Negotiated orders and organizational cultures. In *The annual review of sociology*, vol. 10, edited by R. H. Turner and J. F. Short, Jr., 239–62. Palo Alto, CA: Annual Reviews.

Genovese, E. D. 1974. *Roll, Jordon, roll: The world the slaves made*. New York: Pantheon.

Hollinger, R. C., and J. P. Clark. 1983. *Theft by employees*. Lexington, MA: D. C. Heath.

Homans, G. 1950. *The human group*. New York: Harcourt, Brace & World.

Howard, R. 1985. *Brave new workplace*. New York: Viking.

Hughes, E. C. 1958. *Men and their work*. Glencoe, IL: Free Press.

———.1974. Comments on "Honor in dirty work." *Work and Occupations* 1:284–87.

Juravich, T. 1985. *Chaos on the shop floor*. Philadelphia: Temple University Press.

Lipsky, M. 1981. *Street-level bureaucracy*. New York: Russell Sage.

Mars, G. 1982. *Cheats at work*. London: Unwin.

Mars, G., and M. Nicod 1984. *The world of waiters*. London: Allen & Unwin.

Organ, D. W. 1988. A restatement of the satisfaction-performance hypothesis. *Journal of Management* 14:547–57.

Parker, M. 1985. *Inside the circle: A union guide to QWL*. Boston: South End Press.

Poulantzas, N. 1975. *Classes in contemporary capitalism*. London: New Left Books.

Rothschild, J., and R. Russell. 1986. Alternatives to bureaucracy: Democratic participation in the economy. In *The annual review of sociology*, vol.

12, edited by R. H. Turner and J. F. Short, Jr., 307–28. Palo Alto, CA: Annual Reviews.

Roy, D. 1960. "Banana time": Job satisfaction and informal interaction. *Human Organization* 18:158–68.

Scott, J. C. 1985. *Weapons of the weak: Everyday forms of peasant resistance*. New Haven, CT: Yale University Press.

Shaiken, H. 1984. *Work transformed*. New York: Holt, Rinehart & Winston.

Snow, D. A., and L. Anderson. 1987. Identity work among the homeless: The verbal construction and avowal of personal identities. *American Journal of Sociology* 92:1336–71.

Van Maanen, J. 1977. *Organizational careers*. London: Wiley.

Wardell, M. Forthcoming. Organizations: A bottom-up approach. In *Rethinking organizations*, edited by Michael L. Reed and Michael Hughes. London: Sage.

Willis, P. 1977. *Learning to labor: How working class kids get working class jobs*. New York: Columbia University Press.

Wood, S., ed. 1982. *The degradation of work?* London: Hutchinson.

PORTRAIT

The Story of Edward: The Everyday Geography of Elderly Single-Room Occupancy (SRO) Hotel Tenants

Paul A. Rollinson

This article seeks to provide a rich description of the everyday geography of an often overlooked population in contemporary urban America: elderly tenants of single-room occupancy (SRO) hotels. The term SRO is a recent one, originally coined to describe apartment dwellings that had been subdivided into single rooms in New York City (Shapiro 1966). SRO's have also been described as "flophouses" and "fleabag hotels" (Eckert 1979). These buildings, originally designated as transient facilities, have evolved into largely permanent residences for the single poor of all ages. Today, SRO hotels, which are typically located in dilapidated and deteriorating inner city areas, have been characterized as the nation's least desirable housing (Kasinitz 1984). Some SRO's are in fact old hotels; others are former tenements converted into apartment hotels. For the most part, they offer single, sparsely furnished rooms, with limited cooking facilities and communal bathrooms. The majority have some sort of front desk and lobby. These hotels have traditionally offered housing to the poor elderly, the low-income single working population, the mentally handicapped, and alcohol and narcotic addicts. Today, these hotels are being demolished or converted to other uses at a fast pace (Groth 1983; Hartman et al. 1982; Werner and Bryson 1982). Elderly tenants, faced with this decline, have few if any alternatives, and are often forced to join the ranks of the homeless population (The Coalition for the Homeless and the Gray Panthers of New York City 1984). . . .

Methods

. . . This study evolved out of my role as a consultant to the City of Chicago in its efforts to

From *Journal of Contemporary Ethnography, 19*, pp. 188–206.

understand the problem of the rapid decline of SRO hotels in that city (City of Chicago 1985). I found, in these hotels, a unique, vulnerable, and little understood elderly population. In order to discover more, I conducted fieldwork in a representative neighborhood of Chicago during 1985 and 1986 (Community Emergency Shelter Organization and the Jewish Council on Urban Affairs 1985). . . .

During 1986, I made 19 four-day excursions to the neighborhood. During the month of August I rented a room at one of the four SRO hotels (two were not used in this study because they housed too few elderly tenants). At all four hotels I was introduced to the elderly participants by the desk clerk, either in the hotel lobby or in their rooms. This first meeting rarely led to an interview. Subjects often had other plans, and so I made an appointment for a future interview. Most of the tenants with whom I made contact in their rooms refused to participate. The participants in this exploration, therefore, represented the least withdrawn elderly SRO tenants. Those that remained in their rooms, out of sight or unwilling to be interviewed, were not a part of this study. Discussing the everyday geographical experience proved to be a challenge both to myself and the elderly tenants. It was difficult to identify and articulate themes when no common language was shared. The rule was always to be direct and honest concerning my motives. Since the concept of research was difficult for the tenants to grasp, I simply said I was writing a book about elderly hotel tenants in their neighborhood. These men and women were initially surprised at my interest in them and somewhat skeptical of my motives. Often they would respond with "I don't know nothing," "You don't want to know about me," or "What can I tell you?" Considerable involvement had to be made in the hotel environment before these men and women trusted me. Helping out with messages, the delivery of mail, or other items was essential in gaining their trust. I abandoned the notion of a dispassionate observer role almost at the beginning of this study. . . . I began to be recognized in the hotels as "the professor"[1] and I was allowed to share in the life activities of these men and women. I recorded this population's geographical movement firsthand. I walked with these elderly men and women, I spent time talking in their rooms and the hotel lobbies, I went shopping with them, I shared meal times, I shared recreation time, I shared fears and joys. In summation, I shared as many daily life experiences as possible. I interviewed a total of 53 elderly men and women at the four hotels. Each interview involved at least one daylong firsthand experience. . . .

The Everyday Geography of Edward

This is the story of Edward, an elderly SRO tenant. I compare Edward to the other elderly tenants in the study, briefly describe his life history, how he viewed the SRO hotel and the neighborhood environment, and I discuss his everyday geography and concerns about the future. I met Edward in the lobby of one of the four hotels in August of 1985. Initially he simply agreed to answer some of my questions. Later, he invited me to his room and subsequently to spend time with him traveling around the neighborhood.

Edward was similar to the majority of the elderly SRO tenant population I saw. The elderly SRO tenant population in the study had a mean age of 70 years, was predominantly white (92%), and male (58%). Edward was a 62-year-old white male. Overall, the elderly tenants had a low educational attainment; almost three-quarters (73%) had achieved education levels of high school or lower. Edward, in contrast, had completed two years of college. Elderly SRO tenants were extremely poor; Edward's yearly income ($4,620 in 1986) was even less than the mean of the elderly tenants in the study ($5,559) and well below the mean poverty level ($5,360). Accompanying his low income was a higher than average rent burden of 69% (compared to the already high mean of 46% for all those I interviewed), which exacerbated the tenuousness of Edward's already critical financial status. Nationally, the accepted normal rent-to-income ratio was 30%. Like 62% of his fellow elderly tenants, Edward received most of his income from Social Security. He was fortunate in that he had some savings to rely upon in times of financial need, as only 10% of all the elderly tenants interviewed had any savings.

Edward, like the majority of the study population, was no newcomer to the inner-city environment; he was born and raised in Chicago. However, unlike most other elderly tenants, Edward had lived at his current SRO hotel for only seven months when I met him, compared to a mean of six and one-half years for the other 52 men and women in the study. Like half (46%) of the study population, Edward had lived at another SRO hotel prior to moving to his current SRO residence. He, like most of the other tenants (85%), had moved to his current SRO hotel as a result of a push beyond his control: He was asked to leave by the management at the previous hotel. Edward noted:

> I came from a retirement hotel. Because they served food on the first floor, the only way I could come down was on crutches. That was before I lost my legs, so they had to bring the food upstairs, so I was charged an additional amount to my monthly rate. I thought it was outrageous and after I lost my legs they thought I did not belong there.

The majority of the elderly tenants had worked in sales, administration, and service sectors of the economy. Edward had been a salesman in various businesses all his life. Like the other elderly tenants, Edward found himself alone and in deteriorating health. He stated: "Evidently, when I got in this condition, it seems like I lost a lot of friends. I don't know why, but it happened that way. They're afraid to come into the area, they're always busy and I can't travel to them, so that kinda hurts the situation." Edward had no relatives he felt close to and had made no contact with any in the previous year. However, he did feel close to a few elderly friends in the hotel and contacted them occasionally. Edward, like many other elderly tenants, was handicapped, and this hindered his ability to negotiate both the hotel and the inner-city built environment. In summary, Edward was like most other elderly SRO tenants in the neighborhood.

Edward was born a mere 13 blocks from where I first met him in 1985. He characterized his childhood neighborhood in the 1920's as a mixed neighborhood; it had both working- and middle-class residents. His parents had owned a two-flat in the community. Edward's mother was a homemaker and his father was a blue-collar worker in the trucking industry. Edward characterized his childhood as relatively uneventful. His family was considered fortunate, since his father always had work during the financially difficult years of the Depression. At the age of 18, Edward found himself drawn into World War II and he served in the combat arena in Europe during the latter years of the war. Edward noted emphatically: "The war changed everything." Life was interrupted and forever affected by the conflict. In May, 1946, he was discharged and returned home to Chicago. He found employment first at a neighborhood furniture manufacturer, which Edward described as a "hell hole." Later, Edward found employment as a shipping clerk in a small manufacturing industry in the neighborhood. During this entire time, Edward lived at home with his parents.

In June, 1950, Edward married a woman he had met in the neighborhood who lived about half a mile away from his parents' house. At first, the couple lived with her parents, who had a small two-flat; they then moved to an apartment in his parents' two-flat. They lived at this apartment until 1973. Shortly after the marriage, Edward's parents died and the two-flat was sold. Edward and his wife continued to rent the apartment. During this period, Edward described the constant struggle for financial survival. As a salesman, he lived on commission and he got tired of the "dog-eat-dog situation." He changed jobs frequently, first selling business printing, then office machinery, and then insecticides. In 1973, his wife met a new partner and they were divorced. After this life change, Edward went into selling foreign auto parts. Shortly after his divorce, Edward found a new partner and he lived with her until he encountered problems with his legs. Edward described how he had had problems with his legs for many years, but never went to the doctor because he "could not afford to take time out from work." Up until this time, Edward viewed his life as being a "challenge, a pretty good deal, until I had a problem with my legs."

Edward was admitted to a veterans' hospital and had both his legs amputated to combat a bone disease. He was unclear about the precise reason for the amputation and claims he was never told of the medical diagnosis. After being discharged from hospital, he did not return to his partner's apartment, but was placed in a nursing home. Edward noted emotionally: "They put me in a nursing home when I came out of the hospital. This done me more damage mentally than knowing that I would have to spend time in a cell. This I could cope with, but oh, have you ever been in one of these places. They are something unreal. Poor souls are crawling the walls, they don't get no attention. I told them at the nursing home that I'd crawl across the street just to get the hell out of here, because I ain't staying here." His stay at the nursing home convinced Edward that he desired to maintain his independence at all costs. He commented, "I don't want to be a burden to no one." Edward then moved from the nursing home to a hotel that provided meals. He was asked to leave, and he then moved to the hotel were I met him in 1985.

Edward was satisfied with the hotel as a place to live. His physical disability had significantly constrained his search for accommodation. Edward had two treasured cats that were an integral part of his life; many apartments restricted having pets and this had also constrained Edward's housing search. Living at the hotel meant that Edward had to tolerate its deteriorating physical environment. The most serious problem for him in the hotel was the elevator; when the elevator was not working Edward was trapped in his room, since it was on the seventh floor. His everyday movement was severely constrained during these times. Edward disliked the fact that the hotel was dirty and that many of the other tenants were noisy. However, he was willing to accept these negative characteristics because the hotel was situated in a convenient location and the neighborhood environment provided an exciting atmosphere for observing the "street carnival." Edward commented that "I spend as many hours as I possibly can outside, because I enjoy being with people, it gives me a chance to mingle with the millions in the area."

Edward spent a considerable amount of time outside, weather permitting, on the street in front of the hotel. To Edward, observing the "comings and goings" of street activity provided him with adventure. The street was always active and provided continuous entertainment. Edward would talk to "anyone who is willing to talk." He viewed the hotel and its immediate neighborhood environment as safe. This view changed sharply when he considered the wider neighborhood, particularly the area around the Chicago Transit Authority (CTA) rapid transit elevated railway station just five city blocks east of the hotel. Edward laughed, "There you are taking a calculated risk." This area was dangerous and Edward, confined to a wheelchair, actively avoided the area or steered a cautious course through it.

Edward did not view the SRO as a slum hotel, but as a place of refuge which allowed him to maintain privacy and independence. He was both proud and independent; as Edward said, "It's all I got left." The neighborhood was a place where he felt comfortable: he was born only thirteen blocks away. The hotel environment provided him with the opportunity to observe and interact with people. Edward was well-known within the hotel and had a number of fellow male tenants with whom he spent time talking. He was also eager to talk to others in the neighborhood. Edward said that "I feel a lot more comfortable out here (in the neighborhood), because I mingle with the people more."

Unlike four-fifths (81%) of the tenants who would spend a typical day inside their rooms, Edward spent his time outside, usually on the street in front of the hotel. During the summer, he typically spent at least ten hours outside his room. In the winter months or during days with inclement weather, he was confined to his room, the lobby, or a neighbor's room. In winter, he typically spent only one hour per day outside of his room. Edward commented, "I'm confined because I can't, you know, I can't roll this wheelchair out in the snow." The winter of 1986 was relatively mild and Edward was not denied his mobility. During the previous winter, he only was able to go outside for basic necessities.

Because Edward had lost both his legs and was confined to a wheelchair, immediate movement within his own room at the hotel was highly constrained. His room, typical of most at SRO hotels, was not designed to be wheelchair accessible. Edward had great difficulty maneuvering his wheelchair around the room, especially in the bathroom, which was very small. He also had difficulty getting from his bed to the wheelchair. He stated, "If I'm lucky I hop in the wheelchair. Sometimes I don't make it and I end up on the floor, that's a hell of a way to start the morning. When I'm in bed I pull the phone over by me and if I can't reach the phone (when I'm on the floor) I'm in big trouble. I have to beat on the floor or holler loud enough until somebody hears me."

Edward was unable to use public transportation. He could not board either the bus or the CTA rapid transit elevated railway. However, if an emergency need for transportation arose, he would be helped into a taxi. With Edward's reliance on his wheelchair, it was important for his access to stores or restaurants that the sidewalks and entrance ways be graded. This posed a particular problem for Edward, since the hotel was located in an area that had very deteriorated sidewalks. It was very difficult for him to negotiate these sidewalks. Often, when traveling through the neighborhood, Edward was forced to go out of his way to avoid a pothole in the sidewalk. Encountering bumps or holes in the sidewalk had caused him to be tossed out of the wheelchair and left him helpless and in a very vulnerable position. Many stores and restaurants had steps that imposed a barrier to Edward. He objected to needing help.

On a typical day, Edward woke up early, approximately at 6:30 A.M., and spent the next three hours in his room, preparing breakfast, washing, and shaving. If the weather was nice, he went downstairs at about 9:30–10:00 to either the lobby or out onto the street in front of the hotel. Once a week, during the morning, he went to the laundromat located on the ground floor of the hotel. The time Edward spent outside observing the other people and talking with friends, neighbors, and anyone who was willing to stop and talk with him, provided him with activity, excitement, and companionship. Edward was alone, but he was neither completely isolated nor was he a recluse. Unlike the majority (83%) of the elderly tenants in the study, he did receive weekly assistance from friends and neighbors. This assistance was usually in the form of grocery shopping. Edward was only able to carry a small amount of groceries at any one time and, as a result, he either traveled to the supermarket more than once a week or he got a friend or neighbor to go for him. Edward did not accept help with anything else. He noted, "Some people will say, 'Can I help you do this and help you do that,' and being bull headed as hell I tell them no, except to go to the store."

Edward's typical day continued with lunch, which he prepared in the small kitchen area in his room. In the afternoon, he returned to the street. His travels were constrained more by the condition of the sidewalks and the provision of off ramps than by his desire to travel. In the evening, Edward prepared supper in his room. Then, he would often return outside to the street in front of the hotel if he thought "something will be going on" or someone would be there to talk to. Otherwise Edward would watch television in his room. If all was quiet, he retired at approximately 10 P.M.

Edward's everyday geography was constrained both by his limited physical capabilities and the inner-city built and social environments. Edward was atypical of the other elderly tenants in the study in his desire to leave the SRO hotel at any opportunity. Unlike the other tenants, who often viewed the hotel as a haven from the inner city, Edward had chosen the hotel because of its location in a neighborhood with which he was familiar and where he found adventure. To Edward, the neighborhood allowed him the opportunity to converse and observe ongoing life, rather than being trapped in what he called "a cage" (a retirement home). Like half (48%) of the elderly tenants in the study, Edward had no idea where he would turn to if he needed help. He noted that no one had reached out to help him recently and that this situation was unlikely to change in the future. He faced a very uncertain future, with regard to both his housing situation and his medical condition. Edward was, however, quite aware of this: "I m not ready for the retirement farm yet, I just look that way. I have young ideas. I want to be with a mixed group, rather than old people, although one day that is going to happen to me."

Conclusions

. . . The story of Edward is the story of a remarkable older man defiantly attempting to maintain his privacy and dignity in the face of powerful environmental constraints. For the majority of the elderly tenants, movement beyond the refuge of their rooms was severely limited both by their own physical capabilities and the powerful constraints imposed by the hotel and neighborhood environments. The elderly tenants in Chicago did not exhibit the presence of considerable ties. With limited capabilities and powers of resistance, they were very vulnerable; many (28%) had been beaten or had their possessions stolen in the hotels. The elderly tenants complained of staff stealing money and other possessions from their rooms. Their daily struggle for survival had meant withdrawal from both the neighborhood and the hotel environment in which they found themselves living. Any ties that did exist were, out of fear and necessity, very limited and ephemeral. The mean journey beyond the hotel extended a mere three city blocks. Major roads in the study neighborhood were significant barriers to movement. The timing of the traffic lights on these roads was such that the lights changed too rapidly to allow safe crossing by the slow-moving elderly. Crime was omnipresent in the neighborhood and these men and women were very vulnerable to attack and robbery. Stories of the danger on the street ran rampant throughout the hotels, causing the elderly tenants to restrict movement even further, thus exacerbating their geographical and social isolation.

The majority of these elderly tenants had experienced long periods of living alone and, in an attempt to provide stability in an uncertain environment, had become proudly independent, believing and persevering in their own independence and their ability to make it by themselves. They were hidden from mainstream society, victims of the barriers they had erected to protect themselves from an uncertain, uncaring, and often hostile environment. This population took self-reliance and self-sufficiency to the extreme, which was problematic in at least two ways. First, these elderly men and women exhibited many symptoms of the aging process and had chronic medical problems that went unattended because of their fear of losing their independence by seeking help. Second, social service agencies assume that anyone who is really ill or in need of assistance will seek it. This is a dangerous fallacy with regard to this population since they did not seek help.

The problems faced by elderly tenants of SRO hotels are numerous and often life-threatening. Their treasured independence is encumbered by their poverty-level incomes, their wide range of chronic disabilities, and their inappropriate housing environments. Their desire to make choices and remain independent is all-important to these men and women. Their residence in the SRO hotels was not a genuine choice. Policymakers and social service agencies must strive to create a genuine choice for these men and women and they must also honor the right of this population to choose their unique and independent life-style. Given the fact that this elderly population had few resources and alternatives, the current and rapid decline in the SRO housing stock poses a serious threat to their ability to secure shelter. SRO hotels were inappropriate to the needs of the elderly tenants, but they did provide shelter at a time when homelessness was on the rise throughout the nation. Tenants of SRO hotels are labeled both deviant and undesirable, as "bums" or "derelicts." These men and women suffer greatly as a result of these inaccurate labels and they are consequently left in isolation, and the hotels are allowed to be removed from the housing stock. Edward noted, "[To] whoever is out there I'd like to say that one day you are going to be old. You will never know what it's like until it happens. A lot of us thought that there would always be someone to look out for us. It's a shock to us all to be in this situation."

NOTE

1. This term was given affectionately and, although I had yet to earn my doctorate, I accepted the title without discussion.

REFERENCES

City of Chicago. 1985. *Housing needs of Chicago's single low-income renters.* Department of Planning.

The Coalition for the Homeless and the Gray Panthers of New York City. 1984. *Crowded out: Homelessness and the elderly poor in New York City.* New York: Author.

Community Emergency Shelter Organization and the Jewish Council on Urban Affairs. 1985. *SRO's. An endangered species. Chicago's Single Room Occupancy Hotels.* Chicago: Author.

Eckert, J. K. 1979. The unseen community. *Aging* 291–292:28–35.

———. 1980. *The unseen elderly.* San Diego: Campanile Press, San Diego State University.

Groth, P. E. 1983. Forbidden housing: The evolution and exclusion of hotels, boarding houses, rooming houses, and lodging houses in American cities, 1880–1930. Ph.D. dissertation, University of California, Berkeley.

Hartman, C. H., D. Keating, R. LeGates, and S. Turner. 1982. *Displacement—how to fight it.* Berkeley, CA: Legal Services Anti-Displacement Project.

Kasinitz, P. 1984. Gentrification and homelessness: The single room occupant and the inner city revival. *Urban and Social Change Review* 17:9–14.

Shapiro, J. H. 1966. Single-room occupancy: Community of the alone. *Social Work* 11:24–33.

Werner, F. and D. Bryson. 1982 A guide to the preservation and maintenance of SRO housing. *Clearinghouse Review* 15:999–1009.

DEVELOPING YOUR OWN SNAPSHOTS *About the Group Experience*

1. *Research topic:* One of the most fundamental forms of social order is contained in the concept of *role,* the set of expected behaviors associated with a particular social position like teacher, doctor, son, mother, student, and so on. What is OK in one role may be totally inappropriate in another. For example, we expect students to take exams, write papers, and attend class. We do not expect them to stick their fingers in someone's mouth. But dentists do this daily (we actually pay dentists to stick their fingers in our mouths), and we don't expect dentists to write papers. What is proper or improper depends on the role.

   As we have discussed, there is a role of elevator rider. Similarly, there is a role of passenger, whether on a bus, train, or airplane. While riding with strangers on public transportation, we are expected to behave in a certain way. To examine the requirements of this role, take a ride on a bus or other form of public transportation. (If this is too difficult, try riding in an elevator.) While you are a passenger, notice how other riders are sitting or standing, whether there is any conversation (if so, about what and under what circumstances?), and how you feel when the vehicle is crowded and why you feel that way. If you are not too embarrassed, you might try starting a conversation with another passenger. What is the reaction? And why?
2. *Research topic:* Do college organizations really compensate for a lack of informal interaction? If so, students who spend much time with family, partners, or friends shouldn't join many clubs and organizations on campus; students who don't hang out with family, partners, or friends should make up the difference by joining. Interview a number of students on your campus to find out as much as you can about their social activities: how often they are with friends or family, how many campus organizations they belong to, and any leadership positions they hold in these organizations. What do your results indicate about college organizations as compensatory groups?
3. *Writing topic:* Examine an institutionalized practice—for example, a wedding or a funeral—for all of the latent functions it might perform.
4. *Writing topic:* Most elderly Americans live in independent households, not with their adult children or in a nursing home. In Paul Rollinson's "The Story of Edward: The Everyday Geography

of Elderly Single-Room Occupancy Hotel Tenants," we observed the plight of impoverished older Americans who find themselves alone. Unfortunately, even for more economically advantaged elderly Americans, old age also means a loss of primary group ties. In a brief essay, describe the situation of loneliness among elders in America and explain why their primary ties are not stronger. Wherever possible, draw upon your personal experiences with older people.

5. *Research topic:* Just how restrictive is a formal organization? To what extent does holding a job in a large corporation necessitate a loss of personal freedom for the individual who works there? In Randy Hodson's study "The Active Worker: Compliance and Autonomy at the Workplace," employees were observed to be extremely creative in seeking to overcome feelings of alienation. At the same time, conformity and obedience were often stressed at the expense of individualism. To provide a case study of your own, visit a large company in your local community. For at least a few hours, observe the patterns of behavior—including dress, speech, arrangement of furniture in offices, any uniformity of color, hairstyles, cars in the parking lot, schedule for lunch and breaks, and so on. Don't forget to take notes concerning your observations in some systematic way. For example, before beginning, you might want to make a partial list of the patterns of behavior you expect to find, to be expanded during the study. You might even want to visit, only briefly, another large company in order to get ideas about how employees conform. By the way, in order to avoid looking suspicious while collecting data, you should inform someone at the company of your purpose and ask permission to observe.
6. *Writing topic:* Thinking of the various forms of group experience depicted in the photo essay for this section, describe a situation where you were caught in a social web—that is, "trapped" by your group experience, constrained in your behavior by what other members of a group expected you to do. Indicate whether this was a good or a bad experience for you, and then explain what made it so.

CHAPTER 4

Institutions

WHAT'S A FAMILY?

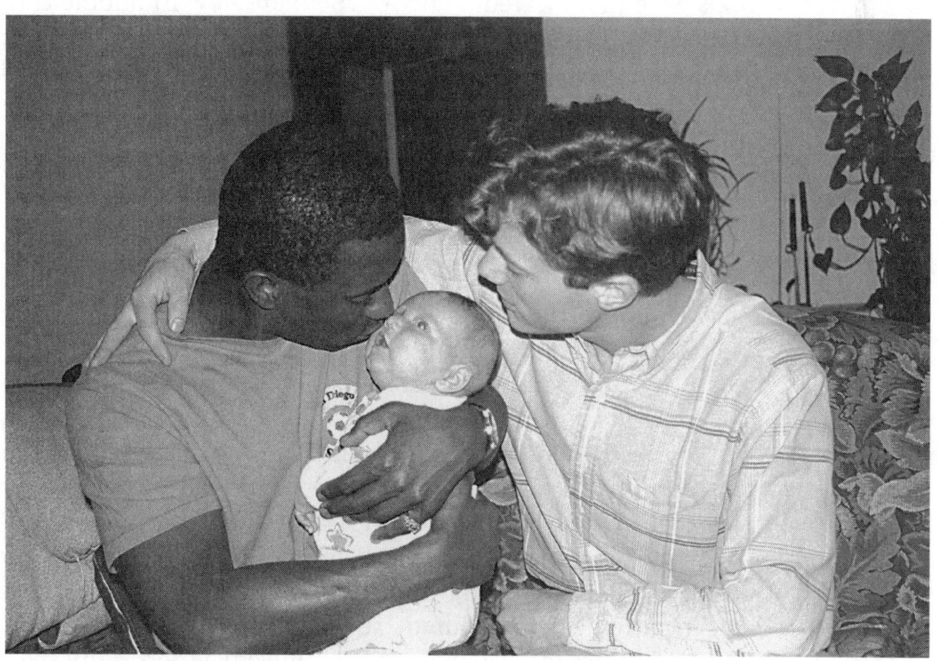

SNAPSHOT

Let the System Do It!

Taking Care of Society's Problems Can Hurt

Less than a century ago, the middle-class family still was involved in almost every aspect of its members' lives. Mother, father, grandparents, and children all worked the farm (or in the family firm). Together, they educated the offspring, treated illnesses, and provided a role for elders. After death, family members were buried in the family plot in the backyard, not miles away in some cemetery with thousands of strangers.

In responding to social problems, we have similarly constructed hospitals, prisons, nursing homes, and special schools for the retarded and the emotionally disturbed. We have also built mental institutions, cancer wards, soup kitchens, and retirement communities—all in the name of efficiency and humanitarian motivation.

Clearly, there are compelling administrative, medical, and economic reasons why many of our thorniest human problems—illness, poverty, and old age—are better handled by specialized formal organizations than by families. But there may be other, less rational reasons as well.

One clue is to look at where our nation's prisons and mental hospitals were first located. Many of them are now in middle-class suburban areas, an easy drive from the urban core. But at the time they were built, these same areas were quite different—they were almost invariably secluded rural settings, located many miles from large population centers and hidden from daily view. Even cemeteries were typically built some distance from major cities, allowing friends and relatives to pay only limited visits.

Remember the cliché "Out of sight, out of mind"? Let's face it: Middle-class Americans would prefer to set aside many problems to put them out of easy reach. The attitude too often is "Let somebody else take care of it. We aren't trained and they are."

Thus, our formal organizations help us displace the things we simply don't want to see. By constructing a formal response, we are able to avoid a whole range of human misery that might otherwise disrupt our personal lives and make us uncomfortable. Of course, many reluctant caregivers cannot bear the misery of seeing their loved ones suffer. In some cases, however, there may be another reason as well. By letting the formal system take care of terminal cancer patients, drug addicts, severely disfigured individuals, and Alzheimer's victims, we increase the subjective probability that these hideous things won't happen to us or to our loved ones. By distancing ourselves from human frailty and misery, we become free to pursue our individual goals and objectives—at work and at home—without fear that the same thing might (or will) happen to us.

Specialized institutions give us the false security of being able to go through life avoiding problems—until we are forced to deal with them. This may be one reason that community-based forms of treatment for mental illness, retardation, and juvenile delinquency have so often been opposed by Americans. In too many cases the thinking is that halfway houses belong on someone else's block, even when their residents pose little if any risk to the neighbors.

Of course, not everyone opts to put blinders on. Recognizing American myopia, educators are beginning to stress the importance of exposing young people to the entire range of social problems that they might otherwise not encounter. In one special program for high school students, for example, each teenager in the program spends a day working in a home for retarded children; each spends a few hours in a jail cell; and each visits a morgue. They thus learn about the possible consequences of their own behavior as well as the inevitable consequences of being human. They are forced to see the world as it really is, not as they'd like it to be. In the process, they may unexpectedly meet themselves.

SNAPSHOT Diversity on Campus

College Students Aren't Immune from Bigotry and Hatred

Howard V. Ehrlich reports that college students on campuses aren't necessarily getting along with their diverse classmates, roommates, and schoolmates. Indeed, the institute has discovered a dramatic increase in racial and anti-Semitic incidents on campuses around the country. At more than 160 colleges, there has been at least one intergroup episode during a three-year period, ranging from insensitive acts to episodes of open warfare. The institute estimates that 20 percent of all minority college students are either physically or verbally harassed. In one year the rise in anti-Semitic incidents alone approached 30 percent.

Such incidents, usually initiated by college students, have included shattering the windows of a Jewish student center in a burst of gunfire, publishing Hitler's statements in the campus newspaper, assaulting members of a Jewish fraternity, spray-painting the words *white power* on the walls of an African American cultural center, airing racist jokes on a campus radio station, harassing a black professor, and scribbling racist graffiti on restroom doors. In a few cases students have actually been murdered simply because they are different.

The targets of campus hate crimes have encompassed a broad range of students besides African Americans and Jews, including whites, Asians, Latinos, Native Americans, and women. Moreover, during the war in the Persian Gulf, dark-skinned students with foreign accents—especially those coming from Middle Eastern nations—were frequently regarded as the enemy by American college students looking for someone, perhaps anyone, to blame.

The most persecuted students on college campuses do not, however, necessarily differ from their assailants with respect to race, religion, national origin, or even gender; they differ in terms of sexual orientation. According to many observers, lesbian and gay students have been most frequently targeted for victimization. On some college campuses gay students have been held hostage, have been verbally insulted, have had their books and clothing defaced, and have received anonymous death threats. During Gay Pride Week on one campus a number of men burst into a movie being watched by a gay group on campus and then blocked the exits to the room. On another campus several students wore sweatshirts bearing the logo "Anti-Fag Society." After a college dance marathon in the Midwest, a gay couple was threatened with death on their answering machine. At an East Coast university antigay slurs were scrawled on sidewalks on the central campus.

You don't even have to be gay to be victimized—you need only "look gay." Thus, male students who have effeminate body language or speech may be harassed by their peers in college dormitories or campus centers. But such indicators of sexual orientation are unreliable; there are effeminate men who aren't gay and gay men who aren't effeminate.

This is one reason that attacks against gays and lesbians are so often targeted at their campus offices and organizational meetings. On the basis of appearance alone, haters cannot always identify students who are gay. As a result, they look for places where they are sure to find a number of "them" together. Frequently flyers announcing meetings are torn down or defaced. At one university campus bigots recently scribbled their message, "All faggots must die," across the announcements. At the same university an anonymous caller phoned the office of the campus Gay and Lesbian Coalition to say, "I'm a Nazi skinhead . . . I'm going to bomb your office and blow all you fags up."

Some college students sincerely believe, often on religious grounds, that homosexuality is immoral. It would be difficult, if not impossible, to convince such students otherwise. But even the most homophobic people on campus can usually be dissuaded from attacking gays in a violent or hurtful way. First, however, they must come to see gay people as what they are: human beings.

SNAPSHOT

Who's Minding the Kids?

Is Violence Filling the Void in Our Teenagers' Lives?

The headlines scream daily of hideous crimes—drive-by shootings, carjackings, and senseless murders—committed by our nation's teenagers. What makes violence so appealing to so many youngsters? Why is it that, in many quarters around the country, guns have replaced leather jackets and CD players as the status symbols of choice?

According to police reports to the FBI, the number of homicides committed by youngsters in their early teens has recently skyrocketed. Between 1985 and 1991, arrest rates for homicide increased among 13- and 14-year-old males by 140 percent and among 15-year-old males by 217 percent.

Actually, the problem is even worse than these dreadful statistics might suggest. While relatively few of our youngsters are committing hideous murders, the crimes are being tolerated—perhaps even honored—by their friends and classmates. Millions of teenagers may not be able to shoot or stab someone themselves, but they are capable of looking on as others do so.

Several years ago, a case of bystander apathy raised enough concern to inspire the motion picture *River's Edge.* A teenager in Milpitas, California, murdered his 14-year-old girlfriend and then returned to the scene with a dozen classmates to show them the corpse. One student covered the body with leaves to keep it from being discovered; others threw rocks at it. None of them contacted the police or told their parents.

More recently, the nation was shocked to learn that an attractive New Hampshire schoolteacher, Pam Smart, had inspired her 15-year-old student and his friends to kill her husband Greg by shooting him in the head. Attorney Marsha Kazarosian subsequently filed suit against the Winnecunnet, New Hampshire, school district on behalf of the families of the three youngsters convicted in the murder. Kazarosian claimed that Pam Smart's love affair with her student was made possible because she was negligently unsupervised by the

Winnecunnet High School administration; somebody in charge should have been keeping a watchful eye on Smart.

Whether or not school officials should have known, it appears that they may have been the only ones at Winnecunnet High who didn't. Statements made during the police investigation indicated clearly that at least one month before the police finally broke the case, the corridors of Winnecunnet High were already abuzz with rumors implicating the three students and their teacher. Yet nobody bothered to inform an adult.

More incredibly, statements later made to law enforcement officials indicate that students at Winnecunnet High were talking about Greg Smart's murder for two months *before* it actually occurred. With a simple phone call, any one of them might have prevented a murder. But nobody wanted to snitch or tattle on a classmate. Everybody was concerned about being rejected by friends. So they all kept quiet and let the murder plot proceed according to plan.

Too many of our teenagers have become desensitized to the consequences of violence. They have been raised on a steady diet of slasher films filled with explicit scenes of sex, murder, and mayhem. After school they come home to empty houses where they daily spend hours listening to rap and heavy metal lyrics or watching MTV videos that glorify violence. For economic reasons, more and more of our teenagers are left to fend for themselves, unsupervised after school and during vacations.

Only a few of our youngsters are willing to shoot someone in the head. But many others participate from a distance. Even if breaking their silence might stop a murder, they do not want to get involved.

It may have happened in New Hampshire, but it could have been anywhere. Marsha Kazarosian's lawsuit reflects an unpleasant truth about American society today. It isn't that TV, motion pictures, and popular music are so powerful. Rather, our traditional institutions have become weak. Our schools, religions, and families have lost their moral authority. And in their place we have allowed the peer group to fill the void in our youngsters' lives.

SNAPSHOT Dirty Work

Who's Going to Do the Unpleasant Jobs?

Every society has its "dirty work": jobs that are considered repugnant, undignified, or menial. They may also be regarded as absolutely essential for the well-being of society. Throughout the world, much of the dirtiest work of a society has been reserved for individuals considered to be outside the mainstream—for example, Pakistanis in England, Iraqis in Kuwait, and Turks in Germany. At the same time, even the most prestigious occupations may include at least a few tasks that could be regarded as dirty.

As a historical trend, the increasing rationalization of American society has created a proliferation of specialized occupations from what was formerly thought of as merely another field's dirty work. Indeed, millions of Americans currently work in jobs that never even existed a few decades earlier: assistants to activity directors in nursing homes and day care centers, emergency medical technicians, dental hygienists, data entry personnel, paralegals, associate producers, home care workers, audiovisual equipment aides, television and radio interns, and so on. To an increasing extent, therefore, one occupation's dirty work has become another's raison d'être!

In the midst of the expansion of specialized occupational roles, some professionals have gained enough resources to subcontract much, if not all, of their dirty work to lower-paid specialists. For example, professors may assign the task of grading multiple-choice exams to their teaching assistants; many dentists have hygienists who perform routine dental care; and nurses often enlist nurses' aides to change bandages and bedpans. Accountants have bookkeepers, physicians have physicians' assistants, and lawyers have paralegals.

What comes to be viewed as dirty work need not be the least bit dirty, at least in a physical sense. There is really nothing intrinsically repulsive about what we might choose to call dirty work. Instead, jobs are labeled as respectable or dirty typically based on a social construction: The members of a society share an understanding of the nature of their environment and apply that understanding to their definitions of occupational tasks.

In contemporary American society, for example, bankers are generally seen as holding a reputable occupational position. During the Middle Ages, however, the same job was regarded as too dirty for Christians to perform and was instead assigned to outsiders—specifically, to European Jews who were systematically excluded from such respectable activities as farming, owning land, and joining the guilds of craftsmen. Jews at that time were generally restricted to the despised occupation of lending money for interest, an activity that was regarded as essential by the church and the nobility as a source of outside financing for building, farming, waging war, or engaging in political affairs.

Despite its economic importance, usury was absolutely forbidden to the Christian majority on religious grounds. As viewed by the church, the lending of money for interest was sinful regardless of the amount of interest charged or the purpose for which money was borrowed. Thus, any Christian who lent money during the Middle Ages would have committed a mortal sin. In the view of the medieval church, however, Jews were headed for hell anyway, so their participation in money lending could add little to the eternal punishment that already awaited them.

Dirty work in America has traditionally been performed for low wages by poor people, newcomers, and minorities who have had few other choices. In the southern colonies, slaves were forced to play the role of field hands or domestic servants, and indentured servants performed heavy labor to buy their freedom. During the 19th century, Chinese newcomers toiled to build the railroads and work the crops. At the turn of the 20th century, European immigrants performed unskilled, backbreaking labor for poor wages and under miserable working conditions.

Even today many economic activities involving dirty work in such areas as restaurants, hospitals, and industrial agriculture continue to rely heavily on people from outside the mainstream—Americans of color as well as newcomers from Latin America, Asia, and Eastern Europe. According to sociologist Herbert Gans, these activities could not survive in their present form without depending on the substandard wages paid to their employees. More generally, Gans suggests that poverty may actually persist in part because it serves the important function of providing a low-wage labor pool that is willing to perform dirty work at low cost.

Of course, many respectable jobs also involve at least some tasks that most people would consider boring and unpleasant, even if they don't require getting dirty hands. Take, for example, the role of police officer, which, according to the television image, consists exclusively of battling the forces of evil. Actually, police spend much of their time and energy on more mundane matters such as removing dead mice, controlling traffic, doing paperwork, helping citizens who have fallen out of bed, and answering false alarms. Many police officers actually go through an entire career without ever having to fire their weapons in the line of duty.

To complicate matters, the very meaning of what comes to be regarded as dirty work is partially determined by the prestige level of an occupation. The same tasks may be considered dirty when performed for low wages but respectable and clean when performed for a lot of money. Homemakers who are unpaid for providing services to the members of their family may occasionally feel bored with routine child rearing and the daily drudgery of preparing the evening meal, yet such tasks are not intrinsically boring. In fact, they can be quite pleasant and satisfying—when carried out by a well-paid teacher or by a chef in a gourmet restaurant. One can only wonder what might happen to the desirability ratings of cooking and child rearing if homemakers were paid a decent wage.

Many people are physically sickened by the image of doctors performing surgery on their patients or, worse yet, conducting an autopsy. More than a few neophyte medical students have been known to go rubbery at the sight of a cadaver being anatomized. Yet Americans would hardly identify the role of doctor as dirty work. Instead, physicians continue to enjoy extremely high status with the American public, invariably being ranked ahead of most other occupations with respect to prestige. Apparently, even the most repulsive job is not necessarily thought of as dirty work. Is it a doctor's life-and-death struggle that makes the difference? In part, perhaps. But high income, prestige, and power can usually be counted on to turn the dirtiest work into good, clean fun.

SEEING INSTITUTIONS THROUGH SNAPSHOTS AND PORTRAITS

At a time when today's aging baby boomers were still hippies—during the late sixties and early seventies—I was just finishing my graduate degree and making plans for the future. My primary objective was to teach at the college level. Yet, like many of my friends and fellow graduate students in sociology, I also thought long and hard about the possibility of dropping out of the mainstream of competitive American society and establishing instead an alternative lifestyle that would be less demanding and repressive. In retrospect, it sounds kind of silly; but at the time, it seemed to make sense.

During the late sixties, many young people claimed to have given up on American institutions—the nuclear family, organized religion, capitalism, constitutional government, and traditional forms of public education—and it was relatively easy to find support and encouragement for going in a different direction. The more politically motivated students of the day referred to anyone in charge of almost anything—whether the police, the chair of the sociology department, or the president of the United States—as "pigs" and to conventional, middle-class political institutions, in the most negative sense possible, as "the establishment." Even among students who weren't inclined toward politics, the operating principle of everyday life seemed to be "do your own thing." Mainstream institutions—the conventional ways of meeting basic needs—were often viewed as irrelevant if not as the enemy.

Of course, though many hip students paid lip service to the idea of an alternative lifestyle, most never went much beyond the hippie fashion (wearing love beads, jeans, and long hair) in seeking to throw off what they saw as the yoke of oppression represented by American institutions. Even the antiwar demonstrations and those for civil rights and women were, for the most part, designed to reform but not overthrow traditional institutional arrangements. After all, many of those young people who demonstrated loudly for equal rights or against the war were students enrolled in the very colleges and universities they were fiercely attacking. Moreover, only a relatively few young people actually left school to drop out of American society.

Over time, those who did leave to take up residence in a commune attempted to establish their own institutions—frequently collective arrangements for feeding their families, building shelter, making clothing, teaching the basic skills of everyday life to children, and attending to their spiritual needs. Many communes failed to survive for more than a few months, however, because they also failed to develop collective ways to meet their members' basic human needs. In a word, they never developed viable alternative institutions.

The collective ways developed by any society for meeting the economic, religious, familial, political, and educational needs of its members are known as *institutions*. The lesson to be learned from the failure of many hippie communes of the 1960s and 1970s is simply that people cannot survive very long as a group without generating some effective institutional arrangements. The more recent demise of the Soviet Union was, in part, a result of a profound failure of its institutions in terms of meeting the basic needs of its members. It can happen to a small commune or to an entire society of millions of people.

The following institutions are commonly found in human societies.

The *economy* is the focal point for developing ways to procure the material necessities of everyday life. One of the most important functions of the economic institution involves getting the unpleasant but necessary jobs done. In "Dirty Work" we were reminded that dirty work in America has traditionally been performed for low wages by poor people, newcomers, and minorities with few other choices. We also saw that the dirtiness of a job has little, if anything, to do with its being physically unclean, but can be changed profoundly depending on how much we pay people to do it.

The *family* ensures the reproduction of society's members and controls sexual behavior so that adults will assume responsibility for socializing their offspring. In 1949 anthropologist George Murdock observed a sample of families located in 250 different societies in order to develop his definition of the family:

> A social group characterized by common residence, economic cooperation, and reproduction. It includes adults of both sexes, at least two of whom maintain a socially approved sexual relationship, and one or more children, own or adopted, of the sexually cohabiting adults.

Although Murdock argued that the family as he defined it was universal, his conception fails to cover the entire range of family forms throughout history and around the world. According to Melvin Spiro, for example, the Israeli kibbutzim that he observed in 1956 assigned responsibility for care of children not to the parents but to communal child care centers and schools.

Contemporary American society provides yet another possible exception. If the family, by Murdock's definition, contains adults of both sexes who maintain a socially acceptable relationship, where do we place gay or childless couples? Where do we place the large and growing number of single-mother households in which a husband or father is totally missing? In the portrait "Men Who Share 'The Second Shift,'" Arlie Hochschild and Anne Machung note that many husbands are conspicuously absent from family activities, even where divorce has not occurred and a marriage remains intact.

Education is responsible for providing specialized occupational training and general information necessary for citizenship. It is easy to envision our educational institutions as being receptive to change and diversity. There is a good deal of evidence, however, that schools are resistant to change—and so are the students who attend them.

The students who attend our institutions of higher education have undoubtedly changed in important ways. They now represent a much wider range of differences, and they are organized. Twenty-five years ago, special-interest organizations on campus included fraternities and a few religious groups. Today, however, there are likely to be organized groups for African Americans, gays and lesbians, Latinos, Asians, women, students with disabilities, and international students, just to mention a few. In "Diversity on Campus" we saw that college students aren't always prepared to deal with their schoolmates who are different with respect to race, religion, sexual orientation, disability status, or even gender.

Religion provides a unified system of beliefs and rituals directed toward answering the ultimate questions of human life. French sociologist Emile Durkheim identified an essential element in defining religion when he distinguished between the *sacred* (beliefs, objects, and customs seen as having special, divine, or otherworldly qualities) and the *profane* (beliefs, objects, and customs seen as mundane, ordinary, and of this world). Religion, according to Durkheim, focuses on sacred things; and particular religious groups differ in terms of what they regard as sacred: the Ten Commandments for both Christians and Jews, the Torah for Jews but not Christians, the coming of Jesus Christ for Christians but not Jews, and so on. Almost anything can assume the sacred status, no matter how nonconventional, frivolous, or ordinary it might appear to be. According to Michael Jindra (in the portrait "Star Trek Fandom as a Religious Phenomenon"), for example, the Star Trek television series has evolved into a religious phenomenon by giving its most ardent fans "something to believe in."

The *political order* sets the stage for some members of society to acquire and maintain power over other members of society. In "The Power Elite at the Bohemian Grove: Has Anything Changed in the 1990s?" Kevin Wehr examines the part played by a club in San Francisco, membership in which is important for maintaining the cohesion of the power elite—the leadership group of the ruling class in America. Interestingly, Clinton administration appointees were noticeably absent from the club's membership list.

Medicine is concerned with the prevention and treatment of disease. But those who practice medicine (e.g., physicians) are also members of society who have been socialized to respond to the human body with deep feelings. When they enter medical school, potential doctors must therefore learn to become comfortable with dead bodies (i.e., autopsies and dissections) and intimate contact with living bodies (i.e., pelvic, rectal, and breast examinations). According to Allen Smith III and Sherryl Kleinman ("Managing Emotions in Medical School"), students must draw upon aspects of their medical training to manage their emotions.

Sport provides competitive physical activities as governed by a set of conventional norms. Douglas Foley's "The Great American

Football Ritual" suggests that high school football is deeply involved in maintaining the status quo. According to Foley, football helps to preserve the inequalities between classes, genders, and races in American society.

Institutions often provide an efficiency in meeting human needs that would be impossible to achieve by sheer individual effort alone. But on the social psychological level, institutional responsiveness to difficult social problems also allows human beings to avoid dealing firsthand with what they would rather pretend doesn't exist: death, illness, disaster, disfigurement, and disability. In "Let the System Do It" this idea was introduced and illustrated. We have developed a set of institutions—schools, political systems, corporations, legal units, and religions—each of which now carries out specialized functions that used to be performed by family members. So as individual members of society, we escape the burden of having to face the entire range of human issues and frailties.

"Let the System Do It" focused attention on the rise of specialized institutions that, for the sake of efficiency, may have reduced the psychological burden of death and illness in our daily lives. In simple societies, the family takes primary responsibility for educating youngsters, performing religious rituals, governing the life of the community, and providing food and shelter (e.g., the family farm). As societies become more industrialized and technologically sophisticated, however, they tend to develop specialized institutions. Through a process that sociologist Talcott Parsons once called *structural differentiation,* tasks previously carried out by the family unit are now performed by highly specialized economic institutions (such as General Electric and Chrysler Corporation), specialized educational institutions (such as high schools and colleges), and specialized religious institutions (such as the Catholic Church). In the process, the family is left with narrowly specialized tasks of its own: socializing children and caring for the emotional needs of family members.

German sociologist Max Weber long ago discussed this trend in modern society when he wrote that industrial societies tend toward greater *rationalization*—the process whereby our lives become increasingly dominated by institutions dedicated to efficiency and to the domination of human beings by technology. Weber recognized that we pay a price for this efficiency: the dehumanization of everyday life. In the process of becoming ever more rationalized, industrial societies reduce activities that might be regarded as sentimental and spontaneous.

Weber identified *bureaucracy* as a particularly dehumanizing characteristic of formal organizations that develops in order to manipulate human beings in the interest of enhancing technical rationality. For Weber, bureaucracy contains a hierarchy of authority in the shape of a pyramid. A few at the top control many at the bottom. There is also an elaborate set of written rules and regulations, which forms the basis for the decisions of the organization. Most disturbing, perhaps, is Weber's contention that bureaucrats treat people as "cases" rather than as whole human beings. Any personal feelings tend to be placed aside and excluded from consideration in favor of interacting with people in highly specialized roles.

How well do American institutions meet human needs? In "Who's Minding the Kids?" we were offered a very negative answer: Our families, schools, and religious institutions are so weak that the adolescent peer group has all but taken over. Too many young people now raise one another. As a result, violence among teenagers has taken on epidemic proportions.

PORTRAIT

Men Who Share "The Second Shift"

Arlie Hochschild and Anne Machung

One out of five men in this study was as actively involved in the home as his wife—some were like Greg Alston, working the same hours as their wives but sharing in a more "male" way, doing such things as carpentry; others, like Art Winfield, shared the cooking and being a primary parent. In my study the men who shared the second shift had a happier family life, so I wanted to know what conditions produce such men. How do men who share *differ* from other men?

The men in this study who shared the work at home were no more likely than others to have "model" fathers who helped at home. Their parents were no more likely to have trained them to do chores when they were young. Michael Sherman and Seth Stein both had fathers who spent little time with them and did little work around the house. But Michael became extremely involved in raising his twin boys, whereas Seth said hello and goodbye to his children as he went to and from his absorbing law practice. Sharers were also as likely to have had mothers who were homemakers or who worked *and* tended the home as non-sharers. . . .

Did the men who shared the work at home love their wives more? Were they more considerate? It's true, egalitarian men had more harmonious marriages, but I would be reluctant to say that men like Peter Tanagawa or Ray Judson loved their wives less than men like Art

Winfield or Michael Sherman, or were less considerate in other ways. One man who did very little at home said, "Just last week I suddenly realized that for the first time I feel like my wife's life is more valuable than mine, because my son needs her more than he needs me." Men who shared were very devoted to their wives; but, in a less helpful way, so were the men who didn't.

Two other, more external factors also did *not* distinguish men who did share from men who didn't: the number of hours they worked or how much they earned. Husbands usually work a longer "full-time" job than wives. But in the families I studied, men who worked fifty hours or more per week were just *slightly* less likely to share housework than men who worked forty-five, forty, or thirty-five hours a week. In addition, fifty-hour-a-week *women* did far *more* child care and housework than men who worked the same hours. Other national studies also show that the number of hours a man works for pay has little to do with the number of hours he works at home.

Of all the factors that influence the relations between husbands and wives, I first assumed that money would loom the largest. The man who shared, I thought, would need his wife's salary more, would value her job more, and as a result also her time. . . .

I assumed that the man who shares would not earn more, and that the wage gap between other husbands and their wives might *cause* the leisure gap between them. Both spouses might agree that because his job came first, his leisure did, too. Leaving child care aside (since most men would want to do some of that), I assumed that men who earned *as much or less* than their wives would do more housework. I assumed that a woman who wanted fifty-fifty in the second shift but had married a high-earning man would reconcile herself to the family's greater need for her husband's work, set aside her desires, and work the extra month a year. By the same token, a traditional man married to a high-earning woman would swallow his traditional pride and pitch in at home. I assumed that money would talk louder than ideals, and invisibly shape each partner's gender strategy.

If money is the underlying principle behind men's and women's strategies, that would mean that no matter how much effort a woman put into her job, its lower pay would result less help from her husband at home. Research about on-the-job stress suggests that jobs in the low-level service sector, where women are concentrated, cause more stress than blue-and-white-collar jobs, where men are concentrated. Although working mothers don't work as long hours as working fathers, they devote as much *effort* to earning money as men, and many women earn less for work that's more stressful. Thus, by using his higher salary to "buy" more leisure at home, he inadvertently makes his wife pay indirectly for an inequity in the wider economy that causes her to get paid less. If money is the key organizing principle to the relations between men and women in marriage, it's a pity for men because it puts their role at home at the mercy of the blind fluctuations of the marketplace and for women because if money talks at home, it favors men. The extra month a year becomes an indirect way in which the woman pays *at home* for *economic* discrimination *outside* the home.

The Limits of Economic Logic

Money mattered in the marriages I studied, but it was not the powerful "invisible hand" behind the men who shared. For one thing, this is clear from the family portraits. Michael Sherman earned much more than Adrienne but his job didn't matter more, and he shared the work at home. For years Ann Myerson earned more than her husband but put her husband's job first anyway. John Livingston valued his wife's job as he did his own, but she took more responsibility at home.

A number of researchers have tried to discover a link between the *wage* gap between working parents and the *leisure* gap between them, and the results have been confusing. All but one study found no significant relation between the amount a man earns relative to his wife and how much housework or child care he does. Among couples in this study, these two factors were not related in a statistically significant way.

An intriguing clue appeared, however, when I divided all the men into three groups: men who earn more than their wives (most men), men who earn the same amount, and men who earn less. Of the men who earned more than their wives, 21 percent shared housework. Of the men who earned about the same, 30 percent. But among men who earned less than their wives, *none* shared.

If a logic of the pocketbook is only a logic of the *pocketbook*, it should operate the same whether a man earns more or a woman earns more. But this "logic of the pocketbook" didn't work that way. It only worked as long as men earned as much or more than their wives. Money frequently "worked" for men (it excused them from housework) but it didn't work for women (it didn't get them out of it).

Another principle—the principle of "balancing"—seems to be at work. According to this principle, if men lose power over women in one way, they make up for it in another way—by avoiding the second shift, for example. In this way they can maintain dominance over women. How much responsibility these men assumed at home was thus related to the deeper issue of male power. Men who earn much more than their wives already have a power over their wives in that they control a scarce and important resource. The more severely a man's financial identity is threatened—by his wife's higher salary, for example—the less he can afford to threaten it further by doing "women's work" at home.

Men who shared the second shift weren't trying to make up for losing power in other realms of their marriage; they didn't feel the need to "balance." Michael Sherman had given up the *idea* that he should have more power than Adrienne. Art Winfield talked playfully about men being "brought up to be kings."

But Peter Tanagawa felt a man *should* have more power, and felt he'd given a lot of it up when Nina's career rose so dramatically. He's adjusted himself to earning much less, but to a man of his ideas, this had been a sacrifice. By making up for his sacrifice by doing more at home, Nina engaged in "balancing." Among other couples, too, it's not only men who "balance"; women do too.

Thus, more crucial than cultural beliefs about men's and women's *spheres*, were couples' beliefs about the right degree of men's and women's *power*. Women who "balanced" felt "too powerful." Sensing when their husbands got "touchy," sensing the fragility of their husbands' "male ego," not wanting them to get discouraged or depressed, such women restored their men's lost power by waiting on them at home.

Wives did this "balancing"—this restoring power to their husbands—for different reasons. One eccentric Englishman and father of three children, aged six, four, and one, took responsibility for about a third of the chores at home. A tenured member of the English department of a small college, he taught classes, and held obligatory office hours, but had abandoned research, minimized committee work, avoided corridor conversations, and had long since given up putting in for a raise. He claimed to "share" housework and child care, but what he meant by housework was working on a new den, and what he meant by child care was reflected in this remark, "The children do fine while I'm working on the house; they muck about by themselves." He was touchy about his accomplishments and covertly nervous, it seemed, about what he called the "limitless" ambitions of his workaholic wife. Without asking him to do more, perhaps his wife was making up for her "limitless ambitions" by carrying the load at home. In the meantime, she described herself as "crushed with work."

I looked again at other interviews I'd done with men who worked less than full time. One architect, the fourth of four highly successful brothers in a prosperous and rising black family, had lost his job in the recession of the late 1970s, become deeply discouraged, taken occasional contracting jobs, and otherwise settled into a life of semi-unemployment. His wife explained: "Eventually we're going to have to make it on my salary. But it's awfully hard on my husband right now, being trained as an architect and not being able to get a job. I take that into account." Her husband did no housework and spent time with his son only when the spirit moved him. "I do very little around the house," he said frankly, "but Beverly doesn't complain, bless her heart." Meanwhile, they lived in near-poverty, while Beverly worked part time, cared for their baby and home, and took courses in veterinary science at night, her overload the result of their economic need added to her attempt to restore a sense of power to her discouraged husband. As she let fall at the end of the interview, "Sometimes I wonder how long I can keep going."

Other men earned less and did less at home but weren't "balancing." They were going back to get a degree, and their wives were temporarily giving them the money and the time to do this. The husband's training for a job counted as much in their moral accounting system as it would if he already had that more important job. For example, one husband was unemployed while studying for a degree in pediatric nursing. His wife, a full-time administrator, cared for their home and their nine-month-old baby. The rhythm of their household life revolved around the dates of his exams. His wife explained: "My husband used to do a lot around here. He used to puree Stevy's carrots in the blender. He used to help shop, and weed the garden. Now he studies every evening until ten. His exams come first. Getting that "A" is important to him. He plays with the baby as a study break." She said she didn't mind doing the housework and caring for the baby and got upset when he complained the house was messy. She said, "I keep myself going by reminding myself this is *temporary*, until Jay gets his degree."

I heard of no women whose husbands both worked and cared for the family while the wives studied for a degree. For a women, getting a degree was not so honored an act. There was no tradition of "putting your wife through college" analogous to the recent tradition of "putting your husband through college." A wife could imagine being supported or being better off when her husband got his degree. Husbands usually couldn't imagine either situation. One husband *had* shared the work at home fifty-fifty when his wife worked, but came to resent it terribly and finally stopped when his wife quit her job and went back to school to get a Ph.D. A job counted as legitimate recompense, but working toward a degree did not. Feeling deprived of attention and service, one man shouted into my tape recorder—half in fun and half not: "You can't eat it. You can't talk to it. It doesn't buy a vacation or a new car. I *hate* my wife's dissertation!" Women who put their husbands through school may have resented the burden, but they didn't feel they had as much right to complain about it.

Taken as a whole, this group of men—semi-unemployed, hanging back at work, or in training—neither earned the bread nor cooked it. And of all the wives, theirs were the least happy. Yet, either because they sympathized with their husbands, or expected the situation to improve, or because they felt there was no way to change it, and because they were, I believe, unconsciously maintaining the "right" balance of power in their marriage, such women worked the extra month a year. Meanwhile, their lower-earning husbands often saw their wives as intelligent, strong, "a rock"; at the same time these men could enjoy the idea that, though not a king at work, a man still had a warm throne at home.

Some women had other ways of accumulating more power than they felt "comfortable" with. One woman I know, an M.D., not in this study, married a former patient, a musician who earned far less than she. Perhaps the feeling that her status was "too great" for their joint notion of the "right" balance, she—a feminist on every other issue—quietly did all the second shift and, as her husband put it, "She never asks." Another woman, a teacher, secretly upset the power balance by having a long-term extra-marital affair almost like another marriage. Life went on as usual at home, but she quietly made up for her secret life by being "wonderful" about all the chores at home.

In these marriages, money was not the main determinant of which men did or didn't share. Even men who earned much more than their wives didn't get out of housework *because* of it. One college professor and father of three, for example, explained why he committed himself to 50 percent of housework and child care:

> My wife earns a third of what I earn. But as a public school teacher she's doing a job that's just as important as mine. She's an extraordinarily gifted teacher, and I happen to know she works just as hard at her teaching as I do at mine. So, when we come home, she's as tired as I am. We share the housework and childcare equally. But [in a tone of exasperation] if she were to take a job in insurance or real estate, she'd just be doing another job. She wouldn't be making the contribution she's making now. We haven't talked about it, but if that were the case, I probably wouldn't break my back like this. She would have to carry the load at home.

Ironically, had his wife earned *more* at a job he admired less—had she worked only for *money*—he would *not* have shared the second shift. . . .

That doesn't mean that money has nothing to do with sharing the second shift. In two different ways, it does. In the first place, couples do not need to think about and plan around financial need. Most of the men who shared at home had wives who pretty much shared at work. The men earned some but not much more. And whatever their wives earned, working-class men like Art Winfield really needed their wives' wages to live. Second, future changes in the general economy may press more couples to do "balancing." Some experts predict that the American economy will split increasingly between an elite of highly paid, highly trained workers and an enlarging pool of poorly paid, unskilled workers. Jobs in the middle are being squeezed out as companies lose out to foreign competition or seek cheaper labor pools in the Third World. The personnel rosters of the so-called sunrise industries, the rapidly growing, high-technology companies, already reflect this split. Companies with many jobs in the middle are in the so-called sunset industries, such as car manufacturing. As the economist Bob Kuttner illustrates: "The fast food industry employs a small number of executives and hundreds of thousands of cashiers and kitchen help who make $3.50 an hour. With some variation, key punchers, chambermaids, and retail sales personnel confront the same short job ladder." In addition, unions in the sunrise industries often face companies' threats to move their plants to cheap labor markets overseas, and so these unions press less hard for better pay.

The decline in jobs in the middle mainly hits men in blue-collar union-protected jobs. Unless they can get training that allows them to compete for a small supply of highly skilled jobs, such men will be forced to choose between unemployment and a low-paid service job.

The "declining middle" is thus in the process of creating an economic crisis for many men. This crisis can lead to two very different results: As economic hardship means more women have to work, their husbands may feel it is "only fair" to share the work at home. Or, there may be a countervailing tendency for men and women to compensate for economically induced losses in male self-esteem by engaging in "balancing." If the logic of the pocketbook affects the way men and women divide the second shift, I think it will affect it in this way, through its indirect effect on male self-esteem.

All in all, men who shared were similar to men who didn't in that their fathers were just as unlikely to have been model helpers at home, and just as unlikely to have done housework as boys themselves. But the men who shared at home seemed to have more distant ties with their fathers, and closer ones with their mothers. They were similar to non-sharing men in the hours they worked, but they tended not to earn a great deal more or less than their wives.

Sharing men seemed to be randomly distributed across the class hierarchy. There were the Michael Shermans and the Art Winfields. In the working class, more men shared without believing it corresponded to the kind of man they wanted to be. In the middle class, more men didn't share even though they believed in it. Men who both shared the work at home and believed in it seemed to come from every social class. Everything else equal, men whose wives had advanced degrees and professional careers—who had what the sociologist Pierre Bourdieu call "cultural capital"—were more likely to share than men whose wives lacked such capital. Men with career wives were more likely to share than men with wives in "jobs." All these factors were part of the social backdrop to the working man's gender strategy at home.

Added to these was also the strategy of his wife. Nearly every man who shared had a wife whose strategy was to urge—or at least welcome—his involvement at home. Such women did not emotionally hoard their children, as Nancy Holt came to do with Joey. When Evan had been about to leave to take Joey to the zoo for a father-son outing, Nancy had edged Evan out by deciding at the last minute to "help" them get along. At first awkward and unconfident with children, Michael Sherman could well have developed a "downstairs" retreat had it not been for Adrienne's showdown and continual invitation to join in the care of their twins. Often, something simple as the way a mother holds her baby so he or she can "look at Dad" indicates her effort to share. Adrienne Sherman didn't just leave her twins with Daddy; she talked to them about what Daddy could do with them; consciously or not, she fostered a tie to him. She didn't play expert. She made room.

As a result, such men were—or became—sensitive to their children's needs. They were more realistic than other fathers about the limits of what their wives provide, and about what their children really need.

Limiting the Idea of Fatherhood

Involved fathers had a much fuller, more elaborate notion of what a father was than uninvolved fathers did. Involved fathers talked about fathering much as mothers talked about mothering. Uninvolved fathers held to a far more restricted mission—to discipline the child or to teach him about sports. For example, when asked what he thought was important about being a father, one black businessman and father of two said:

> Discipline. I don't put up with whining. It bothers me. I'm shorter tempered and my wife is longer tempered. I do a significant amount of paddling. I grew up with being paddled. When I got paddled I knew damn good and well that I deserved it. I don't whip them. One good pop on their bottom and I send them down to their room. I've scared them. I've never punched them.

> And I'll spank them in front of people as well as not in front of them.

To him, being a disciplinarian *was* being a father. As a result, his children gravitated to their mother. She had worked for an insurance company but, under pressure of home and work, finally quit her job. In a strangely matter-of-fact way, she remarked that she didn't "feel comfortable" leaving the children with her husband for long periods. "If I go out to the hairdresser's on Saturday, I might come back and find he didn't fix them lunch; I don't leave them with him too much." If it wasn't a matter of discipline, he didn't think caring for children was his job.

Other fathers limited their notion of fathering mainly to teaching their children about the events in the newspaper, baseball, soccer. When I asked uninvolved fathers to define a "good mother" and "good father," they gave elaborate and detailed answers for "good mothers," and short, hazy answers for "good father," sometimes with a specific mission attached to it, like "teach them about cars."

I asked one man, "What's a good mother?" and he answered: "A good mother is patient. That's the first thing. Someone who is warm, caring, who can see what the child needs, physically, who stimulates the child intellectually, and helps the child meet his emotional challenges."

"What is a good father?" I asked. "A good father is a man who spends time with his children." Another man said, "A good father is a man who is around."

It is not that men have an elaborate idea of fatherhood and then don't live up to it. Their idea of fatherhood is embryonic to being with. They often limit that idea by comparing themselves only to their own fathers and not, as more involved men did, to their mothers, sisters, or other fathers. As a Salvadoran delivery man put it, "I give my children everything my father gave me." But Michael Sherman have his twins what his *mother* gave him.

Curtailing the Idea of What a Child Needs

Men who were greatly involved with their children react against two cultural ideas: one idea removes the actual care of children from the definition of *manhood*, and one curtails the notion of how much care a child needs. As to the first idea, involved fathers' biggest struggle was against the doubts they felt about not "giving everything to get ahead" in their jobs. But even when they conquered this fear, another cultural idea stood in the way—the idea that their child is "already grown-up," "advanced," and doesn't need much from him. A man's individual defense against seeing his children's need for him conspires with this larger social idea.

Just as the archetype of the supermom—the woman who can do it all—minimizes the real needs of women, so too the archetype of the "superkid" minimizes the real needs of children. It makes it all right to treat a young child as if he or she were older. Often uninvolved parents remarked with pride that their small children were "self-sufficient" or "very independent."

I asked the fifth-grade teacher in a private school how she thought her students from two-job families were doing. She began by saying that they did as well as the few children she had whose mothers stayed home. But having said that, her talk ran to the problems: "The good side of kids being on their own so much is that it makes them independent really early. But I think they pay a price for it. I can see them sealing off their feelings, as if they're saying, 'That's the last time I'll be vulnerable.' I can see it in their faces, especially the sixth-grade boys."

Throughout the second half of the nineteenth century, as women were increasingly excluded from the workplace, the cultural notion of what a child "needs" at home correspondingly grew to expand the woman's role at home. As Barbara Ehrenreich and Deirdre English point out in *For Her Own Good*, doctors and ministers argued strongly that a woman's place was at home. The child needed her there. As the economic winds have reversed, so has the idea of a woman's proper place—and the child's real needs. Nowadays, a child is increasingly imagined to need time with other children, to need "independence-training," not to need "quantity time" with a parent but only a small amount of "quality time." As one working father remarked: "Children need time to play with other children their age. It's stimulating for them. Nelson enjoyed it, I think, from when he was six months."

If in the earlier part of the century, middle-class children suffered from overattentive mothers, from being "mother's only accomplishment," today's children may suffer from an underestimation of their needs. Our idea of what a *child* needs in each case reflects what *parents* need. The child's needs are thus a cultural football in an economic and marital game.

An Orwellian "superkid" language has emerged to consolidate this sense of normality. In a September 1985 *New York Times* article entitled "New Programs Come to Aid of Latch Key Children," Janet Edder quotes a child-care professional as follows: "Like other child-care professionals, Mrs. Selgison prefers to use the phrase 'Children in Self Care' rather than "Latch Key Children,' a term coined during the depression when many children who went home alone wore a key around their necks." "Children in Self Care" suggests that the children *are* being cared for, but by themselves, independently. Unlike the term "Latch Key Children," which suggests a child who is sad and deprived, the term "Children in Self Care" suggests a happy superkid.

Another article, in the August 1984 *Changing Times*, entitled "When You Can't Be Home, Teach Your Child What to Do," suggests that working parents do home-safety checkups so that a pipe won't burst, a circuit breaker won't blow, or an electrical fire won't start. Parents should advise children to keep house keys out of sight and to conceal from callers the fact that they're alone at home. It tells about "warm lines"—a telephone number a child can call for advise or simple comfort when he or she is alone. Earlier in the century, advice of this sort was offered to destitute widows or working wives of disabled or unemployed men while the middle class shook its head in sympathy. Now the middle class has "children in self-care" too.

The parents I talked to had younger children, none of whom were in "self-care." The children I visited seemed to me a fairly jolly and resilient lot. But parents I spoke to did not feel very supported in their parenthood; like Ann Myerson, many parents in the business world felt obligated to hide concerns that related to a child. Many female clerical workers were discouraged from making calls home. Many men felt that doing anything for family reasons—moving to another city, missing the office party, passing up a promotion—would be taken as a sign they lacked ambition or manliness. As for John Livingston's coworkers, the rule of thumb was: don't go home until your wife calls.

For all the talk about the importance of children, the cultural climate has become subtly less hospitable to parents who put children first. This is not because parents love children less, but because a "job culture" has expanded at the expense of a "family culture."

As motherhood as a "private enterprise" declines and more mothers rely on the work of lower-paid specialists, the value accorded the work of mothering (not the value of children) had declined for women, making it all the harder for men to take it up.

My Wife Is Doing It

Involved fathers are aware that their children depend on them. Every afternoon Art Winfield knew Adam was waiting for him at daycare. Michael Sherman knew that around six A.M. one of his twins could call out "Daddy." John

Livingston knew that Cary relied on him to get around her mother's discipline. Such men were close enough to their children to know what they were and weren't getting from their mothers.

Uninvolved fathers were not. They *imagined* that their wives did more with the children than they did. For example, one thirty-two-year-old grocery clerk praised his wife for helping their daughter with reading on the weekends—something his wife complained he didn't make time for. But when I interviewed her, I discovered that her weekends were taken with housework, church, and visiting relatives.

Sometimes I had the feeling that fathers were passing the childcare buck to their wives while the wives passed it to the baby-sitter. Each person passing on the role wanted to feel good about it, and tended to deny the problems. Just as fathers often praised their wives as "wonderful mothers," so mothers often praised their baby-sitters as "wonderful." Even women who complain about daycare commonly end up describing the daycare worker as "great." So important to parents was the care of their child that they almost had to believe that "everything at daycare was fine." Sadly, not only was the role of caretaker transferred from parent to baby-sitter, but sometimes also the illusion that the child was "in good hands."

The reasons men have for why their wives were wonderful—for example, that they were patient—were often reasons women gave for why the baby-sitters were wonderful. Just as uninvolved fathers who praised their wives often said they wouldn't want to trade places with their wives, so wives often said they wouldn't want to trade places with their daycare worker.

As one businesswoman and mother of a three-year-old boy commented: "Our baby-sitter is just fantastic. She's with the kids from seven o'clock in the morning until six o'clock at night. And some kids stay later. I don't know how she does it. *I* couldn't" Another working mother commented: "I couldn't be as patient as Elizabeth [the daycare worker] is. I love my child, but I'm not a baby person."

The daycare worker herself was often in a difficult spot. She depended economically on the parents, so she didn't want to say anything so offensive it might lead them to withdraw the child. On the other hand, sometimes she grew concerned about a child's behavior. Typical of many daycare workers, Katherine Wilson, who had cared for children for fifteen years, remarked:

> One out of five parents just drop their children off and run. Another three will come in and briefly talk with you. Then the last person will come and in talk to you quite a bit. Not too many call during the day. A lot of parents aren't too concerned with day-to-day activities. They just trust we know what we're doing.

Some daycare centers even established a policy of check-in sheets that required parents to come inside the daycare center and sign their child in each morning, thus preventing the hurried few who might otherwise leave their children off at the sidewalk.

Pickup time was often hectic, and not a good time to talk. As one daycare worker observed:

> It's a hell of a life the parents lead. Every time I see them they're in a rush. It's rush in the morning and rush in the evening. They barely ask me what Danny had for lunch or how he seemed. I think they might feel bad when they see him around four o'clock in the afternoon. He gets kind of restless then. He's waiting. He sees the parents of the other children come and each time the doorbell rings he hopes its his parents. But, see, they come in the last—six-thirty.

Sometimes a daycare worker becomes worried about a child. As Alicia Fernandez confided:

> I've had Emily for a year and a half now. She's never been real open with me and I don't think she is with her mother either. I think, in a way, Emily was hurt that her former sitter had to give her up. It was a hard adjustment coming in to me and in fact I don't think she has adjusted. One day she took the money out of my wallet—the money her mother had given me—and tore it up. I was so shocked. It was my pay. I slapped her across the knees. She didn't even cry. I felt bad I'd done that, but even worse that she didn't even cry. I thought, hey, something's wrong.

Had she mentioned this to Emily's mother and father? I asked. She replied quickly and quietly: "Oh no. It's hard to talk about that. I feel badly about it but on the other hand if I told her mother, she might take Emily away."

The daycare worker, who could best judge how Emily's day had gone, felt afraid to confide her concerns to Emily's parents, who badly needed to hear them. Other daycare workers also kept their opinions to themselves. As another daycare worker noted: "You can feel sorry for them. I have Tim for nine hours. I have Jessica for ten and a half—now Jessie's mother is a single mother. Like I say, at the end of the day they cry." "Do you talk to their parents about the crying?" I asked. "They don't ask, and I don't bring it up." She continued, echoing a thought other daycare workers expressed as well:

> Don't get me wrong. These children are adaptable. They're pliant. As long as there's a sense of love here and as long as you feed them, they know I'm the one who satisfies their needs. That's all I am to them. The children love me and some little children, like Nelson, don't want to go home. He's three now, but I've had him since he was seven months old; Stephanie's three and I've had her since she was six weeks. But I do feel sorry for the children, I do. Because I know there are days when they probably don't feel like coming here, especially Mondays.

When daycare workers feel sorry for the children they care for something is wrong. This woman, a thirty-year-old black mother of three, was gentle and kindly, a lovely person to care for children. What seemed wrong to me was the overly long hours, the blocked channels of communication, and the fathers who imagined their wives were "handling it all."

A Father's Influence

In a time of stalled revolution—when women have gone to work, but the workplace, the culture, and most of all, the men, have not adjusted themselves to this new reality—children can be the victims. Most working mothers are already doing all they can, doing that extra month a year. It is men who can do more.

Fathers can make a difference that shows in the child. I didn't administer tests to the children in the homes I visited nor gather systematic information on child development. I did ask the baby-sitters and daycare workers for their general impressions of differences between the children of single parents, two-job families in which the father was uninvolved, and two-job families in which the father was actively involved. All of them said that the children of fathers who were actively involved seemed to them "more secure" and "less anxious." Their lives were less rushed. On Monday, they had more to report about Sunday's events: "Guess what I did with my dad. . . ."

But curiously little attention has been paid to the effect of fathers on children. Current research focuses almost exclusively on the influence on children of the working *mother*. A panel of distinguished social scientists chosen by the National Academy of Sciences to review the previous research on children of working mothers concluded in 1982 that a mother's employment has no consistent ill effects on a child's school achievement, IQ, or social and emotional development. Other summary reviews offer similar but more complex findings. For example, in charting fifty years of research on children of working mothers, Lois Hoffman, a social psychologist at the University of Michigan, has concluded that most girls of all social classes and boys from working-class families, whose mothers worked, were more self-confident and earned better grades than children whose mothers were housewives. But she also found that compared to the sons of housewives, middle-class boys raised by working mothers were less confident and did less well in school. But what about the influence of the fathers?

Apart from my study, other systematic research has documented a fact one might intuitively suspect: the more involved the father, the better developed the child intellectually and socially. Professor Norma Radin and her students at the University of Michigan have conducted a number of studies that show that, all else being equal, the children of highly involved fathers are better socially and emotionally adjusted than children of noninvolved fathers and score higher on academic tests. In Professor Radin's research, "highly involved" fathers are those who score in the top third on an index compromised of questions concerning responsibility for physical care (e.g., feeding the children), responsibility for socializing the child (e.g., setting limits), power in decision-making regarding the child, availability to the child, and an overall estimate of his involvement in raising his preschooler. In one study of fifty-nine middle-class families with children between the ages of three and six, Professor Radin found that highly involved fathers had sons who were better adjusted and more socially competent, more likely to perceive themselves as masters of their fate, and a higher mental age on verbal intelligence tests. A 1985 study of Abraham Sagi found Israeli children of highly involved fathers to be more empathetic than other children.

A 1985 comprehensive and careful study by Carolyn and Phil Cowan, two psychologists at the University of California, Berkeley, found that three-and-a-half-year-old children of involved fathers achieved higher scores on certain playroom tasks (classifying objects, putting things in a series, role-taking tasks) than other children. When fathers worked longer hours outside the home, the Cowans found in their observation sessions, the three-and-a-half-year-olds showed more anxiety. The daughters of long-hours men were, in addition, less warm and less task oriented at playroom tasks, although they had fewer behavior problems. When fathers worked long hours, mothers tended to "compensate" by establishing warm relations with their sons. But when mothers worked long hours, husbands did not "compensate" with their daughters. In spite of this, the girls did well in the playroom tasks. When fathers *or* mothers worked more outside the home, the parent established a closer bond with the *boy*.

Finally, the results of active fatherhood seem to last. In one study, two psychologists asked male undergraduates at the University of Massachusetts, Amherst, to respond to such statements as "My father understood my problems and worries and helped with them, hugged or kissed me goodnight when I was small, was able to make me feel better when I was upset, gave me a lot of care and attention." They were also asked to describe his availability ("away from home for days at a time, . . . out in the evening at least two nights a week, . . . home afternoons when children came home from school" and so on). The young men who ranked their fathers highly—or even moderately—nurturant and available were far more likely to describe themselves as "trusting, friendly, loyal, and dependable, industrious and honest."

In the end, caring for children is the most important part of the second shift, and the effects of a man's care or his neglect will show up again and again through time—in the child as a child, in the child as an adult, and probably also in the child's own approach to fatherhood, and in generations of fathers to come. Active fathers are often in reaction against a passive detached father, a father like Seth Stein. But an exceptionally warmhearted man, like the stepfather of Art Winfield, could light the way still better. In the last forty years, many women have made a historic shift, into the economy. Now it is time for a whole generation of men to make a second historic shift—into work at home.

PORTRAIT

Managing Emotions in Medical School

Allen C. Smith, III and Sherryl Kleinman

All professionals develop a perspective different from, and sometimes at odds with, that of the public (Friedson 1970). "Professionals" are supposed to know more than their clients and to have personable, but not personal, relationships with them. Social distance between professional and client is expected (Kadushin 1962). Except for scattered social movements within the professions in the late 1960s and 1970s that called for personal and egalitarian relationships with clients (Haug and Sussman 1969; Kleinman 1984), professionals expect to have an "affective neutrality" (Parsons 1951) or a "detached concern" for clients (Lief and Fox 1963). Because we associate authority in this society with an unemotional persona, affective neutrality reinforces professionals' power and keeps clients from challenging them. One element of professional socialization, then, is the development of appropriately controlled affect.

Medicine is the archetypal profession, and norms guiding the physician's feelings are strong. Physicians ideally are encouraged to feel moderate sympathy toward patients, but excessive concern and all feelings based on the patient's or the physician's individuality are proscribed (Daniels 1960). Presumably, caring too much for the patient can interfere with delivering good service. Other feelings such as disgust or sexual attraction, considered natural in the personal sphere, violate fundamental medical ideals. Doctors are supposed to treat all patients alike (that is, well) regardless of personal attributes, and without emotions that might disrupt the clinical process or the doctor–patient relationship. As several sociologists have shown, both doctor and patient use dramaturgical strategies to act "as if" the situation were neutral (Emerson 1970; Goffman 1974, p. 35). Such detachment presumably helps doctors to deal with death and dying (Sudnow 1967), with the pressure of making mistakes (Bosk 1979), and with the uncertainty of medical knowledge (Fox 1980b).

In this paper we examine another provocative issue—the physical intimacy inherent in medicine—and ask how medical students manage their inappropriate feelings as they make contact with the human body with all of their senses. We look closely at the situations that make them most uncomfortable: disassembling the dead human body (i.e., autopsy and dissection) and making "intimate" contact with living bodies (i.e., pelvic, rectal, and breast examinations). From the beginning of medical training, well before students take on clinical responsibility, dealing with the human body poses a problem for them (Mudd and Siegel

From "Managing Emotions in Medical School: Students' Contacts with the Living and the Dead" by A. Smith and S. Kleinman, 1989, *Social Psychology Quarterly 52:* 56–69.

1969). Clothed in multiple meanings and connected to important rituals and norms, the body demands a culturally defined respect and provokes deep feelings. Even a seemingly routine physical exam calls for a physical intimacy that would evoke strong feelings in a personal context, feelings which are unacceptable in medicine.

The ideology of affective neutrality is strong in medicine; yet no courses in the medical curriculum deal directly with emotion management, specifically learning to change or eliminate inappropriate feelings (Hochschild 1983). Rather, two years of participant observation in a medical school revealed that discussion of the students' feelings is taboo; their development toward emotional neutrality remains part of the hidden curriculum. Under great pressure to prove themselves worthy of entering the profession, students are afraid to admit that they have uncomfortable feelings about patients or procedures, and hide those feelings behind a "cloak of competence" (Haas and Shaffir 1977, 1982). Beneath their surface presentations, how do students deal with the "unprofessional" feelings they bring over from the personal realm? . . .

Methods

We studied students as they encountered the human body in clinical situations during the first three years of their training at a major medical school in the Southeast. . . . [We] observed for 35 hours in the gross anatomy laboratory, 34 hours in the physical diagnosis course (classroom, session on the pelvic examination, and practice with patients), and 168 hours in the five third-year clinical clerkships. We selected sites that included major body contact situations: dissection, practice sessions on physical examination skills, and services in the clerkships where contact with the breasts, genitals, and rectum is officially routine.

Over the same period we conducted open-ended, in-depth interviews with 16 first-year, 13 second-year, and 15 third-year students and with 18 others, including residents, attending physicians, nurses, spouses, and a counselor in the student health service. . . .

The Students' Problem

As they encounter the human body, students experience a variety of uncomfortable feelings including embarrassment, disgust, and arousal. Medical school, however, offers a barrier against these feelings by providing the anesthetic effect of long hours and academic pressure. . . . These difficulties and the sacrifices that they entail legitimate the special status of the profession the students are entering. They also blunt the students' emotional responses.

Yet uncomfortable feelings break through. Throughout the program, students face provocative situations—some predictable, others surprising. They find parts of their training, particularly dissection and the autopsy, bizarre or immoral when seen from the perspective they had "for 25 years" before entering medical school.

> Doing the pelvis, we cut it across the waist. . . . Big saws! The mad scientist! People wouldn't believe what we did in there. The cracking sound! That day was more than anxiety. We were really violating that person . . . Drawn and quartered (first-year male).

> I did my autopsy 10 days ago. That shook me off my feet. Nothing could have prepared me for it. The person was my age . . . She just looked (pause) asleep. Not like the cadaver. Fluid, blood, smell. It smelled like a butcher shop. And they handled it like a butcher shop. The technicians. Slice, move, pull, cut . . . all the organs, insides, pulled out in ten minutes. I know it's absurd, but what if she's not really dead? She doesn't look like it (second-year female).

The "mad scientist" and the "butcher" violate the students' images of medicine. Even in more routine kinds of contact, the students sometimes feel that they are ignoring the sanctity of the body and breaking social taboos.

Much of the students' discomfort is based on the fact that the bodies they have contact with are or were *people*. Suddenly students feel uncertain about the relationship of the person to the body, a relationship they had previously taken for granted. . . .

Students find contact with the sexual body particularly stressful. In the anatomy lab, in practice sessions with other students, and in examining patients, students find it difficult to feel neutral as contact approaches the sexual parts of the body.

> When you listen to the heart you have to work around the breast, and move it to listen to one spot. I tried to do it with minimum contact, without staring at her tit . . . breast . . . The different words (pause) shows I was feeling both things at once (second-year male).

Though they are rarely aroused, students worry that they will be. They feel guilty, knowing that sexuality is proscribed in medicine, and they feel embarrassed. . . .

Students also feel disgust. They see feces, smell vomit, touch wounds, and hear bone saws, encountering many repulsive details with all their senses.

> One patient was really gross! He had something that kept him standing, and coughing all the time. Coughing phlegm, and that really bothers me. Gross! Just something I don't like. Some smelled real bad. I didn't way to examine their axillae. Stinking armpits! It was just not something I wanted to do (second-year female).

When the ugliness is tied to living patients, the aesthetic problem is especially difficult. On opening the bowels of the cadaver, for example, students permit themselves some silent expressions of discomfort, but even a wince is unacceptable with repugnant living patients.

To make matters worse, students learn early on that they are not supposed to talk about their feelings with faculty members or other students. Feelings remain private. The silence encourages students to think about their problem as an individual matter, extraneous to the "real work" of medical school. They speak of "screwing up your courage," "getting control of yourself," "being tough enough," and "putting feelings aside." They worry that the faculty would consider them incompetent and unprofessional if they admitted their problem. . . . Exemplifying pluralistic ignorance, each student feels unrealistically inadequate in comparison with peers (yet another uncomfortable feeling). Believing that other students are handling the problem better than they are, each student manages his or her feelings privately, only vaguely aware that all students face the same problem. . . .

Emotion Management Strategies

How do students manage their uncomfortable and "inappropriate" feelings? The deafening silence surrounding the issue keeps them from defining the problem as shared, or from working out common solutions. They cannot develop strategies collectively, but their solutions are not individual. Rather, students use the *same* basic emotion management strategies because social norms, faculty models, curricular priorities, and official and unofficial expectations provide them with uniform guidelines and resources for managing their feelings.

Transforming the Contact

Students feel uncomfortable because they are making physical contact with people in ways they would usually define as appropriate only in a personal context, or as inappropriate in any context. Their most common solution to this problem is cognitive (Hochschild 1979; Thoits 1985). Mentally they transform the body and their contact with it into something entirely different from the contacts they have in their personal lives. Students transform the person into a set of esoteric body parts and change their intimate contact with the body into a mechanical or analytic problem.

> I just told myself, "OK, doc, you're here to find out what's wrong, and that includes the axillae (armpits)." And I detach a little, reduce the person for a moment . . . Focus real hard on the detail at hand, the fact, or the procedure or the question. Like with the cadaver. Focus on a vessel. Isolate down to whatever you're doing (second-year female).

. . . Students also transform the moment of contact into a complex intellectual puzzle, the kind of challenge they faced successfully during previous years of schooling. They interpret details according to logical patterns and algorithms, and find answers as they master the rules. . . .

> The patient is really like a math word problem. You break it down into little pieces and put them together. The facts you get from a history and physical, from the labs and chart. They fit together, once you begin to see how to do it . . . It's an intellectual challenge (third-year female).

. . . The scientific, clinical language that the students learn also supports intellectualization. It is complex, esoteric, and devoid of personal meanings. "Palpating the abdomen" is less personal than "feeling the belly."

> When we were discussing the pelvis, the wrong words kept coming to mind, and it was uncomfortable. I tried to be sure to use the right words, penis and testicles (pause) not cock and balls. Even just thinking. Would have been embarrassing to make that mistake that day. School language, it made it into a science project (first-year female).

Further, the structure of the language, as in the standard format for the presentation of a case, helps the students to think and speak impersonally. Second-year students learn that there is a routine, acceptable way to summarize a patient: chief complaint, history of present illness, past medical history, family history, social history, review of systems, physical findings, list of problems, medical plan. . . .

Transformation sometimes involves changing the body into a nonhuman object. Students think of the body as a machine or as an animal specimen, and recall earlier comfortable experiences in working on that kind of object. The body is no longer provocative because it is no longer a body. . . .

> (The pelvic exam) is pretty much like checking a broken toaster. It isn't a problem. I'm good at that kind of thing (second-year male). . . .

Accentuating the Positive

. . . Students identify much of their contact with the body as "real medicine," asserting that such contact separates medicine from other professions. As contact begins in dissection and continues through the third-year clinical clerkships, students feel excited about their progress. . . .

> This (dissection) is the part that is really medical school. Not like any other school. It feels like an initiation rite, something like when I joined a fraternity. We were really going to work on people (first-year male).

After years of anticipation, they are actually entering the profession; occasions of body contact mark their arrival and their progress. The students also feel a sense of privilege and power.

> This is another part that is unique to med school. The professor told us we are the only ones who can do this legally. It is special (pause) and uneasy (first-year female).

. . . Contact also provides a compelling basis for several kinds of learning, all of which the students value. They sense that they learn something important in contact, something richer than the "dry facts" of textbooks and lectures. Physicians, they believe, rely on touch, not on text. . . .

> We learned a lot about the body before, and about the disease in the abstract. Now, those abstractions are right in front of us. We can begin to connect the abstract lessons to the facts we find with the patients (third-year female).

Students also develop clinical intuition and a fascination for the body and the "personality" of its parts. They find the learning that occurs with contact gratifying, sometimes satisfying a long-standing curiosity, and frequently symbolizing the power of medicine.

Similarly, students can intensify the good feelings that come with practicing medical ideals. By attending to those ideals, students can feel a pride which overrides any spontaneous discomfort.

> If it's something uneasy, like moving her (breast) to listen to her heart, I also know that I'm doing the right thing. It's both, and it fells good to know I'm doing it right (second-year male). . . .

Using the Patient

. . . When they are uncomfortable, students can control their feelings by shifting their awareness away from their own feelings and to the patient's. Empathizing with the patient, they distract themselves from their own feelings. At the same time, they can feel good about "putting the patient first."

> Sure, my feelings matter. But theirs do too, even more. I'm here for them, and it's only right to give theirs priority. It feels good to listen to them, to try to understand (pause) to care. And I don't feel so weird (second-year male).

. . . Students sometimes use the patient as an external locus for their own uncomfortable feelings. They make the patient responsible for their feelings, blaming the patient or simply projecting their own feelings onto the patient. A student can manage feelings of sexual awkwardness, for example, by defining the patient as inappropriately sexual. . . .

> My very first patient was a young girl, 14 years old. I had been told she was a pediatrics patient, but I sure didn't expect a 14-year-old (pause) and well-developed. I think she was promiscuous. I forgot to do the heart at first. Went all the way to the end and then said, "I'll have to listen to your heart." It was extremely uncomfortable (third-year male).

Labeling the patient as "promiscuous," the student can forgive himself his awkwardness and perhaps replace it with feelings of superiority or anger. . . .

Laughing about It

. . . Humor is an acceptable way for people to acknowledge a problem and to relieve tension without having to confess weaknesses. In this case, joking also lets other students know that they are not alone with the problem.

> When the others are talking it's usually about unusual stuff, like jokes about huge breasts . . . Talking in small groups would help. The sexual aspect is there. Are they normal or abnormal? What's going on? (second-year male)

. . . By redefining the situation as at least partially humorous, students reassure themselves that they can handle the challenge. They believe that the problem can't be so serious if there is a funny side to it. Joking also allows them to relax a little and to set ideals aside for a time.

Where do students learn to joke in this way? The faculty, including the residents (who are the real teachers on the clinical teams), participate freely, teaching the students that humor is an acceptable way to talk about uncomfortable encounters in medicine. . . .

> If I had to examine her I'd toss my cookies. I mean she is enormous. That's it! Put it in the chart! Breasts too large for examination! (resident). (The team had just commented on a variety of disturbing behaviors that they observed with the patient.)

. . . Eager to please the faculty and to manage their emotions, students quickly adopt the faculty's humor. Joking about patients and procedures means sharing something special with the faculty, becoming a colleague. The idea implicit in the humor, that feelings are real despite the rule against discussing them, is combined with an important sense of "we-ness" that the students value. . . .

Avoiding the Contact

Students sometimes avoid the kinds of contact that give rise to unwanted emotions. They control the visual field during contact, and eliminate or abbreviate particular kinds of contact.

> We did make sure that it was covered. The parts we weren't working on. The head, the genitals. All of it really. It is important to keep them wrapped and moist, so they wouldn't get moldy. That made sense. But when the cloth slipped, someone made sure to cover it back up, even if just a little (pubic) hair showed (first-year female).

. . . Students also avoid contact by abbreviating or eliminating certain parts of the physical examination, moving or looking away, or being absent. Absence is usually not an option, but many students use the less obvious variations. . . .

> At the genitals, I was embarrassed. I had never touched a guy's genitals before. Even though this was medical, it was a pretty quick exam. I mimicked the preceptor, but I didn't really have any knowledge of it. It was not comfortable (second-year female).

The students explain their limited and "deferred" examinations by claiming inexperience or appealing to the patient's needs: "Four or five others will be doing it. Why should I make the patient uncomfortable?" Some students admit they use these arguments to avoid or postpone disturbing contact.

. . . When the faculty members are present they do the work themselves, leaving the students to observe. This lack of supervision gives students the freedom to learn without the pressure of criticism. It also gives them opportunities to avoid the kinds of contact that make them uncomfortable.

Also, faculty members protect students from contact with the parts of the body that make them most uneasy. . . . The faculty rarely challenge students to "defer" the breast, rectal and genital examinations in the clerkships, and they abbreviate such contact in their own work. . . .

Taking Medicine Home

In their studies, students gradually come to see the human body as an interesting object, separate from the person. This new, intellectualized body is stripped of the meanings the students knew before coming to medical school. The impersonal body is relatively neutral and easy to contact clinically, but students have a vague and unsettling sense of loss. . . .

> I had to confront the fact that we are just flesh, made of flesh, like the animals we

eat. It took a week to work it out, partly (second-year male).

According to the official perspective of the school, the body is "just" a complex object. The heart may be an awesome, marvelous pump, but something which has been valuable is lost during professionalization. Mysterious and romantic meanings are publicly discarded, and students are not sure what their world will be like without them. . . .

For some students, medical training creates a problem as new meanings for the body and for body contact go home with them at night. The clinical perspective enters into moments of contact with spouses and friends, an arena where personal meanings are important.

> I have learned enough to find gross problems. And they taught us that breast cancer is one of the biggest threats to a woman's health. OK. So I can offer my expertise. But I found myself examining her, right in the middle of making love. Not cool! (second-year male)

. . . Particularly in the sexual domain, the progressive neutralization of the body threatens personal meanings that the students have long attached to physical intimacy. . . . Acknowledging the threatening quality of intimacy in personal life, some students are also concerned that they may bring their emotion management strategies home and use them in unhealthy ways to minimize personal pains.

For other students, neutralizing the body at school helps them to achieve greater intimacy at home. If intimacy has been overromanticized in their personal relationships, for example, it can become less awesome and more manageable as they redefine it for medicine.

> Well, it's been fun, trying things on him. I'd practice things like the ear exam, or (pause) we didn't do the (male) genitals at school. I tried it at home. He was real good about it, and I think I learned something. I was glad to have a chance before trying it on a real patient. And we talked afterward, more than we usually do (second-year female).

Conclusion

. . . The five emotion management strategies used by the students illustrates the culture of modern Western medicine. In relying on these strategies, the students reproduce that culture (Foucault 1973), creating a new generation of physicians who will support the biomedical model of medicine and the kind of doctor–patient relationship in which the patient is too frequently dehumanized. . . .

Analytic transformation is the students' primary strategy, and it does tend to produce affective neutrality. As we stated, however, the medical culture provides other strategies that involve strong feelings instead of the neutrality of medical ideals. The particular feelings allowed by faculty members and by the culture fit with the basis of all occupations that have achieved the honorific title of "profession": acquiring hierarchical distance from clients (if not always emotional indifference). Much of the humor that students learn puts down patients who are aesthetically, psychologically, or socially undesirable (Papper 1978). Blaming patients and avoiding uncomfortable contact lend power to the physician's role. Even the effort to accentuate the comfortable feelings which come with learning contributes to the distance. In concentrating on the medical problem, students distance themselves from their patients. As Becker et al. (1961) observed years ago, uninteresting patients who have nothing to teach are "crocks." All of these strategies maintain the kind of professional distance that characterizes modern medical culture, a distance which provides for comfortable objectivity as well as scientific medical care.

One of the students' strategies, however, operates differently. Empathizing with patients diminishes the students' discomfort and directs attention to the patient's feelings and circumstances. Students are taught that excessive concern for patients can cloud their clinical judgment, but moderate concern allows them to manage their own feelings *and* to pay close attention to the patient.

Depending on how easily they can switch their strategies on and off, students and physicians may influence the character of their personal relationships as well as their medical practice. For some the effects can be healthy, enhancing personal intimacy by diminishing its mystique. Yet for others the results, particularly the long-term results, may be disruptive (Hochschild 1983). We speculate that the professionalization of private emotions may help to explain some of the health problems associated with the practice of medicine.

It would be unfair to conclude that medical training is uniquely responsible for the specific character of the students' emotion management problem and for its unspoken solution. The basic features of the culture of medicine are consistent with the wider cultural context in which medicine exists. Biomedicine fits with the emphasis in Western culture on rationality and scientific "objectivity." In Western societies the mind is defined as superior to the body, and thoughts are defined as superior to feelings (Mills and Kleinman 1988; Tuan 1982; Turner 1984). Not surprisingly, students know the feeling rules of professional life before they arrive at medical school. Childhood socialization and formal education teach them to set aside their feelings in public, to master "the facts," and to present themselves in intellectually defensible ways (Bowers 1984). Medical situations provide vivid challenges, but students come equipped with emotion management skills that they need only to strengthen.

We suspect that the patterns we found in medical education occur as well in other professional schools and situations. Most health professionals face similar challenges and maintain a similar silence about them (Pope, Keith-Spiegel, and Tabachnik 1986). Comparably provocative challenges exist elsewhere, requiring potentially similar strategies of change and control.

The generality of the questions and the answers is illustrated by fundamental aspects of military life. Missions, tactics, and equipment are all designed to kill, and the possibility of death is real. Combat training would provoke uncomfortable disruptive feelings if individual and collective emotion management strategies were not at work. The first author recalls that in his basic training in the army, instructors required recruits to learn that "an M-1 rifle is a 30-caliber, gas-operated, clip-fed, semiautomatic, repeating rifle with an effective range of 600 yards." The military perspective and nomenclature neutralize the moral dimension of the gun in the same way as the medical perspective and nomenclature neutralize the moral dimension of the cadaver. In combat and in preparation for combat, soldiers and sailors reduce the enemy to "slopes" and "gooks," making it easier to transform the enemy solider into a target or a devil. The names are similar to the medical students' "crocks" and "gomers"—blunt, blaming names for disturbing patients. Fatigue is an accepted feature of both military and medical training, blunting emotions for solider and for physician.

Our study suggests that the emotional socialization of professional training will influence the character of performance in the workplace and will have consequences for life outside the workplace. Medical students accept that they must change their perspective on the body in order to practice medicine, but they worry about the consequences. Often using the word "desensitization," they are concerned that medical training will dull their emotional responses too generally.

> Those feelings just get in the way. They don't fit, and I'm going to learn to get rid of them. Don't know how yet, and some of the possibilities are scary. What's left when

you succeed? But what choice is there? (second-year female)

It's kind of dehumanizing. We just block off the feelings, and I don't know what happens to them. This is pretty important to me. I'm working to keep a sense of myself through all this (third year male).

Quietly, because their concern is private and therefore uncertain, students ask questions we might all ask. Will we lose our sensitivity to those we serve? To others in our lives? To ourselves? Will we even know it is happening?

REFERENCES

Becker, H., B. Geer, E. Hughes, and A. Strauss. 1961. *Boys in White*. New Brunswick, NJ: Transaction.

Bosk, C. 1979. *Forgive and Remember*. Chicago: University of Chicago Press.

Bowers, C. 1984. *The Promise of Theory: Education and the Politics of Cultural Change*. New York: Longmans.

Daniels, M. 1960. "Affect and Its Control in the Medical Intern." *American Journal of Sociology* 55:259–67.

Emerson, J. 1970. "Behavior in Private Places: Sustaining Definitions of Reality in Gynecological Examinations." Pp. 74–97 in *Recent Sociology Number 2*, edited by H. P. Dreitzel. London: Macmillan.

Foucault, M. 1973. *The Birth of the Clinic: An Archaeology of Medical Perception*. New York: Pantheon.

Fox, R. 1980b. "The Evolution of Medical Uncertainty." *Millbank Memorial Fund Quarterly: Health and Society* 58(1):1–49.

Friedson, E. 1970. *The Profession of Medicine*. New York: Dodd, Mead.

Goffman, E. 1974. *Frame Analysis*. New York: Harper.

Haas, J., and W. Shaffir. 1977. "The Professionalization of Medical Students: Developing Competence and a Cloak of Competence." *Symbolic Interaction* 1:71–88.

———. 1982. "Taking on the Role of Doctor: A Dramaturgical Analysis of Professionalization." *Symbolic Interaction* 5:187–203.

Haug, M., and M. Sussman. 1969. "Professional Autonomy and the Revolt of the Client." *Social Problems* 17:153–60.

Hochschild, A. 1979. "Emotion Work, Feeling Rules, and Social Structure." *American Journal of Sociology* 85(3):551–75.

———. 1983. *The Managed Heart*. Berkeley: University of California Press.

Kadushin, C. 1962. "Social Distance between Client and Professional." *American Journal of Sociology* 67:517–31.

Kleinman, S. 1984. *Equals before God: Seminarians as Humanistic Professionals*. Chicago: University of Chicago Press.

Lief, H., and R. Fox. 1963. "Training for Detached Concern in Medical Students." Pp. 12–35 in *The Psychological Basis of Medical Practice*, edited by H. Lief. New York: Harper and Row.

Mills, T., and S. Kleinman. 1988. "Emotions, Reflexivity, and Action: An Interactionist Analysis." *Social Forces* 66(4):1009–27.

Mudd, J., and R. Siegel. 1969. "Sexuality—The Experiences and Anxieties of Medical Students." *New England Journal of Medicine* 281:1397–403.

Papper, S. 1978. "The Undesirable Patient." Pp. 166–68 in *Dominant Issues in Medical Sociology*, edited by H. Schwartz and C. Kart. Reading, MA: Addison-Wesley.

Parsons, T. 1951. *The Social System*. New York: Free Press.

Pope, K., P. Keith-Spiegel, and B. Tabachnik. 1986. "Sexual Attraction to Clients: The Human Therapist and the (Sometimes) Inhuman Training System." *American Psychologist* 41(2): 147–58.

Sampson, E. E. 1988. "The Debate on Individualism: Indigenous Psychologies of the Individual and Their Role in Personal and Societal Functioning." *American Psychologist* 43(1):15–22.

Sudnow, D. 1967. *Passing On*. Englewood Cliffs, NJ: Prentice-Hall.

Thoits, P. 1985. "Self-Labeling Processes in Mental Illness: The Role of Emotional Deviance." *American Journal of Sociology* 91:221–49.

Tuan, Y.-F. 1982. *Segmented Worlds and Self: Group Life and Individual Consciousness*. Minneapolis: University of Minnesota Press.

Turner, B. *The Body and society*. 1984. New York: Basil Blackwell.

PORTRAIT

The Great American Football Ritual: Reproducing Race, Class, and Gender Inequality

Douglas E. Foley

. . . The setting of this field study was "North Town," a small (8,000 population) South Texas farming/ranching community with limited industry, considerable local poverty, and a population that was 80% Mexican-American. . . . "North Town High" had an enrollment of 600 students and its sports teams played at the Triple-A level in a five-level state ranking system.

During the football season described here, I attended a number of practices, rode on the players' bus, and hung out with the coaches at the fieldhouse and with players during extensive classroom and lunchtime observations. I also participated in basketball and tennis practices and interviewed students extensively about student status groups, friendship, dating, and race relations. The participant-observation and interviewing in the sports scene involved hundreds of hours of fieldwork over a 12-month period. . . .

The Ritual Complex

The Weekly Pep Rally

Shortly after arriving in North Town I attended my first pep rally. Students, whether they liked football or not, looked forward to Friday afternoons. Regular 7th-period classes were let out early to hold a mass pep rally to support the team. Most students attended these events but a few used it to slip away from school early. During the day of this pep rally I overheard a number of students planning their trip to the game. Those in the school marching band (80) and in the pep club (50) were the most enthusiastic. . . .

[The] Friday afternoon . . . pep rally was age-graded. The older, most prominent students took the center seats, thus signaling their status and loyalty. Younger, first- and second-year students sat next to the leaders of the school activities if they were protégés of those leaders.

In sharp contrast, knots and clusters of the more socially marginal students, the "druggers," and the "punks and greasers," usually claimed the seats nearest the exits, thus signaling their indifference to all the rah-rah speeches they had to endure. The "nobodies" or "nerds," those dutiful, conforming students who were followers, tended to sit in the back of the center regions. Irrespective of the general territory, students usually sat with friends from their age group. Teachers strategically placed themselves at the margins and down in front to assist in crowd control.

The pep rally itself was dominated by the coaches and players, who were introduced to the audience to reflect upon the coming contest. In this particular pep rally the team captains led the team onto the stage. All the Anglo players entered first, followed by all the Mexicano players. Coach Trujillo started out with the classic pep talk that introduced the team captains, who in turn stepped forward and spoke in an awkward and self-effacing manner, thus enacting the ideal of a sportsman—a man of deeds, not words. They all stuttered through several "uhs" and "ers," then quickly said, "I hope y'all come support us.

A very edited version of the original article from *Sociology of Sport Journal, 7,* pp. 111–135.

Thanks." Generally students expected their jocks to be inarticulate and, as the cliché goes, strong but silent types. . . .

The Marching Band and Band Fags

The quality of the marching band was as carefully scrutinized as the football team by some community members. The band director, Dante Aguila, was keenly aware of maintaining an excellent winning band. Like sport teams, marching bands competed in local, district, and statewide contests and won rankings. The ultimate goal was winning a top rating at the state level. In addition, each band sent its best players of various instruments to district contests to compete for individual rankings. Individual band members could also achieve top rankings at the state level.

A certain segment of the student body began training for the high school marching band during their grade-school years. Band members had a much more positive view of their participation in band than the players did. The band was filled with students who tended to have better grades and came from the more affluent families. The more marginal, deviant students perceived band members as "goodie goodies," "richies," and "brains." This characterization was not entirely true because the band boosters club did make an effort to raise money to help low-income students join the band. Not all band students were top students, but many were in the advanced or academic tracks. Band members were generally the students with school spirit who were proud to promote loyalty to the school and community. The marching band was also a major symbolic expression of the community's unity and its future generation of good citizens and leaders.

The view that band members were the cream of the crop was not widely shared by the football players. Many female band members were socially prominent and "cool," but some were also studious homebodies. On the other hand, "real men" supposedly did not sign up for the North Town band. According to the football players, the physically weaker, more effeminate males tended to be in the band. Males in the band were called "band fags." The only exceptions were "cool guys" who did drugs, or had their own rock and roll band, or came from musical families and planned to become professional musicians. The males considered to be fags were sometimes derided and picked on as "sissies." Occasional gender jokes were made about their not having the "balls" to date the cute female band members.

The main masculinity test for band fags was to punch their biceps as hard as possible. If the victim returned this aggression with a defiant smile or smirk, he was a real man; if he winced and whined, he was a wimp or a fag. The other variations on punching the biceps were pinching the forearm and rapping the knuckles. North Town boys generally punched and pinched each other, but this kind of male play toward those considered fags was a daily ritual degradation. These were moments when physically dominant males picked on allegedly more effeminate males and reaffirmed their place in the male pecking order. Ironically, however, the players themselves rarely picked on those they called band fags. Males who emulated jocks and hoped to hang out with them were usually the hit men. The jocks signaled their real power and prestige by showing restraint toward obviously weaker males.

Cheerleaders and Pep Squads

As in most pep rallies, on the Friday I am describing, the cheerleaders were in front of the crowd on the gym floor doing dance and jumping routines in unison and shouting patriotic cheers to whip up enthusiasm for the team. The cheerleaders were acknowledged as some of the prettiest young women in the school and they aroused the envy of nobodies and nerds. Male students incessantly gossiped and fantasized about these young women and their reputations. . . .

. . . Students invariably had their favorites to adore and/or ridicule. Yet they told contradictory stories about the cheerleaders. When privately reflecting on their physical attributes and social status, males saw going with a cheerleader as guaranteeing their coolness and masculinity. Particularly the less attractive males plotted the seduction of these young women and reveled in the idea of having them as girlfriends. When expressing their views of these young women to other males, however, they often accused the cheerleaders of being stuck-up or sluts.

This sharp contradiction in males' discourse about cheerleaders makes perfect sense, however, when seen as males talking about females as objects to possess and dominate and through which to gain status. Conversations among males about cheerleaders were rhetorical performances that bonded males together and established their rank in this patriarchal order. In public conversations, males often expressed bravado about conquest of these "easy lays." In private conversations with intimate friends, they expressed their unabashed longing for, hence vulnerable emotional need for, these fantasized sexual objects. Hence, cheerleaders as highly prized females were dangerous, status-confirming creatures who were easier to relate to in rhetorical performances than in real life. Only those males with very high social status could actually risk relating to and being rejected by a cheerleader. The rest of the stories the young men told were simply male talk and fantasy.

Many young women were not athletic or attractive enough to be cheerleaders, nevertheless they wanted to be cheerleaders. Such young women often joined the pep squad as an alternative, and a strong esprit de corps developed among the pep squad members. They were a group of 50 young women in costume who came to the games and helped the cheerleaders arouse crowd enthusiasm. The pep squad also helped publicize and decorate the school and town with catchy team-spirit slogans such as "Smash the Seahawks" and "Spear the Javelinos." In addition, they helped organize after-the-game school dances. Their uniforms expressed loyalty to the team, and pep squad members were given a number of small status privileges in the school. They were sometimes released early for pep rallies and away games. . . .

Homecoming: A Rite of Community Solidarity and Status

Ideally, North Town graduates would return to the homecoming bonfire and dance to reaffirm their support and commitment to the school and team. They would come back to be honored and to honor the new generation presently upholding the name and tradition of the community. In reality, however, few ex-graduates actually attended the pregame bonfire rally or postgame school dance. Typically, the game itself drew a larger crowd and the local paper played up the homecoming game more. College-bound youth were noticeably present at the informal beer party after the game. Some townspeople were also at the pregame bonfire rally, something that rarely happened during an ordinary school pep rally. . . .

Three groups of boys with pickup trucks eventually created a huge pile of scrap wood and burnable objects that had been donated. The cheerleaders, band, and pep squad members then conducted the bonfire ceremonies. Several hundred persons, approximately an equal number of Anglo and Mexicano students, showed up at the rally along with a fair sprinkling of older people and others who were not in high school. Nearly all of the leaders were Anglos and they were complaining that not enough students supported the school or them. The cheerleaders led cheers and sang the school fight song after brief inspirational speeches from the coaches and players. . . .

The huge blazing fire in the school parking lot made this pep rally special. The fire added to the festive mood, which seemed partly adolescent high jinks and partly serious communion with the town's traditions. The collective energy of the youth had broken a property law or two to stage this event. Adults laughed about the "borrowed" packing crates and were pleased that others "donated" things from their stores and houses to feed the fire. The adults expressed no elaborate rationale for having a homecoming bonfire, which they considered nice, hot, and a good way to fire up the team.[1] Gathering around the bonfire reunited all North Towners, past and present, for the special homecoming reunion and gridiron battle. . . .

After the homecoming game, a school dance was held featuring a homecoming court complete with king and queen. The queen and her court and the king and his attendants, typically the most popular and attractive students, were elected by the student body. Ideally they represented the most attractive, popular, and successful youth. They were considered the best of a future generation of North Towners. Following tradition, the queen was crowned during halftime at midfield as the band played and the crowd cheered. According to tradition, the lovely queen and her court, dressed in formal gowns, were ceremoniously transported to the crowning in convertibles. The king and his attendants, who were often football players and dirty and sweaty at that, then came running from their halftime break to escort the young women from the convertibles and to their crowning. The king and his court lingered rather uneasily until the ceremony was over and then quickly returned to their team to rest and prepare for the second half. . . .

The Powder-Puff Football Game: Another Rite of Gender Reproduction

A powder-puff football game was traditionally held in North Town on a Friday afternoon before the seniors' final game. A number of senior football players dressed up as girls and acted as cheerleaders for the game. A number of the senior girls dressed up as football players and formed a touch football team that played the junior girls. The male football players served as coaches and referees and comprised much of the audience as well. Perhaps a quarter of the student body, mainly the active, popular, successful students, drifted in and out to have a laugh over this event. More boys than girls, both Anglo and Mexicano, attended the game.

The striking thing about this ritual was the gender difference in expressive manner. Males took the opportunity to act in silly and outrageous ways. They pranced around in high heels, smeared their faces with lipstick, and flaunted their padded breasts and posteriors in a sexually provocative manner. Everything, including the cheers they led, was done in a very playful, exaggerated, and burlesque manner.

In sharp contrast, the females donned the football jerseys and helmets of the players, sometimes those of their boyfriends, and proceeded to huff and puff soberly up and down the field under the watchful eyes of the boys. They played their part in the game as seriously as possible, blocking and shoving with considerable gusto. This farce went on for several scores, until one team was the clear winner and until the females were physically exhausted and the males were satiated with acting in a ridiculous manner. . . .

. . . Anthropologists have come to call such curious practices "rituals of inversion" (Babcock, 1978), specially marked moments when people radically reverse everyday cultural roles and practices. During these events people break, or humorously play with, their own cultural rules. Such reversals are possible without suffering any sanctions or loss of face. These moments are clearly marked so that no one familiar with the culture will misread such reversals as anything more than a momentary break in daily life.

Males of North Town High used this moment of symbolic inversion to parody females in a burlesque and ridiculous manner. They took great liberties with the female role through this humorous form of expression. The power of these young males to appropriate and play with female symbols of sexuality was a statement about males' social and physical dominance. Conversely, the females took few liberties with their expression of the male role. They tried to play a serious game of football. The females tried earnestly to prove they were equal. Their lack of playfulness was a poignant testimony to their subordinate status in this small town. . . .

Prominent Citizens and Their Booster Club: Reproducing Class Privileges

North Town was the type of community in which male teachers who had athletic or coaching backgrounds were more respected than other teachers. For their part, the other teachers often told "dumb coach" jokes and expressed resentment toward the school board's view of coaches. North Town school board members, many of them farmers and ranchers—rugged men of action—generally preferred that their school leaders be ex-coaches. Consequently a disproportionate number of ex-coaches became school principals and superintendents. . . . School board members invariably emphasized an ex-coach's ability to deal with the public and to discipline the youth.

Once gridiron warriors, coaches in small towns are ultimately forced to become organization men, budget administrators, and public relations experts. . . . Ultimately they must appease local factions, school boards, administrators, booster clubs, angry parents, and rebellious teenagers. The successful North Town coaches invariably become excellent public relations men who live a "down home" rural lifestyle; they like to hunt and fish and join local coffee klatches or Saturday morning quarterback groups. They must be real men who like fraternizing with the entrepreneurs, politicians, and good ole' boys who actually run the town. This role as a local male leader creates a web of alliances and obligations that put most coaches in the debt of the prominent citizens and their booster club.

North Town's booster club, composed mainly of local merchants, farmers, and ranchers, had the all-important function of raising supplementary funds for improving the sports program and for holding a postseason awards banquet. The club was the most direct and formal link that coaches had with the principal North Town civic leaders. Some prominent merchants and ranchers were absent from these activities, however, because they disliked sports or because they left it to those with more time and enthusiasm. North Town had a long history of booster club and school board interference in coaching the team. One coach characterized North Town as follows: "One of the toughest towns around to keep a job. Folks here take their football seriously. They are used to winning, not everything, not the state, but conference and maybe bidistrict, and someday even regional. They put a lot of pressure on you to win here."

The booster club that coach Trujillo had to deal with was run by a small clique of Anglos . . . "good ole' boys and redneck types." They became outspoken early in the season against their "weak Mexican coach." They fanned the fires of criticism in the coffee-drinking sessions over which of the two freshman quarterbacks should start, the "strong-armed Mexican boy" or the "all-around, smart Anglo boy." The Anglo boy was the son of a prominent car dealer and . . . booster club activist. The Mexican boy was the son of a migrant worker and small grocery store manager. The freshman coach, Jim Ryan, chose the Anglo boy. . . . In a similar vein, conflict also surfaced over the selection of the varsity quarterback. Coach Trujillo chose the son of an Anglo businessman, an underclassman, over a senior, the son of a less prominent Anglo. The less educated Anglo faction lambasted the coach for this decision, claiming he showed his preference for the children of the more socially and politically prominent [families]. . . .

The pattern of community pressures observed in North Town was not particularly exceptional. A good deal of the public criticism and grumbling about choices of players had racial overtones. The debate over which Anglo varsity quarterback to play also reflected community class differences among Anglos. North Town students and adults often expressed their fears and suspicion that racial and class prejudices were operating. It would be an exaggeration, however, to portray the North Town football team as rife with racial conflict and disunity. Nor was it filled with class prejudice. On a day-to-day basis there was considerable harmony and unity. Mexicanos and Anglos played side by side with few incidents. A number of working-class Mexicano youths and a few low-income Anglos were also members of the football program. At least in a general way, a surface harmony and equality seemed to prevail. . . .

Local sports enthusiasts are fond of arguing that coaches select players objectively, without class or racial prejudices, because their personal interest, and that of the team, is served by winning. Unfortunately, this free-market view glosses over how sport actually functions in local communities. Small-town coaches are generally subjected to enormous pressures to play everyone's child, regardless of social class and race. Success in sport is an important symbolic representation of familial social position. Men can reaffirm their claim to leadership and prominence through the success of their offspring. A son's athletic exploits relive and display the past physical and present social dominance of the father. In displaying past and present familial prominence, the son lays claim to his future potential. Every North Town coach lived and died by his ability to win games *and* his social competence to handle the competing status claims of the parents and their children.

Socially prominent families, who want to maintain their social position, promote their interests through booster clubs. The fathers of future community leaders spend much time talking about and criticizing coaches in local coffee shops. These fathers are more likely to talk to the coaches privately. Coaches who have ambitions to be socially prominent are more likely to "network" with these sports-minded community leaders. A symbiotic relationship develops between coaches, especially native ones, and the traditional community leaders. Preferential treatment of the sons of prominent community leaders flows from this web of friendships, hunting privileges, Saturday morning joking, and other such exchanges.

Moreover, considerable pressure to favor the sons of prominent citizens comes from within the school as well. The school and its classrooms are also a primary social stage upon which students enact their social privilege. These youths establish themselves as leaders in academic, political, and social affairs, and teachers grant them a variety of privileges. This reinforces the influence of their parents in the PTA, the sports and band booster clubs, and the school board. Both generations, in their own way, advance the interests of the family on many fronts.

The Spectators: Male Socialization through Ex-Players

Another major aspect of the football ritual is how the spectators, the men in the community, socialize each new generation of players. In North Town, groups of middle-aged males with families and businesses were influential in socializing the new generation of males. These men congregated in various restaurants for their morning coffee and conversation about business, politics, the weather, and sports. Those leading citizens particularly interested in sports could be heard praising and criticizing "the boys" in almost a fatherly way. Some hired the players for part-time or summer jobs and were inclined to give them special privileges. Athletes were more likely to get well-paying jobs as road-gang workers, machine operators, and crew leaders. Most players denied that they got any favors, but they clearly had more prestige than other high school students who worked. Nonplayers complained that jocks got the good jobs. On the job site the men regaled players with stories of male conquests in sports, romance, and business.

Many players reported these conversations, and I observed several during Saturday morning quarterback sessions in a local restaurant and gas station. One Saturday morning after the all-important Harris game, two starters and their good buddies came into the Cactus Bowl Café. One local rancher-businessman shouted, "Hey, Chuck, Jimmie, get over here! I want to talk to you boys about that Harris game!" He then launched into a litany of mistakes each boy and the team had made. Others in the group chimed in and hurled jokes at the boys about "wearing skirts" and being "wimps." Meanwhile the players stood slope-shouldered and "uh-huhed" their tormentors. One thing they had learned was never to argue back too vociferously. The players ridiculed such confrontations with "old-timers" privately, but the proper response from a good kid was tongue-biting deference. . . .

Some ex-players led the romanticized life of tough, brawling, womanizing young bachelors. These young men seemed suspended in a state of adolescence while avoiding becoming responsible family men. They could openly do things that the players had to control or hide because of training rules. Many of these ex-players were also able to physically dominate the younger high school players. But ex-players no longer had a stage upon which to perform heroics for the town. Consequently they often reminded current players of their past exploits and the superiority of players and teams in their era. Current players had to "learn" from these tormentors and take their place in local sports history.

Players Talking about Their Sport: The Meaning of Football

The preceding portrayal of the community sports scene has already suggested several major reasons why young males play football. Many of them are willing to endure considerable physical pain and sacrifice to achieve social prominence in their community. Only a very small percentage are skilled enough to play college football, and only one North Towner has ever made a living playing professional football. The social rewards from playing football are therefore mainly local and cultural.

However, there are other more immediate psychological rewards for playing football. When asked why they play football and why they like it, young North Town males gave a variety of answers. A few openly admitted that football was a way for them to achieve some social status and prominence, to "become somebody in this town." Many said football was fun, or "makes a man out of you," or "helps you get a cute chick." Others parroted a chamber of commerce view that it built character and trained them to have discipline, thus helping them be successful in life. Finally, many evoked patriotic motives—to beat rival towns and to "show others that South Texas plays as good a football as East Texas."

These explicit statements do not reveal the deeper psychological lessons learned in sports combat, however. In casual conversations, players used phrases that were particularly revealing. What they talked most about was "hitting" or "sticking" or "popping" someone. These were all things that coaches exhorted the players to do in practice. After a hard game, the supreme compliment was having a particular "lick" or "hit" singled out. Folkloric immortality, endless stories about that one great hit in the big game, was what players secretly strove for. For most coaches and players, really "laying a lick on" or "knocking somebody's can off" or "taking a real lick" was that quintessential football moment. Somebody who could "take it" was someone who could bounce up off the ground as if he had hardly been hit. The supreme compliment, however, was to be called a hitter or head-hunter. A hitter made bone-crushing tackles that knocked out or hurt his opponent.

Players who consistently inflicted outstanding hits were called animals, studs, bulls, horses, or gorillas. A stud was a superior physical specimen who fearlessly dished out and took hits, who like the physical contact, who could dominate other players physically. Other players idolized a "real stud," because he seemed fearless and indomitable on the field. Off the field a stud was also cool, or at least imagined to be cool, with girls. Most players expected and wanted strong coaches and some studs to lead them into battle. They talked endlessly about who was a real stud and whether the coach "really kicks butt."

The point of being a hitter and stud is proving that you have enough courage to inflict and take physical pain. Pain is a badge of honor. Playing with pain proves you are a man. In conventional society, pain is a warning to protect your body, but the opposite ethic rules in football. In North town bandages and stitches and casts became medals worn proudly into battle. Players constantly told stories about overcoming injuries and "playing hurt." A truly brave man was one who could fight on; his pain and wounds were simply greater obstacles to overcome. Scars were permanent traces of past battles won, or at the very least fought well. They became stories told to girlfriends and relatives. . . .

Many players, particularly the skilled ones, described what might be called their aesthetic moments as the most rewarding thing about football. Players sitting around reviewing a game always talked about themselves or others as "making a good cut" and "running a good route," or "trapping" and "blindsiding" someone. All these specific acts involved executing a particular type of body control and skill with perfection and excellence. Running backs made quick turns or cuts that left would-be tacklers grasping for thin air. Ends "ran routes" or a clever change of direction that freed them to leap into the air and catch a pass. Guards lay in wait for big opposing linemen or aggressive linebackers to enter their territory recklessly, only to be trapped or blindsided by them. Each position had a variety of assignments or moments when players used their strength and intelligence to defeat their opponents. The way this was done was beautiful to a player who had spent years perfecting the body control and timing to execute the play. Players talked about "feeling" the game and the ball and the pressure from an opponent.

Team sports, and especially American football, generally socialize males to be warriors. The young men of North Town were being socialized to measure themselves by their animal instincts and aggressiveness. Physicality, searching for pain, enduring pain, inflicting pain, and knowing one's pain threshold emphasizes the biological, animal side of human beings. These are the instincts needed to work together and survive in military combat and, in capitalist ideology, in corporate, academic, and industrial combat. The language used—head-hunter, stick'em, and various aggressive animal symbols—conjures up visions of Wall Street stockbrokers and real estate sharks chewing up their competition.

Other Males: Brains, Farm Kids, and Nobodies

What of those males who do not play high school football? Does this pervasive community ritual require the participation of all young males? Do all non-athletes end up in the category of effeminate "band fags"? To the contrary, several types of male students did not lose gender status for being unathletic. There were a small number "brains" who were obviously not physically capable of being gridiron warriors. Some of them played other sports with less physical contact such as basketball, tennis, track, or baseball. In this way they still upheld the ideal of being involved in some form of sport. Others, who were slight of physique, wore thick glasses, lacked hand-eye coordination, or ran and threw poorly, sometimes ended up hanging around jocks or helping them with their schoolwork. Others were loners who were labeled nerds and weirdos.

In addition, there were many farm kids or poor kids who did not participate in sports. They were generally homebodies who did not participate in many extracurricular activities. Some of them had to work to help support their families. Others had no transportation to attend practices. In the student peer groups they were often part of the great silent majority called "the nobodies."

Resistance to the Football Ritual: The Working-Class Chicano Rebels

There were also a number of Mexicano males who formed anti-school oriented peer groups. They were into a "hip" drug oriented lifestyle. These males, often called "vatos" (cool dudes), made it a point to be anti-sports, an activity they considered straight. Although some were quite physically capable of playing, they rarely tried out for any type of team sports. They made excuses for not playing such as needing a job to support their car or van or pickup. They considered sports "kids' stuff," and their hip lifestyle as more adult, cool, and fun.

Even for the vatos, however, sports events were important moments when they could publicly display their lifestyle and establish their reputation. A number of vatos always came to the games and even followed the team to other towns. They went to games to be tough guys and "enforcers" and to establish "reps" as fighters. The vatos also went to games to "hit on chicks from other towns." During one road game, after smoking several joints, they swaggered in with cocky smiles plastered on their faces. The idea was to attract attention from young women and hopefully provide a fight while stealing another town's women. Unlike stealing watermelons or apples from a neighbor, stealing women was done openly and was a test of courage. A man faced this danger in front of his buddies and under the eyes of the enemy.

Ultimately, only one minor scuffle actually occurred at the Larson City game. Some days after the game the vatos told many tales about their foray into enemy territory. With great bravado they recounted every unanswered slight and insult they hurled at those "geeks." They also gloried in their mythical conquests of local young women. For the vatos, fighting, smoking pot, and chasing females were far better sport than huffing and puffing around for "some fucking coach." As the players battled on the field, the vatos battled on the sidelines. They were another kind of warrior that established North Town's community identity and territoriality through the sport of fighting over and chasing young women.

The Contradiction of Being "In Training"

In other ways, even the straight young men who played football also resisted certain aspects of the game. Young athletes were thrust into a real dilemma when their coaches sought to rationalize training techniques and forbade various pleasures of the flesh. Being in training meant no drugs, alcohol, or tobacco. It also meant eating well-balanced meals, getting at least 8 hours of sleep, and not wasting one's emotional and physical energy chasing women. These dictates were extremely difficult to follow in a culture where drugs are used regularly and where sexual conquest and/or romantic love are popular cultural ideals. Add a combination of male adolescence and the overwhelming use of sex and women's bodies to sell commodities, and you have an environment not particularly conducive to making sacrifices for the coach and the team. North Town athletes envied the young bachelors who drank, smoked pot, and chased women late into the night. If they wanted to be males, American culture dictated that they break the rigid, unnatural training rules set for them.

Contrary to the vatos' caricature of jocks as straight and conformist, many North Town football players actually broke their training rules. They often drank and smoked pot at private teen parties. Unlike rebellious vatos, who publicly flaunted their drinking and drugs, jocks avoided drinking in public. By acting like all-American boys, jocks won praise from adults for their conformity. Many of them publicly pretended to be sacrificing and denying themselves pleasure. They told the old-timers stories about their "rough practices" and "commitment to conditioning." Consequently, if jocks got caught breaking training, the men tended to overlook these infractions as slips or temptations. In short, cool jocks know how to manage their public image as conformists and hide their private nonconformity. . . .

Fathers who had experienced this training contradiction themselves made the boys-will-be-boys argument on behalf of their sons. They gave their sons and other players stern lectures about keeping in shape, *but* they were the first to chuckle at the heroic stories of playing with a hangover. They told these same stories about teammates or about themselves over a cup of coffee or a beer. As a result, unless their youth were outrageously indiscreet—for example passing out drunk on the main street or in class, getting a "trashy girl" pregnant—a "little drinking and screwing around" was overlooked. They simply wanted the school board to stop being hypocritical and acknowledge that drinking was all part of growing up to be a prominent male.

In the small sports world of North Town, a real jock actually enhances his public image of being in shape by occasionally being a "boozer" or "doper." Indeed, one of the most common genres of stories that jocks told was the "I played while drunk/stoned," or the "I got drunk/stoned the night before the game" tale. Olmo, a big bruising guard who is now a hard-living, hard-drinking bachelor, told me a classic version of this before the homecoming game:

> Last night we really went out and hung one on. Me and Jaime and Arturo drank a six-pack apiece in a couple of hours. We were cruising around Daly City checking out the action. It was real dead. We didn't see nobody we knew except Arturo's cousin. We stopped at his place and drank some more and listened to some music. We stayed there till his old lady [mom] told us to go home. We got home pretty late, but before the sun come up, 'cause we're in training, ha ha. . . .

Conclusions

. . . The football ritual remains a powerful metaphor of American capitalist culture. In North Town, football is still a popular cultural practice deeply implicated in the reproduction of the local ruling class of white males, hence class, patriarchal, and racial forms of dominance. The larger ethnographic study (Foley, 1990) details how the football ritual was also tied to student status groups, dating, friendship, and social mobility patterns. Local sports, especially football, are still central to the socialization of each new generation of youth and to the maintenance of the adolescent society's status system. In addition, this ritual is also central to the preservation of the community's adult status hierarchy. The local politics of the booster club, adult male peer groups, and Saturday morning coffee klatches ensnare coaches and turn a son's participation in the football ritual into an important symbolic reenactment of the father's social class and gender prominence. . . .

NOTE

1. The firing-up-the-team pun was actually a fairly good explanation of the bonfire. It was a kind of tribal fire around which the community war dance was held. The event was preparing these young warriors for battle, and the cheerleaders and band replaced painted dancers and tom tom drums. In addition, the fire was a kind of community hearth. At least some people were literally returning to the "home fires" of their village and tribe.

REFERENCES

Babcock, B. (Ed.) (1978). *The reversible world: Symbolic inversion in art and society*. Ithaca, NY: Cornell University Press.

Foley, D. (1990). *Learning capitalist culture: Deep in the heart of Texas*. Philadelphia: University of Pennsylvania Press.

PORTRAIT

Star Trek Fandom as a Religious Phenomenon

Michael Jindra

Star Trek (ST) fandom is a phenomenon unlike any other. Now over 25 years old, it originated when the original *Star Trek* television series was threatened with cancellation after its first year. Fans immediately sprang into action with a letter-writing campaign to keep it going (Trimble 1983). When it finally was canceled after its third year, the show went into syndication, and ironically, that is when the "fandom" phenomenon really started to take off.[1] The first convention was in New York in 1972. A centralized fan clearinghouse organization, the Welcommittee, was established in 1972 to introduce fans to ST fandom (Van Hise 1990; Bacon-Smith 1992). . . .

No other popular culture phenomenon has shown the depth and breadth of "creations" or "productions" (in the broad sense of "cultural productions") that Star Trek has, both officially and unofficially. The numbers are staggering: over $2 billion in merchandise sold over the last 25 years, over 4 million novels sold *every year* (often bestsellers), dictionaries of ST alien languages, institutes that study them, "fanzines" numbering in the thousands, hundreds of fan clubs, conventions, on-line computer discussion groups, and tourist sites, plus of course the endless reruns, broadcast in over 100 countries. Captain Kirk and Mr. Spock, the two main characters on the original series (TOS), are household names not only in the United States but in other English-speaking countries, as is the spaceship on which they travel, the *Enterprise*. . . .

. . . Drawing on recent discussions concerning the changing form and meaning of contemporary religion (Luckmann 1991; Swatos 1983), I will attempt to show the ST fandom is one location in which to find religion in our society.

Methods

. . . I set out . . . to look at fan "culture" itself, for it is in the practice of the fans that we better understand the nature of any social group. The ethnographic method (mainly interviews and participant/observation) provided by my training in cultural anthropology allowed me to undertake this kind of study. . . .

. . . When I mentioned to friends that I was undertaking this project, I was deluged with names of people who were "big" fans of the show. Almost everyone seemed to know someone who was a serious ST fan. I struck up conversations with strangers who turned out to be fans. Soon I had more names of fans than I could possibly interview.

. . . I went to the public library and to bookstores and found a whole section of Star Trek-related materials, most of which were (of course) checked out. . . .

I attended a local ST convention and enjoyed several hours of conversation with fans about ST and why they liked it. I went to meetings of local science fiction clubs. I was also introduced to a different kind of "community," that of the computer on-line networks, and quickly found there was no way I could follow all of the ST talk on these nets, for the volume of the ST newsgroups exceeded 1,000 messages every week. . . .

. . . I also posted a 28-question questionnaire on a net, from which I received 33 responses, almost all of them through electronic mail. . . .

From *Sociology of Religion, 55,* pp. 27–51, Spring 1994, published and copyright 1994 by the Association for the Sociology of Religion. Reprinted by permission.

Religion in Contemporary American Society

The "folk" definition of religion, that is, how most Americans think of religion, is that of a system of private, conscious and articulated beliefs set off from the other "spheres" of life such as work, politics or leisure. . . .

Without its institutional and confessional form, we often fail to recognize religion in our own society, or . . . it becomes "disguised" under various political or cultural forms (Luckmann 1991:169). . . .

. . . In many people's minds, the world has become "disenchanted" of gods, ancestral spirits and nature deities, "men have become like gods" and science "offers us total mastery over our environment and over our destiny" (Lessa and Vogt 1979:413, citing Edmund Leach). This modern-day religion is expressed in many areas of our culture, including popular culture, as in the case of ST, I will argue. . . .

The "secularization" of Western society does mean the removal of religion to its own separate sphere, but also, Luckmann argues, its replacement with an emergent form of religion, best described as the privatization of religion. . . .

Religious practice, in other words, is carried on not only in large institutions, but increasingly in smaller networks, with features and practices that vary from place to place, but with a commonality often fostered by commercialization. Kenneth Thompson argues that symbolic communities are a part of the "sacralization" that resists processes of secularization. These communities become sacred to the extent they are "socially transcendent," that is, marked off from "the mundane world of everyday routine" (Thompson 1990:179). This essay will seek to demonstrate that ST fandom is among the chief locations of this kind of religious practice and forms of a type of "symbolic community" that identifies itself in opposition to the "mundane" (in the words of fans themselves) world of non-ST fans.

First, however, I will look at ST as a fixed set of consciously maintained beliefs. This is in part the "folk" conception of religion in our own society, as a fixed set of consciously maintained beliefs. Some ST fans do adhere to ST "philosophies" (Paulson 1991), and others are simply attracted by the world it portrays, a reflection of dominant American cultural themes (Kottak 1990). For both, however, the content of ST provides them with an orientation to the world, and to its (our) future.

Something to "Believe" In: The World View of Star Trek

. . . ST history shows that war on Earth eventually stopped, and nations and planets joined together in a "United Federation of Planets" for which the *Enterprise* is an ambassador, explorer and defender. This "positive view of the future" is one of the most popular reasons fans like the show, as they often state themselves. . . . Faith is placed in the power of the human mind, in humankind, and in science. On ST, threats are normally from alien forces, as problems such as poverty and war and disease on Earth have been eliminated. . . .

ST mixes the scientific and technical ideals of America with its egalitarian ideology to produce a progressive world where people from all races work together in a vast endeavor to expand knowledge. The following was written by a fan about the first public viewing of ST, at a World Science Fiction convention in 1966: "We noticed people of various races, genders and planetary origins working together. Here was a future it did not hurt to imagine. Here was a constructive tomorrow for mankind, emphasizing exploration and expansion" (Asherman 1989:2). . . .

That ST has progress and a "positive view of the future" as central themes is reaffirmed in writing by ST fans themselves (Lichtenberg et al. 1975; Gerrold 1984) and very directly by its late founder Gene Roddenberry, "the man who created an American myth." In 1991, just months before he died, a 30-page interview with Roddenberry was published in *The Humanist*, the official magazine of the American Humanist Association, to which Roddenberry had belonged since 1986. In the interview he reveals that he had a very conscious humanist philosophy that saw humans taking control of their own destiny, their ability to control the future. Rodenberry's intention was to express his philosophy in ST, but he had to keep this intention secret lest the network pull the plug on him (Alexander 1991).

Others, like Roddenberry, have used ST to express their philosophy publicly. Jeffrey Mills has taught courses at various colleges on the "cultural relevance of Star Trek." He points to the Prime Directive (forbidding interference in another culture), the Vulcan philosophy of IDIC (Infinite Diversity in Infinite Combination), and the governing structure of the United Federation of Planets as the kinds of ideas upon which we need to act if we are to survive into the twenty-first century. By watching ST, studying it and applying its lessons, we can make the world a better place, Mills has written. "[I]n this light Star Trek almost becomes a sort of scripture, doesn't it? What the Bible does in 66 books, Star Trek does in 79 episodes. . . . I can't think of a series that really spoke to the future of humankind with as much clarity and vision as Star Trek" (quoted in Paulson 1991:29) In this sense ST may be akin to an American "civil religion," about which I will speak more later. . . .

Star Trek Fandom

. . . The story of the origin and growth of ST fandom has itself attained a level of mythology, as a kind of origin myth of the movement. One of the first showings of ST, at a science fiction convention in 1966, is recounted in the following manner in the *Star Trek Compendium*. The author talks of the event almost in terms of a conversion experience:

> After the film was over we were unable to leave our seats. We just nodded at each other and smiled, and began to whisper. We came close to lifting the man (Roddenberry) upon our shoulders and carrying him of the room. . . . [H]e smiled, and we returned the smile before we converged on him (Asherman 1989:2).

From then on, according to the author, the convention was divided into two factions, the "enlightened" (who saw the preview) and the "unenlightened."

ST's exposure to a prime-time television audience, however, began to give it a wider audience than science fiction ever had. The letter-writing campaigns to save the series are now legendary, as is the leader of this movement, Bjo Trimble, who later published her memoirs (1983). In it she details the organization of the campaign and the massive numbers of letters that were sent to NBC, which saved the show from being canceled after its first year. The movement became even stronger after the series was finally canceled (largely due to a bad time slot) in 1969 after three seasons. Here is how ST fandom is described by one of its earliest fans:

> All in all, fans literally starved for new information, new material, more fuel for their fiery obsession—for their almost-religion of a more-than-promising future. Because of a lack of material to placate a mind hungry for ST, fans had to be creative. . . . [E]very fan of ST was family—a distant friend we had not met. Conventions were like stepping through an enchanted doorway into another world. The force of fandom was palpable and we longed for rebirth. We believed we could make it a reality so we wrote letters and scripts and reviews and novels. We wished. We dreamt. We burned with inspiration.

The author goes on to speak of "suffering," which made the revival all the sweeter. ST "brought hope." It also brought "intolerance and prejudice" against fans. Why? "Probably because Trek somehow threatens their perfect little microcosm of existence." The writer then speaks about the "cultural acceptance" of ST. "ST and its fans still have the powerful magic to make an impact on society; even to manipulate the future. That ability has been proven" (Van Hise 1990:11–12).

Fan Networks

Organizations

. . . The fan clubs have grown into a worldwide circuit of clubs, with nearly 200 in several countries, boasting approximately 100,000 members (Paikert 1991), which include both Starfleet chapters and chapters of the newer "Klingon Assault Group" (KAG). A hierarchy of Starfleet clubs is established by naming them after Star Trek vessels, with larger, more established clubs given status as starships (e.g., USS *Excelsior*) while smaller ones are called "shuttles."

Hierarchy is established within each club by the titles given to leaders (Admiral, Captain). Biographies are written of the leadership for the Starfleet newsletter (*Starfleet Communique*), which includes photos of them posing in uniform with their rank and title (e.g., Admiral John Dow, Communications Chief). Members move up the hierarchy by being active in group events, much like the Boy Scouts. Both Starfleet and KAG organizations stress community service projects; this aspect distinguishes them from a mere fan group and underlies the seriousness with which they take their beliefs about building a better world.

Included among the fan organizations is a central clearing house for information called "Welcommittee" that connects fans and introduces new fans to the world of Star Trek fandom. They provide free advice of where clubs are, how to start clubs, and how to host conventions. They also provide information on fanzines and just about any other question one might have about Star Trek fandom. The ST Welcommittee began in 1972 and now comprises at least fourteen geographic areas, each with its own "captain" and "crew," working in many states and six foreign countries (Van Hise 1990). . . .

Computer Networks and Electronic Billboards

Another fan "community" exists in the computer "on-line" networks that have Star Trek billboards or live discussion groups. On these nets, individuals "discuss" the show, posting comments, questions, or responding to other posts. Fans often take on pseudonyms from the characters in the show. There are over 3,000 postings/month on the biggest USENET newsgroup that is devoted solely to Star Trek talk, called rec.arts.startrek (r.a.s.).

A similar type network is BITNET, which also has a very active ST newsgroup (70–90 messages/day during the academic year). Other computer nets, such as Prodigy, Genie, Compuserve, and America-On-Line, all have ST newsgroups or have regularly scheduled live discussion groups. These users work primarily from their homes. . . .

Women

. . . Women, in contrast to the ST male "geek" stereotype, have been leaders in the ST fan movement from the very beginning, have written many of the ST novels, and were also instrumental in setting up the earliest fan clubs (Lichtenberg et al. 1975:ch. 1).

. . . These women writers "steal characters" from the show and flesh them out in ways that enable them to live outside the boundaries of a restrictive society. Rather than focusing on the more science and action-adventure aspects of the ST universe, female fans focus on the relationships of the characters. . . . These fans, "reconstruct their own reality" and "create a community" under the guise of play, protecting them from the masculine gaze that portrays play as trivial. Through the stories women are allowed to play roles and express feelings that masculine culture does not allow.

Community

Much of ST fandom seems to revolve around certain "communities" (e.g., electronic bulletin boards, women writers) that discuss ST, and remake it in various ways. The local groups such as Star Fleet are face-to-face communities tied into a national organization, much like denominations. The electronic and women's networks are a little more diffuse, yet in some ways deal more with the "philosophical" issues of ST. . . . Taken as a whole, ST fandom forms a type of "symbolic community" where people seek to form identities distinct from the outside world. . . . Communities such as these are often a response to the breakdown of traditional structural communities based more on face-to-face relations between relatives and neighbors. This loss of community allows (or forces) people to choose or construct their own identities (Lash and Friedman 1992:7). . . .

In ST fandom, these identities become quite personal when Starfleet members take on specific ranks and titles and use them in all correspondence of the groups, including signatures on their e-mail posts. The fans' distinctiveness is expressed in their disdain of the "mundanes" who do not consider the alternative worlds and futures that science fiction constructs. ST fandom provides an opportunity for fans to build common links at a time when people's mobility and lifestyle make this problematic. It is very easy to strike up conversations with strangers about ST, and it is frequently reported among fans that a group of strangers found common ground in their love of ST (Amesley 1989). . . .

Conventions

The different communities described above are rather isolated from each other, but there are opportunities for them to meet at other locations such as conventions and tourist sites, which also serve as locations where serious fans meet casual fans.

ST conventions were among the earliest fan activities. The first ST convention ever held, in New York in 1972, entered ST mythology after 3,000 people showed up when only 300–400 people were expected (Van Hise 1990:87–88). Since then, conventions have grown until there are now more than 90 annually. They feature trivia and costume contests, artwork, literature, bridge mock-ups, and appearances by actors. James Van Hise, the author of the *Trek Fan's Handbook*, described a convention in the following way:

> If you've never been to a convention, it's an experience that is difficult to explain. It's like being ushered into another world, where every facet of the day has something to do with STAR TREK. It might be seeing the incredible variety of merchandise in the dealers' room or seeing a star of the series in person and having the opportunity to ask questions. To describe it as a time warp would not be far from wrong. You're very much cut off from the real world in a convention. You can easily forget your own troubles as well as those of the world until the con ends and you have to come down to earth again. It's no wonder many people attend as many conventions as they can. It is an intense two or three day vacation and is quite a stimulating experience (1990:90).

Conventions are an opportunity to immerse oneself further in the ST "experience," much as one immerses oneself in ritual. Using the religious language of "immersion" is not just a rhetorical move on my part. Witness the following quote, taken from a questionnaire response:

> At a convention I went to a while back they had this thing about the "Temple of Trek." I stayed and watched—even partici-

> pated in the chanting. They had some woman who was there with her baby—fairly newborn. And they "baptized" the kid into this pseudo-church. Pretty bizarre—even though it was all just a joke. But I must admit—I was kind of wondering at the time if everyone there was really taking it all as a joke.

The ambiguity over the seriousness of Trek practice reveals, I believe, its underlying religious potential. . . .

Star Trek Tourism and "Pilgrimage"

In recent years the number of Star Trek places of "pilgrimage" and commemorative exhibitions has been increasing. The twenty-fifth anniversary served as the occasion for some of the exhibitions, such as one at the Smithsonian. The Oregon Museum of Science and Industry has opened a 6,000 square foot permanent Trek exhibit. Other places allow fans to experience the show. As part of their park in California, Universal Studios has a ST set in which they film selected tourists, in full uniform, acting out a ST plot.

I visited one fan who proudly showed me the video of her visit there. The video spliced footage of the tourists acting out parts with actual footage from one of the movies, giving the appearance that they were actually part of a ST movie. This fan described the experience "as a dream come true" which made the 2,000 mile trip "worthwhile." "We pilgrimage out there; it's our Mecca," she told me. Another fan showed me numerous pictures of her posing in uniform on a mockup of the Enterprise bridge built for a convention.

Various towns are now taking up the ST theme in order to attract tourists. Vulcan, Canada has turned itself into a ST "theme" town. A town in Iowa proclaimed itself Captain Kirk's hometown (the Kirk character does come from Iowa) and has an annual Captain Kirk festival. Though this may be pure commercialism on the part of the towns, their success is contingent on their appeal to fans as a place of tourism. . . .

. . . The experience of sitting on the bridge in uniform and being photographed or filmed brings one into direct participation in the universe, much as many rituals do, for the only way really to "connect" with something is to participate in it. Cultural productions can carry individuals beyond themselves and the restrictions of everyday experiences. . . . It is the fan's dream actually to be on the show, and the closest thing to it are bridge mock-ups and studio tours.[2] Out of this experience comes a closer identification with the universe they seek.

Linking the Star Trek Universe to the Present

This universe, however, is not a totally separate, fantastical universe unconnected to the present. In various ways, the Star Trek universe is "linked" with the contemporary world. The lead-in to every TNG episode ("Space: the final frontier. These are the voyages of the Starship Enterprise . . .") begins with a shot of the Earth from close in, and then a gradual "tour" through the other planets of the solar system until it finally focuses on the *Enterprise*. This sequence orients the viewer to envision the events as taking place in his own universe.

Other "linkage" is accomplished by some of the Trek manuals and novels. The recently published *Star Trek Chronology: A History of the Future* (Okuda and Okuda 1993) compiles a history of the world from the present to the time of the latest *Enterprise* in the twenty-fourth century.

This world is a direct projection into the future from the present, for the show continually refers to historical events from the twentieth century and before. Through time travel, many plots actually take place in pre-twenty-first century time. Episodes that have done this are frequently among the most popular.[3] . . .

ST has also affected the fans' lives. Actors often relate how they get letters from fans telling them how the show inspired them to become engineers or doctors, or to do well in school (also see Lichtenberg et al. 1975). ST has given people hope for the future, inspiring them to take control of their lives in the same way many self-help and quasi-religions do (Greil and Rudy 1990).

Fans also want to bring ST into the present time, to order things along the lines of the ST universe. ST fans have had an impact on the United States space program, supporting increased funding and specific programs involving manned and exploratory space missions. Science fiction becomes science fact (Asherman 1989:151) as "fans actively engineer events to make it true" (Van Hise 1990:14), such as naming the first space shuttle the USS *Enterprise*. . . .

The Reality of the Star Trek Universe

ST, like many other shows, actively encourages a "suspension of disbelief" and sets itself up as a reality in which fans can "exist." The reality of this universe is important to many people. . . .

This perception is what William Shatner, in a controversial *Saturday Night Live* skit set at a ST convention, poked fun at when he implored the fans to "Get a life!" after they asked him questions that assumed the reality of the ST universe. At ST conventions, where cast members of ST are often paid hefty fees to make personal appearances, these actors are sometimes questioned as if they are the characters they portray. Actors have had uncomfortable moments answering such questions as "What is Vulcan really like?" and "Why did you marry Spock's mother?" (Irwin and Love 1978:69).

Filling Out the Star Trek Universe

There has been a virtual industry built up around "filling out" the ST universe. Reference books such as the *Star Trek Technical Manual*, which lists the specifications of Starfleet ships, and *Worlds of the Federation*, which details planets and the races that live on them, have been among the most popular. Dozens of other books are in existence, with titles such as the *Starfleet Marriage Manual, Starfleet Cook Book*, and *Starfleet Officer Requirements* (Van Hise 1990:41–50). Languages and dictionaries have been compiled for the Klingon, Vulcan, and Romulan worlds, three of the best known aliens of ST. The entire history, geography, philosophy and even the actual location of the planet Vulcan has been described, sometimes with the full cooperation of people at academic institutions and even NASA.[4] A journal for the study of the Klingon language (HolQed) has also been introduced recently, and one can attend a Klingon language camp. Other literature includes more conventional encyclopedias, handbooks, and "crew books" that delve into the characters and actors in the series. Stories in *Trek* magazine have also filled out the biographies of the characters (Irwin and Love 1990).

The ST universe has been filled out with just about everything to make it a full, consistent reality, to enable one to live within this universe. This is a universe much larger and more complex and complete than any other fictional universe. . . .

The Consistency of the Star Trek Universe

The fan literature and manuals have brought about the completion of an alternate universe, in which the coherence of the universe must be maintained for fans to continue their "suspension of disbelief." Fans go to extraordinary lengths to do this, for instance, often focusing on the consistency and reality of the technical details of the ship: "The trek universe is possibly the most complex and self-consistent fictional reality ever created. We all know how the phaser, transporter, et al. work. We know that you can't beam through a shield or communicate through 'sub space interference.'"[5] . . .

. . . References to the Star Trek "canon" are frequent on . . . newsgroups and form the rules for . . . debate. A regularly posted "netiquette" (which gives guidelines for posting on r.a.s.) gives the definition of canon:

> "Canon" means that Gene Roddenberry (or his duly appointed representative) has declared something to be officially part of the "Star Trek" universe. This includes the TV episodes and the movies, primarily. "Non-canon" is everything else (the books, the animated series, comic books, the story you made up when you were playing "Star Trek" with your friends during recess back in kindergarten, etc.) . . .

. . . In effect, the "canon" forms the cosmology of the ST world, giving it the coherence that ties together the many fans of the show who devote many hours to discussing the show. Episodes are heavily critiqued after they are broadcast. Fans seem to "reject" some shows and accept others as up to the standards of the show. What is authentic or "pure" Trek is often debated. . . .

The fans of ST have constructed their own world—a consistent utopian world where science has given us control over the problems of life we experience and read about in the papers. In order to complete their created universe, both the creators of the show and the fans have to rely, ironically, on "science/magic." As shown above, the science on the show is one of the most common topics of fan discussion. The technology used is given a veneer of scientific reality, but most fans, even while trying to make it as close to reality as possible, recognize that most of the technology is made up and is thus closer to magic. . . .

ST is a body of knowledge that is continually being added to and revised. The on-line comments and novels are oriented to maintaining its reality, to maintaining the coherence of the show. . . .

What can be made of all this creativity, this invention and filling out of an entire other universe? I would argue that this is a creation of mythology in much the same way that any Levi-Straussian *bricoleur* would do it (Levi-Strauss 1966). Levi-Strauss used this term (French for "handy-man") to illustrate the process of creating mythology where *bricoleurs* use the available "tools" and "materials" of the culture to create a mythological structure over a period of time. In this situation, the *bricoleurs* act not on their own culture, but on the alternative one they have constructed (but which of course cannot be totally separated). The creation of new plots and stories and the ironing out of existing ones is essentially the mediating of contradictions in the story (universe). In this universe, the contradictions are an affront to the consistent universe that fans so desperately want to see created. . . .

The Stigma of Fandom

Religious movements often have a sense of being persecuted or looked down upon because of their zealousness. And indeed, there is a stigma associated with ST fandom. . . . Disclaimers on the part of fans that they are not "hardcore" fans are common. Many (if not most) fans want to distance themselves from a segment of fans that they believe to have gone "too far" in their fan activities. . . .

An astounding 80 percent of *fans* in one nonscientific poll taken at a convention said that some fans are "excessively active and devoted." It is believed that these people confuse fiction or entertainment with reality, and neglect "real" issues and sometimes their own material needs in the pursuit of fan activities and memorabilia. Stories are passed around among fans about people who confuse reality with unreality. One person claimed he knew what he called a "Dataite," a fan who would allow no criticism of the character "Data" on TNG. . . .

. . . Nonfans sense the "seriousness" of Star Trek when they witness fandom activities and react against it because they believe it should remain totally in the realm of entertainment.

That people take it seriously offends them. ST fans, on the other hand, want to be respected and understood, and want their devotion to be recognized as legitimate. I believe it is in this interplay between "seriousness and diversion," a common feature of religion (Lessa and Vogt 1979:414), that we see the roots of the tension over ST, its fandom and the general public.

Whether serious ST fandom is becoming culturally acceptable is not certain. Over 50 percent of Americans now say they are fans, but since ST has it roots in an entertainment medium there are likely going to be fans who resent those who take it more seriously, who "transport" themselves to the ST universe through viewing it, discussing it, attending conventions and belonging to fan groups. Were it not for the stigma, we would probably see even higher attendance at conventions and in fan clubs.

Conclusion

Is Star Trek fandom a religion, or at least a religious phenomenon? . . . ST fandom does not seem to fit the more restrictive, substantive definition of religion that posits belief in a deity or in the supernatural. It does, however, have some commonalties with broader definitions of religion that come under the rubric "quasi-religions," such as Alcoholics Anonymous and New Age groups. These organizations "ride the fence between the sacred and secular" (Greil and Rudy 1990:221), between religion and nonreligion. . . .

These new religions often have "no stable organization, canonized dogmas, recruitment system, or disciplining apparatus" (Luckmann 1991:178). They tend to be more therapeutically oriented, qualifying as "Identity Transformation Organizations" (ITOs), which "encourage adherents to undergo radical shifts in worldview and identity" (Greil and Rudy 1990:226–27).This element is less explicit in ST fandom, but it is there. George Takei (who played Sulu in TOS), one of the more popular convention speakers, usually gives an inspirational-type speech detailing the history of ST and fandom, how they both show the potential of humankind and help inspire people to get their lives together and make career decisions. . . .

ST fandom, however, differs in some significant ways from the quasi-religions described above. It is more organized than many of these other groups. ST fandom may not have a disciplining apparatus (outside of "flaming" someone on the computer nets), but it does have an organization, dogmas, a low-key recruitment system, and a "canon." . . . ST fandom cuts across class, gender, and ethnicity more than many other quasi-religions. Fans come both from working-class and academic and professional backgrounds (though what they like about the show often differs). Even though there is a stigma associated with serious fandom, ST does provide a certain commonality and unity of purpose for a wide variety of people.

Indeed, I would argue that ST fandom has strong elements of a "civil religion." Robert Bellah, who popularized the notion of a civil religion, calls it "an understanding of the American experience in the light of ultimate and universal reality" (1974:40) that seeks to become a world civil religion, which is exactly what we seem to have in the assimilationist, homogeneous Earth of twenty-fourth century Star Trek. A civil religion is a "generalizing" of religious belief necessary to have an integrated society, as a counter to "pluralizing" trends that divide society (Tschannen 1991:400). The generalized beliefs involved in ST fandom consist, as detailed above, in putting faith in science, humanity and a positive future. . . .

For many fans of popular culture, organized religion seemingly has less relevance, partially because they perceive it not as forward looking but as backward looking. Exceptions are, of course, to be found among millennial denominations that speak in specific terms about the future. But for the bulk of the population whose relations to organized religion is more nominal, mainline denominations are often seen either as status-quo and backward looking, or perhaps concerned too much with present-day politics to provide any real meaning for the future. Americans are traditionally forward looking, and it is events like the space race that animate them. ST fandom embodies this idealism and offers fans reasons to hope.

ST fandom does not have the thoroughgoing seriousness of established religions, but it is also not mere entertainment. This interplay of seriousness and entertainment, I argue, is a sign of its vitality. The communities, both symbolic and geographic, that are formed by ST fandom are evidence of the ongoing sacralization of elements of our modernist culture that express hope in the future. It is a phenomenon that relates to deep-seated American beliefs about the nature of humankind, the world and its future, and encourages the practices that parallel religious processes of codifying, forming a community and developing institutions to guide its practices.

NOTES

1. People identify themselves according to certain "fandoms," such as TV and film fandoms (Quantum Leap, Dr. Who, Star Trek, etc.), science fiction, comic books and other pop culture phenomena (Bacon-Smith 1992:309).
2. Many celebrity fans are attempting to become part of the ST universe by making appearances on the show. When planning for TNG ["The Next Generation"] was under way, Whoopie Goldberg called Paramount in order to play a part in the series, asking only a nominal fee.
3. A number of sources have listed the most popular episodes. One that is generally recognized to be among the best, if not the best, is *City on the Edge of Forever* from TOS, which takes Kirk, Spock and McCoy back to the 1930's. The best TNG episode is said by many to be *Yesterday's Enterprise,* which also involved time travel.
4. In a July 1991 letter to *Sky & Telescope* magazine, three scientists at the Harvard-Smithsonian Center for Astrophysics coauthored a letter with Gene Roddenberry that identified the star 40 Eradani as the sun around which the planet Vulcan revolves. This was based on recent astronomical observations that reveal the age of the star as being compatible with a planet that hosts life, whereas the previously named Vulcan sun (Epsilon Eridani) could not have.
5. In the magazine *Trek,* there is a column called "Star Trek Mysteries Explained" which attempts to explain the technical details of the series.

REFERENCES

Alexander, D. 1991. "Gene Roddenberry." *Humanist* (March/April):5–38.

Amesley, C. 1989. "How to watch Star Trek. *Cultural Studies* 3:323–39.

Asherman, A. 1989. *The Star Trek Compendium* (updated). New York: Pocket Books.

Bacon-Smith, C. 1992. *Enterprising Women.* Philadelphia: University of Pennsylvania Press.

Bellah, R. 1974 [1967]. "Civil religion in America," pp. 21–44 in R. Richey and D. Jones (eds.), *American Civil Religion.* New York: Harper & Row.

Gerrold, D. 1984 [1973]. *The World of Star Trek.* New York: Bluejay Books.

Greil, A. and D. Rudy. 1990. "On the margins of the sacred," pp. 219–32 in T. Robbins and D. Anthony (eds.), *In Gods We Trust.* New Brunswick, NJ: Transaction.

Irwin, W. and G. B. Love (eds.). 1978. *The Best of "Trek,"* vol. 1. New York: Signet.

Kottak, C. 1990. *Prime Time Society.* Belmont, CA: Wadsworth.

Lash, S. and J. Friedman (eds.). 1992. *Modernity and Identity.* Oxford: Blackwell.

Lessa, W. and E. Vogt. 1979. *Reader in Comparative Religion,* 4th ed. New York: Harper & Row.

Levi-Strauss, C. 1966. *The Savage Mind.* Chicago: University of Chicago Press.

Lichtenberg, J., S. Marshak, and J. Winston. 1975. *Star Trek Lives!* New York: Bantam.

Luckmann, T. 1991. "Religion old and new," pp. 167–82 in P. Bourdieu and J. Coleman (eds.),

Social Theory in a Changing Society. Boulder, CO: Westview.

Okuda, M. and D. Okuda. 1993. *Star Trek Chronology*. New York: Pocket Books.

Paikert, C. 1991. "Special Report on *Star Trek*." *Variety* (Dec. 2):49ff.

Paulson, S. 1991. "Free enterprise." *Isthmus*. Madison, WI (Sept. 27).

Swatos, W. H., Jr. 1983. "Enchantment and disenchantment in modernity." *Sociological Analysis* 44:321–38.

Thompson, K. 1990. "Secularization and sacralization," pp. 161–81 in J. Alexander and P. Sztompka (eds.), *Rethinking Progress*. Boston: Unwin Hyman.

Trimble, B. 1983. *On the Good Ship Enterprise*. Norfolk, VA: Donning.

Tschannen, O. 1991. "The secularization paradigm." *Journal for the Scientific Study of Religion* 30:395–415.

Van Hise, J. 1990. *The Trek Fan's Handbook*. Las Vegas: Pioneer Books.

PORTRAIT

The Power Elite at the Bohemian Grove: Has Anything Changed in the 1990s?

Kevin Wehr

The Bohemian Grove is a place of power and prestige. Located in the redwoods of Northern California, it is the retreat grounds of the exclusive Bohemian Club of San Francisco. It has been claimed by Domhoff (1974) that membership in the club represents a cross-section of the power elite, the leadership group of the ruling class in America. However, this work was done 20 years ago during Republican administrations. Anecdotal evidence suggests that the situation has not changed significantly (Weiss, 1989; Domhoff, 1981). However, there is a need for a systematic update.

This study presents new information on the Bohemian Grove as a playground for the powerful by looking at the presidential campaign contributions of club members from five key states in the 1992 federal elections and at the business and government affiliations of the guests at the 1993 summer retreat.

Campaign Finance Analysis

Using 1968 campaign finance data, Domhoff (1974:32) found that only 13 percent of Bohemian Club members gave to either presidential campaign. Further, he reported that 90 percent of the donations were to Republicans.

The present study utilized the Federal Election Commission listing of individual contributions for the states which represent the bulk of members in the Bohemian Club: California, New York, Connecticut, Illinois, and the District of Columbia. Only 8 percent of members gave, which is consistent with Domhoff's 1968 findings and other studies of the low rates of giving by club members, corporate directors, and wealthy families (Alexander, 1972; Domhoff, 1972; Allen and Broyles, 1989; Webber, 1990).

The Bohemians from the five key states who donated at the presidential level overwhelmingly supported the Bush campaign and gave more money on average than those who supported Clinton or Perot. One hundred forty-two members, 91 percent of the total, gave $235,150 to Bush, an average gift of $1,656. By contrast, eleven members gave $8,750 to Clinton, an average of $795. Only three members gave a total of $459 to Perot. Two members gave to multiple candidates; one gave $1,000 to Clinton and $500 to Bush, and the other gave $2,000 to Bush and $131 to Perot.

A closer look at the eleven Democratic donors suggests that they are consistent with earlier studies. Four were from the Jewish community, which has been suggested in other studies to provide a large minority of major Democratic donors (Fuchs, 1956; Domhoff, 1972; Isaacs, 1974; Lipset and Raab, 1984; Cohen, 1989). Three others were former Democratic appointees, one of whom, Henry H. Fowler, was the Secretary of the Treasury under Lyndon B. Johnson and a partner at Goldman Sachs on Wall Street. Another, Francis Wheat, was a member of the Securities and Exchange Commission under Lyndon B. Johnson. The third, Harold Brown, was the Secretary of Defense under Jimmy Carter. All but two of the donors to Clinton's campaign were from California.

The Guest List

The guest list shows the names of all the guests and their hosts, and thus makes it possible to search for patterns within elite groups. Domhoff (1974:40) claims that guest lists would be invaluable documents for studying cohesion within the nation's elite, should the lists be available over time.

Republican presidents or candidates have been regular guests since the turn of the century, if they were not already members (Van der Zee, 1974; Domhoff, 1974). However, even at the height of the New Deal in 1934, the guest list included Harold L. Ickes, Secretary of the Interior for Franklin D. Roosevelt (Ickes, 1953). Most members of Reagan's cabinet were guests during the 1980s (Domhoff, 1981; Weiss, 1989); many of those in Reagan's higher administration have been long-time members through their previous business connections.

Analyzing the 1970 guest list, Domhoff (1974:40–43) claimed that many guests fit into the following three classifications: father–son connections, business affiliations, and government–industry associates. There were still many examples of father–son connections in the 1993 guest list. For example, William M. Rees brought his son, William M. Rees, Jr. This can be understood as an introduction—a debutante ball for the male offspring of the power elite.

There were also many examples of business affiliations in 1993. Members of corporate boards, cronies from college, associates of private councils and think-tanks, and powerful men in connected industries use the Grove as a stomping ground. For example, Henry H. Fowler of Cave Man camp (the camp of the late Richard Nixon and Herbert Hoover), former Secretary of the Treasury and limited partner at Goldman Sachs investment company, invited Roy C. Smith IV, lawyer and also a limited partner at Goldman Sachs. The glue and the go-betweens of the power elite are lawyers and investment bankers (Mills, 1956). Often the member–guest connection has to do with a banker or lawyer inviting an important client to vacation at the Grove. Examples of these connections are numerous. To detail one instance, John H. F. Haskell, Jr., managing director and investment banker with Dillon, Read sponsored James K. Baker, CEO of Arvin Industries, a Fortune 500 company.

There were also Republicans from past administrations who were hosts or guests. Richard Cheney, Secretary of Defense under Bush, was the guest of George R. Roberts, a venture capitalist from Uplifters camp. Henry Kissinger, Secretary of State under Nixon, brought Charles R. Lee, a fellow Harvard graduate who now consults for U.S. Steel. From James Baker to George Shultz, former officials make up a core of active members at the Grove.

However, there were *no* members of the Clinton administration who were hosts or guests. The eleven donors to the Clinton campaign sponsored several guests, none of whom had any connections with the Clinton administration specifically, although Robert Trent Jones, Jr., brought Peter G. Kelly, who has been an active member in the Democratic National Committee for many years. Reinforcing these findings, my study of the major Clinton appointees shows no members of the Bohemian Club.

Conclusions

There are both similarities and differences between this study and past findings. Campaign contributions show that Club members who gave donations are still overwhelmingly pro-Republican. The 1993 guest list shows father–son connections and business affiliations. These findings lend support to the idea that the Bohemian Grove is an arena where processes of social interaction can help develop ruling-class cohesion.

However, Democrats are missing from the Grove, including Clinton appointees. Rather than showing that democratic donors and Clinton appointees are integral members of the power elite, this study suggests that Democrats may represent the "out-groups" within the power elite. It will be interesting to see if more Democratic appointees appear at the Grove in the future years of the Clinton administration.

REFERENCES

Alexander, Herbert. 1971. *Financing the Election 1968*. Lexington, MA: Heath Lexington Books.

Allen, Michael P. and Philip Broyles. 1989. "Class Hegemony and Political Finance." *American Sociological Review* 54:275–287.

Cohen, Stephen M. 1989. *The Dimensions of American Jewish Liberalism*. New York: The American Jewish Committee.

Domhoff, G. William. 1972. *Fat Cats and Democrats*. Englewood Cliffs, NJ: Prentice-Hall.

———. 1974. *The Bohemian Grove and Other Retreats*. New York: Harper and Row.

———. 1981. "Politics Among the Redwoods." *The Progressive* 45(1):32–36.

Fuchs, Lawrence H. 1956. *The Political Behavior of American Jews*. New York: Free Press.

Ickes, Harold L. 1953. *The Secret Diary of Harold L. Ickes, Vol. 1. The First Thousand Days, 1933–36*. New York: Simon and Schuster.

Isaacs, Stephen D. 1974. *Jews and American Politics*. Garden City, NJ: Doubleday.

Lipset, Seymour and Earl Raab. 1984. "The American Jews, the 1984 Elections, and Beyond." *Tocqueville Review* 6:401–419.

Van der Zee, John. 1974. *The Greatest Men's Party on Earth*. New York: Harcourt Brace Jovanovich.

Webber, Michael. 1990. "The Material Bases of the Democratic Party: Class and Campaign Finance in the 1930s." Ph.D. dissertation, University of California, Santa Cruz.

Weiss, Phillip. 1989. "Inside Bohemian Grove" *Spy Magazine* (November):58–76.

DEVELOPING YOUR OWN SNAPSHOTS *About Institutions*

1. *Writing topic:* Imagine that all institutions suddenly ceased to exist and that you personally had no choice but to take care of satisfying your own needs (and the needs of family members) on a daily basis. Write a short essay in which you describe a typical day in your life.

2. *Writing topic:* In a short essay, try to explain why students on campuses around the country are having so much trouble getting along with their schoolmates who are different. As indicated earlier, diversity on campus is on the rise. Do you sense that the level of competition—for popularity, status, grades, grants, scholarships, and jobs—has become more fierce? Could this be a factor in explaining the rise of intergroup hostility among college students? Before writing, you might want to jump ahead in this book and read the snapshot about "The Economic Escalator" in the section on Social Inequality. Certainly, the educational institution has changed in important ways. Students attending colleges and universities in the 1960s were far less likely to work part-time while attending classes on a full-time basis. They were also less concerned about finding a good job after they graduated—after all, Americans enjoyed an unparalleled level of prosperity during the 1960s, and optimism abounded—at least among those who were fortunate enough to graduate from college.
3. *Research topic:* What is a family and what is not? To study the range of family conceptions held by college students, construct a short questionnaire and give it to a small sample of students on your campus. One approach would be for you to ask your respondents to evaluate a list of possible family arrangements as legitimate family forms. On this list you might include (a) mother, father, and children, (b) mother and children, (c) father and children, (d) mother, boyfriend, and children, (e) father, girlfriend, and children, (f) gay couple and children, (g) mother, stepfather, and children, (h) woman living alone, (i) college roommates, (j) grandparents and grandchildren, and so on. How many of your fellow students' family conceptions fall within the broad definition of family proposed by anthropologist George Murdock?
4. *Writing topic:* In a short essay, discuss changes in the structure and functions of the family over the last 30 years. If you have completed the research topic in question 3, how do you think your respondents would have answered the same question about family 30 years ago?
5. *Research topic:* Garbage collecting has traditionally been viewed as dirty work, not only because it was physically unclean but also because it was a low-paying job. Collecting garbage is still physically dirty, but does it still offer low pay? To see how the

dirtiness of garbage collecting may have changed over the years, compare the average income of garbage collectors in your town or state now versus 10, 20, and 30 years ago. Also determine whether the collectors are unionized and how often they have threatened to strike. If possible, compare the racial or ethnic characteristics of garbage collectors over time. Why might you expect change in race or ethnic group? As a final possibility, examine in detail the circumstances of any strike that might have occurred among garbage collectors in your town. How long did it last? How many garbage pickups were missed during the strike? Did the strike disrupt business or school? How was the strike resolved?

6. *Writing topic:* In response to Kevin Wehr's "The Power Elite at the Bohemian Grove," write a short essay in which you explain how club memberships might sustain or strengthen the position of powerful people in society.
7. *Writing topic:* The photo essay for this section asks, "What's a family?" In a brief essay, describe when and where you have experienced a sense of family outside your own childhood home. In what ways do these experiences differ from those you might have had in your family of origin?

CHAPTER 5

Deviance

WHAT'S NORMAL AND NATURAL?

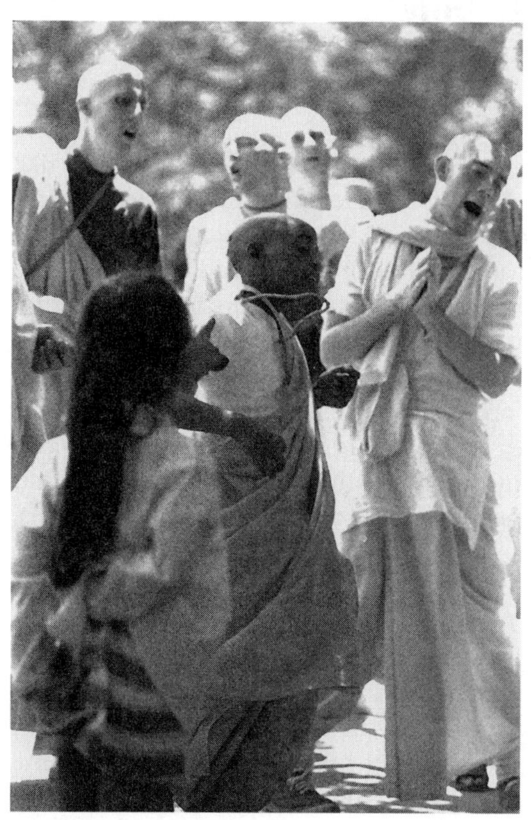

PEEP LAND
LIVE NUDE GIRLS
VIDEO 25¢ BOOTHS
SHOW FOLLIES
4 THEATERS
XXX
MOVIES
PEEPLAND
LIVE GIRLS
LIVE GIRLS

SNAPSHOT

Is the Death Penalty Only a Vehicle for Revenge?

An Ardent Abolitionist States His Case

Whenever I articulate my opposition to the death penalty, I feel like a voice in the wilderness. Almost 86 percent of all Americans favor the death penalty; and the remaining 14 percent would probably be willing to make an exception to eliminate the Ted Bundys of the world. In fact, the United States has the dubious distinction of being the only remaining Western nation not to have abolished the death penalty for homicide.

The reason underlying our overwhelming support of executions, according to a recent survey conducted for *ABC News* and *The Washington Post,* is usually revenge or retribution. Americans believe that the most serious crimes deserve the most severe punishment. Thus, as the Old Testament points out," . . . thou shalt give life for life, eye for eye, tooth for tooth. . . . "

And, I admit, it's not hard to understand why revenge seems sweet. People are fed up with violent crime, believing that it is out of control and of epidemic proportions. They want to do something about it. Many idolize Bernard Goetz, the so-called subway vigilante, because he refused to passively accept his victimization. The same appeal can be seen cinematically in Charles Bronson's *Death Wish* and in Sylvester Stallone's portrayals of Rambo and Rocky. Whether or not I agree with the extremity of the public reaction, I can understand why Bundy's execution by the state of Florida was seen by many as a cause for celebration. The world lost one of its most despicable killers.

The arguments for the death penalty, however, typically fall outside the realm of empirical inquiry. Instead they are often emotionally charged, arguing that convicted killers deserve to die or that getting even is valuable as a measure of psychological compensation for victims and society. As an abolitionist, however, I rest my entire case on the weight of economic and social issues that can be demonstrated by empirical inquiry. These three important issues involve cost, deterrence, and protection.

Many people ask why we should spend hard-earned taxpayer money to imprison a murderer when we could just as easily execute him at much lower cost. But the fixed costs of running a maximum-security prison are little affected by the presence of a few additional inmates serving life sentences for first-degree murder. The warden still has to be paid, and the heat still has to be kept on. Moreover, because of the lengthy appeals process required by the Supreme Court in capital cases, it actually costs less to imprison a killer than to execute him. In Florida, for example, the average cost of a case that results in execution is $3.2 million, whereas the estimated cost of imprisonment for 40 years is slightly more than $500,000. And those who argue, "If it costs so much to carry out the appeals process, then take him out back and string him up," should consider the number of errors that have been made under less stringent requirements: Since 1900, 139 people have been sentenced to death who were later proven innocent. Twenty-three of them were exonerated only after the executions had been carried out. In addition, the typical length of imprisonment between sentencing and execution is actually only three years, not the 11 years that Ted Bundy manipulated out of the court system.

Proponents of the death penalty also claim that it deters violent criminals. They believe we need to execute murderers to send a message to potential killers that if they can't control their murderous behavior, the same thing will happen to them.

Yet the death penalty has little if any effect on killings. In a study of 14 nations in which the death penalty was eliminated, criminologists Dane Archer and Rosemary Gantner report, for example, that abolition was followed more often than not by a reduction in national homicide rates. For example, homicide dropped 59 percent in Finland, 30 percent in Italy, 63 percent in Sweden, and 46 percent in Switzerland. In only five of these 14 countries did homicide increase at all. Even more ironically, research conducted by criminologist William Bowers suggests that the murder rate actually rises for a short period after the killer has been executed, apparently as a result of what he calls a "brutalization effect." That is, would-be murderers seem to identify more with the state executioner than they do with the inmate.

The third argument, of course, is that capital punishment protects society by guaranteeing that killers like Charles Manson will never be paroled. And certainly, capital punishment does make sure that particular murderers never kill again. But before I support the death penalty, I want to know whether an alternative exists for protecting society—for making sure that a killer isn't granted another opportunity—without taking human life. If the alternative response to a brutal, hideous murder is life imprisonment with parole eligibility, then I indeed favor the death penalty. If, however, the alternative is a life sentence without any possibility of parole, then capital punishment becomes unnecessary for the protection of society and I am therefore against it.

In fact, I cringe whenever I hear that Charles Manson is being considered for parole because I know what people will say: "The criminal justice system is soft on murderers. We should be executing those who commit heinous crimes." Actually, Charles Manson did receive the death penalty. But in 1972 the Supreme Court struck down capital punishment because it was being applied in an uneven, capricious manner. At that point any murderer on death row was instead given the next most severe sentence under state law; in California that sentence was a life sentence with parole eligibility. As a result, Charles Manson was eligible for parole after serving only seven years.

A series of rulings by the Supreme Court in 1976 paved the way for states to restore the death penalty, but only under strict guidelines. In some states (for example, California) those convicted of murder continue to become eligible for parole after serving only several years in prison; but if the court adds the "special circumstances provision," the only possible sentences are either death or life imprisonment without parole.

Most states now have special circumstances statutes for heinous crimes such as multiple murder or murder with rape. In some states (for example, Massachusetts) all first-degree murderers are ineligible for parole, so that no special statute is required. Under such conditions, the death penalty is unnecessary for protecting society from vicious killers because we can instead lock them up and throw away the key.

Actually, many proponents of the death penalty raise the issues of cost, deterrence, and protection of society only to rationalize what essentially is a thirst for revenge. This can be seen most clearly in the public response to heinous crimes.

In December 1987 Ronald Gene Simmons brutally murdered 16 people in Russellville, Arkansas, in the largest family massacre in American history. When the residents of Russellville learned that Simmons had suffocated the young children in his family and that he had had an incestuous relationship with his married daughter, cries for the death penalty were heard loud and clear throughout Arkansas. In 1989 Simmons was convicted of multiple murder and sentenced to die by means of lethal injection. Similarly, in October 1989 a young pregnant woman from Reading, Massachusetts, was shot to death by her husband, Charles Stuart. Public outrage quickly took the form of demands for Massachusetts legislators to enact a death penalty statute.

Florida certainly did get a measure of satisfaction by electrocuting serial killer Ted Bundy; the same can be said for the state of Illinois when it executed notorious serial killer John Wayne Gacy in 1994. For many Americans the opportunity to get even with a serial killer is reason enough to apply the death penalty. But for those few who instead believe that capital punishment can be justified only to the extent that it protects society's members or serves as an effective deterrent, then execution by the state is cruel and unnecessary punishment. In a civilized society, our best defense against "wild animals" is to lock them in cages so they can't get to the rest of us.

SNAPSHOT

Mass Murder

Summer's Fatal Time Bomb

I hate to be a prophet of doom, but it is entirely conceivable—no, probable—that our local newspapers will soon carry the gruesome details of yet another massacre in the United States. My prediction is feasible because there are at least 20 mass killings in the United States every year, and a disproportionate number of them occur during July and August.

This concentration of massacres during the summer is nothing new. Remember, it was August 1, 1966, when Charles Whitman climbed to the top of the tower at the University of Texas and fired on the crowd below. From that vantage point he extinguished the lives of 14 and injured another 30 before being gunned down by police. More recently, James Huberty went "hunting for humans" in a San Ysidro, California, McDonald's on July 18, 1984. With his rifle, a shotgun, and a pistol, Huberty entered the fast-food restaurant and opened fire on patrons eating lunch. Newspapers called it "the Big Mac Attack" and "Mass McMurder," but there was nothing funny about slaying 21 innocent victims. And three summers later, this time in August, a 23-year-old Vietnamese immigrant went on a shooting spree in Dorchester, Massachusetts, in a bloody act of retaliation against those he believed responsible for tarnishing his reputation. The young killer ended his own life, but not before he had murdered five and wounded two others.

So if recent history repeats itself, we're in for big trouble this summer. Another random slaughter of strangers could take place on a street corner or in a crowded supermarket parking lot. Some distraught husband may massacre his family, taking them with him to the hereafter. Another mass murderer may gun down customers and employees during an armed robbery.

Why do so many massacres occur during the summer? The image of a crazed killer who is driven beyond the edge of sanity by excessive heat and humidity comes immediately to mind. It is an ancient belief that the weather has important effects on what we do and how we feel. The Greek philosopher Hippocrates talked about health in relation to changes of the seasons and the rising and setting of the stars. The Talmud suggests that certain illnesses are caused by standing nude under the spell of a full moon. Certainly, you wouldn't have trouble convincing astrology buffs or even radio talk show hosts, who claim that every lunatic in town calls when the moon is full and the humidity rises.

Research suggests that hot, muggy weather puts people in a bad mood. During an oppressive hot spell, customers in restaurants are less generous with tips, and witnesses are less likely to help others in an emergency. When the humidity rises, so do the use of harsh discipline and punishment in schools, the suicide rate, and admissions to mental hospitals.

Clearly, then, weather influences human behavior. Under extreme conditions, it might even precipitate violence. But it takes more than a few hot, sticky days to create a mass murderer or even to push him over the edge.

In our book *Mass Murder: America's Growing Menace,* criminologist James A. Fox and I studied 42 mass murderers who had each killed four or more victims between 1974 and 1979. We searched newspaper accounts, conducted telephone and personal interviews, and studied biographies and in-depth interviews with mass killers. We were also able to compare massacres with single-victim homicides by studying FBI information available on the 96,263 homicides in the United States for the years 1976 through 1980, including 156 incidents of mass murder.

In almost every case of mass murder we discovered that the killer had experienced profound frustration in his personal life, often over a period of many years or even decades. In addition, there was usually a precipitating event in the killer's life, much more than just a change in the weather. At some point before the mass murder, the killer had typically experienced the actual or threatened loss of a job or a loved one, causing him to become despondent and hopeless. We also learned that most mass murderers had access to and training in the use of firearms. This fact alone may explain why 95 percent of all mass killers are men; they have unequal access to weapons of mass destruction, having traditionally monopolized the military, fields of law enforcement, and hunting as a hobby.

James Ruppert is an appropriate example. Like the majority of mass killers, Ruppert is a white, middle-aged male. In 1975 this resident of Hamilton, Ohio—at the time 40 years old—committed one of the worst mass murders in the history of the United States: He shot to death 11 members of his family—his mother, his brother and sister-in-law, and their eight children.

Ruppert had led a life of frustration, beginning with childhood. As a young boy he was asthmatic, shy, and clumsy. He walked hunched over from illness, so sickly that he was not permitted to take gym at school or play sports with the neighborhood kids. In high school he was teased and harassed by schoolmates, never dating or participating in extracurricular activities. As an adult he flunked out of college, had no sexual relations with women, and drifted from job to job. And as if this weren't enough, Ruppert's mother threatened to evict him from the house in which they had lived together for many years unless he repaid his debts to her and stopped his excessive drinking. It was against this background that Ruppert came down the stairs of his mother's home carrying two handguns and a rifle for a few rounds of target practice on the banks of the local river. But before he reached the front door, he instead slaughtered his family.

Another element of mass murder may be based more on common sense than behavioral science theory: During July and August many people spend more time together, stay up later, congregate on the streets, and are therefore available to be killed simultaneously. For similar reasons mass murder is also overrepresented during winter or at any time when family and friends come together for their annual holiday reunion, sometimes traveling great distances to be with their loved ones. Holidays heighten emotions, both positive and negative; they also provide an opportunity for killers to get even with everyone they believe has conspired against them.

In December 1987, for example, the largest family slaughter in U.S. history occurred in Dover, Arkansas, when Gene Simmons murdered 14 members of his family as they convened for their Christmas reunion. At any other time of the year there would have been fewer family members available to massacre. A few days later, seven members of the Dreesman family were found shot to death in their

Algona, Iowa, home. Four of them had traveled from Hawaii for the holiday and would probably still be alive if the murders had taken place in February or May. Also during December there have been mass killings in Long Beach, California; Dayton, Texas; Nashua, New Hampshire; and Wichita, Kansas. James Ruppert's 1975 massacre also occurred during an annual family reunion on Easter Sunday. If Ruppert had gotten angry on a Monday morning in June, probably only one person—his mother—would have died.

Because so many mass killings occur in July and August, during the hottest months of the year *and* during some of the coldest months of the year, it's not the weather per se but changes in the way people interact during these periods that really make a difference. Sunny California, Texas, and Florida have more than their share of mass murders, but so does New York. All of these states have large numbers of transient, rootless people who have no place to turn when the frustrations of everyday life become intolerable. And despite their hot and humid climate, states in the Deep South have fewer mass killings than you would expect based on population alone. Unlike other regions of the country, Georgia, Mississippi, and Tennessee continue to have strong local institutions—family, religion, and fraternal organizations—that provide support and guidance when times get tough, therefore helping to protect their residents against mass murder.

So consider yourselves warned. During July and August, people get together for pool parties, shopping sprees, and family barbecues. In many sections of the city they attempt to recover from the heat of the day by staying up late, sitting together on the front stoop of their sweltering apartment houses, and talking with their neighbors. Feelings of anger, resentment, and argument can build; the potential for victimizing large numbers of people also escalates, simply because more people are available for simultaneous killing. For these reasons we may soon again read the details of yet another gruesome killing . . . unless, of course, we are able to change the *social* climate.

SNAPSHOT Getting Away with Murder

For Some Accused, "Snitching" Means Beating the Rap

This was to be Kelly Keniston's big break in journalism. For four straight months she corresponded with Douglas Clark, the man known as the Sunset Strip Killer, while he was serving time on San

Quentin's death row. According to the State of California, in 1980 Clark and a female accomplice had murdered and mutilated at least seven people. Some of the victims were adults; others were juveniles. Some were prostitutes, and one was a male. All were slain in an unusually brutal manner including decapitation.

Keniston's plan was simple. She would meet the convicted killer, gain his confidence, pump him for information, and then write an article about him for a major magazine. But Keniston never penned the story that was to launch her journalistic career. Instead, in October 1984 she married Douglas Clark and became an advocate not only for her husband but also for "returning integrity to the American concept of justice."

To this day, Keniston argues that her husband is innocent, that he was victimized by a shoddy legal defense and by a secret plea bargain with the woman whom the prosecution claimed was his accomplice. That woman, Carol Bundy, was able to convince the court by her testimony that Douglas Clark was the main culprit in their killing spree and that, mesmerized by his charm, she merely went along for the ride to please her lover. Despite assurances to the jury that the district attorney would go for the death penalty, Carol Bundy received a parolable sentence; Douglas Clark is scheduled to die in the gas chamber.

Whether her husband is guilty or innocent, Kelly Keniston's mission directs attention to the use of a controversial procedure in the prosecution of certain killers, especially serial killers. In order to secure a conviction, one of the defendants is convinced by the prosecuting attorney to turn state's evidence in return for a lesser sentence. From the prosecution's standpoint it makes good sense to convict at least one defendant on the word of another rather than convicting no one at all. But this advantage is not always properly weighed against its potential for abuse. How much credibility should the court give to the testimony of an accomplice who is eager to escape execution or a lifetime behind bars? To what extent does this plea bargaining with accomplices actually promote lying and perjury? The importance of such questions is highlighted by the fact that some 30 percent of all serial murders are committed by teams of assailants—usually brothers, cousins, friends or coworkers. If they are caught and tried, one defendant often ends up informing on another.

The extreme absurdity as well as the logic of this kind of snitching can be seen in the case of the Zebra killers, members of a Black Muslim cult called the Death Angels who, during 1973 and early 1974, killed 14 and injured eight on the streets of San Francisco. In the absence of an eyewitness account, the Zebra killers may never have come to justice. But on the basis of the testimony of one of their own members, Anthony Harris, four defendants were found guilty and sentenced to life in prison. Under oath, Harris described the slayings in detail and identified the killers by name. In return he was granted immunity.

Prosecuting attorneys' use of informants under bizarre circumstances is well illustrated by the case of the Johnson brothers, who during the 1970s operated a million-dollar crime ring in the tri-state region of Pennsylvania, Maryland, and Delaware. To silence some of their disloyal accomplices who were scheduled to testify to the FBI, during the summer of 1978 the Johnson brothers shot to death six members of their gang.

In 1980 Bruce, Norman, and David Johnson were tried, found guilty of murder, and given life sentences. Their conviction depended a good deal on the cooperation of gang members who were willing to snitch. For example, in return for his testimony, the gang's hit man, Leslie Dale, received 10 to 40 years. Another gang member, Richard Donnell, got a sentence of one to three years concurrent with a term he was already serving.

In the Sunset Strip Killer case one defendant, Douglas Clark, was a man; the other, Carol Bundy, was a woman. The prosecution chose to plea-bargain with the female rather than the male defendant, using Carol Bundy's version of the crimes against Douglas Clark.

This is nothing new. In fact, there seems to be a general willingness for juries, prosecuting attorneys, and citizens to side with female defendants who stand accused of committing heinous crimes. In 1958, for example, Charlie Starkweather and Caril Fugate went on an eight-day killing spree across Nebraska and Wyoming that resulted in the slaughter of 10 innocent people. Jurors heard testimony that implicated both defendants. Yet only Charlie Starkweather went to the electric chair. His partner, Caril Fugate, was released from prison in 1976 and is now a homemaker living in Michigan.

By lightening the burden on our courts, plea bargaining may be essential to the justice system. In cases of serial murder, however, bargaining with one defendant against another can be justified only as a tactic of last resort. Most serial killers are sociopaths. They lack conscience and empathy. They have no feelings of remorse. But serial killers do excel at manipulating other people. They are exceptionally convincing liars who successfully lure victims into their trap and, if apprehended, skillfully defend themselves in court.

Is Douglas Clark an expert liar or an innocent man? He remains on death row, still waiting for his case to be reviewed and hoping to have his conviction overturned. And his wife Kelly continues to agitate. She has proclaimed her husband's innocence on television programs around the country, including "People Are Talking" in Baltimore, Pittsburgh, and San Francisco. She has established the Information Clearinghouse on Justice in San Rafael, California, which publishes a quarterly newsletter containing information and editorials concerning the death penalty, prosecutorial immunity, and related issues. Kelly also writes articles, but they don't get printed in major magazines. After all, who would believe a writer who is also the wife of the Sunset Strip Killer?

SNAPSHOT

Fat Chance in a Slim World

We Believe It's the Size of a Book's Cover That Counts

A black woman in Philadelphia wrote recently to complain about the way she was treated by other people. Among other things, she rarely dated, had few friends, and was forced to settle for a job for which she was overqualified. Moreover, passengers on buses and trains often stared at her with pity or scorn, while workers at the office rarely included her in their water cooler conversations.

The letter writer attributed these difficulties not to her gender or race but to the fact that she was vastly overweight by conventional standards. Her letter brought to mind the unfortunate victims of such illnesses as cancer, heart disease, and Alzheimer's who have the unavoidable symptoms of an illness over which they have little, if any, control. But they are typically treated with compassion and sympathy.

Curiously enough, fat people frequently receive contempt rather than compassion, unless their obesity can be attributed to some physical ailment (for example, a glandular condition). Otherwise, they are seen as having caused their own problem by some combination of excessive impulsivity and lack of moral fiber. Not unlike prostitutes, ex-cons, and skid row bums, they may be regarded as lacking the self-control and willpower necessary to lead a healthy, normal life. In addition, this discrimination has been directed more often at women than at men over the years.

The term *fat person* is therefore more than a description of somebody's weight, body type, or illness; more often than not it is also used to stigmatize or discredit an entire group of human beings by making their belt size an excuse for bigotry. The woman from Philadelphia may have been correct: Research suggests that people who are overweight by our standards are often viewed as undesirable dates and mates. They frequently have trouble getting married, going to college, obtaining credit from a bank, or being promoted. In short, they are excluded, exploited, and oppressed.

Stigmatizing fat people is, of course, only one expression of a much more general tendency in our culture: the tendency to judge others by their looks rather than their intelligence, talent, or character. Study after study suggests that what is beautiful is considered good. That is, attractive individuals are more likely to be preferred as dates, to be popular with their friends, to be cuddled and kissed as newborns, to achieve high grades in school, to be disciplined less severely by their parents, to be recommended for a job after a personal interview, and to have their written work judged favorably.

By conventional American wisdom, fat is as ugly and deviant as thin is beautiful and conformist. We are so infatuated with being slim and trim that it is indeed hard to imagine anything else. Yet the desirability of particular body types and body weight varies from culture to culture; fat has not always been universally despised. Beginning with the ancient world, fat people have often been respected, if not admired, throughout history. Even Cleopatra was fat by our standards; but by the standards of her own time and culture, she was a raving beauty. Renoir's French impressionist masterpieces portrayed a version of the female body that today would be considered massive, huge, and fat rather than beautiful. And in cultures where food was in short supply, obesity was often used to validate personal success. Under such circumstances rich people could afford to eat enough to be fat and therefore to survive. Skinniness was therefore a sign of neither good health nor beauty but rather of poverty and illness.

Until the roaring twenties the large and voluptuous version of feminine beauty continued to dominate our culture. But the flappers changed all this by bobbing their hair, binding their breasts, and, by some accounts, trying to resemble adolescent boys. While many women of the 1920s moved toward feminine power, others retreated from it by shrinking their bodies in fad diets. During this era, the suffragette movement succeeded and women got the vote, but many men felt threatened. Suddenly, they preferred women who were small, petite, and thin and who looked powerless.

Given the importance of physical attractiveness in defining the value and achievement of females, it should come as no surprise that American women have come under extreme pressure to be unrealistically slim and trim. This has made many women dissatisfied with their bodies and mistakenly convinced them that mastery was possible only by controlling their weight. Women constitute 90 percent of those afflicted with the eating disorder anorexia nervosa and are the majority of those who join organizations such as Weight Watchers and Diet Workshop. Women are also more likely than men to suffer from compulsive overeating and obesity.

Since the women's movement of the 1960s, we seem to have become even more preoccupied with being slim and trim. Playboy's centerfolds and contestants in the Miss America pageant have become increasingly thin. Leading women's magazines publish more and more articles about diets and dieting. Physicians offer drastic medical "cures" such as stomach stapling for obesity and liposuction surgery for "problem areas" like "saddlebag" thighs, "protuberant" abdomens, buttocks, "love handles," fatty knees, and redundant chins. And the best-seller list inevitably contains a disproportionate number of books promising miraculous methods of weight reduction. According to sociologist Naomi Wolf, our preoccupation with this "beauty myth" is designed to control the behavior of women who might otherwise be less concerned about their attractiveness.

In the face of all this, signs of an incipient cultural rebellion against crash dieting and irrational thinness have also emerged. Popular books like Millman's *Such a Pretty Face,* Orbach's *Fat Is a Feminist Issue,* and Chernin's *The Obsession: Reflections on the Tyranny of Slenderness* have taken their place in bookstores alongside the diet manuals. Rather than urge obedience to the conventional standards of beauty, these books expose the dangers to physical and mental health caused by rapid and repeated weight loss. Instead of focusing on individual change, they place the blame for our excessive concern with being skinny on sexism and the socialization of women to absurd cultural standards.

The merchants of fashion have also sensed a cultural change in the offing. Growing numbers of dress shops now specialize in designer fashions for size 14 and over and "flattering designs in better plus size fashions." Moreover, on the basis of much evidence from around the world, physicians have revised their weight standards so that what was formerly considered 10 or 15 pounds overweight is now regarded as optimal.

In addition, organizations such as the National Association to Aid Fat Americans (NAAFA) have helped fat people—even those who are considered obese—to gain a more favorable self-image. Rather than automatically advising its members to diet, NAAFA calls attention to the fact that fat people are often the victims of prejudice and discrimination. The organization focuses on improving the way that fat people are treated on the job, as customers, and in social situations. Taking its cue from black organizations, which reject words originating in the white community such as *Negro* and *colored,* NAAFA prefers to use the term *fat* rather than *overweight* or *obese*. In this way it refuses to conceal the issue in euphemisms, refuses to accept the stigma, and tries to emphasize that fat can be beautiful.

Unfortunately, however, our culture continues to give fat people a double message. We advise them to be themselves and to accept their body image regardless of social pressures to conform to some arbitrary standard of beauty. But we also urge them to go on a diet so that they will no longer be fat. While the rhetoric may confuse, it is also revealing. All things considered, our aversion to fat is deeply embedded in our culture and is likely to remain with us for some time to come.

SEEING DEVIANCE THROUGH SNAPSHOTS AND PORTRAITS

The last time I visited a state prison, it was to interview a notorious serial killer. As you might expect, our conversation began rather tentatively. I tried to figure out what he was thinking; he tried to figure out what I was up to. I sized him up; he sized me up. Our first 30 minutes together consisted of an exchange of polite trivialities. We talked about almost everything—everything, that is, except what I had come to discuss in the first place: the heinous crimes of which he had been convicted.

If you've ever visited a prison, you probably know how uncomfortable it can be to talk with inmates, at least initially. There is usually a great deal of anxiety, which gets in the way of honest communication.

Part of the problem involves what sociologist Erving Goffman referred to as "the management of spoiled identity." An imprisoned serial murderer has been stigmatized; he is discredited among those who live beyond the prison walls. He knows that I know; and I know that he knows that I know. There is no way for him to conceal the fact that he has been found guilty of murdering 12 young women, even if he continues to proclaim his innocence (which serial killers almost always do). The prison walls tell it all. So the best we can expect to do is to minimize the discomfort generated by his deviance . . . and that takes both time and effort.

Deviance refers to any behavior of an individual that is seen as violating the norms and values of a group or society generally. It is important that we examine the sources and consequences of deviant behavior; otherwise, we might mistakenly come to see society as a perfectly integrated, totally cohesive unit. We might even conclude that all individuals in society are conformists. A quick scan of the headlines in a daily newspaper—the rapes, murders, robberies, embezzlements, and car thefts—will show that this is clearly not the case. You don't have to visit a prison to see nonconformity; it can be observed in the everyday behavior of ordinary and not-so-ordinary people.

Many acts of deviance are rather harmless—for example, parking in a loading zone or breaking a curfew. Other acts of deviance are incredibly dangerous and violent—for example, armed robbery, rape, and murder.

According to sociologist Erich Goode, three important factors help to determine the degree of deviance. First, *the larger the number of people who disapprove of some behavior, the more deviant it is.* Twenty-five years ago, for example, so many Americans disapproved of divorce that large numbers of couples opted to stay married, even if they were miserable, rather than risk becoming stigmatized by a divorce. By contrast, divorce has become so commonplace in contemporary America that it has lost much of the stigma that it once had. In a similar process, cheating among college students used to be regarded as a major violation of cultural norms. A couple of decades ago, relatively few students even tried it once, let alone became habitual cheaters. As shown in Donald McCabe's "The Influence of Situational Ethics on Cheating among College Students," however, the act of cheating is more and more regarded as a minor violation of institutional norms, while growing numbers of college students are experimenting with it.

Second, *the greater the power of the individuals who disapprove of a certain behavior, the more deviant it is*. Looting from local stores may be seen as a form of political protest by impoverished members of a community. But it may be regarded as nothing less than a major offense against society by wealthy and powerful members of society who are eager to protect their own business investments. Similarly, behavior disapproved by a youngster's parents may be regarded as more deviant than behavior disapproved by his or her peers.

Third, *the more severe the penalty for committing a particular act, the more deviant it is.* As penalties such as restraining orders, arrests, and prison sentences have, during recent years, been applied more and more to cases of domestic violence, the perpetrators of such crimes have found themselves increasingly stigmatized. In a second example of the influence of the effect of penalizing nonconformist behavior, Craig Reinarman ("The Social Construction of Drug Scares") shows that politicians, journalists, and even scientists have periodically created drug scares, even if the facts surrounding the prevalence of illicit drug use did not warrant "getting tough on drugs." In the process of "waging a war against drugs," repressive drug laws have been passed and increasing numbers of drug offenders imprisoned. Drug users have become regarded as evil, sinful transgressors worthy of punishment rather than as suffering victims in need of treatment.

When someone commits a severely deviant act, he or she may be stigmatized. In other words, the violation of society's rules is regarded as so extreme that an entire human being, not just a particular behavior, gets discredited. Clearly serial killers fit this category. But as suggested in "Fat Chance in a Slim World," so do individuals who are overweight by conventional standards . . . and they haven't broken any laws at all! Fat is too often regarded as a symptom of not just illness but also lack of moral fiber or willpower. To some extent people who are very short, tall, or thin also bear the burden.

Mentally ill patients represent another group of stigmatized people. Some very depressed individuals would rather conceal their pain and suffering than risk being rejected by the important people in their lives. As suggested in D. L. Rosenhan's "On Being Sane in Insane Places," mental patients who are hospitalized also risk being labeled as psychotic ("crazy," "sick," "nuts," "schizo") by other people—in this case, the people in charge of running the institution. Initially the nonconformist behavior of an individual may go unnoticed. As with many other people, his or her bizarre behavior may be concealed from others or may be a short-term, temporary violation of the norms. From the point of view of *labeling theory,* however, the very act of being "discovered" as violating a norm is regarded as creating the conditions for *secondary deviance:* an individual who is labeled by others as "crazy" or "sick" is seen as continuing to act in a deviant manner because he or she has been stigmatized. Having been brought to public attention, he or she is segregated from normal people and forced to associate with others defined as deviant. In the process such individuals come to regard themselves as others see them—as deviant members of society.

Sociologist Erving Goffman has done a good deal to enlighten us about the labeling process in the way patients are treated in a mental hospital. In a major study of asylums conducted in 1958, Goffman found that the hospital staff assumes absolute power to define how patients should think and behave. The institution seeks to gain total control over the terms by which its patients define themselves. Inmates are resocialized, so that they can be easily managed and controlled.

According to Goffman, new patients learn quickly what is required of them to get along while institutionalized and later to be released. They are asked to discard their old self-concepts—those they had used on the outside—and to adopt a new set of self-definitions taught by the staff. First and foremost, inmates must abandon the normal concept that they are sane or healthy and instead see themselves as sick and therefore in need of help. Admitting that he or she is psychologically ill is regarded as a patient's first step along the road to recovery. Conversely, any claim that an inmate is well tends to be regarded as a symptom of severe mental disease.

As patients spend more and more time in the hospital, larger areas of their self-concept are turned upside down. Boredom is regarded as a sign of depression, anger as acting out, independence as rebelliousness and irrationality, and a desire for privacy as withdrawal. It takes no time at all for inmates to recognize that being resocialized by the institution to accept the role of a mentally ill person is the only way to be rewarded while confined and then later regarded as cured. This means not being a management problem for the staff: submitting to the hospital routines, which includes cooperation in taking medications and going to therapy sessions. Otherwise, a patient might remain in the institution indefinitely.

Ideally, of course, whether a patient is defined by the hospital staff as healthy or sick and viewed as ready for release should be based strictly on his or her symptoms. In reality, however, the social setting of a mental hospital also comes into play in defining the situation. This brings up an interesting question that sounds very much like the plot from an old movie: If a random selection of people from our society were secretly admitted to a mental hospital, would they be able to convince the staff that they were well, that they didn't belong, that they should be released? Or would they be defined by the rules of hospital life as rebellious, irrational, depressed, and therefore in need of continuing hospitalization? The classic study by D. L. Rosenhan looked at exactly this question.

French sociologist Emile Durkheim once observed that deviant behavior actually helps to unite the members of a society by focusing attention on the validity of its moral order. In the face of a deviant act—for example, a heinous crime—the members of a group feel challenged, even threatened. They no longer take for granted the important values they share. Instead they rally their forces to encourage and support the legitimacy of behaving "correctly." Durkheim also suggested that punishing the individual who commits a deviant act similarly reconfirms behavior that conforms to a group's cultural standards. Punishment sends a message to every member of society: "Listen up now. Break the rules and the same thing will happen to you!"

Numerous Americans, concerned about our soaring crime rate, would gladly base their support of capital punishment on Durkheim's view of deviance: Sending a killer to the electric chair also sends a message to potential killers everywhere. Thus capital punishment is often justified by the fact that it might deter violent crime. However, as indicated in "Is the Death Penalty Only a Vehicle for Revenge?" very little evidence suggests that capital punishment actually deters future murders (although it definitely keeps the condemned killer from killing again). Even if most Americans favor capital punishment, most criminologists seem to agree that the swift and certain imposition of a life sentence without parole is an effective alternative to the death penalty. First-degree murderers should never be eligible for parole, and their sentence should never be commuted by a future governor who believes in their rehabilitation. As criminologist James A. Fox and I have argued, we need a "life sentence without hope."

Let me pause, at this point, to once again raise the question of "value-free" sociology. In "Is the Death Penalty Only a Vehicle for Revenge?" I took a definite stand—based on evidence collected by criminologists, but nevertheless a definite stand on a controversial issue. You should be aware that some sociologists would cringe at the very thought. In their view, advocacy is antithetical to the goals of the "science of sociology." Not everyone would agree, however. Sociologist Howard Becker has in fact argued just the opposite: that sociologists must take sides in favor of important values and pressing concerns. For him advocacy is not only consistent with but also essential to the work of sociology. Feminist sociologists have similarly taken issue with the value-free position.

I am especially sure that the death penalty would have little impact on mass murderers. Those who kill several victims at a time would hardly be deterred by either a life sentence or an execution. Indeed, their killing spree is usually an act of suicide anyway; but before taking their own lives, they have decided to get even with all of the individuals they blame for having caused their problems—women, foreigners, postal workers, and so on.

Historically, the death penalty has been applied with discrimination. For crimes of equivalent severity, black defendants have been more likely than their white counterparts to be executed. In 1972 the Supreme Court declared the death penalty unconstitutional because it was being applied in an uneven, capricious manner. In 1976 it was reinstated, but only if applied under strict guidelines. Even today there is evidence that the death penalty is administered unevenly. Offenders who kill white victims "get the chair" more often than offenders who kill black victims.

In "Getting Away with Murder" I discussed another possible basis for discrimination in the application of the death penalty. We learned that prejudice against women may actually be used to justify discrimination against men. When a man and a woman team up to commit serial murder, it is the man who is usually executed. Apparently the court simply cannot believe that women are capable of committing cold-blooded murder; they are probably seen stereotypically as followers rather than as initiators—even when they commit heinous crimes.

"Mass Murder: Summer's Fatal Time Bomb" indicated that the rate of horrific crime varies with social climate. What happens when individuals interact seems to account for monthly variations in the level of mass murder. During the hot summer months, people get together more and their conversations heat up.

PORTRAIT

The Social Construction of Drug Scares

Craig Reinarman

Drug "wars," anti-drug crusades, and other periods of marked public concern about drugs are never merely reactions to the various troubles people can have with drugs. These drug scares are recurring cultural and political phenomena *in their own right* and must, therefore, be understood sociologically on their own terms. It is important to understand why people ingest drugs and why some of them develop problems that have something to do with having ingested them. But the premise of this chapter is that it is equally important to understand patterns of acute societal concern about drug use and drug problems. This seems especially so for U.S. society, which has had *recurring* anti-drug crusades and a *history* of repressive anti-drug laws.

Many well-intentioned drug policy reform efforts in the U.S. have come face to face with staid and stubborn sentiments against consciousness-altering substances. The repeated failures of such reform efforts cannot be explained solely in terms of ill-informed or manipulative leaders. Something deeper is involved, something woven into the very fabric of American culture, something which explains why claims that some drug is the cause of much of what is wrong with the world are *believed* so often by so many. The origins and nature of the *appeal* of anti-drug claims must be confronted if we are ever to understand how "drug problems" are constructed in the U.S. such that more enlightened and effective drug policies have been so difficult to achieve.

From *Constructions of Deviance,* edited by Patricia Adler and Peter Adler (pp. 92–104), 1994, Belmont, CA: Wadsworth.

In this [article] I take a step in this direction. First, I summarize briefly some of the major periods of anti-drug sentiment in the U.S. Second, I draw from them the basic ingredients of which drug scares and drug laws are made. Third, I offer a beginning interpretation of these scares and laws based on those broad features of American culture that make *self-control* continuously problematic.

Drug Scares and Drug Laws

What I have called drug scares (Reinarman and Levine, 1989a) have been a recurring feature of U.S. society for 200 years. They are relatively autonomous from whatever drug-related problems exist or are said to exist.[1] I call them "scares" because, like Red Scares, they are a form of moral panic ideologically constructed so as to construe one or another chemical bogeyman, à la "communists," as the core cause of a wide array of pre-existing public problems.

The first and most significant drug scare was over drink. Temperance movement leaders constructed this scare beginning in the late 18th and early 19th century. It reached its formal end with the passage of Prohibition in 1919.[2] As Gusfield showed in his classic book *Symbolic Crusade* (1963), there was far more to the battle against booze than long-standing drinking problems. Temperance crusaders tended to be native born, middle-class, non-urban Protestants who felt threatened by the working-class, Catholic immigrants who were filling up America's cities during industrialization.[3] The latter were what Gusfield termed "unrepentant deviants" in that they continued their long-standing drinking practices despite middle-class W.A.S.P. norms against them. The battle over booze was the terrain on which was fought a cornucopia of cultural conflicts, particularly over whose morality would be the dominant morality in America.

In the course of this century-long struggle, the often wild claims of Temperance leaders appealed to millions of middle-class people seeking explanations for the pressing social and economic problems of industrializing America. Many corporate supporters of Prohibition threw their financial and ideological weight behind the Anti-Saloon League and other Temperance and Prohibitionist groups because they felt that traditional working-class drinking practices interfered with the new rhythms of the factory, and thus with productivity and profits (Rumbarger, 1989). To the Temperance crusaders' fear of the barroom as a breeding ground of all sorts of tragic immorality, Prohibitionists added the idea of the saloon as an alien, subversive place where unionists organized and where leftists and anarchists found recruits (Levine, 1984).

This convergence of claims and interests rendered alcohol a scapegoat for most of the nation's poverty, crime, moral degeneracy, "broken" families, illegitimacy, unemployment, and personal and business failure—problems whose sources lay in broader economic and political forces. This scare climaxed in the first two decades of this century, a tumultuous period rife with class, racial, cultural, and political conflict brought on by the wrenching changes of industrialization, immigration, and urbanization (Levine, 1984; Levine and Reinarman, 1991).

America's first real drug law was San Francisco's anti-opium den ordinance of 1875. The context of the campaign for this law shared many features with the context of the Temperance movement. Opiates had long been widely and legally available without a prescription in hundreds of medicines (Brecher, 1972; Musto, 1973; Courtwright, 1982; cf. Baumohl, 1992), so neither opiate use nor addiction was really the issue. This campaign focused almost exclusively on what was called the "Mongolian vice" of opium *smoking* by Chinese immigrants (and white "fellow travelers") in dens (Baumohl, 1992). Chinese immigrants came to California as "coolie" labor to build the railroad and dig the gold mines. A small minority of them brought along the practice of smoking opium—a practice originally brought to China by British and American traders in the 19th century. When the railroad was completed and the gold dried up, a decade-long depression ensued. In a tight labor market, Chinese immigrants were a target. The white Workingman's Party fomented racial hatred of the low-wage "coolies" with whom they now had to compete for work. The first law against opium smoking was only one of many laws enacted to harass and control Chinese workers (Morgan, 1978).

By calling attention to this broader political-economic context I do not wish to slight the specifics of the local political-economic context. In addition to the Workingman's Party, downtown businessmen formed merchant associations and urban families formed improvement associations, both of which fought for more than two decades to reduce the impact of San Francisco's vice districts on the order and health of the central business district and on family neighborhoods (Baumohl, 1992).

In this sense, the anti-opium den ordinance was not the clear and direct result of a sudden drug scare alone. The law was passed against a specific form of drug use engaged in by a disreputable group that had come to be seen as threatening in lean economic times. But it passed easily because this new threat was understood against the broader historical backdrop of long-standing local concerns about various vices as threats to public health, public morals, and public order. Moreover, the focus of attention were dens where it was suspected that whites came into intimate contact with "filthy, idolatrous" Chinese (see Baumohl, 1992). Some local law enforcement leaders, for example, complained that Chinese men were using this vice to seduce white women into sexual slavery (Morgan, 1978). Whatever the hazards of opium smoking, its initial criminalization in San Francisco had to do with both a general context of recession, class conflict, and racism, and with specific local interests in the control of vice and the prevention of miscegenation.

A nationwide scare focusing on opiates and cocaine began in the early 20th century. These drugs had been widely used for years, but were first criminalized when the addict population began to shift from predominately white, middle-class, middle-aged women to young, working-class males, African-Americans in particular. This scare led to the Harrison Narcotics Act of 1914, the first federal anti-drug law (see Duster, 1970).

Many different moral entrepreneurs guided its passage over a six-year campaign: State Department diplomats seeking a drug treaty as a means of expanding trade with China, trade which they felt was crucial for pulling the economy out of recession; the medical and pharmaceutical professions whose interests were threatened by self-medication with unregulated propriety tonics, many of which contained cocaine or opiates; reformers seeking to control what they saw as the deviance of immigrants and Southern Blacks who were migrating off the farms; and a pliant press which routinely linked drug use with prostitutes, criminals, transient workers (e.g., the Wobblies), and African-Americans (Musto, 1973). In order to gain the support of Southern Congressmen for a new federal law that might infringe on "states' rights," State Department officials and other crusaders repeatedly spread unsubstantiated suspicions, repeated in the press, that, e.g., cocaine induced African-American men to rape white women Musto, 1973:6–10, 67). In short, there was more to this drug scare, too, than mere drug problems.

In the Great Depression, Harry Anslinger of the Federal Narcotics Bureau pushed Congress for a federal law against marijuana. He claimed it was a "killer weed" and he spread stories to the press suggesting that it induced violence—especially among Mexican-Americans. Although there was no evidence that marijuana was widely used, much less that it had any untoward effects, his crusade resulted in its criminalization in 1937—and not incidentally a turnaround in his Bureau's fiscal fortunes (Dickson, 1968). In this case, a new drug law was put in place by a militant moral-bureaucratic entrepreneur who played on racial fears and manipulated a press willing to repeat even his most absurd claims in a context of class conflict during the Depression (Becker, 1963). While there was not a marked scare at the time, Anslinger's claims were never contested in Congress because they played upon racial fears and widely held Victorian values against taking drugs solely for pleasure.

In the drug scare of the 1960s, political and moral leaders somehow reconceptualized this same "killer weed" as the "drop out drug" that was leading America's youth to rebellion and ruin (Himmelstein, 1983). Bio-medical scientists also published uncontrolled, retrospective studies of very small numbers of cases suggesting that, in addition to poisoning the minds and morals of youth, LSD produced broken chromosomes and thus genetic damage (Cohen et al., 1967). These studies were soon shown to be seriously misleading if not meaningless (Tijo et al, 1969), but not before the press, politicians, the medical profession, and the National Institute of Mental Health used them to promote a scare (Weil, 1972:44–46).

I suggest that the reason even supposedly hard-headed scientists were drawn into such propaganda was that dominant groups felt the country was at war—and not merely with Vietnam. In this scare, there was not so much a "dangerous class" or threatening racial group as multi-faceted political and cultural conflict, particularly between generations, which gave rise to the perception that middle-class youth who rejected conventional values were a dangerous threat.[4] This scare resulted in the Comprehensive Drug Abuse Control Act of 1970, which criminalized more forms of drug use and subjected users to harsher penalties.

Most recently we have seen the crack scare, which began in earnest *not* when the prevalence of cocaine use quadrupled in the late 1970s, nor even when thousands of users began to smoke it in the more potent and dangerous form of freebase. Indeed, when this scare was launched, crack was unknown outside of a few neighborhoods in a handful of major cities (Reinarman and Levine, 1989a) and the prevalence of illicit drug use had been dropping for several years (National Institute on Drug Use, 1990). Rather, this most recent scare began in 1986 when freebase cocaine was renamed crack (or "rock") and sold in precooked, inexpensive units on ghetto street corners (Reinarman and Levine, 1989b). Once politicians and the media linked this new form of cocaine use to the inner-city, minority poor, a new drug scare was under way and the solution became more prison cells rather than more treatment slots.

The same sorts of wild claims and Draconian policy proposals of Temperance and Prohibition leaders re-surfaced in the crack scare. Politicians have so outdone each other in getting "tough on drugs" that each year since crack came on the scene in 1986 they have passed more repressive laws providing billions more for law enforcement, longer sentences, and more drug offenses punishable by death. One result is that the U.S. now has more people in prison than any industrialized nation in the world—about half of them for drug offenses, the majority of whom are racial minorities.

In each of these periods more repressive drug laws were passed on the grounds that they would reduce drug use and drug problems. I have found no evidence that any scare actually accomplished those ends, but they did greatly expand the quantity and quality of social control, particularly over subordinate groups perceived as dangerous or threatening. Reading across these historical episodes one can abstract a recipe for drug scares and repressive drug laws that contains the following *seven ingredients*:

1. **A Kernel of Truth** Humans have ingested fermented beverages at least since human civilization moved from hunting and gathering to primitive agriculture thousands of years ago (Levine, forthcoming). The pharmacopia has expanded exponentially since then. So, in virtually all cultures and historical epochs, there has been sufficient ingestion of consciousness-altering chemicals to provide some basis for some people to claim that it is a problem.
2. **Media Magnification** In each of the episodes I have summarized and many others, the mass media has engaged in what I call the *routinization of caricature*—rhetorically re-crafting worst cases into typical cases and the episodic into the epidemic. The media dramatize drug problems, as they do other problems, in the course of their routine news-generating and sales-promoting procedures (see Brecher, 1972:321–34; Reinarman and Duskin, 1992; and Molotch and Leste, 1974).
3. **Politico-Moral Entrepreneurs** I have added the prefix "politico" to Becker's (1963) seminal concept of moral entrepreneur in order to emphasize the fact that the prominent and powerful moral entrepreneurs in drug scares are often political elites. Otherwise, I employ the term just as he intended: to denote the *enterprise*, the work, of those who create (or enforce) a rule against what they see as a social evil.[5]

   In the history of drug problems in the U.S., these entrepreneurs call attention to drug using behavior and define it as a threat about which "something must be done." They also serve as the media's primary source of sound bites on the dangers of this or that drug. In all the scares I have noted, these entrepreneurs had interests of their own (often financial) which had little to do with drugs. Political elites typically find drugs a functional demon in that (like "outside agitators") drugs allow them to deflect attention from other, more systemic sources of public problems for which they would otherwise have to take some responsibility. Unlike almost every other political issue, however, to be "tough on drugs" in American political culture allows a leader to take a firm stand without risking votes or campaign contributions.

4. **Professional Interest Groups** In each drug scare and during the passage of each drug law, various professional interests contended over what Gusfield (1981:10–15) calls the "ownership" of drug problems—"the ability to create and influence the public definition of a problem" (1981: 10), and thus to define what should be done about it. These groups have included industrialists, churches, the American Medical Association, the American Pharmaceutical Association, various law enforcement agencies, scientists, and most recently the treatment industry and groups of those former addicts converted to disease ideology.[6] These groups claim for themselves, by virtue of their specialized forms of knowledge, the legitimacy and authority to name what is wrong and to prescribe the solution, usually garnering resources as a result.

5. **Historical Context of Conflict** This trinity of the media, moral entrepreneurs, and professional interests typically interacts in such a way as to inflate the extant "kernel of truth" about drug use. But this interaction does not by itself give rise to drug scares or drug laws without underlying conflicts which make drugs into functional villains. Although Temperance crusaders persuaded millions to pledge abstinence, they campaigned for years without achieving alcohol control laws. However, in the tumultuous period leading up to Prohibition, there were revolutions in Russia and Mexico, World War I, massive immigration and impoverishment, and socialist, anarchist, and labor movements, to say nothing of increases in routine problems such as crime. I submit that all this conflict made for a level of cultural anxiety that provided fertile ideological soil for Prohibition. In each of the other scares, similar conflicts—economic, political, cultural, class, racial, or a combination—provided a context in which claims makers could viably construe certain classes of drug users as a threat.

6. **Linking a Form of Drug Use to a "Dangerous Class"** Drug scares are never about drugs per se, because drugs are inanimate objects without social consequence until they are ingested by humans. Rather, drug scares are about the use of a drug by particular groups of people who are, typically, *already* perceived by powerful groups as some kind of threat (see Duster, 1970; Himmelstein, 1978). It was not so much alcohol problems *per se* that most animated the drive for Prohibition but the behavior and morality of what dominant groups saw as the "dangerous class" of urban, immigrant, Catholic, working-class drinkers (Gusfield, 1963; Rumbarger, 1989). It was *Chinese* opium smoking dens, not the more widespread use of other opiates, that prompted California's first drug law in the 1870s. It was only when smokable cocaine found its way to the African-American and Latino underclass that it made headlines and prompted calls for a drug war. In each case, politico-moral entrepreneurs were able to construct a "drug problem" by linking a substance to a group of users perceived by the powerful as disreputable, dangerous, or otherwise threatening.

7. **Scapegoating a Drug for a Wide Array of Public Problems** The final ingredient is scapegoating, i.e., blaming a drug or its

alleged effects on a group of its users for a variety of pre-existing social ills that are typically only indirectly associated with it. Scapegoating may be the most crucial element because it gives great explanatory power and thus broader resonance to claims about the horrors of drugs (particularly in the conflictual historical contexts in which drug scares tend to occur).

Scapegoating was abundant in each of the cases noted above. To listen to Temperance crusaders, for example, one might have believed that without alcohol use, America would be a land of infinite economic progress with no poverty, crime, mental illness, or even sex outside marriage. To listen to leaders of organized medicine and the government in the 1960s, one might have surmised that without marijuana and LSD there would have been neither conflict between youth and their parents nor opposition to the Vietnam War. And to believe politicians and the media in the past 6 years is to believe that without the scourge of crack the inner cities and the so-called underclass would, if not disappear, at least be far less scarred by poverty, violence, and crime. There is no historical evidence supporting any of this.

In short, drugs are richly functional scapegoats. They provide elites with fig leaves to place over unsightly social ills that are endemic to the social system over which they preside. And they provide the public with a restricted aperture of attribution in which only a chemical bogeyman or the lone deviants who ingest it are seen as the cause of a cornucopia of complex problems.

Toward a Culturally Specific Theory of Drug Scares

Various forms of drug use have been and are widespread in almost all societies comparable to ours. A few of them have experienced limited drug scares, usually around alcohol decades ago. However, drug scares have been *far* less common in other societies, and never as virulent as they have been in the U.S. (Brecher, 1972; Levine, 1992; MacAndrew and Edgerton, 1969). There has never been a time or place in human history without drunkenness, for example, but in *most* times and places drunkenness has not been nearly as problematic as it has been in the U.S. since the late 18th century (Levine, forthcoming). Moreover, in comparable industrial democracies, drug laws are generally less repressive. Why then do claims about the horrors of this or that consciousness-altering chemical have such unusual power in American culture?

Drug scares and other periods of acute public concern about drug use are not just discrete, unrelated episodes. There is a historical pattern in the U.S. that cannot be understood in terms of the moral values and perceptions of individual anti-drug crusaders alone. I have suggested that these crusaders have benefitted in various ways from their crusades. For example, making claims about how a drug is damaging society can help elites increase the social control of groups perceived as threatening (Duster, 1970), establish one class's moral code as dominant (Gusfield, 1963), bolster a bureaucracy's sagging fiscal fortunes (Dickson, 1968), or mobilize voter support (Reinarman and Levine, 1989a, b). However, the recurring character of pharmaco-phobia in U.S. history suggests that there is something about our *culture* which makes citizens more vulnerable to anti-drug crusaders' attempts to demonize drugs. Thus, an answer to the question of America's unusual vulnerability to drug scares must address why the scapegoating of consciousness-altering substances regularly *resonates* with or appeals to substantial portions of the population.

There are three basic parts to my answer. The first is that claims about the evils of drugs are especially viable in American culture in part because they provide a welcome *vocabulary of attribution* (cf. Mills, 1940). Armed with

"DRUGS" as a generic scapegoat, citizens gain the cognitive satisfaction of having a folk devil on which to blame a range of bizarre behaviors or other conditions they find troubling but difficult to explain in other terms. This much may be true of a number of other societies, but I hypothesize that this is particularly so in the U.S. because in our political culture individualistic explanations for problems are so much more common than social explanations.

Second, claims about the evils of drugs provide an especially serviceable vocabulary of attribution in the U.S. in part because our society developed from a *temperance culture* (Levine, 1992). American society was forged in the fires of ascetic Protestantism and industrial capitalism, both of which demand *self-control.* U.S. society has long been characterized as the land of the individual "self-made man." In such a land, self-control has had extraordinary importance. For the middle-class Protestants who settled, defined, and still dominate the U.S., self-control was both central to religious world views and a characterological necessity for economic survival and success in the capitalist market (Weber, 1930 [1985]). With Levine, (1992), I hypothesize that in a culture in which self-control is inordinately important, drug-induced altered states of consciousness are especially likely to be experienced as "loss of control," and thus to be inordinately feared.[7]

Drunkenness and other forms of drug use have, of course, been present everywhere in the industrialized world. But temperance cultures tend to arise only when industrial capitalism unfolds upon a cultural terrain deeply imbued with the Protestant ethic.[8] This means that only the U.S., England, Canada, and parts of Scandinavia have Temperance cultures, the U.S. being the most extreme case.

It may be objected that the influence of such a Temperance culture was strongest in the 19th and early 20th century and that its grip on the American *zeitgeist* has been loosened by the forces of modernity and now, many say, postmodernity. The third part of my answer, however, is that on the foundation of a Temperance culture, advanced capitalism has built a *postmodern, mass consumption culture* that exacerbates the problem of self-control in new ways.

Early in the 20th century, Henry Ford pioneered the idea that by raising wages he could simultaneously quell worker protests and increase market demand for mass-produced goods. This mass consumption strategy became central to modern American society and one of the reasons for our economic success (Marcuse, 1964; Aronowitz, 1973; Ewen, 1976; Bell, 1978). Our economy is now so fundamentally predicated upon mass consumption that theorists as diverse as Daniel Bell and Herbert Marcuse have observed that we live in a mass consumption culture. Bell (1978), for example, notes that while the Protestant work ethic and deferred gratification may still hold sway in the workplace, Madison Avenue, the media, and malls have inculcated a new indulgence ethic in the leisure sphere in which pleasure-seeking and immediate gratification reign.

Thus, our economy and society have come to depend upon the constant cultivation of new "needs," the production of new desires. Not only the hardware of social life such as food, clothing, and shelter but also the software of the self—excitement, entertainment, even eroticism—have become mass consumption commodities. This means that our society offers an increasing number of incentives for indulgence—more ways to lose self-control—and a decreasing number of countervailing reasons for retaining it.

In short, drug scares continue to occur in American society in part because people must constantly manage the contradiction between a Temperance culture that insists on self-control and a mass consumption culture which renders self-control continuously problematic. In addition to helping explain the recurrence of drug scares, I think this contradiction helps account for why in the last dozen years millions of Americans have joined 12-Step groups, more than 100 of which have nothing whatsoever to do with ingesting a drug (Reinarman, forthcoming). "Addiction," or the generalized loss of self-control, has become the meta-metaphor for a staggering array of human troubles. And, of course, we also seem to have a staggering array of politicians and other moral entrepreneurs who take advantage of such cultural contradictions to blame new chemical bogeymen for our society's ills.

NOTES

1. In this regard, for example, Robin Room wisely observes "that we are living at a historic moment when the rate of (alcohol) dependence as a cognitive and existential experience is rising, although the rate of alcohol consumption and of heavy drinking is falling." He draws from this a more general hypothesis about "long waves" of drinking and societal reactions to them: "[I]n periods of increased questioning of drinking and heavy drinking, the trends in the two forms of dependence, psychological and physical, will tend to run in opposite directions. Conversely, in periods of a "wettening" of sentiments, with the curve of alcohol consumption beginning to rise, we may expect the rate of physical dependence . . . to rise while the rate of dependence as a cognitive experience falls" (1991:154).
2. I say "formal end" because Temperance ideology is not merely alive and well in the War on Drugs but is being applied to all manner of human troubles in the burgeoning 12-Step Movement (Reinarman, forthcoming).
3. From Jim Baumohl I have learned that while the Temperance movement attracted most of its supporters from these groups, it also found supporters among many others (e.g., labor, the Irish, Catholics, former drunkards, women), each of which had its own reading of and folded its own agenda into the movement.
4. This historical sketch of drug scares is obviously not exhaustive. Readers interested in other scares should see, e.g., Brecher's encyclopedic work *Licit and Illicit Drugs* (1972), especially the chapter on glue sniffing, which illustrates how the media actually created a new drug problem by writing hysterical stories about it. There was also a PCP scare in the 1970s in which law enforcement officials claimed that the growing use of this horse tranquilizer was a severe threat because it made users so violent and gave them such super-human strength that stun guns were necessary. This, too, turned out to be unfounded and the "angel dust" scare was short-lived (see Feldman et al., 1979). The best analysis of how new drugs themselves can lead to panic reactions among users is Becker (1967).
5. Becker wisely warns against the "one-sided view" that sees such crusaders as merely imposing their morality on others. Moral entrepreneurs, he notes, do operate "with an absolute ethic," are "fervent and righteous," and will use "any means" necessary to "do away with" what they see as "totally evil." However, they also "typically believe that their mission is a holy one," that if people do what they want it "will be good for them." Thus, as in the case of abolitionists, the crusades of moral entrepreneurs often "have strong humanitarian overtones" (1963:147–8). This is no less true for those whose moral enterprise promotes drug scares. My analysis, however, concerns the character and consequences of their efforts, not their motives.
6. As Gusfield notes, such ownership sometimes shifts over time, e.g., with alcohol problems, from religion to criminal law to medical science. With other drug problems, the shift in ownership has been away from medical science toward criminal law. The most insightful treatment of the medicalization of alcohol/drug problems is Peele (1989).
7. See Baumohl's (1990) important and erudite analysis of how the human will was valorized in the therapeutic temperance thought of 19th-century inebriate homes.
8. The third central feature of Temperance cultures identified by Levine (1992), which I will not dwell on, is predominance of spirits drinking, i.e., more concentrated alcohol than wine or beer and thus greater likelihood of drunkenness.

REFERENCES

Aronowitz, Stanley, *False Promises: The Shaping of American Working Class Consciousness* (New York: McGraw-Hill, 1973).

Baumohl, Jim, "Inebriate Institutions in North America, 1840–1920," *British Journal of Addiction* 85:1187–1204 (1990).

Baumohl, Jim, "The 'Dope Fiend's Paradise' Revisited: Notes from Research in Progress on Drug Law Enforcement in San Francisco, 1875–1915," *Drinking and Drug Practices Surveyor* 24:3–12 (1992).

Becker, Howard S., *Outsiders: Studies in the Sociology of Deviance* (Glencoe, IL: Free Press, 1963).

Becker, Howard S., "History, Culture, and Subjective Experience: An Exploration of the Social Bases of Drug-Induced Experiences," *Journal of Health and Social Behavior* 8:162–176 (1967).

Bell, Daniel, *The Cultural Contradictions of Capitalism* (New York: Basic Books, 1978).

Brecher, Edward M., *Licit and Illicit Drugs* (Boston: Little Brown, 1972).

Cohen, M. M., K. Hirshorn, and W. A. Frosch, "In Vivo and in Vitro Chromosomal Damage Induced by LSD-25." *New England Journal of Medicine* 227:1043 (1967).

Courtwright, David, *Dark Paradise: Opiate Addiction in America before 1940* (Cambridge, MA: Harvard University Press, 1982).

Dickson, Donald, "Bureaucracy and Morality," Social Problems 16:143–156 (1968).

Duster, Troy, *The Legislation of Morality: Law, Drugs, and Moral Judgment* (New York: Free Press, 1970).

Ewen, Stuart, *Captains of Consciousness: Advertising and the Social Roots of Consumer Culture* (New York: McGraw-Hill, 1976).

Feldman, Harvey W., Michael H. Agar, and George M. Beschner, *Angel Dust* (Lexington, MA: Lexington Books, 1979).

Gusfield, Joseph R., *Symbolic Crusade: Status Politics and the American Temperance Movement* (Urbana: University of Illinois Press, 1963).

Gusfield, Joseph R., *The Culture of Public Problems: Drinking-Driving and the Symbolic Order* (Chicago: University of Chicago Press, 1981).

Himmelstein, Jerome, "Drug Politics Theory," *Journal of Drug Issues* 8 (1978).

Himmelstein, Jerome, *The Strange Career of Marihuana* (Westport, CT: Greenwood Press, 1983).

Levine, Harry Gene, "The Alcohol Problem in America: From Temperance to Alcoholism," *British Journal of Addiction* 84:109–119 (1984).

Levine, Harry Gene, "Temperance Cultures: Concern about Alcohol Problems in Nordic and English-Speaking Cultures," in G. Edwards et al., Eds. *The Nature of Alcohol and Drug Related Problems* (New York: Oxford University Press, 1992).

Levine, Harry Gene, *Drunkenness and Civilization* (New York: Basic Books, forthcoming).

Levine, Harry Gene, and Craig Reinarman, "From Prohibition to Regulation: Lessons from Alcohol Policy for Drug Policy." *Milbank Quarterly* 69:461–494 (1991).

MacAndrew, Craig, and Robert Edgerton, *Drunken Comportment* (Chicago: Aldine, 1969).

Marcuse, Herbert, *One-Dimensional Man: Studies in the Ideology of Advanced Industrial Society* (Boston: Beacon Press, 1964).

Mills, C. Wright, "Situated Actions and Vocabularies of Motive," *American Sociological Review,* 5:904–913 (1940).

Molotch, Harvey, and Marilyn Lester, "News as Purposive Behavior: On the Strategic Uses of Routine Events, Accidents, and Scandals," *American Sociological Review* 39:101–112 (1974).

Morgan, Patricia, "The Legislation of Drug Law: Economic Crisis and Social Control, *Journal of Drug Issues* 8:53–62 (1978).

Musto, David, *The American Disease: Origins of Narcotic Control* (New Haven, CT: Yale University Press, 1973).

National Institute on Drug Abuse, *National Household Survey on Drug Abuse: Main Findings 1990* (Washington, DC: U.S. Department of Health and Human Services, 1990).

Peele, Stanton, *The Diseasing of America: Addiction Treatment Out of Control* (Lexington, MA: Lexington Books, 1989).

Reinarman, Craig, "The 12-Step Movement and Advanced Capitalist Culture: Notes on the Politics of Self-Control in Postmodernity," in B. Epstein, R. Flacks, and M. Darnovsky, Eds. *Contemporary Social Movements and Cultural Politics* (New York: Oxford University Press, forthcoming).

Reinarman, Craig, and Ceres Duskin, "Dominant Ideology and Drugs in the Media," *International Journal on Drug Policy* 3:6–15 (1992).

Reinarman, Craig, and Harry Gene Levine, "Crack in Context: Politics and Media in the Making of a Drug Scare," *Contemporary Drug Problems* 16:535–577 (1989a).

Reinarman, Craig, and Harry Gene Levine, "The Crack Attack: Politics and Media in America's Latest Drug Scare: pp. 115–137 in Joel Best, Ed., *Images of Issues: Typifying Contemporary Social Problems* (New York: Adline de Gruyter, 1989b).

Room, Robin G. W., "Cultural Changes in Drinking and Trends in Alcohol Problems Indicators: Recent U.S. Experience," pp. 149–162 in Walter B. Clark and Michael E. Hilton, Eds. *Alcohol in America: Drinking Practices and Problems* (Albany: State University of New York Press, 1991).

Rumbarger, John J., *Profits, Power, and Prohibition: Alcohol Reform and the Industrializing of America. 1800–1930* (Albany: State University of New York Press, 1989).

Tijo, J. H., W. N. Pahnke, and A. A. Kurland, "LSD and Chromosomes: A Controlled Experiment," *Journal of the American Medical Association* 210:849 (1969).

Weber, Max, *The Protestant Ethic and the Spirit of Capitalism* (London: Unwin, 1985 [1930]).

Weil, Andrew, *The National Mind* (Boston: Houghton Mifflin, 1972).

PORTRAIT

On Being Sane in Insane Places

D. L. Rosenhan

If sanity and insanity exist, how shall we know them?

The question is neither capricious nor itself insane. However much we may be personally convinced that we can tell the normal from the abnormal, the evidence is simply not compelling. It is commonplace, for example, to read about murder trials wherein eminent psychiatrists for the defense are contradicted by equally eminent psychiatrists for the prosecution on the matter of the defendant's sanity. More generally, there are a great deal of conflicting data on the reliability, utility, and meaning of such terms as "sanity," "insanity," "mental illness," and "schizophrenia."[1] Finally, as early as 1934, Benedict suggested that normality and abnormality are not universal.[2] What is viewed as normal in one culture may be seen as quite aberrant in another. Thus, notions of normality and abnormality may not be quite as accurate as people believe they are.

To raise questions regarding normality and abnormality is in no way to question the fact that some behaviors are deviant or odd. Murder is deviant. So, too, are hallucinations. Nor does raising such questions deny the existence of the personal anguish that is often associated with "mental illness." Anxiety and depression exist. Psychological suffering exists. But normality and abnormality, sanity and insanity, and the diagnoses that flow from them may be less substantive than many believe them to be.

At its heart, the question of whether the sane can be distinguished from the insane (and whether degrees of insanity can be distinguished from each other) is a simple matter: do the salient characteristics that lead to diagnoses reside in the patients themselves or in the environments and contexts in which observers find them? From Bleuler, through Kretchmer, through the formulators of the recently revised *Diagnostic and Statistical Manual* of the American Psychiatric Association, the belief has been strong that patients present symptoms, that those symptoms can be categorized, and, implicitly, that the sane are distinguishable from the insane. More recently, however, this belief has been questioned. Based in part on theoretical and anthropological considerations, but also on philosophical, legal, and therapeutic ones, the view has grown that psychological categorization of mental illness is useless at best and downright harmful, misleading, and pejorative at worst. Psychiatric diagnoses, in this view, are in the minds of the observers and are not valid summaries of characteristics displayed by the observed.[3, 4, 5]

Gains can be made in deciding which of these is more nearly accurate by getting normal people (that is, people who do not have, and have never suffered, symptoms of serious psychiatric disorders) admitted to psychiatric hospitals and then determining whether they were discovered to be sane and, if so, how. If the sanity of such pseudopatients were always detected, there would be prima facie evidence that a sane individual can be distinguished from the insane context in which he is found. Normality (and presumably abnormality) is distinct enough that it can be recognized wherever it occurs, for it is carried within the person. If, on the other hand, the sanity of the pseudopatients were never discovered, serious difficulties would arise for those who support traditional modes of psychiatric diagnosis. Given that the hospital staff was not incompetent, that the pseudopatient had been behaving as sanely as he had been outside of the hospital, and that it had never been previously suggested that he belonged in a psychiatric hospital, such an unlikely outcome would support the view that psychiatric diagnosis betrays little about the patient but much about the environment in which an observer finds him.

This article describes such an experiment. Eight sane people gained secret admission to 12 different hospitals.[6] Their diagnostic experiences constitute the data of the first part of this article; the remainder is devoted to a description of their experiences in psychiatric institutions. Too few psychiatrists and psychologists, even those who have worked in such hospitals, know what the experience is like. They rarely talk about it with former patients, perhaps because they distrust information coming from the previously insane. Those who have worked in psychiatric hospitals are likely to have adapted so thoroughly to the settings that they are insensitive to the impact of that experience. And while there have been occasional reports of researchers who submitted themselves to psychiatric hospitalization,[7] these researchers have commonly remained in the hospitals for short periods of time, often with the knowledge of the hospital staff. It is difficult to know the extent to which they were treated like patients or like research colleagues. Nevertheless, their reports about the inside of the psychiatric hospital have been valuable. This article extends those efforts.

Pseudopatients and Their Settings

The eight pseudopatients were a varied group. One was a psychology graduate student in his 20's. The remaining seven were older and "established." Among them were three psychologists, a pediatrician, a psychiatrist, a painter, and a housewife. Three pseudopatients were women, five were men. All of them employed pseudonyms, lest their alleged diagnoses embarrass them later. Those who were in mental health professions alleged another occupation in order to avoid the special attentions that might be accorded by staff, as a matter of courtesy or caution, to ailing colleagues.[8] With the exception of myself (I was the first pseudopatient and my presence was known to the hospital administrator and chief psychologist and, so far as I can tell, to them alone), the presence of pseudopatients and the nature of the research program were not known to the hospital staffs.[9]

The settings were similarly varied. In order to generalize the findings, admission into a variety of hospitals was sought. The 12 hospitals in the sample were located in five different states on the East and West coasts. Some were old and shabby, some were quite new. Some were research-oriented, others not. Some had good staff–patient ratios, others were quite understaffed. Only one was a strictly private hospital. All of the others were supported by state or federal funds or, in one instance, by university funds.

After calling the hospital for an appointment, the pseudopatient arrived at the admissions office complaining that he had been hearing voices. Asked what the voices said, he replied that they were often unclear, but as far as he could tell they said "empty," "hollow," and "thud." The voices were unfamiliar and were of the same sex as the pseudopatient. The choice of these symptoms was occasioned by their apparent similarity to existential symptoms. Such symptoms are alleged to arise from painful concerns about the perceived meaninglessness of one's life. It is as if the hallucinating person were saying, "My life is empty and hollow." The choice of these symptoms was also determined by the *absence* of a single report of existential psychoses in the literature.

Beyond alleging the symptoms and falsifying name, vocation, and employment, no further alterations of person, history, or circumstances were made. The significant events of the pseudopatient's life history were presented as they had actually occurred. Relationships with parents and siblings, with spouse and children, with people at work and in school, consistent with the aforementioned exceptions, were described as they were or had been. Frustrations and upsets were described along with joys and satisfactions. These facts are important to remember. If anything, they strongly biased the subsequent results in favor of detecting sanity, since none of their histories or current behaviors were seriously pathological in any way.

Immediately upon admission to the psychiatric ward, the pseudopatient ceased simulating *any* symptoms of abnormality. In some cases, there was a brief period of mild nervousness and anxiety, since none of the pseudopatients really believed that they would be admitted so easily. Indeed, their shared fear was that they would be immediately exposed as frauds and greatly embarrassed. Moreover, many of them had never visited a psychiatric ward; even those who had, nevertheless had some genuine fears about what might happen to them. Their nervousness, then, was quite appropriate to the novelty of the hospital setting, and it abated rapidly.

Apart from the short-lived nervousness, the pseudopatient behaved on the ward as he "normally" behaved. The pseudopatient spoke to patients and staff as he might ordinarily. Because there is uncommonly little to do on a psychiatric ward, he attempted to engage others in conversation. When asked by staff how he was feeling, he indicated that he was fine, that he no longer experienced symptoms. He responded to instructions from attendants, to calls for medication (which was not swallowed), and to dining-hall instructions. Beyond such activities as were available to him on the admissions ward, he spent his time writing down his observations about the ward, its patients, and the staff. Initially these notes were written "secretly," but as it soon became clear that no one much cared, they were subsequently written on standard tablets of paper in such public places as the dayroom. No secret was made of these activities.

The pseudopatient, very much as a true psychiatric patient, entered a hospital with no foreknowledge of when he would be discharged. Each was told that he would have to get out by his own devices, essentially by convincing the staff that he was sane. The psychological stresses associated with hospitalization were considerable, and all but one of the pseudopatients desired to be discharged almost immediately after being admitted. They were, therefore, motivated not only to behave sanely, but to be paragons of cooperation. That their behavior was in no way disruptive is confirmed by nursing reports, which have been obtained on most of the patients. These reports uniformly indicate that the patients were "friendly," "cooperative," and "exhibited no abnormal indications."

The Normal Are Not Detectably Sane

Despite their public "show" of sanity, the pseudopatients were never detected. Admitted, except in one case, with a diagnosis of schizophrenia,[10] each was discharged with a diagnosis of schizophrenia "in remission." The label "in remission" should in no way be dismissed as a formality, for at no time during any hospitalization had any question been raised about any pseudopatient's simulation. Nor are there any indications in the hospital records that the pseudopatient's status was suspect. Rather, the evidence is strong that, once labeled schizophrenic, the pseudopatient was stuck with that label. If the pseudopatient was to be discharged, he must naturally be "in remission"; but he was not sane, nor, in the institution's view, had he ever been sane.

The uniform failure to recognize sanity cannot be attributed to the quality of the hospitals, for, although there were considerable variations among them, several are considered excellent. Nor can it be alleged that there was simply not enough time to observe the pseudopatients. Length of hospitalization ranged from 7 to 52 days, with an average of 19 days. The pseudopatients were not, in fact, carefully observed, but this failure clearly speaks more to traditions within psychiatric hospitals than to lack of opportunity.

Finally, it cannot be said that the failure to recognize the pseudopatients' sanity was due to the fact that they were not behaving sanely. While there was clearly some tension present in all of them, their daily visitors could detect no serious behavioral consequences—nor, indeed, could other patients. It was quite common for the patients to "detect" the pseudopatients' sanity. During the first three hospitalizations, when accurate counts were kept, 35 of a total of 118 patients on the admissions ward voiced their suspicions, some vigorously, "You're not crazy. You're a journalist or a professor [referring to the continual note-taking]. You're checking up on the hospital." While most of the patients were reassured by the pseudopatient's insistence that he had been sick before he came in but was fine now, some continued to believe that the pseudopatient was sane throughout his hospitalization.[11] The fact that the patients often recognized normality when staff did not raises important questions.

Failure to detect sanity during the course of hospitalization may be due to the fact that physicians operate with a strong bias toward what statisticians call the type 2 error.[5] This is to say that physicians are more inclined to call a healthy person sick (a false positive, type 2) than a sick person healthy (a false negative, type 1). The reasons for this are not hard to find: it is clearly more dangerous to misdiagnose illness than health. Better to err on the side of caution, to suspect illness even among the healthy.

But what holds for medicine does not hold equally well for psychiatry. Medical illnesses, while unfortunate, are not commonly pejorative. Psychiatric diagnoses, on the contrary, carry with them personal, legal, and social stigmas.[12] It was therefore important to see whether the tendency toward diagnosing the sane insane could be reversed. The following experiment was arranged at a research and teaching hospital whose staff had heard these findings but doubted that such an error could occur in their hospital. The staff was informed that at some time during the following 3 months, one or more pseudopatients would attempt to be admitted into the psychiatric hospital. Each staff member was asked to rate each patient who presented himself at admissions or on the ward according to the likelihood that the patient was a pseudopatient. A 10-point scale was used, with a 1 and 2 reflecting high confidence that the patient was a pseudopatient.

Judgments were obtained on 193 patients who were admitted for psychiatric treatment. All staff who had had sustained contact with or primary responsibility for the patient—attendants, nurses, psychiatrists, physicians, and psychologists—were asked to make judgments. Forty-one patients were alleged, with high confidence, to be pseudopatients by at least one member of the staff. Twenty-three were considered suspect by at least one psychiatrist. Nineteen were suspected by one psychiatrist *and* one other staff member. Actually, no genuine pseudopatient (at least from my group) presented himself during this period.

The experiment is instructive. It indicates that the tendency to designate sane people as insane can be reversed when the stakes (in this case, prestige and diagnostic acumen) are high. But what can be said of the 19 people who were suspected of being "sane" by one psychiatrist and another staff member? Were these people truly "sane," or was it rather the case that in the course of avoiding the type 2 error the staff tended to make more errors of the first sort—calling the crazy "sane"? There is no way of knowing. But one thing is certain: any diagnostic process that lends itself so readily to massive errors of this sort cannot be a very reliable one.

The Stickiness of Psychodiagnostic Labels

Beyond the tendency to call the healthy sick—a tendency that accounts better for diagnostic behavior on admission than it does for such behavior after a lengthy period of exposure—the data speak to the massive role of labeling in psychiatric assessment. Having once been labeled schizophrenic, there is nothing the pseudopatient can do to overcome the tag. The tag profoundly colors others' perceptions of him and his behavior.

From one viewpoint, these data are hardly surprising, for it has long been known that elements are given meaning by the context in which they occur. Gestalt psychology made this point vigorously, and Asch[13] demonstrated that there are "central" personality traits (such as "warm" versus "cold") which are so powerful that they markedly color the meaning of other information in forming an impression of a given personality.[14] "Insane," "schizophrenic," "manic-depressive," and "crazy" are probably among the most powerful of such central traits. Once a person is designated abnormal, all of his other behaviors and characteristics are colored by that label. Indeed, that label is so powerful that many of the pseudopatients' normal behaviors were overlooked entirely or profoundly misinterpreted. Some examples may clarify this issue.

Earlier I indicated that there were no changes in the pseudopatient's personal history and current status beyond those of name, employment, and, where necessary, vocation. Otherwise, a veridical description of personal history and circumstances was offered. Those circumstances were not psychotic. How were they made consonant with the diagnosis of psychosis? Or were those diagnoses modified in such a way as to bring them into accord with the circumstances of the pseudopatient's life, as described by him?

As far as I can determine, diagnoses were in no way affected by the relative health of the circumstances of pseudopatient's life. Rather, the reverse occurred: the perception of his circumstances was shaped entirely by the diagnosis. A clear example of such translation is found in the case of a pseudopatient who had had a close relationship with his mother but was rather remote from his father during his early childhood. During adolescence and beyond, however, his father became a close friend, while his relationship with his mother cooled. His present relationship with his wife was characteristically close and warm. Apart from occasional angry exchanges, friction was minimal. The children had rarely been spanked. Surely there is nothing especially pathological about such a history. Indeed, many readers may see a similar pattern in their own experiences, with no markedly deleterious consequences. Observe, however, how such a history was translated in the psychopathological context, this from the case summary prepared after the patient was discharged.

> This white 39-year-old male . . . manifests a long history of considerable ambivalence in close relationships, which begins in early childhood. A warm relationship with his mother cools during his adolescence. A distant relationship to his father is described as becoming very intense. Affective stability is absent. His attempts to control emotionality with his wife and children are punctuated by angry outbursts and, in the case of the children, spankings. And while he says that he has several good friends, one senses considerable ambivalence embedded in those relationships also. . . .

The facts of the case were unintentionally distorted by the staff to achieve consistency with a popular theory of the dynamics of a schizophrenic reaction.[15] Nothing of an ambivalent nature had been described in relations with parents, spouse, or friends. To the extent that ambivalence could be inferred, it was probably not greater than is found in all human relationships. It is true the pseudopatient's relationships with his parents changed over time, but in the ordinary context that would hardly be remarkable—indeed, it might very well be expected. Clearly, the meaning ascribed to his verbalizations (that is, ambivalence, affective instability) was determined by the diagnosis: schizophrenia. An entirely different meaning would have been ascribed if it were known that the man was "normal."

All pseudopatients took extensive notes publicly. Under ordinary circumstances, such behavior would have raised questions in the minds of observers, as, in fact, it did among patients. Indeed, it seemed so certain that the notes would elicit suspicion that elaborate precautions were taken to remove them from the ward each day. But the precautions proved needless. The closest any staff member came to questioning these notes occurred when one pseudopatient asked his physician what kind of medication he was receiving and began to write down the response. "You needn't write it," he was told gently. "If you have trouble remembering, just ask me again."

If no questions were asked of the pseudopatients, how was their writing interpreted? Nursing records for three patients indicate that the writing was seen as an aspect of their pathological behavior. "Patient engages in writing behavior" was the daily nursing comment on one of the pseudopatients who was never questioned about his writing. Given that the patient is in the hospital, he must be psychologically disturbed. And given that he is disturbed, continuous writing must be a behavioral manifestation of that disturbance, perhaps a subset of the compulsive behaviors that are sometimes correlated with schizophrenia.

One tacit characteristic of psychiatric diagnosis is that it locates the sources of aberration within the individual and only rarely within the complex of stimuli that surrounds him. Consequently, behaviors that are stimulated by the environment are commonly misattributed to the patient's disorder. For example, one kindly nurse found a pseudopatient pacing the long hospital corridors. "Nervous, Mr. X?" she asked. "No, bored," he said.

The notes kept by pseudopatients are full of patient behaviors that were misinterpreted by well-intentioned staff. Often enough, a patient would go "berserk" because he had, wittingly or unwittingly, been mistreated by, say, an attendant. A nurse coming upon the scene would rarely inquire even cursorily into the environmental stimuli of the patient's behavior. Rather, she assumed that his upset derived from his pathology, not from his present interactions with other staff members. Occasionally, the staff might assume that the patient's family (especially when they had recently visited) or other patients had stimulated the outburst. But never were the staff found to assume that one of themselves or the structure of the hospital had anything to do with a patient's behavior. One psychiatrist pointed to a group of patients who were sitting outside the cafeteria entrance half an hour before lunchtime. To a group of young residents he indicated that such behavior was characteristic of the oral-acquisitive nature of the syndrome. It seemed not to occur to him that there were very few things to anticipate in a psychiatric hospital besides eating.

A psychiatric label has a life and an influence of its own. Once the impression has been formed that the patient is schizophrenic, the expectation is that he will continue to be schizophrenic. When a sufficient amount of time has passed, during which the patient has done nothing bizarre, he is considered to be in remission and available for discharge. But the label endures beyond discharge, with the unconfirmed expectation that he will behave as a schizophrenic again. Such labels, conferred by mental health professionals, are as influential on the patient as they are on his relatives and friends, and it should not surprise anyone that the diagnosis acts on all of them as a self-fulfilling prophecy. Eventually, the patient himself accepts the diagnosis, with all of its surplus meanings and expectations, and behaves accordingly.[5]

The inferences to be made from these matters are quite simple. Much as Zigler and Phillips have demonstrated that there is enormous overlap in the symptoms presented by patients who have been variously diagnosed,[16] so there is enormous overlap in the behaviors of the sane and the insane. The sane are not "sane" all of the time. We lose our tempers, "for no good reason." We are occasionally depressed or anxious, again for no good reason. And we may find it difficult to get along with one or another person—again for no reason that we can specify. Similarly, the insane are not always insane. Indeed, it was the impression of the pseudopatients while living with them that they were sane for long periods of time—that the bizarre behaviors upon which their diagnoses were allegedly predicated constituted only a small fraction of their total behavior. If it makes no sense to label ourselves permanently depressed on the basis of an occasional depression, then it takes better evidence than is presently available to label all patients insane or schizophrenic on the basis of bizarre behaviors or cognitions. It seems more useful, as Mischel[17] has pointed out, to limit our discussions to *behaviors,* the stimuli that provoke them, and their correlates.

It is not known why powerful impressions of personality traits, such as "crazy" or "insane," arise. Conceivably, when the origins of and stimuli that give rise to a behavior are remote or unknown, or when the behavior strikes us as immutable, trait labels regarding the *behaver* arise. When, on the other hand, the origins and stimuli are known and available, discourse is limited to the behavior itself. Thus, I may hallucinate because I am sleeping, or I may hallucinate because I have ingested a peculiar drug. These are termed sleep-induced hallucinations, or dreams, and drug-induced hallucinations, respectively. But when the stimuli to my hallucinations are unknown, that is called craziness, or schizophrenia—as if that inference were somehow as illuminating as the others. . . .

The Consequences of Labeling and Depersonalization

Whenever the ratio of what is known to what needs to be known approaches zero, we tend to invent "knowledge" and assume that we understand more than we actually do. We seem unable to acknowledge that we simply don't know. The needs for diagnosis and remediation of behavioral and emotional problems are enormous. But rather than acknowledge that we are just embarking on understanding, we continue to label patients "schizophrenic," "manic-depressive," and "insane," as if in those words we had captured the essence of understanding. The facts of the matter are that we have known for a long time that diagnoses are often not useful or reliable, but we have nevertheless continued to use them. We now know that we cannot distinguish insanity from sanity. It is depressing to consider how that information will be used.

Not merely depressing, but frightening. How many people, one wonders, are sane but not recognized as such in our psychiatric institutions? How many have been needlessly stripped of their privileges of citizenship, from the right to vote and drive to that of handling their own accounts? How many have feigned insanity in order to avoid the criminal consequences of their behavior, and, conversely, how many would rather stand trial than live interminably in a psychiatric hospital—but are wrongly thought to be mentally ill? How many have been stigmatized by well-intentioned, but nevertheless erroneous, diagnoses? On the last point, recall again that a "type 2 error" in psychiatric diagnosis does not have the same consequences it does in medical diagnosis. A diagnosis of cancer that has been found to be in error is cause for celebration. But psychiatric diagnoses are rarely found to be in error. The label sticks, a mark of inadequacy forever.

NOTES AND REFERENCES

1. P. Ash (1949), *J. Abnorm. Soc. Psychol. 44*, 272 (1949); A. T. Beck (1962), *Amer. J. Psychiat. 119*, 210; A. T. Boisen (1938), *Psychiatry 2*, 233; N. Kreitman (1961), *J. Ment. Sci. 107*, 876; N. Kreitman, P. Sainsbury, J. Morrisey, J. Towers, J. Scrivener (1961), *J. Ment. Sci. 107*, 887; H. O. Schmitt & C. P. Fonda (1956), *J. Abnorm. Soc. Psychol. 52*, 262; W. Seeman (1953), *J. Nerv. Ment. Dis. 118*, 541. For an analysis of these artifacts and summaries of the disputes, see J. Zibin (1967), *Annu. Rev. Psychol. 18*, 373; L. Phillips & J. G. Draguns (1971), *Annu. Rev. Psychol. 22*, 447.
2. R. Benedict (1934), *J. Gen. Psychol. 10*, 59.
3. See in this regard H. Becker (1963), *Outsiders: Studies in the sociology of deviance*, New York: Free Press; B. M. Braginsky, D. D. Braginsky, & K. Ring (1969), *Methods of Madness: The mental hospital as a last resort*, New York:Holt, Rinehart & Winston; G. M. Crocetti & P. V. Lemkau (1965), *Amer. Sociol. Rev. 30*, 577; E. Goffman (1964), *Behavior in public places*, New York: Free Press; R. D. Laing (1960), *The divided self: A study of sanity and madness*, Chicago: Quadrangle; D. L. Phillips (1963), *Amer. Sociol. Rev. 20*, 963; T. R. Sarbin (1972), *Psychol. Today 6*, 18; E. Schur (1969), *Amer. J. Sociol. 75*, 309; T. Szasz (1963), *Law, liberty and psychiatry*, New York: Macmillan; (1963b), *The myth of mental illness: Foundations of a theory of mental illness*, New York: Hoeber Harper. For a critique of some of these views, see W. R. Gove (1970), *Amer. Sociol. Rev. 35*, 873.
4. E. Goffman (1961), *Asylums*, Garden City, NY: Doubleday.
5. T. J. Scheff (1966), *Being mentally ill: A sociological theory*, Chicago: Aldine.
6. Data from a ninth pseudopatient are not incorporated in this report because, although his sanity went undetected, he falsified aspects of his personal history, including his marital status and parental relationships. His experimental behaviors therefore were not identical to those of the other pseudopatients.
7. A. Barry (1971), *Bellevue is a state of mind*, New York: Harcourt Brace Jovanovich; I. Belknap (1956), *Human problems of a state mental hospital*, New York: McGraw-Hill; W. Caudill, F. C. Redlich, H. R. Gilmore, E. B. Brody (1952), *Amer. J. Orthopsychiat. 22*, 314; A. R. Goldman, R. H. Bohr, T. A. Steinberg (1970), *Prof. Psychol. 1*, 427; *Roche Report 1* (13[1971]), 8.
8. Beyond the personal difficulties that the pseudopatient is likely to experience in the hospital, there are legal and social ones that, combined, require considerable attention before entry. For example, once admitted to a

psychiatric institution, it is difficult, if not impossible, to be discharged on short notice, state law to the contrary notwithstanding. I was not sensitive to these difficulties at the outset of the project, nor to the personal and situational emergencies that can arise, but later a writ of habeas corpus was prepared for each of the entering pseudopatients and an attorney was kept "on call" during every hospitalization. I am grateful to John Kaplan and Robert Bartels for legal advice and assistance in these matters.

9. However distasteful such concealment is, it was a necessary first step to examining these questions. Without concealment, there would have been no way to know how valid these experiences were; nor was there any way of knowing whether whatever detections occurred were a tribute to the diagnostic acumen of the staff or to the hopsital's rumor network. Obviously, since my concerns are general ones that cut across individual hopsitals and staffs, I have respected their anonymity and have eliminated clues that might lead to their identification.

10. Interestingly, of the 12 admissions, 11 were diagnosed as schizophrenic and one, with the identical symptomatology, as manic-depressive psychosis. This diagnosis has a more favorable prognosis, and it was given by the only private hospital in our sample. On the relations between social class and psychiatric diagnosis, see A. deB. Hollingshead & F. C. Redlich (1958), *Social class and mental illness: A community study*, New York: John Wiley.

11. It is possible, of course, that patients have quite broad latitudes in diagnosis and therefore are inclined to call many people sane, even those whose behavior is patently aberrant. However, although we have no hard data on this matter, it was our distinct impression that this was not the case. In many instances, patients not only singled us out for attention, but came to imitate our behaviors and styles.

12. J. Cumming & E. Cumming (1965), *Community Ment. Health 1*, 135; A. Farina & K. Ring (1965), *J. Abnorm. Psychol. 70*, 47; H. E. Freeman & O. G. Simmons (1963), *The mental patient comes home*, New York: John Wiley; W. J. Johannsen (1969), *Ment. Hygiene 53*, 218; A. S. Linsky (1970), *Soc. Psychiat. 5*, 166.

13. S. E. Asch (1946), *J. Abnorm. Soc. Psychol. 41*, 258; *Social Psychology*, New York: Prentice-Hall.

14. See also I. N. Mensh & J. Wishner (1947), *J. Personality 16*, 188; J. Wishner (1960), *Psychol. Rev. 67*, 96; J. S. Bruner & R. Tagiuri (1954), in G. Lindzey (Ed.), *Handbook of social psychology*, (Vol. 2, pp. 634–654), Cambridge, MA: Addison-Wesley; J. S. Bruner, D. Shapiro, & R. Tagiuri (1958), in R. Tagiuri & L. Petrullo (Eds.), *Person perception and interpersonal behavior* (pp. 277–288), Stanford, CA: Stanford University Press.

15. For an example of a similar self-fulfilling prophecy, in this instance dealing with the "central" trait of intelligence, see R. Rosenthal & L. Jacobson, *Pygmalion in the classroom*, New York: Holt, Rinehart & Winston.

16. E. Zigler & L. Phillips (1961), *J. Abnorm. Soc. Psychol. 63*, 69. See also R. K. Freudenberg & J. P. Robertson (1956), *A.M.A. Arch. Neurol. Psychiatr. 76*, 14.

17. W. Mischel (1968), *Personality and assessment*, New York: John Wiley.

PORTRAIT

The Influence of Situational Ethics on Cheating among College Students

Donald L. McCabe

Introduction

Numerous studies have demonstrated the pervasive nature of cheating among college students (Baird 1980; Haines, Diekhoff, LaBeff, and Clark 1986; Michaels and Miethe 1989; Davis, et al. 1992). This research has examined a variety of factors that help explain cheating behavior, but the strength of the relationships between individual factors and cheating has varied considerably from study to study (Tittle and Rowe 1973; Baird 1980; Eisenberger and Shank 1985; Haines, et al. 1986; Ward 1986; Michaels and Miethe 1989; Perry, Kane, Bernesser, and Spicker 1990; Ward and Beck 1990).

Although the factors examined in these studies (for example, personal work ethic, gender, self-esteem, rational choice, social learning, deterrence) are clearly important, the work of LaBeff, Clark, Haines, and Diekhoff (1990) suggests that the concept of situational ethics may be particularly helpful in understanding student rationalizations for cheating. . . . LaBeff et al. conclude

> that students hold qualified guidelines for behavior which are situationally determined. As such, the concept of situational ethics might well describe . . . college cheating [as] rules for behavior may not be considered rigid but depend on the circumstances involved. (1990, p. 191)

LaBeff et al. believe a utilitarian calculus of "the ends justifies the means" underlies this reasoning process and "what is wrong in most situations might be considered right or acceptable if the end is defined as appropriate" (1990, p. 191). As argued by Edwards (1967), the situation determines what is right or wrong in this decision-making calculus and also dictates the appropriate principles to be used in guiding and judging behavior.

Sykes and Matza (1957) hypothesize that such rationalizations, that is, "justifications for deviance that are seen as valid by the delinquent but not by the legal system or society at large" (p. 666), are common. However, they challenge conventional wisdom that such rationalizations typically follow deviant behavior as a means of protecting "the individual from self-blame and the blame of others after the act" (p. 666). They develop convincing arguments that these rationalizations may logically precede the deviant behavior and "[d]isapproval from internalized norms and conforming others in the social environment is neutralized, turned back, or deflated in advance. Social controls that serve to check or inhibit deviant motivational patterns are rendered inoperative, and the individual is freed to engage in delinquency without serious damage to his self image." (pp. 666–667) . . .

Methodology

The data discussed here were gathered as part of a study of college cheating conducted during the 1990–1991 academic year. A seventy-two item questionnaire concerning cheating behavior was administered to students at thirty-one

---

From "The Influence of Situational Ethics on Cheating among College Students" by D. McCabe, 1992, *Sociological Inquiry 62:* 365–343.

highly selective colleges across the country. Surveys were mailed to a minimum of five hundred students at each school and a total of 6,096 completed surveys were returned (38.3 percent response rate). Eighty-eight percent of the respondents were seniors, nine percent were juniors, and the remaining three percent could not be classified. Survey administration emphasized voluntary participation and assurances of anonymity to help combat issues of non-response bias and the need to accept responses without the chance to question or contest them. . . .

Results

Of the 6,096 students participating in this research, over two-thirds (67.4 percent) indicated that they had cheated on a test or major assignment at least once while an undergraduate. This cheating took a variety of different forms, but among the most popular (listed in decreasing order of mention) were: (1) a failure to footnote sources in written work, (2) collaboration on assignments when the instructor specifically asked for individual work, (3) copying from other students on tests and examinations, (4) fabrication of bibliographies, (5) helping someone else cheat on a test, and (6) using unfair methods to learn the content of a test ahead of time. Almost one in five students (19.1 percent) could be classified as active cheaters (five or more self-reported incidents of cheating). . . . Students in this research were asked to report all cheating in which they had engaged while an undergraduate—a period of three years for most respondents at the time of this survey.

Students admitting to any cheating activity were asked to rate the importance of several specific factors that might have influenced their decisions to cheat. These data establish the importance of denial of responsibility and condemnation of condemners as neutralization techniques. For example, 52.4 percent of the respondents who admitted to cheating rated the pressure to get good grades as an important influence in their decision to cheat with parental pressures and competition to gain admission into professional schools singled out as the primary grade pressures. Forty-six percent of those who had engaged in cheating cited excessive workloads and an inability to keep up with assignments as important factors in their decisions to cheat.

In addition to rating the importance of such preselected factors, 426 respondents (11.0 percent of the admitted cheaters) offered their own justifications for cheating in response to an open-ended question on motivations for cheating. These responses confirm the importance of denial of responsibility and condemnation of condemners as neutralization techniques. They also support LaBeff et al.'s (1990) claim that appeal to higher loyalties is an important neutralization technique. . . .

. . . Denial of responsibility was the technique most frequently cited (216 responses, 61.0 percent of the total) in the 354 responses classified into one of Sykes and Matza's five categories of neutralization. The most common responses in this category were mind block, no understanding of material, a fear of failing, and unclear explanations of assignments. (Although it is possible that some instances of mind block and a fear of failing included in this summary would be more accurately classified as rationalization, the wording of all responses included here suggests that rationalization preceded the cheating incident. . . . Condemnation of condemners was the second most popular neutralization technique observed (99 responses, 28.0 percent) and included such explanations as pointless assignments, lack of respect for individual professors, unfair tests, parents' expectations, and unfair professors. Twenty-four respondents (6.8 percent) appealed to higher loyalties to explain their behavior. In particular, helping a friend and responding to peer pressures were influences some students could not ignore. Finally, fifteen students (4.2 percent) provided responses that clearly fit into the category of denial of injury. These students dismissed their cheating as harmless since it did not hurt anyone or they felt cheating did not matter in some cases (for example, where an assignment counted for a small percentage of the total course grade).

Detailed examination of selected student responses provides additional insight into the neutralization strategies they employ.

Denial of Responsibility

Denial of responsibility invokes the claim that the act was "due to forces outside of the individual and beyond his control such as unloving parents" (Sykes and Matza 1957, p. 667). For example, many students cite an unreasonable workload and the difficulty of keeping up as ample justification for cheating.

> Here at . . . , you must cheat to stay alive. There's so much work and the quality of materials from which to learn, books, professors, is so bad that there's no other choice.
>
> It's the only way to keep up.
>
> I couldn't do the work myself.

The following descriptions of student cheating confirm fear of failure is also an important form of denial of responsibility:

> . . . a take-home exam in a class I was failing.
>
> . . . was near failing.

Some justified their cheating by citing behavior of peers:

> Everyone has test files in fraternities, etc. If you don't, you're at a great disadvantage.
>
> When most of the class is cheating on a difficult exam and they will ruin the curve, it influences you to cheat so your grade won't be affected.

All of these responses contain the essence of denial of responsibility: the cheater has deflected blame to others or to a specific situational context.

Denial of Injury

. . . [D]enial of injury was identified as a neutralization technique employed by some respondents. A key element in denial of injury is whether one feels "anyone has clearly been hurt by (the) deviance." In invoking this defense, a cheater would argue "that his behavior does not really cause any great harm despite the fact that it runs counter to the law" (Sykes and Matza 1957, pp. 667–668). For example, a number of students argued that the assignment or test on which they cheated was so trivial that no one was really hurt by their cheating.

> These grades aren't worth much therefore my copying doesn't mean very much. I am ashamed, but I'd probably do it the same way again.
>
> If I extend the time on a take home it is because I feel everyone does and the teacher kind of expects it. No one gets hurt. . . .

The Denial of the Victim

. . . At least four students (0.1% of the self-admitted cheaters in this study) provided comments elsewhere on the survey instrument which involved denial of the victim. The common element in these responses was a victim deserving of the consequences of the cheating behavior and cheating was viewed as "a form of rightful retaliation or punishment" (Sykes and Matza 1957, p. 668).

This feeling was extreme in one case, as suggested by the following student who felt her cheating was justified by the

> realization that this school is a manifestation of the bureaucratic capitalist system that systematically keeps the lower classes

down, and that adhering to their rules was simply perpetuating the institution.

This "we" versus "they" mentality was raised by many students, but typically in comments about the policing of academic honesty rather than as justification for one's own cheating behavior. When used to justify cheating, the target was almost always an individual teacher rather than the institution and could be more accurately classified as a strategy of condemnation of condemners rather than denial of the victim.

The Condemnation of Condemners

Sykes and Matza describe the condemnation of condemners as an attempt to shift "the focus of attention from [one's] own deviant acts to the motives and behavior of those who disapprove of [the] violations. [B]y attacking others, the wrongfulness of [one's] own behavior is more easily repressed or lost to view" (1957, p. 668). The logic of this strategy for student cheaters focused on issues of favoritism and fairness. Students invoking this rationale describe "uncaring, unprofessional instructors with negative attitudes who were negligent in their behavior" (LaBeff et al. 1990, p. 195). For example:

> In one instance, nothing was done by a professor because the student was a hockey player.

> The TAs who graded essays were unduly harsh.

> It is known by students that certain professors are more lenient to certain types, e.g., blondes or hockey players.

> I would guess that 90% of the students here have seen athletes and/or fraternity members cheating on an exam or papers. If you turn in one of these culprits, and I have, the penalty is a five-minute lecture from a coach and/or administrator. All these add up to a "who cares, they'll never do anything to you anyway" attitude here about cheating.

Concerns about the larger society were an important issue for some students:

> When community frowns upon dishonesty, then people will change.

> If our leaders can commit heinous acts and then lie before Senate committees about their total ignorance and innocence, *then why can't I cheat a little?*

> In today's world you do anything to be above the competition.

In general, students found ready targets on which to blame their behavior and condemnation of the condemners was a popular neutralization strategy.

The Appeal to Higher Loyalties

The appeal to higher loyalties involves neutralizing "internal and external controls . . . by sacrificing the demands of the larger society for the demands of the smaller social groups to which the [offender] belongs. [D]eviation from certain norms may occur not because the norms are rejected but because other norms, held to be more pressing or involving a higher loyalty, are accorded precedence" (Sykes and Matza 1957, p. 669). For example, a difficult conflict for some students is balancing the desire to help a friend against the institution's rule on cheating. The student may not challenge the rules, but rather views the need to help a friend, fellow fraternity/sorority member, or roommate to be a greater obligation which justifies the cheating behavior.

Fraternities and sororities were singled out as a network where such behavior occurs with some frequency. For example, a female student at a small university in New England observed:

> There's a lot of cheating within the Greek system. Of all the cheating I've seen, it's often been men and women in fraternities

> & sororities who exchange information or cheat.

The appeal to higher loyalties was particularly evident in student reactions concerning the reporting of cheating violations. Although fourteen of the thirty-one schools participating in this research had explicit honor codes that generally require students to report cheating violations they observe, less than one-third (32.3 percent) indicated that they were likely to do so. When asked if they would report a friend, only four percent said they would and most students felt that they should not be expected to do so. Typically student comments included:

> Students should not be sitting in judgment of their own peers.
>
> The university is not a police state.

For some this decision was very practical:

> A lot of students, 50 percent, wouldn't because they know they will probably cheat at some point themselves.

For others, the decision would depend on the severity of the violation they observed and many would not report what they considered to be minor violations, even those explicitly covered by the school's honor code or policies on academic honesty. Explicit examination or test cheating was one of the few violations where students exhibited any consensus concerning the need to report violations. Yet even in this case many students felt other factors must be considered. For example, a senior at a woman's college in the Northeast commented:

> It would depend on the circumstances. If someone was hurt, *very likely*. If there was no single victim in the case, if the victim was [the] institution . . . , then *very unlikely*.

Additional evidence of the strength of the appeal to higher loyalties as a neutralization technique is found in the fact that almost one in five respondents (17.8 percent) reported that they had helped someone cheat on an examination or major test. The percentage who have helped others cheat on papers and other assignments is likely much higher. Twenty-six percent of those students who helped someone else cheat on a test reported that they had never cheated on a test themselves, adding support to the argument that peer pressure to help friends is quite strong.

Conclusions

From this research it is clear that college students use a variety of neutralization techniques to rationalize their cheating behavior, deflecting blame to others and/or the situational context, and the framework of Sykes and Matza (1957) seems well supported when student explanations of cheating behavior are analyzed. Unlike prior research (LaBeff et al. 1990), however, the present findings suggest that students employ all of the techniques described by Sykes and Matza, including denial of injury and denial of victim. Although there was very limited evidence of the use of denial of victim, denial of injury was not uncommon. Many students felt that some forms of cheating were victimless crimes, particularly on assignments that accounted for a small percentage of the total course grade. The present research does affirm LaBeff et al.'s finding that denial of responsibility and condemnation of condemners are the neutralization techniques most frequently utilized by college students. Appeal to higher loyalties is particularly evident in neutralizing institutional expectations that students report cheating violations they observe.

. . . This research ultimately involved 6,096 students at thirty-one geographically dispersed institutions ranging from small liberal arts colleges in the Northeast to nationally prominent research universities in the South and West. Fourteen of the thirty-one institutions have long-standing honor-code traditions. The code tradition at five of these schools dates to the late 1800s and all fourteen have codes that survived the student unrest of the 1960s. In such a context, the strength of the appeal to higher loyalties and the denial of responsibility as justifications for cheating is a very persuasive argument that neutralization techniques are salient to today's college student. More importantly, it may suggest fruitful areas of future discourse between faculty, administrators, and students on the question of academic honesty.

REFERENCES

Baird, John S. 1980, "Current Trends in College Cheating," *Psychology in Schools* 17:512–522.

Davis, Stephen F., Cathy A. Grover, Angela H. Becker, and Loretta N. McGregor. 1992. "Academic Dishonesty: Prevalence, Determinants, Techniques, and Punishments." *Teaching of Psychology.* In press.

Edwards, Paul. 1967. *The Encyclopedia of Philosophy,* no. 3, edited by Paul Edwards. New York: MacMillan Company and Free Press.

Eisenberger, Robert, and Dolores M. Shank. 1985. "Personal Work Ethic and Effort Training Affect Cheating." *Journal of Personality and Social Psychology* 49:520–528.

Haines, Valerie J., George Dickhoff, Emily LaBeff, and Robert Clark. 1986. "College Cheating: Immaturity, Lack of Commitment, and the Neutralizing Attitude." *Research in Higher Education* 25:342–354.

LaBeff, Emily E., Robert E. Clark, Valerie J. Haines and George M. Dickhoff. 1990. "Situational Ethics and College Student Cheating." *Sociological Inquiry* 60:190–198.

Michaels, James W., and Terance Miethe. 1989. "Applying Theories of Deviance to Academic Cheating." *Social Science Quarterly* 70:870–885.

Perry, Anthony R., Kevin M. Kane, Kevin J. Bernesser, and Paul T. Spicker. 1990. "Type A Behavior, Competitive Achievement-Striving, and Cheating among College Students." *Psychological Reports* 66:459–465.

Sykes, Gresham M., and David Matza. 1957. "Techniques of Neutralization: A Theory of Delinquency." *American Sociological Review* 22: 664–670.

Tittle, Charles, and Alan Rowe. 1973. "Moral Appeal, Sanction Threat, and Deviance: An Experimental Test." *Social Problems* 20:488–498.

Ward, David. 1986. "Self-Esteem and Dishonest Behavior Revisited." *Journal of Social Psychology* 123:709–713.

Ward, David, and Wendy L. Beck. 1990. "Gender and Dishonesty." *The Journal of Social Psychology* 130:333–339.

DEVELOPING YOUR OWN SNAPSHOTS *About Deviance*

1. *Writing topic:* Max Weber urged sociologists to attempt to be objective, even when their personal views were contradicted. Gun control is a controversial issue that has many proponents on both sides. In writing, state your own personal opinion—either for or against the restriction of firearms as a national policy. Then, in a short essay, defend the point of view that opposes your own.
2. *Research topic:* Every year the U.S. Department of Justice publishes the Uniform Crime Reports for the United States. In *Crime in the United States,* you will find a number of different statistics concerning the serious crimes reported to the F.B.I. by local

police departments. This book is easily available in libraries or from the U.S. Government Printing Office. Using *Crime in the United States* for a recent year, find monthly variations in murder and verify that murder rates peak during July, August, and December. Now do the same for property crimes like larceny and burglary. Do these offenses also peak during the relatively cold month of December? Why or why not? Explain how the social climate may have more influence than the weather on monthly variations in homicide. Do you think that the social climate has the same impact on property crimes?

3. *Research topic:* Based on public opinion surveys, we know that most Americans favor the death penalty. But we also know that support for capital punishment decreases if people see an alternative that protects society just as well. For example, in a 1994 survey of Massachusetts citizens, William J. Bowers found that 54 percent prefer life without parole over the death penalty. In a paper-and-pencil questionnaire, ask 20 students to indicate whether they support or oppose capital punishment. Also ask the supporters of the death penalty to indicate whether they would support or oppose it under the following conditions: (a) if life imprisonment with possible parole were the only alternative sentence available; (b) if life imprisonment without parole eligibility were the only alternative sentence available; (c) if "life without hope"—that is, life imprisonment without parole eligibility, pardon, or commutation of sentence—were the only alternative available; or (d) if life imprisonment without parole eligibility plus victim restitution were the only alternative sentence available. What do your results indicate about protection of society as a motivation for supporting the death penalty?
4. *Research topic:* With your instructor's assistance, commit an act of deviance to see how others respond to you. Select an act that is neither illegal nor unethical. Also, make sure that your deviant behavior will not permanently affect the way you are treated by others! Because it isn't always easy to think of a safe act of deviance, let me suggest one. Try marking your forehead with a meaningless symbol—for example, two black and green circles. Then walk on campus and observe the reactions (or lack of reactions). Do strangers and friends respond differently to you? Try the same experiment again, but this time walk on campus with two other students whose foreheads have been painted like yours. Do you notice a difference in the way you are treated?

What do you think people assume when they encounter three students wearing the same unknown symbol?

5. *Research topic:* Interview an individual who seems to be stigmatized because of appearance (someone considered fat, short, tall, unattractive, and so on). In your interview, try to determine at what age your respondent first remembers being considered different. Have your respondent indicate the specific ways in which he or she has been discriminated against—at work, in dating, and at school. Also try to discover how he or she manages the stigma (for example, denial or avoidance). Note: Please be careful not to approach a stigmatized person in a hurtful or insensitive way. You might want to place an ad in your college newspaper asking for volunteers to participate in your study who have been labeled as too short, too tall, or too fat. Or you might invite volunteers from among your classmates. It may even be possible to locate an organization to which stigmatized people belong—for example, Little People of America or National Association to Aid Fat Americans. In any case, it is important to use extreme sensitivity in locating a potential respondent.
6. *Writing topic:* Name a group in American society, other than fat people, whose members have been stigmatized. How do you think they would be treated in some other culture? Why?
7. *Writing topic:* Reinarman discusses what he calls the "social construction of drug scares." Consider another social problem that has recently been in the news and is widely believed to be dramatically on the rise—for example, abducted children, serial murder, or domestic homicide. Which groups, agencies, and political figures might benefit by exaggerating the prevalence of the problem you choose to examine? Going to appropriate books and articles, attempt to document its actual occurrence and growth.
8. *Research topic:* The photo essay for this section asks, "What's normal and natural?" One way to find out is to put yourself in the shoes of someone who is deviant. For example, walk around for one day as a fat person to see how other people treat you. With the help of a friend, "put on weight" by wearing large clothing and padding yourself in a realistic way. Then take written notes about any differences you detect in the reactions of others. Also notice any differences in how you feel about yourself and about the way you are treated.

CHAPTER 6

Social Inequality

RAGS TO RICHES: MYTH OR REALITY?

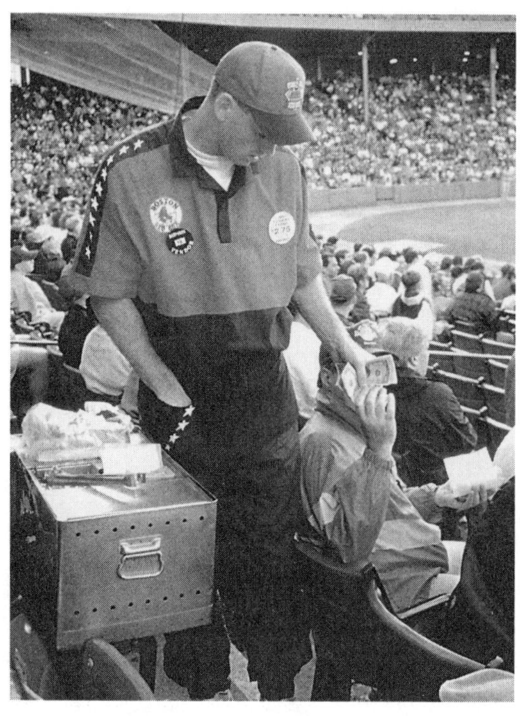

THE LOTTERY
JUNE

SNAPSHOT

The Economic Escalator

Americans on Their Way Down

The term *downward mobility* is being used to characterize the economic plight of an entire generation of middle-class Americans who are slipping and sliding their way down the socioeconomic ladder. Forget about the short-term effects of recession. According to political analyst Kevin Phillips, the culprit is an economic trend that began in the 1980s and will likely continue indefinitely.

The rich really have been getting much richer, apparently at the expense of poor and middle-income Americans who have seen their status deteriorate. Through at least the last decade, the biggest losers have been African Americans, Latinos, young men, female heads of households, farmers, and steelworkers; but almost everyone else has also suffered to some extent.

In a shift away from manufacturing toward services, we have been transformed into a postindustrial society. In 1959 production of goods represented some 60 percent of all American employment; but by 1985 this figure had dropped to only 26 percent. The overwhelming majority of Americans are now employed in the service sector of the economy. During this transitional period new jobs were created, but in the main these were poorly paid and provided few opportunities for upward mobility. Thus, large numbers of Americans were forced to take a substantial drop in pay and, therefore, in their way of life.

According to Phillips, the widening gap between rich and poor may have been encouraged by national economic policies of the 1980s—a period that represented a strong reversal of almost four decades of downward income redistribution. At the upper end of our class system, the after-tax proportion of income for the wealthiest 1 percent of Americans climbed from 7 percent in 1977 to 11 percent in 1990. Even when adjusted for inflation, the number of millionaires doubled between the late seventies and the late eighties, resulting in a record one million households reporting a net worth of at least $1 million.

For families on lower rungs of the socioeconomic ladder, however, living standards have deteriorated. Since 1977, the average after-tax family income of the bottom 10 percent of Americans has declined 10.5 percent in current dollars. According to a recent study by Professor Timothy Smeeding, the percentage of U.S. children living in poverty rose from less than 15 percent in 1978 to 20 percent today. Compared with seven other industrial countries (Sweden, West Germany,

Australia, Canada, Britain, France, and the Netherlands), the United States has the dubious distinction of being the most unequal.

Growing income inequality has already been linked with a worsening of our most stubborn and perplexing social ailments. Professor Henry Miller of the University of California notes that homelessness is a growing problem in our major cities—a problem that is not easily solved.

He suggests that we were previously able as a society to assimilate many of the homeless into the military or industry. In today's economy, however, those who lack education or marketable skills remain permanently unemployed or take dead-end jobs. What is more, in the process of converting inexpensive rooming houses into high-priced condominiums for the affluent, the gentrification of urban areas during the 1980s forced even more of the poverty-stricken onto the streets.

According to *American Demographics,* young adults have been hit particularly hard by downward mobility. As a result, they are taking longer to finish school, living longer with their parents or other relatives, and delaying their plans to marry. Young married couples today are less likely to own their own homes. Quite a few return to live with their parents.

Comparing their worsening economic circumstances with those of their parents, millions of young people—members of what the media have called Generation X—have begun to question the validity of the American Dream and are less optimistic about the future. Called "selfish," "passive," and "ultraconservative" by those who remember the liberal activism of the prosperous 1960s, many young adults are merely trying to maintain or improve their standard of living. In the face of an erosion in their incomes, they frequently regard tax increases as a burden they cannot afford.

American business leaders are beginning to understand that America's economic problems have a long-term basis in reality. The Business Council, whose members consist of 100 executives from America's largest companies, suggested recently that the current recession will be succeeded by a prolonged period of lean economic times. The public seems to agree: A recent *Business Week* survey determined that 64 percent of Americans predict that the economy of the United States will be dominated by foreign companies within 10 years.

The continuing trends away from manufacturing and toward increasing inequality between rich and poor are, of course, far from inevitable. But a reversal would necessitate a major commitment on the part of political leaders, business, and members of the public who recognize the urgency of finding a solution. The urban underclass is now at least four times larger than it was during the turbulent 1960s, when our major cities were burning. Disturbances have already begun to erupt in some large cities. Some predict that there will be riots of earthshaking proportions within two to three years in at least four major cities: New York, Chicago, Los Angeles, and Miami. At that point, there will probably be widespread support for making essential changes in our economy. The real question is one of timing: Will we be too late?

SNAPSHOT

Images of Aging

Are the Elderly Too Powerful?

Several years ago 80-year-old Clara Peller achieved overnight fame for her line in a Wendy's ad: "Where's the beef?" Peller's comic portrayal of a cantankerous old lady reflects a familiar stereotype: Older people are seen as entering a second childhood in which they become bossy, irritable, feeble, and possibly weakened in intellect, making unreasonable demands on others. With low incomes and high health costs, elderly consumers are seen as especially concerned about getting good value for their money.

Studies of age stereotyping conducted over the past 50 years show that this image of aging has been widely accepted. Gerontologists' research among graduate students of psychology in the 1950s showed that most believed that old people are set in their ways, walk slowly, have poor coordination, are bossy, and like to doze. These results have been duplicated in more recent research. A 1988 study by William C. Levin reported in *Research on Aging* showed that Americans characterize older people as less intelligent, competent, healthy, active, creative, attractive, reliable, energetic, flexible, educated, wealthy, and socially involved than younger people.

Most of my students routinely overestimate the percentage of the elderly who live below the poverty line or in nursing homes. For example, the average estimate was that 37 percent of all Americans 65 years or older are now residing in a nursing home, while the actual figure is only 4 percent.

Surprisingly, these same students also overestimated the percentage of senators, judges, and former presidents who were at least 65, and the proportion of billionaires, CEOs of major corporations, and corporate stockholders who are elderly. The same students who were unrealistic about poverty and dependence exaggerated the wealth and power of the elderly: Fewer than 5 percent of major American corporations are actually headed by a CEO who is 65 or older, but the average estimated by the students was 43 percent. In this latter stereotype, older people are often seen as powerful and rich—perhaps too powerful and rich for their own good.

Traditionally, older people were blamed for their own plight; their poverty and dependence were regarded as an inevitable part of the life cycle. In the new view, however, the aged are seen as having disproportionate influence in the government, as having garnered too large a share of the country's economic resources, and as responsible for a national debt of unprecedented proportions and for health care costs that seem to be out of control.

The former view long justified encouraging the elderly to disengage from work despite evidence that older workers are as productive as their younger counterparts. The new stereotype is potentially even more dangerous. It justifies organizing against the interests of the elderly, cutting the government expenditures that benefit them, perhaps even eliminating social security, and reducing efforts to keep the aged alive. In this view, since the elderly have so much wealth and political clout, they do not need the help of younger Americans.

Some have already begun to exploit the new stereotype. In politics, the interests of the elderly and the young have been pitted against one another as though they were in essential conflict. This is often a substitute for the real battle that is so carefully avoided—that of the poor and the middle class against the rich. Thus, Americans for Generational Equity (AGE) argues that the status of the elderly has greatly improved at the expense of the well-being of the young. The leaders of AGE cite statistics showing high rates of poverty among children, a decline in real income among baby boomers, and a massive federal debt. AGE blames the elderly for consuming too much of the national budget and enjoying increases in social security benefits, while inflation-adjusted wages for the rest of the population have declined.

Even more disturbing is the extent to which this perception may be influencing medical personnel who make life-and-death decisions. Studies have shown that emergency room personnel tend to expend greater effort resuscitating younger patients. In a 1984 television interview, Colorado's former governor Richard Lamm said that the elderly "have a duty to die" because of the financial cost of health care needed to prolong the lives of the elderly. According to Lamm, it might cost too much to keep them alive.

Now the Clara Peller image is of someone who has found the beef and refuses to share it with her grandchildren. Older Americans deserve a better commercial.

SNAPSHOT

The Functions of Immigrant Bashing

When Hospitality Turns Hostile

Voices of xenophobia and racism once again reverberate throughout German society, and concerned observers want to know why. East Germany has struggled to make the transition from communism to a free-market economy; but its high unemployment and inefficient use of resources have inspired violent attacks on refugees and workers from Eastern European and third world countries. During 1991 alone there were more than 1500 attacks against foreigners. In September 1991, for example, 600 right-wing German youths firebombed a home for foreigners and then attacked 200 Vietnamese and Mozambicans in the streets of Hoyerswerde.

Even West Germany has not been totally immune from the effects of economic tension, although episodes of violence have been far less severe and less frequent. In an apparent act of racially inspired arson, a 25-year-old Ghanaian was burned to death and his two Nigerian roommates seriously injured in a fire that swept through a hotel for foreigners seeking asylum in the city of Saarlouis.

Much of the violence in Germany has been perpetrated by a relatively small number of extremists—an estimated 5,000 hard-core neo-Nazis and another 30,000 racist skinheads. In East Berlin a chapter of neo-Nazis recruited only a few hundred unemployed and alienated young men who gave voice to racism and xenophobia as a way of "fighting back."

Yet the degree of resentment in Germany can be easily underestimated. Based on the results of a recent national poll, up to 40 percent of all German citizens can be characterized as silent sympathizers. They express at least some sympathy for the issues—"Germany for Germans," "racial purity," and "foreigners out"—espoused by right-wing extremists. Moreover, 15 percent of Germany's youths say they now consider Adolf Hitler to be a great man. In the underground computer game "Concentration Camp Manager," xenophobia takes a macabre twist. German high school students who play it are challenged by the task of killing as many Turks with as little gas as possible.

We must be careful not to view anti-immigrant sentiment as an exclusively German problem. In reality, violence against foreigners has recently increased in countries around the world, mainly in response to a burgeoning presence of immigrant workers. Across the globe, millions are leaving their homelands for a better life, and they do not always receive a friendly welcome from the citizens of their host country.

Even in China, where foreigners have long enjoyed deferential treatment, there are signs that resentment against the 1,500 African students who study there is on the rise. Formerly minor incidents have become major points of conflict. For example, hearing that African male students had taken Chinese women to a Christmas Eve dance, thousands of Chinese demonstrators amassed in the streets of Nanjing, shouting racial insults like "Beat the blacks."

In France, mounting resentment against 2 million Muslim Arab immigrants has provoked the government to speed up the process of integrating newcomers into French society and to tighten controls against illegal immigration. In March 1990 three men of North African origin were brutally murdered in separate racially motivated attacks. Public opinion pollsters report that 76 percent of all French citizens now believe there are too many Arabs in their country.

In Italy, a traditional haven for newcomers, hospitality has similarly turned cold. Hardly a week passes without some episode of conflict between immigrants and Italians. In March 1990, for example, a large gang of Florentine youths battered their way into an immigrant dormitory and beat up immigrant workers. In May 1991 a crowd of Italians cheered as the police arrested a group of Albanians who were demonstrating in the city of Asti to protest the living conditions in their refugee camp. Seventy-five percent of all Italians now favor closing the borders to all new immigration.

The United States has always been a nation of immigrants. In 1830 the largest number of our newcomers were Irish; in 1890 they were German. In 1900 they were Italian; after that they were Canadian. During the 1980s four out of five immigrants came from Asia, Latin America, and the Caribbean. By 1990 the newcomers were coming in great numbers from Mexico, the Philippines, Vietnam, China, Taiwan, South Korea, and India. Smaller numbers also entered from the Dominican Republic, El Salvador, Jamaica, and Iran.

The foreign-born population of the United States is currently more than 14 million, by far the largest in the world. Moreover, we are presently in the midst of possibly the largest wave of immigration in U.S. history. Between 1981 and 1990, more than 7 million newcomers pulled up their roots for political as well as economic reasons and left their homelands to begin new lives in the United States. There will be more newcomers in America in the 1990s than in any previous decade.

In America, as is true elsewhere, the welcome wagon has not always been out for our newcomers, despite their enormous numbers. During the 1982 recession, for example, many Americans held Japanese car manufacturers responsible for massive layoffs in our automobile industry. A 27-year-old Chinese American, Vincent Chin, was spending his Saturday night drinking in a bar located in one of Detroit's working-class neighborhoods. Shouting "It's because of you we're out of work," a Chrysler autoworker and his stepson bludgeoned Chin to death with a baseball bat. From their point of view, *any* Asian was the enemy.

Violence against newcomers also increased during the recession of the early 1990s. In central New Jersey, gangs of white men drove through local areas populated by Asian Indians, smashing their automobile windshields and shouting anti-Indian slurs. On New Year's Day, 1991, several Indians were assaulted in a diner in the town of Iselin. In May 1991 a young Indian man was hospitalized after being attacked behind a local convenience store.

In May 1990 three Vietnamese men were assaulted on the streets of Brooklyn, New York. Shouting racial insults, the attackers repeatedly hit one of the victims on his head with a claw hammer. He was hospitalized with a fractured skull.

To some extent, violence directed against newcomers may reflect an almost constant mixture of such irrational factors as racism, ethnocentrism, and xenophobia. Regardless of the state of the economy at any given point in history, certain members of society—especially those who can trace their own ancestry in a country back several generations—are bound to be offended by, and seek to remove, the strange customs, rituals, and appearance of "inferior outsiders."

At the same time, however, anti-immigrant violence also may have a more practical political and economic basis. First, during periods of economic retrenchment, it sends a powerful message to foreigners from those who seek to reduce competition for jobs. Anti-immigrant violence says to everyone and anyone who might consider emigrating for the sake of a better standard of living, "Your kind is not welcome in *our* country. Don't bother to come. If you do, the same thing will happen to *you*." And to newcomers, it says loud and clear, "Go back where you came from . . . or else."

As a form of collective scapegoating, violence aimed at newcomers serves the rulers of a nation as well. Sociologist Lewis Coser once referred to this phenomenon as a "safety valve." He suggested that when times are bad, hostility that might otherwise be directed at the leaders of a society—its president, prime minister, senators, king, and so on—is instead aimed at its marginal members, those located along the bottom rungs of the socioeconomic ladder. Thus, by focusing blame on the "outsiders," the rulers of a society are able to preserve their positions of power, even if their policies and programs are in fact responsible for pervasive economic hardships. According to Jorge Bustamante, the president of El Colegio de la Frontera Norte in Tijuana, Mexico, it invariably becomes politically correct to capitalize on anti-immigrant sentiments whenever the U.S. unemployment rate rises above politically acceptable levels. Politicians then conveniently forget about the role that newcomers play in providing a cheap source of labor that helps keep American industry competitive. They also forget that growing numbers of immigrants spur investments, help revitalize decaying communities, and pay taxes. When Americans are out of work, we can expect to hear our public officials call for repatriating recent arrivals, establishing more stringent criteria for accepting refugees, and closing the borders with Mexico. This is when immigrants are routinely blamed for Americans being out of work, for trafficking in drugs, for increasing the cost of social services, and for committing violent crime. In 1994, as unemployment rates hovered at 8.5 percent statewide, Californians passed Proposition 187 in an effort to reduce the cost of providing social services and education to the state's immigrant population.

So what else is new? If there are hard times in America, it must be time to pick on the newcomers!

SNAPSHOT Race, IQ, and Hysterectomies

Scientists Are Human Beings Too

A study published recently in *The American Journal of Public Health* suggests that a doctor's age and regional location contribute to his or her odds of doing surgery on women. Specifically, it reports that older gynecologists and doctors living in the South are particularly likely to perform hysterectomies. This may be important information because critics argue that between 25 and 50 percent of the hundreds of thousands of hysterectomies done every year may be unnecessary, no matter who performs the operation.

If the decision to do surgery were based strictly on medical evidence, we would expect age and region to have no effect on hysterectomy rates. This is not the case. In reality, doctors' medical decisions seem to be based in part on where they grew up, what their peers believe to be correct, and what their culture tells them is appropriate. Fad and fashion are as much a part of science as they are of dress design or popular music. What is stylish in one generation or area of the country may be out of style in another. Objectivity is a scientific goal, but it is not always a reality.

We should keep this in mind when evaluating the heated public debate about race and IQ that has emerged (or reemerged) with the recent publication of *The Bell Curve* by Charles Murray and the late Richard J. Herrnstein. Behavioral scientists once again inform us that the average black American has a lower IQ than the average white American and that this IQ gap is hereditary.

This is nothing new. In 1969 Arthur Jenson, an educational psychologist, hypothesized that "genetic factors are strongly implicated in the average Negro–White intelligence difference." A survey of the members of the American Psychological Association showed at the time that older psychologists and psychologists living in the South were especially likely to agree with Jenson's thesis.

If agreement with the genetic racial argument were based strictly on scientific evidence, we would expect age and region to have no effect on the conclusions that psychologists draw regarding race and IQ. This is not the case. Instead, psychologists' judgments seem to be based in part on where they grew up, what their peers believe to be correct, and what their culture tells them is appropriate. Fad and fashion apparently are a part of psychology as well as of dress design and gynecology.

The argument that minority members are genetically inferior is by no means restricted to African Americans. During the early part of this century psychologists found that immigrants coming from Poland, Russia, Greece, Turkey, and Italy tended to score lower on intelligence tests than immigrants from northwestern Europe. In support of revising immigration and naturalization laws, psychologists argued in 1923 that newcomers from southern and eastern Europe were polluting the stream of intelligence in America. In 1924, based on the testimony of these "objective psychologists," the

United States imposed immigration quotas aimed at reducing the flow of "undesirables."

Given the present stage of our knowledge about human behavior, it makes little sense to speculate about racial differences in IQ. First we must work to wipe out the really important differences that divide us as a people—lack of opportunity, low self-esteem, hopelessness, and despair. We must fight against racism and poverty. Only when these vital differences have been held constant will any possible racial differences in intelligence be made clear. In a society where equality of opportunity is a reality, we won't need scientists to justify our selfishness.

SEEING SOCIAL INEQUALITY THROUGH SNAPSHOTS AND PORTRAITS

"Can you spare some change for a cup of coffee, mister?" I never know what to do when I am confronted by a panhandler asking for a handout, especially if he looks like he's been drinking. If I give him what he wants, I might only be supplying him with his next drink of booze and his next hangover. But if I don't give him anything, I feel guilty. Who knows, maybe he hasn't eaten in three days, and my small contribution will keep him going until the next handout comes along.

Homeless people in the streets of our major cities represent an extreme example of *social inequality*—the unequal distribution of wealth, power, and prestige among the members of society. At the other end of that distribution are entertainers and professional athletes who earn millions of dollars a year and enjoy tremendous popularity. Most of us fall in between the panhandler and the famous ballplayer.

We clearly are not a classless society. In fact, social inequality in America is highly structured and is passed from one generation to another. This characteristic of society is known as *social stratification.* In fact, almost all sociologists agree that social inequality is stratified or layered. Historically, they have debated two important issues about stratification. First, what is the basis on which society has been structured into social classes? Second, exactly what does that stratification system look like?

The 19th-century theorist Karl Marx tended to think of stratification in economic terms alone. He believed the development of social classes to be primarily determined by the economic forces in society. Power and prestige also existed, but only as a result of economic position.

For Marx, two distinct and unequal classes emerge to determine the direction of a capitalist economy: the *bourgeoisie,* those who own property and the means of production, and the *proletariat,* those who work the means of production. Marx argued that members of the bourgeoisie, given their ownership position in the economy, are able to control their own lives. By contrast, members of the proletariat, because they merely sell their labor in order to survive, are generally at the mercy of the bourgeoisie. They must go where the work is, live within a careful budget, and hope they are not laid off or fired.

According to Marx, capitalism produces the seeds of its own destruction. Over time, the exploitation of the proletariat inevitably grows so great that workers become conscious of their common enemy and rise up to overthrow the capitalist system. After a revolution of the proletariat, capitalism is replaced with a utopian state of communism, a classless society in which the proletariat both own and work the means of production and all property. Social stratification then dissolves into history.

The German sociologist Max Weber also recognized the importance of economic forces in generating social classes. Unlike Marx, however, Weber also recognized that social class is not exclusively a result of an individual's role in economic production—that is, either working or owning the machinery of production. Weber wrote that individuals can be located in a system of stratification based not only on their possession of material goods or *wealth* but also on their social honor or *prestige* in a community and their ability to make decisions affecting the lives of others, or *power.*

Weber's conception of stratification was important in emphasizing that any of the three characteristics of social class—wealth, prestige, or power—can help determine the others. Thus, in June 1995 a young American pilot from Spokane, Washington, was downed by the Bosnian Serbs and spent six grueling days behind enemy lines before being rescued by helicopter. Widely hailed as a hero, Captain Scott O'Grady was honored with parades, television interviews, and newspaper profiles. This national prestige brought opportunities to increase his wealth (for example, lectures, popular articles, and public appearances). As in the case illustrated by Captain O'Grady, social honor has been known to precede and contribute to an individual's ability to acquire both power and wealth.

Weber's view also allows the possibility that more than two important social classes can emerge. At the upper end of the rankings are wealthy individuals who inherit most of their money; at the other end are severely impoverished people. In between are numerous individuals who are middle-class with respect to income, prestige, and power.

Actually, sociologists have been able to identify a number of different social classes whose members share similar occupational positions, opportunities, attitudes, and lifestyles. In a widely accepted classification system, sociologists have categorized Americans into an upper class containing the wealthiest and most powerful people in the country; an upper-middle class made up of the families of business executives and professionals who have high income; a lower-middle class consisting of average-income Americans; a working class containing primarily blue-collar workers; and a lower class made up of both the working poor and the "disreputable poor."

Life chances is Max Weber's term referring to an individual's probability of securing the "good things of life." Sociologists are well aware that an individual's life chances definitely vary by social class. Thus, regardless of their intelligence and steadfastness, people who are born into a low social class will likely benefit less from society's opportunities than people born into a higher social class. Members of lower classes are less likely to vote, obtain favors from politicians, go to college, receive adequate public services, be in good physical and mental health, have decent working conditions, or feel they have control over their everyday lives. They are more likely to give birth out of wedlock, grow up in single-parent families, be arrested and imprisoned after committing a crime, and die at an early age. Many observers have suggested that the gap between rich and poor has widened over the last decade or so. Clearly, there are now more homeless people on the streets of our major cities and more middle-class families whose members have skidded in terms of social class. In "The Economic Escalator" we found that intergenerational mobility seems increasingly to be heading downward. As a result, millions of young people have begun to question the validity of the American Dream. Young adults have been particularly hard hit. As a result, they are staying in school longer, delaying their marriage plans, and moving back in with their parents.

An individual's life chances also vary by gender, race, and age. African Americans continue to be disproportionately represented in poverty. Affirmative action legislation may have helped create a large and viable black middle class, but it has hardly touched the lives of the members of the black underclass who continue to live in chronic poverty.

How do we explain the fact that poverty is overrepresented among African Americans? Do we blame racism? Job loss? Family structure? In "Race, IQ, and Hysterectomies," I examined the controversial hypothesis that racial groups differ with respect to intelligence. Rather than enter the debate, however, I examined the debaters, the psychologists who express an opinion that blacks are, on average, genetically inferior to whites in terms of intelligence. If the link between race and IQ were objective science, psychologists' age and region would have no effect on their opinions about this controversy. But scientists are human beings, too. They are influenced by where they grow up, what their parents have told them is right and wrong, and what their friends believe.

It doesn't take much intelligence to know that in our postindustrial society we lack the jobs that could propel large numbers of young black males out of the underclass. Jobs that exist tend to pay little, lead nowhere, or be located so far away from concentrations of black Americans as to be inaccessible.

Racial discrimination also continues to affect the life chances of black Americans. Diana Pearce's study, "Gatekeepers and Homeseekers: Institutional Patterns in Racial Steering," suggests that real estate agents play an active role in perpetuating racial segregation by their steering of black homeseekers away from white neighborhoods.

American women continue to earn less than their male counterparts. Moreover, when both husband and wife hold full-time jobs, it is usually the working woman who is expected to do the household chores and childrearing as well. She continues to be the main source of advice and guidance for their children and the one who is held responsible for cleaning and cooking. Perhaps this fact of life helps explain the American female's disadvantage on the job: Because of the extra burden placed on her shoulders, the working woman is often unable to make the same commitment to her career that her husband can.

Just as African Americans are influenced by continuing discrimination, so women's life chances are affected by structural conditions that serve to maintain gender inequality. As shown by Mindy Stombler and Patricia Yancey Martin in "Fraternity Little Sister Organizations," gender discrimination occurs in places where you might least expect it to occur—such as in higher education.

Stombler and Martin conclude that fraternity little sister organizations provide an organized outlet for a type of gender relations that sustains the power of men over women.

In the early 1980s we were in the grip of a recession, and older Americans suffered more than their share of economic hardship. Some were eating dogfood in order to survive. Perhaps fewer elders are now in critical economic condition, but their image continues to give them problems. In "Images of Aging" I suggested that the old stereotype that all older people are poor, sickly, and incompetent has been joined by a new stereotype that they are *also* powerful and wealthy—perhaps too much so for their own good. The new view may turn out to be particularly dangerous by inspiring conflict between the generations for increasingly scarce economic resources. Indeed, there already exist political pressure organizations designed to minimize the influence of older people in the area of social security and health care. Americans for Generational Equity represents the interests of young people, and the American Association of Boomers represents the interests of middle-aged Americans.

The United States is in the midst of a possibly unprecedented period of immigration, and not everyone is delighted. In "The Functions of Immigrant Bashing" I discussed the violence perpetrated against newcomers, not only in the United States but around the world, as increasing numbers of frustrated individuals look for someone to blame for their declining economic situation. Using the framework laid out by sociologist Lewis Coser in his modern classic, *The Functions of Social Conflict,* I also raised the possibility that immigrant bashing helps protect the leaders of a society from the unmitigated hostility of its citizens.

Some sociologists believe that social inequality is functional and even necessary to the operation of a society. In an early article, Kingley Davis and Wilbert Moore argued in 1945 that at least some degree of social stratification is necessary as a means for rewarding the really important positions in a society. Without an adequate system of unequal rewards, the most capable persons would not be placed into society's most important occupational roles—those requiring talent and training. In his highly critical response to Davis and Moore, sociologist Melvin Tumin later wrote that institutionalized social inequality was also dysfunctional for society. In other words, stratification has some negative consequences that were ignored by Davis and Moore. He argued, in particular, that inequality limits the development of talent in a society and actually serves the interests of only the power elite whose members are eager to maintain their advantaged positions in society.

Sociologist Herbert J. Gans takes a modified version of the functional position when he argues in "Positive Functions of the Undeserving Poor: Uses of the Underclass in America" that the presence of poverty has negative consequences for both the poor and society in general. But Gans also recognizes that the image of the undeserving poor has certain benefits for Americans who aren't impoverished. For example, by being thought of as undeserving, poor people can be blamed for almost any problem, whether crime, violence, or urban decay. The idea of the undeserving poor also creates many jobs for middle-class Americans who make careers out of controlling, guarding, rehabilitating, or caring for poor people. According to Gans, we must first recognize the positive functions of the underclass before we can effectively eliminate it.

PORTRAIT

Positive Functions of the Undeserving Poor: Uses of the Underclass in America

Herbert J. Gans

I. Introduction

. . . Poverty has many negative functions (or dysfunctions), most for the poor themselves, but also for the nonpoor. Among those of most concern to both populations, perhaps the major one is that a small but visible proportion of poor people is involved in activities which threaten their physical safety, for example street crime, or which deviate from important norms claimed to be "mainstream," such as failing to work, bearing children in adolescence and out of wedlock, and being "dependent" on welfare. In times of high unemployment, illegal and even legal immigrants are added to this list for endangering the job opportunities of native-born Americans.

Furthermore, many better-off Americans believe that the number of poor people who behave in these ways is far larger than it actually is. More important, many think that poor people act as they do because of moral shortcomings that express themselves in lawlessness or in the rejection of mainstream norms. Like many other sociologists, however, I argue that the behavior patterns which concern the more fortunate classes are *poverty-related*, because they are, and have historically been, associated with poverty. After all, mugging is only practiced by the poor. They are in fact caused by poverty, although a variety of other causes must also be at work since most poor people

From *Politics and Society, 22.* Copyright 1994 by Herbert J. Gans. Reprinted by permission of Herbert J. Gans. The author is the Robert S Lynd Professor of Sociology, Columbia University, and author, most recently, of *The War Against the Poor: The Underclass and Antipoverty Policy* (Basic Books, 1995).

are not involved in any of these activities, including mugging.

Because their criminal or disapproved behavior is ascribed to moral shortcomings, the poor people who resort to it are often classified as unworthy or *undeserving*. For example, even though the failure of poor young men (or women) to work may be the effect of a lack of jobs, they are frequently accused of laziness, and then judged undeserving. Likewise, even though poor young mothers may decide not to marry the fathers of their children, because they, being jobless, cannot support them, the women are still accused of violating conventional familial norms, and also judged undeserving. Moreover, once judged to be undeserving, poor people are then no longer thought to be deserving of public aid that is financially sufficient and secure enough to help them escape poverty.

Judgments of the poor as undeserving are not based on evidence, but derive from a stereotype, even if, like most others, it is a stereotype with a "kernel of truth" (e.g., the monopolization of street crime by the poor). . . .

One reason, if not the only one, for the exaggeration and the stereotyping, and for the continued attractiveness of the concept of the undeserving poor itself, is that undeservingness has a number of *positive* functions for the better-off population. Some of these functions, or uses, are positive for everyone who is not poor, but most are positive only for some people, interest groups, and institutions, ranging from moderate income to wealthy ones. Needless to say, that undeservingness has uses for some people does not justify it; the existence of functions just helps to explain why it persists.

My notion of function, or empirically observable adaptive consequence, is adapted from the classic conceptual scheme of Robert K. Merton.[1] My analysis will concentrate on those positive functions which Merton conceptualized as *latent*, which are unrecognized and/or unintended, but with the proviso that the functions which are identified as latent would probably not be abolished once they were widely recognized. Positive functions are, after all, also benefits, and people are not necessarily ready to give up benefits, including unintended ones, even if they become aware of them.[2]

The rest of this article deals only with functions of the poor labeled undeserving. . . .

II. Functions of the Undeserving Poor[3]

I will discuss five sets of positive functions: microsocial, economic, normative-cultural, political, and macrosocial, which I divide into 13 specific functions, although the sets are arbitrarily chosen and interrelated, and I could add many more functions. . . .

Two Microsocial Functions

1. Risk Reduction. Perhaps the primary use of the idea of the undeserving poor, primary because it takes place at the microsocial scale of everyday life, is that it distances the labeled from those who label them. By stigmatizing people as undeserving, labelers protect themselves from the responsibility of having to associate with them, or even to treat them like moral equals, which reduces the risk of being hurt or angered by them. Risk reduction is a way of dealing with actual or imagined threats to physical safety, for example from people who might be muggers, or cultural threats attributed to poor youngsters or normative ones imagined to come from welfare recipients. All pejorative labels and stereotypes serve this function, which may help to explain why there are so many such labels.

2. Scapegoating and Displacement. By being thought undeserving, the stigmatized poor can be blamed for virtually any shortcoming of everyday life which can be credibly ascribed to them—violations of the laws of logic or social causation notwithstanding. Faulting the undeserving poor can also support the desire for revenge and punishment. In a society in which punishment is reserved for legislative, judicial, and penal institutions, *feelings* of revenge and punitiveness toward the undeserving poor supply at least some emotional satisfaction.

Since labeling poor people undeserving opens the door for nearly unlimited scapegoating, the labeled are also available to serve what I call the displacement function. Being too weak to object, the stigmatized poor can be accused of having caused social problems which they did not actually cause and can serve as cathartic objects on which better-off people can unload their own problems, as well as those of the economy, the polity, or of any other institution, for the shortcomings of which the poor can be blamed.

Whether societywide changes in the work ethic are displaced onto "shiftlessness," or economic stagnation onto "welfare dependency," the poor can be declared undeserving for what ails the more affluent. This may also help to explain why the national concern with poor Black unmarried mothers, although usually ascribed to the data presented in the 1965 Moynihan Report, did not gather steam until the beginning of the decline of the economy in the mid-1970s. Similarly, the furor about poor "babies having babies" waited for the awareness of rising adolescent sexual activity among the better-off classes in the 1980s—at which point rates of adolescent pregnancy among the poor had already declined. But when the country became ambivalent about the desirability of abortions, the issue was displaced on the poor by making it almost impossible for them to obtain abortions. . . .

Three Economic Functions

3. Economic Banishment and the Reserve Army of Labor. People who have successfully been labeled as undeserving can be banished from the formal labor market. If young people are designated "school dropouts," for example, they can also be thought to lack the needed work habits, such as proper adherence to the work ethic, and may not be offered jobs to begin with. Often, they are effectively banished from the labor market before entering it because employers imagine them to be poor workers simply because they are young, male, and Black.[4] Many ex-convicts are declared unemployable in similar fashion, and some become recidivists because they have no other choice but to go back to their criminal occupations.

Banishing the undeserving also makes room for immigrant workers, who may work for lower wages, are more deferential, and are more easily exploitable by being threatened with deportation. In addition, banishment helps to reduce the official jobless rate, a sometimes useful political function, especially if the banished drop so completely out of the labor force that they are not even available to be counted as "discouraged workers."

The economic banishment function is in many ways a replacement for the old reserve army of labor function, which played itself out when the undeserving poor could be hired as strikebreakers, as defense workers in the case of sudden wartime economic mobilization, as "hypothetical workers," who by their very presence could be used to depress the wages of other workers, or to put pressure on the unions not to make wage and other demands. Today, however, with a plentiful supply of immigrants, as well as of a constantly growing number of banished workers who are becoming surplus labor, a reserve army is less rarely needed—and when needed, can be recruited from sources other than the undeserving poor.[5]

Welfare recipients may, however, turn out to continue to be a part of the reserve army. Currently, they are encouraged to stay out of the labor market by remaining eligible for the Medicaid benefits they need for their children only if they remain on welfare.[6] Should the Clinton administration welfare reform program become reality, however, welfare recipients, who will be required to work for the minimum wage or less, could exert pressure on the wages of the employed, thus bringing them right back into the reserve army.

4. *Supplying Illegal Goods*. The undeserving poor who are banished from other jobs remain eligible for work in the manufacture and sale of illegal goods, including drugs. Although it is estimated that 80 percent of all illegal drugs are sold to Whites who are not poor, the sellers are often people banished from the formal labor market.[7] Other suppliers of illegal goods include the illegal immigrants, considered undeserving in many American communities, who work for garment industry sweatshops manufacturing clothing under illegal conditions.

5. *Job Creation*. Perhaps the most important economic function of the undeserving poor today is that their mere presence creates jobs for the better-off population, including professional ones. Since the undeserving poor are thought to be dangerous or improperly socialized, their behavior either has to be modified so that they act in socially approved ways, or they have to be isolated from the undeserving sectors of society. The larger the number of people who are declared undeserving, the larger also the number of people needed to modify and isolate as well as control, guard, and care for them. Among these are the social workers, teachers, trainers, mentors, psychiatrists, doctors and their support staffs in juvenile training centers, "special" schools, drug treatment centers, and penal behavior modification institutions, as well as the police, prosecutors, defense attorneys, judges, court officers, probation personnel and others who constitute the criminal courts, and the guards and others who run the prisons.

Jobs created by the presence of undeserving poor also include the massive bureaucracy of professionals, investigators, and clerks who administer welfare. Other jobs go to the officials who seek out poor fathers for child support monies they may or may not have, as well as the welfare office personnel needed to take recipients in violation of welfare rules off the rolls, and those needed to put them back on the rolls when they reapply. In fact, one can argue that some of the rules for supervising, controlling, and punishing the undeserving poor are more effective at performing the latent function of creating clerical and professional jobs for the better-off population than the manifest function of achieving their official goals. . . .

Three Normative Functions

6. *Moral Legitimation*. Undeservingness justifies the category of deservingness and thus supplies moral and political legitimacy, almost by definition, to the institutions and social structures that include the deserving and exclude the undeserving.[8] Of these structures, the most important is undoubtedly the class hierarchy, for the existence of an undeserving class or stratum legitimates the deserving classes, if not necessarily all of their class-related behavior.[9] The alleged immorality of the undeserving also gives a moral flavor to, and justification for, the class hierarchy, which may help to explain why upward mobility itself is so praiseworthy.[10]

7. *Norm Reinforcement*. By violating, or being imagined as violating a number of mainstream behavioral patterns and values, the undeserving poor help to reaffirm and reinforce the virtues of these patterns—and to do so visibly, since the violations by the undeserving are highly publicized. As Emile Durkheim pointed out nearly a century ago, norm violations and their punishments also provide an opportunity for preserving and reaffirming the norms. This is not insignificant, for norms sometimes disparaged as "motherhood" values gain new moral power when they are violated, and their violators are stigmatized.

If the undeserving poor can be imagined to be lazy, they help to reaffirm the Protestant work ethic; if poor single-parent families are publicly condemned, the two-parent family is once more legitimated as ideal. In the 1960s, middle-class morality was sometimes criticized as culturally parochial and therefore inappropriate for the poor, but since the 1980s, mainstream values have once more been regarded as vital sources of behavioral guidance for them.[11]

Enforcing the norms also contributes further to preserving them in another way, for one of the standard punishments of the undeserving poor for misbehaving—as well as a standard obligation in exchange for help—is practicing the mainstream norms, including those that the members of the mainstream may only be preaching, and that might die out if the poor were not required to incorporate them in their behavior. Old work rules that can no longer be enforced in the rest of the economy can be maintained in the regulations for workfare; old-fashioned austerity and thrift are built into the consumption patterns expected of welfare recipients. Economists like to argue that if the poor want to be deserving, they should take any kind of job, regardless of its low pay or demeaning character, reflecting a work ethic which economists themselves have never practiced.

Similarly, welfare recipients may be removed from the rolls if they are found to be living with a man—but the social worker who removes them has every right to cohabit and not lose his or her job. In most states, welfare recipients must observe rules of housecleaning and child care that middle-class people are free to ignore without being punished. While there are many norms and laws governing child care, only the poor are monitored to see if they obey these. Should they use more physical punishment on their children than social workers consider desirable, they can be charged with child neglect or abuse and can lose their children to foster care.[12]

The fact is that the defenders of such widely preached norms as hard work, thrift, monogamy, and moderation need people who can be accused, accurately or not, of being lazy, spendthrift, promiscuous, and immoderate. One reason that welfare recipients are a ready target for punitive legislation is that politicians, and most likely some of their constituents, imagine them to be enjoying leisure and an active sex life at public expense. Whether or not very many poor people actually behave in the ways that are judged undeserving is irrelevant if they can be imagined as doing so. Once imagining and stereotyping are allowed to take over, then judgments of undeservingness can be made without much concern for empirical accuracy. For example, in the 1990s, the idea that young men from poor single-parent families were highly likely to commit street crimes became so universal that the news media no longer needed to quote experts to affirm the accuracy of the charge.

Actually, most of the time most of the poor are as law abiding and observant of mainstream norms as are other Americans. Sometimes they are even more observant; thus the proportion of welfare recipients who cheat is always far below the percentage of taxpayers who do so.[13] Moreover, survey after survey has shown that the poor, including many street criminals and drug sellers, want to hold respectable jobs like everyone else, hope someday to live in the suburbs, and generally aspire to the same American dream as most moderate and middle-income Americans.[14]

8. Supplying Popular Culture Villains. The undeserving poor have played a long-term role in supplying American popular culture with villains, allowing the producers of the culture both to reinforce further mainstream norms and to satisfy audience demands for revenge, notably by showing that crime and other norm violations do not pay. Street criminals are shown dead or alive in the hands of the police on local television news virtually every day, and more dramatically so in the crime and action movies and television series.

For many years before and after World War II, the criminal characters in Hollywood movies were often poor immigrants, frequently of Sicilian origin. Then they were complemented for some decades by communist spies and other Cold War enemies who were not poor, but even before the end of the Cold War, they were being replaced by Black and Hispanic drug dealers and gang leaders.

At the same time, however, the popular culture industry has also supplied music and other materials offering marketable cultural and political protest which does not reinforce mainstream norms, or at least not directly. Some of the creators and performers come from poor neighborhoods, however, and it may be that some rap music becomes commercially successful by displacing on ghetto musicians the cultural and political protest of record buyers from more affluent classes.[15]

Three Political Functions

9. Institutional Scapegoating. The scapegoating of the undeserving poor mentioned in Function 2 above also extends to institutions which mistreat them. As a result, some of the responsibility for the existence of poverty, slums, unemployment, poor schools, and the like is taken off the shoulders of elected and appointed officials who are supposed to deal with these problems. For example, to the extent that educational experts decide that the children of the poor are learning disabled or that they are culturally or genetically inferior in intelligence, attempts to improve the schools can be put off or watered down.

To put it another way, the availability of institutional scapegoats both personalizes and exonerates social systems. The alleged laziness of the jobless and the anger aimed at beggars take the heat off the failure of the economy, and the imagined derelictions of slum dwellers and the homeless, off the housing industry. In effect, the undeserving poor are blamed both for their poverty and also for the absence of "political will" among the citizenry to do anything about it.

10. Conservative Power Shifting. Once poor people are declared undeserving, they also lose their political legitimacy and whatever little political influence they had before they were stigmatized. Some cannot vote, and many do not choose to vote or mobilize because they know politicians do not listen to their demands. Elected officials might ignore them even if they voted or mobilized, because these officials and the larger polity cannot easily satisfy their demands for economic and other kinds of justice.[16] As a result, the political system is able to pay additional attention to the demands of more affluent constituents. It can therefore shift to the "right."

The same shift to the right also takes place ideologically. Although injustices of poverty help justify the existence of liberals and the more radical left, the undeserving poor themselves provide justification and opportunities for conservatives to attack their ideological enemies on their left. When liberals can be accused of favoring criminals over victims, their accusers can launch and legitimate incursions on the civil liberties and rights of the undeserving poor, and concurrently on the liberties and rights of defenders of the poor. Moreover, the undeservingness of the poor can be used to justify attacks on the welfare state. Charles Murray understood the essence of this ideological function when he argued that welfare and other welfare state legislation for the poor only increased the number of poor people.[17]

11. Spatial Purification. Stigmatized populations are often used, deliberately or not, to stigmatize the areas in which they live, making such areas eligible for various kinds of purification. As a result, "underclass areas" can be torn down and their inhabitants moved to make room for more affluent residents or higher taxpayers.

However, such areas can also be used to isolate stigmatized poor people and facilities by selecting them as locations for homeless shelters, halfway houses for the mentally ill or for ex-convicts, drug treatment facilities, and even garbage dumps, which have been forced out of middle- and working-class areas following NIMBY (not in my backyard) protests. Drug dealers and other sellers of illegal goods also find a haven in areas stigmatized as underclass areas, partly because these supply some customers, but also because police protection in such areas is usually minimal enough to allow illegal activities without significant interference from the law.[18] In fact, municipalities would face major economic and political obstacles to their operations without stigmatized areas in which stigmatized people and activities can be located.

Two Macrosocial Functions

12. Reproduction of Stigma and the Stigmatized. For centuries now, undeservingness has given rise to policies and agencies which are manifestly set up to help the poor economically and otherwise to become deserving, but which actually prevent the undeserving poor from being freed of their stigma, and which also manage, unwittingly, to see to it that their children face the same obstacles.[19] In some instances, this process works so speedily that the children of the stigmatized face "anticipatory stigmatization," among them the children of welfare recipients who are frequently predicted to be unable to learn, to work, and to remain on the right side of the law even before they have been weaned.

If this outcome were planned deliberately, one could argue that politically and culturally dominant groups are reluctant to give up an easily accessible and always available scapegoat. In actuality, however, the reproduction function results unwittingly from other intended and seemingly popular practices. For example, the so-called War on Drugs, which has unsuccessfully sought to keep hard drugs out of the United States, but has meanwhile done little to provide drug treatment to addicts who want it, thereby aids the continuation of addiction, street crime, and a guaranteed prison population, not to mention the various disasters that visit the families of addicts and help to keep them poor.

The other major source of reproducing stigma and the stigmatized is the routine activities of the organizations which service welfare recipients, the homeless, and other stigmatized poor, and end up mistreating them.[20] For one thing, such agencies, whether they exist to supply employment to the poor or to help the homeless, are almost certain to be underfunded because of the powerlessness of their clientele. No organization has ever had the funds or power to buy, build, or rehabilitate housing for the homeless in sufficient number. Typically, they have been able to fund or carry out small demonstration projects.

In addition, organizations which serve stigmatized people often attract less well-trained and qualified staff than those with high-status clients, and if the clients are deemed undeserving, competence may become even less important in choosing staff.[21] Then too, helping organizations generally reflect the societal stratification hierarchy, which means that organizations with poor, low-status clients frequently treat them as undeserving. If they also fear some of their clients, they may not only withhold help, but attack the clients on a preemptive strike basis. Last but not least, the agencies that serve the undeserving poor are bureaucracies which operate by rules and regulations that routinize the work, encourage the stability and growth of the organizations, and serve the needs of their staffs before those of their clients. . . .

13. Extermination of the Surplus. In earlier times, when the living standards of all poor people were at or below subsistence, many died at an earlier age than the better off, thus performing the set of functions for the latter forever associated with Thomas Malthus. Standards of living, even for the very poor, have risen considerably in the last century, but even today, morbidity and mortality rates remain much higher among the poor than among moderate-income people. To put it another way, various social forces combine to do away with some of the people who have become surplus labor and are no longer needed by the economy.

Several of the killing illnesses and pathologies of the poor change over time; currently, they include AIDS, tuberculosis, hypertension, heart attacks, and cancer, as well as psychosis, substance abuse, street crime, injury and death during participation in the drug trade and other underworld activities, and intraclass homicide resulting from neighborhood conflicts over turf and "respect." Whether the poor people whose only problem is being unfairly stereotyped and stigmatized as undeserving die earlier than other poor people is not known.[22]

Moreover, these rates can be expected to remain high or even to rise as rates of unemployment—and of banishment from the labor force—rise, especially for the least skilled. Even the better-off jobless created by the downsizing of the 1990s blame themselves for their unemployment if they cannot eventually find new jobs, become depressed, and in some instances begin the same process of being extruded permanently from the labor market experienced by the least skilled of the jobless. . . .

III. Conclusion

. . . This analysis does not imply that undeservingness will or should persist. Whether it *will* persist is going to be determined by what happens to poverty in America. If it declines, poverty-related crime should also decline, and then fewer poor people will probably be described as undeserving. If poverty worsens, so will poverty-related crime, as well as the stereotyping and stigmatization of the poor, and any worsening of the country's economy is likely to add to the kinds and numbers of undeserving poor, if only because they make convenient and powerless scapegoats.

The functions that the undeserving poor play cannot, by themselves, perpetuate either poverty or undeservingness, for as I noted earlier, functions are not causes. For example, if huge numbers of additional unskilled workers should be needed, as they were for the World War II war effort, the undeserving poor will be welcomed back into the labor force, at least temporarily. Of course, institutions often try to survive once they have lost both their reasons for existence and their functions. Since the end of the Cold War, parts of the military-industrial establishment both in the United States and Russia have been campaigning for the maintenance of some Cold War forces and weapons to guarantee their own futures, but these establishments also supply jobs to their national economies, and in the United States, for the constituents of elected officials. Likewise, some of the institutions and interest groups that benefit from the existence of undeservingness, or from controlling the undeserving poor, may try to maintain undeservingness and its stigma. They may not even need to, for if Emile Durkheim was right, the decline of undeservingness would lead to the criminalization, or at least stigmatization, of new behavior patterns.

Whether applying the label of undeservingness to the poor *should* persist is a normative question which ought to be answered in the negative. Although people have a right to judge each other, that right does not extend to judging large numbers of people as a single group, with one common moral fault, or to stereotyping them without evidence either about their behavior or their values. Even if a case could be made for judging large cohorts of people as undeserving, these judgments should be distributed up and down the socioeconomic hierarchy, requiring Americans also to consider whether and how people in the working, middle, and upper classes are undeserving. . . .

NOTES

This article should be read as a straightforward analysis, written sans irony, even though the analysis of latent functions, which often debunks the conventional wisdom, can take on an unintentially ironic tone.

1. Robert K. Merton, "Manifest and Latent Functions," in his *Social Theory and Social Structure* (Glencoe, IL, 1949), chap. 1.
2. Actually, some of the functions that follow may in fact have been intended by some interest groups in society, but neither intended nor recognized by others, adding an interesting conceptual variation—and empirical question—to Merton's dichotomy.
3. For brevity's sake, I will hereafter refer to the undeserving poor instead of the poor labeled undeserving, but I always mean the latter.
4. Kathryn M. Neckerman and Joleen Kirschenman, "Hiring Strategies, Racial Bias and Inner-City Workers," *Social Problems* 38, no. 4 (1991); 433–47.
5. Dahrendorf has suggested, surely with Marx's *Lumpenproletariat* in mind, that when the very poor are excluded from full citizenship, they can become "a reserve army for demonstrations . . . including soccer violence, race riots, and running battles with the police." Ralf Dahrendorf, *Law and Order* (London: Stevens, 1985), 107. He is writing with Europe in mind, however.
6. Consequently, they are part of the reserve army only if and when they also work off-the-books in the informal economy. For the argument that recipients are permanently part of the reserve army, see Frances F. Piven and Richard A. Cloward, *Regulating the Poor,* 2d ed. (New York: Pantheon, 1993).
7. Ron Harris, "Blacks Feel Brunt of Drug War," *Los Angeles Times,* 22 April 1990, 1.
8. Since political legitimacy is involved here, these functions could also be listed among the political ones below.
9. That many of the undeserving poor, and literally those of the underclass, are also thought to be *declasse,* adds to the moral and political legitimacy of the rest of the class system.
10. Although Marxists might have been expected to complain that the notion of the undeserving poor enables the higher classes to create a split in the lower ones, instead Marxist theory creates a mirror image of the capitalist pattern. In declaring undeserving the owners of the means of production, and sometimes the entire bourgeoisie, the theorists ennobled the working class and the poor together with it. Nonetheless, Marx found it necessary to make room for the *Lumpenproletariat,* although for him if not all of his successors, its moral failures were largely determined by the needs of the Marxists ideology just as those of the undeserving poor were shaped by capitalist ideology.
11. See Isabel Sawhill, "The Underclass: An Overview," *The Public Interest,* no. 96 (1989): 3–15. For a contrary analysis, which finds and criticizes the acceptance of poverty-related deviance as normal, see Daniel P. Moynihan, "Defining Deviancy Down," *American Scholar* 62, no. 1 (1993): 17–30.
12. Poor immigrants who still practice old-country discipline norms are particularly vulnerable to being accused of child abuse.
13. Teresa Funicello, *Tyranny of Kindness: Dismantling the Welfare System to End Poverty in America* (New York: Atlantic Monthly Press, 1993), 60.
14. See Mark R. Rank, *Living on the Edge: The Realities of Welfare in America* (New York: Columbia University Press, 1994), 93.
15. A sizable proportion of the blues, country music, cowboy songs, and jazz of earlier eras was originally composed and played in prisons, brothels, and slum area taverns. It is probably not coincidental that as far back as the eighteenth century, at least, English "actors, fencers, jugglers, minstrels, and in fact all purveyors of amusements to common folk," were thought undeserving by the higher classes. Webb and Webb, *English Poor Law History,* 354.
16. In addition, the undeserving poor make a dangerous constituency. Politicians who say

kind words about them or who act to represent their interests are likely to be attacked for their words and actions. Jesse Jackson was hardly the first national politician to be criticized for being too favorable to the poor.

17. Charles Murray, *Losing Ground: American Social Policy, 1950–1980* (New York: Basic Books, 1984). Myron Magnet [blames] the increase in undeservingness also on various unnamed radicals associated with the conservative image of the 1960s. Myron Magnet, *The Dream and the Nightmare: The Sixties' Legacy to the Underclass* (New York: Morrow, 1993).
18. Since even middle-class drug buyers are willing to travel to underclass areas for drugs, neighborhoods convenient to expressways and bridges that serve the suburbs often become major shopping centers for hard drugs.
19. . . . Many policies and agencies reproduce the positions and statuses of the people they are asked to raise, notably the public schools.
20. For some examples of the literature on client mistreatment, see Michael B. Katz, *In the Shadow of the Poor House: A Social History of Welfare in America* (New York: Basic Books, 1986); Michael Lipsky, *Street Level Bureaucracy: Dilemmas of the Individual in Public Services* (New York: Russell Sage Foundation, 1980); Piven and Cloward, *Regulating the Poor,* chaps. 4 and 5; and for mistreatment of the homeless, Elliott Liebow, *Tell Them Who I Am: The Lives of Homeless Women* (New York: Free Press, 1993), chap. 4.
21. They may also attract young professionals with reforming or missionary impulses, but many of them either burn out or leave for financial reasons when they begin to raise families.
22. Poor blacks and members of some other racial minorities pay additional "health penalties" for being non-White.

PORTRAIT

Fraternity Little Sister Organizations: Structures of Opportunity or Exploitation?

Mindy Stombler and Patricia Yancey Martin

. . . The structural conditions of universities and colleges contribute to the maintenance and creation of gender inequality on campus. Women students' status on university campuses is not lower than men's solely because gender inequality is imported from outside. Formal structures that are part of university life actively impede women students' progress in higher education (Gabriel and Smithson 1990; Sadker and Sadker 1994). University and college women are structurally devalued, for example, by their less favorable and infrequent representation in textbooks, lectures, and research (Gabriel and Smithson 1990); their receipt of less financial aid (Sadker 1984); male faculty's failure to sponsor, call on, or acknowledge them (Hall and Sandler 1982); and the dedication of more resources and attention to men's activities (Messner 1992).

Although structural factors create and maintain gender inequality on campus, gender inequality is also created and maintained on an informal and interpersonal level. Women students' everyday lives are subjected to male

From *Journal of Contemporary Ethnography, 23,* pp. 150–184. The results presented in this article are based on a study of Euro-American little sisters; other research has since been done comparing Euro-American little sisters with African American little sisters.

domination through their peer relations. Through these peer relations, many women students come to value men's companionship over scholastic and career goals, learning that their attractiveness to men, as well as the high status that accompanies attaining a boyfriend, is an integral part of their self-worth (Holland and Eisenhart 1990). In this way, the high-pressure heterosexual peer group, central to women students' everyday lives, transmits and produces traditional patriarchal gender relations (Gwartney-Gibbs and Stockard 1989; Handler 1993).

In fraternity little sister programs, structural factors and informal interpersonal dynamics converge to create an organizational atmosphere that is conducive to women's subordination. Peer influence is often more pernicious than are structural factors such as sexist school authority, processes, and materials in the transmission of male privilege (Cowie and Lees 1981; Gwartney-Gibbs and Stockard 1989; Holland and Eisenhart 1990; Lees 1986). Fraternity little sister programs combine the worst of both worlds (structural and interpersonal) by providing an organized outlet for, and positively sanctioning, the peer culture and the form of gender relations that give power over women to men. Fraternity little sister programs thus exaggerate the oppressive dynamics that already exist. Men's social fraternities actively create gender inequality (Boeringer, Shehan, and Akers 1991; Boswell and Spade 1993; Bryan 1987; Ehrhart and Sandler 1985; Garrett-Gooding and Senter 1987; Kalof and Cargill 1991; Martin and Hummer 1989; Risman 1982; Sanday 1990), and the fraternity little sister program represents an extension of this practice (McKee 1987; Riker 1983). . . .

Methods

The data come from participant observation, open-ended depth interviews, official reports and documents, newspaper articles, and a survey of a convenience sample of 110 students. We collected most of the interview and archival data on the campuses of five public universities in the Southeast.

The first author conducted participant observation at one fraternity, including observation of little sister rush, several parties and social events, and an orientation meeting of newly chosen little sisters. Because the first author played a "naive student role," several women who were little sisters acted as tour guides through their world. These women told her that they were flattered to be the subjects of her research. To observe little sister/fraternity brother interaction on another campus, the first author also attended intramural sports events where Greeks participate.

We interviewed 17 Euro-American little sisters from seven men's social fraternities. We conducted the interviews in settings of the respondent's own choosing, including restaurants, homes, empty classrooms, and offices. We asked them to tell us their stories of how and why they became little sisters. . . .

We used official inquiry and commission reports about fraternities, sororities, and little sister organizations as well as local and national fraternity and sorority publications as archival data. Newspaper articles and televised reports on sexual assault involving fraternity little sisters provided additional data. . . .

Who Is a Little Sister?

Little sisters are undergraduate women, typically 18 to 20 years of age, whom fraternity men select to associate with them on a formal, quasi-official basis (Martin and Hummer 1989; Sanday 1990). Most women become little sisters early in their college careers or as entering third-year transfer students and are active for one or two semesters, although some remain active longer. Both Greek, or sorority, and independent, or nonsorority, women are little sisters. Our in-class survey identified 24 of 53 women who were little sisters, 14 of whom were independents, and 10 of whom belonged to a sorority. Some women who are little sisters are students at nearby institutions. For instance, Kim, the president of a large fraternity little sister program, joined a little sister group when she was a community college student because it let her "belong to the university system and tie into the Greeks."

In general, the women told us they joined little sister groups for social reasons—to meet men, find someone to date, make friends, and have fun. Many women accomplished these goals. Both sorority and independent women valued the opportunity to make friends and date fraternity men. Although sorority women who were little sisters emphasized meeting and associating with men and seeking an environment with less structure than a sorority has, independent little sisters told us they joined from loneliness, in search of a home away from home, and to gain entree to the Greek system. Fraternities have many parties, and their members often dominate the top positions of student government, service organizations, and intramural sports. Thus both independent and sorority women could gain valuable resources through their association with a fraternity.

Little Sister Criteria

We found that fraternity men selected little sisters for their physical beauty and sociability.[1] Physical beauty means that a woman's face, figure, and hairstyle comply with standards of attractiveness among the young. White fraternity men rarely invited women of color to serve as little sisters for their group. Sociability refers to a woman's charm, friendliness, and outgoingness. Fraternity men wanted women as little sisters who liked to attend parties, smile and laugh, flirt, and who were agreeable (Martin and Hummer 1989). Referred to as "having a good personality," most students interviewed said this criterion ranked far below beauty as a little sister qualification.

Four out of 12 pages of a full-color, slick-paper brochure that enumerated one fraternity's members' accomplishments, honors, and successes were devoted to photographs of little sisters. Significantly, the two center pages showed photos of little sisters in varied social settings in the company of the brothers, a not-so-subtle parody of men's pornographic magazines. Centered was the following message: "Little Sisters—Chosen on the Basis of Beauty, Charm, and Loyalty" and "Their Motto: To Serve the Brothers." The back cover page was an 8 inch by 10 inch photo of a little sister in a bikini climbing out of a swimming pool. In depicting women as its beautifiers and servers, Martin and Hummer (1989) have said that a fraternity uses little sisters to tell potential recruits they will have access to sexy, beautiful women if they join. Fraternity men's selection of women on the basis of beauty commodifies women, thus contributing to the creation and maintenance of gender inequality on campus (see Stombler 1993). . . .

Factors Attracting Little Sisters

If fraternity little sister rush was simply a beauty contest, why would so many women on the college campus want to participate? If fraternity men often exploited and abused women who joined fraternities as little sisters, why did women continue to join? Why did women actively participate in their own exploitation? Not all women who were little sisters were abused by fraternity men, not all women recognized exploitation, and those women who did acknowledge it might weigh the exploitation and abuse against the status and other benefits that accompanied little sisterhood.

Status, Romance, and Affirmation

. . . When women joined little sister groups to gain men's company and approbation, they acted within the constraints of an unequal power structure and a culture of romance (Holland and Eisenhart 1990) that encouraged them to define their identity and self-worth through their relations with men. Little sister groups brought women and men together in highly ritualized and romantic ways, particularly during the recruitment, or rush, stages of the relationship (Martin and Hummer 1989 and Risman 1982 explain Greek "rush"). For women who were young and new to campus, who knew few people except a roommate or friend from home, little sister rush and selection could be exhilarating. On their best behavior and hoping to attract beautiful women, the men shower the women with attention. Some women are understandably flattered. Sarah, the woman who quit little sisters because her friend was expelled, described her pleasure at the way the men treated her during little sister rush:

> We had guys coming up to us all the time. They really wanted us there. We couldn't believe this. . . . My first week up at school, I had a couple of people from the fraternity asking me out and that would happen like in a year's time back at home. I was pretty flattered. We were treated like queens.

Fraternities announced a little sister's selection in ways that publicly advertised her good fortune in being chosen. In some cases, the men dressed in suits or tuxedos, arrived on foot or in limousines, and presented the little sister with flowers and a written invitation. With the flower and invitation in hand, they went to the woman's residence in the early evening when everyone was there to see their display. . . .

Connecting to Campus Social Life, Finding Friends

Women who joined little sister organizations were connected to many high-status men (typically 35 to 150 or more) and to many other women, thus these groups helped women find friends and companions and linked them to other people on campus (see Martin and Hummer 1989). Fraternities engaged in community service activities, competed in sporting events, and participated in student government and other activities. If a fraternity enjoyed high status, women who were associated with it might share that status. Whether a woman's status was raised or lowered by membership depended on how the men treated her. Kim, the 4-year member of a little sister program who joined while a community college student and who was president of her group when little sister groups were abolished on her campus, described the fraternity and the little sister program as a friendship group:

> You really felt like you were part of something when you went there, right from the start. Even if you didn't go through it [rush] with friends, there was always someone to talk to whether it was a guy or a girl. . . . Guys remembered who you were, too. After the [little sister] meetings they would say, "Hey we're going to [a local bar] tonight. You're all welcome to join us." We would go. It was fun.

Women who were little sisters had open invitations to fraternity parties except for sorority–fraternity functions; such parties were closed to nonsorority members. . . . Fraternities had many parties, often three in a weekend, so the women who were little sisters had many chances to socialize. Some parties were elaborate and expensive, and the women were flattered to be included. . . .

Familial Bonds

Some women who were little sisters viewed their relations with fraternity men as family-like, characterized by bonds of closeness, fondness, mutual regard, and support. A sorority adviser said one woman who was a little sister invited an entire fraternity to her wedding and most members attended. She described the men as "the brothers I never had." Consistent with the pseudo-familial ties of brotherhood among fraternity men (see Martin and Hummer 1989; Sanday 1990), the men couched their relations with the women who were little sisters in pseudo-familial terms. . . .

A *big brother* was a fraternity member who usually lived in the fraternity house, was informed about fraternity activities, and was paired in a special relationship with one or more women who were little sisters. Many women who were little sisters described relations with their big brothers as close, supportive, or protective. . . .

A *little brother* was a new fraternity pledge who was affiliated with a woman who was a veteran little sister, whom he refers to as his big sister. Sarah said she hugged the men who were her little brothers when they met on campus: "We hug each other . . . we're so glad to see each other.". . .

Informal norms asserted that brother–sister relations were not sexual or dating relationships, but rather, friendships. Dating between women who were little sisters and big or little brothers was normatively discouraged. . . . Although affectionate bonds developed between some women who were little sisters and their fraternity brothers, they did not generalize to all fraternity members. . . .

Big sister referred to the relationship between a veteran little sister and a male fraternity pledge or the relationship between a veteran little sister and a new little sister. The big sister is expected to make her little sister and/or little brother feel welcome, provide support, and introduce them to others.

Costs and Demands

Little sister groups allowed women to connect to the Greek system at relatively minimal expense. . . . Women who were little sisters paid dues of $10 to $40 a semester and even less after the first semester in most fraternities. Sorority dues and rush fees were, in contrast, $1,000 per year or more. . . .

Some respondents said little sister groups were less demanding and structured than sororities. Caroline said her sorority was more strict about behavioral standards and that fraternities had no standards for either the men who were brothers or the women who were little sisters. . . . Missy, a little sister vice president, said socials thrown by or for the women who were little sisters were more relaxed and friendly than sorority socials. . . .

Although many students said little sister membership required little time or effort (unlike sororities), Kim said her grades dropped when she became president of her little sister group. . . . Barbara held no office in her little sister group yet complained about the time, effort, and money the NM fraternity required of its little sisters. . . .

Paradoxically, fraternities' lower self-imposed behavioral standards, compared to sororities, might have increased little sisters' risk of becoming the prey of unscrupulous men. The informal norms of fraternity life did not prevent brothers from taking advantage of little sisters and placing them at risk, as the next section shows. . . .

Becoming a Little Sister

Little sister rush, as a time period and an activity, was modeled after fraternity and sorority rush (Martin and Hummer 1989; Risman 1982). Temporally, it consisted of a few consecutive weekday evenings, early in the academic terms. Women were invited to attend open-invitation parties or meetings at the fraternity house for the purpose of expressing their interest in becoming little sisters. Going from fraternity house to fraternity house, the young women progressed through rush in small groups consisting of their acquaintances. Friends, often from the same high school, tried to be chosen by the same fraternity. During little sister rush, women actively sought individual and group male approval, which required them to assume a demeaning position. . . .

The Selection Process

Membership selection processes differed across fraternities, depending on who did the selecting, but they invariably devalued women. . . . Larger fraternities generally had a *bid committee* whose say was final in selection decisions. In these cases, rushees had to favorably impress the committee members. . . . Selection committee members "made mental and written notes" about women who interested them. On the final days, they discussed and voted on each woman on their lists.

Most fraternities required current little sisters to attend rush parties and help entertain the rushees but did not allow them to participate in meetings where selection decisions were made. . . .

Although none of the fraternities that we studied allowed women who were little sisters to vote on selection, some did take the opinions of the current little sister officers into account. . . .

On one campus, . . . little sister organizations were allowed to exist only if fraternity members agreed that new little sisters would be selected by an equal number of little sisters and fraternity members, although the selection committee could be chaired by the fraternity's little sister chairperson, who is male (Lil' sister programs 1991). Ironically, this campus abolished little sister groups (Council abolishes 1991) shortly after women were granted some semblance of control over their selection process.

After selections were made, the brothers might don suits or tuxedos and go in groups, often riding in a limousine, to the rushee's residence—sorority house, dorm, or apartment. They would invite the woman to become affiliated with their fraternity, present her with a flower, and sing her a song. This was called *handing out a bid.* A woman who received a bid almost always affiliated with the fraternity because she had expressed her willingness to affiliate by attending the third rush party. Although the performances might be less elaborate at some fraternities or campuses, fraternity men made an effort to make the chosen women feel special and honored in what was a deliberately public display. This display validated a woman's status in her own eyes and the eyes of her peers.

Pledgeship and Initiation

Like male fraternity pledges (see Martin and Hummer 1989), women who were little sisters endured a trial membership stage that usually lasted for most of an academic term. During this period, the brothers decided whether the women were "good enough" to become full-fledged little sisters. During pledgeship, the women who were chosen as little sisters were subjected to demands on their energies and time and were given tests of loyalty and information. Once again, the men controlled the women's experience and evaluation. If they successfully completed the pledgeship, the women were eligible for initiation to full membership as a little sister. These women did not become full-fledged members of the fraternity, however (see Fraternities phase 1989; Georgia Tech 1991). . . .

Interviewing was a frequent component of pledgeship. Interviews consisted of talks between a woman who was pledging little sisters and a brother, where the woman would ask the brother a short series of questions to become acquainted (e.g., his name, hometown, major in college, grade point average, and position in the fraternity). . . . Not all of the women focused on these standard topics. Caroline recalls "getting creative":

> We set up 25 of our 50 questionnaires for pledges. The pledge's questions were a little more sexual. We tried to embarrass them. We asked questions like "What is your favorite position?" "What is the most embarrassing thing that ever happened to you during sex?" "What is your sexual fantasy?" "If I was your sexual partner, what would you do?"

Initiation ceremonies at the end of the pledgeship period required formal, often identical dress. . . . Fraternity men conducted the ceremony and instructed the women about fraternity slogans, colors, and symbols. The ceremony often had a religious theme and might be held in a church, the fraternity house, or a banquet room on campus. The initiates typically passed candles, repeated passages, and pledged loyalty to each other and to the fraternity (See Sanday 1990 on fraternity initiation ceremonies, on which little sister initiation is modeled). When the ceremony ended, the women were declared to be little sisters and the brothers gave them tokens of membership such as pins, certificates, flowers, or gifts. Caroline recalled her initiation as "very short" and described her initiation and new status:

> We didn't learn the secret grip or anything like that [laughs]. It was like you are now formally a member of our associated little group [laughs]. . . .

Fraternity Mens' Expectations of Little Sisters

According to Martin and Hummer (1989), the little sister job was to support the brothers, reinforcing women's subservience to men on campus. Expectations varied from one fraternity to another, but generally the men expected, and in some fraternities required, women who were little sisters to help them raise money for charitable and community service projects; support the fraternity's intramural sports teams; watch television and videos with the brothers at the house; help decorate the house for parties; attend, prepare for, hostess, or clean-up after parties; pay dues to the fraternity; buy the brothers gifts during holidays; attend fraternity functions to which they are invited; organize banquets for the brothers; help with rush week plans, activities, and recruitment; attend little sister meetings, and accompany the men on weekend parties or vacations. The women at some fraternities participated in women's intramural sports and had woman-only retreats, but women themselves initiated these practices. The men showed some interest in women-only events if the women competed against another fraternity's little sister program. When the women expressed dissatisfaction with their role as little sisters, they often lamented the brothers' lack of appreciation for their efforts. Amy resented the fraternity's failure to give credit to her and her peers for the work they did for the fraternity. According to Amy, women who were little sisters helped the fraternity with many community service functions during the year but "they [the brothers] get all the credit. Never once do you read in the newspapers that the little sisters of the fraternity were there too." Some women who were little sisters said they were asked to clean up or do grunt work around the house. Karen described her refusal to do work of this sort: "They would try to get us to help clean up the house sometimes but we were like 'No way!' They are slobs; we are not going to clean up after them."

Most fraternities expected the women who were little sisters to help recruit new women to be little sisters, but under conditions men controlled. According to Missy, the vice president of little sisters at a high-status fraternity, men in XYZ wanted women who were veteran little sisters to participate in "new" little sister rush so rushees will "see nice girls and smiling faces." As noted earlier, the men did not want women who were little sisters to lobby them about who to select, nor did they permit women to vote on new little sisters. Allowing women to vote would acknowledge a membership right. Boundaries set by the men on the quantity, quality, and content of participation were ambiguous.

Ambiguity in Participatory Boundaries

Women who were little sisters were unclear about how much and in what ways they might or should participate in the fraternity. Most fraternity men said they wanted the women to be active, but the underlying message was ambiguous. The men had the power to define the extent of women's participation. On one hand, the men told the women to make the fraternity a high priority in their lives. Several women reported being fined for missing fraternity events; one was fined $10.00 for missing a party. The sorority house mother we interviewed said women who were little sisters in her sorority always put the fraternity ahead of the sorority. If the sorority had a banquet to honor members with good grades and the fraternity wanted its little sisters to attend a softball game, "They [the women who were little sisters] always went to the game. . . . They were afraid the guys would get mad. . . . Yes, they put the fraternity first. It made me so mad."

Yet little sisters were also warned against becoming too wrapped up in the fraternity and its affairs, or becoming too "gung ho." Missy said the brothers at her fraternity became upset when "lots of the girls started to live and breathe XYZ" and when the women who were little sisters were "trying too hard" by interfering in fraternity affairs in ways the men wanted to preserve for themselves. . . .

Erin, a woman who was a little sister at a high-status fraternity whose little sister chairman encouraged the women to join the men at the fraternity for meals, told a story about the mixed messages and expectations that little sisters receive:

> They [the brothers] used to tell us when we first came over not to come to dinner all the time. I mean they don't tell you that but other little sisters do. Because there's always this one little story. I don't know if it's true, but there was some girl that used to come over here every day for lunch. Every single day. And they just kind of got upset because I mean we don't pay for it. I mean we are welcome to come over here you know. We don't have the right to come over here every day for lunch. I mean we're invited but you just don't infringe on what they give you. But no, I don't see any girls, nobody comes around here too much that eats over here all the time. Nobody.

Yet, at the little sister meeting for the newly chosen women, the women who were little sister officers encouraged the new women to attend lunch with the brothers as often as they liked.

Women who were little sisters did not participate fully in fraternity life and activities. One InterFraternity Council (IFC) president, who belonged to a high-status fraternity, led the campaign to abolish little sister programs on his campus. He described women who were little sisters as "half members" who "half belonged" to the fraternity. Consistent with this view, his fraternity required the women who were little sisters to do "half as many interviews" as male pledges during the pledgeship and to learn one half of the rituals and secrets of the fraternity. Ambiguous participatory boundaries obscured women's role in the fraternity and reinforced the men's power to define women's roles.

Ambiguity in Sexual Expectations

Many students believed fraternity men expected women who were little sisters to have sex with them. . . . Many university officials also believed this claim. Most little sisters, and the fraternity men whom we interviewed, admitted the claim had some merit. Still, many women who were little sisters denied that the primary purpose of the program was sex, insisting it was friendship. Kim, one of the little sister presidents, believed this. Yet she acknowledged that some women joined little sister groups to have sex and that fraternity men would sexually exploit any little sister who allowed it. Caroline said fraternity men purposely selected two kinds of women: the kind to make them look good and the kind who would have sex. Kim explained how little sister groups acquired a reputation for sexual availability. She claimed the women who were little sisters rather than fraternity men were responsible for whether they had sex, saying that the women decided whether or not to pursue sex with the men. She described the attitude she had when she entered her fraternity, LLL, during rush week:

> I didn't go in with the attitude or intention of meeting someone and going home with them that night. Of course, there's a lot of hot guys there. A lot of times, and I'm just being realistic, a lot of times that would happen and that's why the little sister program had the reputation it did. This happened a lot in some fraternities. LLL tried not to push this in their program, only because they didn't want to have problems. They were taking us in to be little sisters, to be friends with everybody there, not to have a problem. I'm sure it happened at LLL. I think that was the problem with why our reputation [little sisters generally] was the way it was; it wasn't really that way. It depends on what type of attitude you go in with more than anything else and it really depends on the individual. If you are going in there with the attitude of I'm going to go scam [find someone to have sex with], if you go in with this type of attitude, you're going to get a reputation there. . . . As much as people think that guys are just, you know, hound dogs or whatever, they really aren't. A lot of the guys really do want to be your friend and have a good time.

Sarah criticized fraternity men who were known for having casual sex without a relationship, or "scamming," but she, like most of the women we interviewed, held women who were little sisters primarily responsible:

> Some guys are noted scammers and they go out with little sisters. They would scam at parties and take little sisters upstairs or make out with them on the dance floor. It was all pretty sleazy if you ask me.

Sarah's follow-up comments showed how the men can evict a little sister who has been sexually indiscreet and is no longer wanted around the house. Although the men readily had sex with any woman who was a little sister who allowed it, they defined women who had sex easily or often as sluts, sleazies, or whores. Then the men, sometimes joined by other women who were little sisters, shunned the stigmatized woman until she stopped coming to the house. . . .

Caroline said that different fraternities had different norms for little sister–brother relationships. Some proscribed sexual or dating relations with the women who were little sisters, whereas others allowed the men to date or have sex at will with women who were little sisters. The fraternity men made rules to proscribe dating relationships with women who were little sisters primarily to prevent dissent and competition among the brothers, not to protect the women. Caroline described the variety of rules and norms about little sister–brother relations that she knew about. . . .

Organizational Structure and Issues of Control

Although the structure of little sister groups varied, we found that some features were fairly common, particularly the leadership positions and roles fraternity men and women played in little sister organizations. Conflicts emerged over women's pursuit of, and men's resistance to, women's attempts at self-governance. Little sister organizations encouraged dependence and powerlessness in women. . . .

The Little Sister Chairman or Coordinator

The fraternity president typically appointed a brother as *little sister chairman* or *coordinator* for a semester or year. This chairman formally linked the women who were little sisters to the brotherhood; he informed them of fraternity events and supervised them and their activities. The chairman attended the womens' weekly meeting and told them what they could and could not do at the fraternity. One little sister chairman who talked to us described his rule-maker role as follows: . . .

> They can't write our fraternity letters; they can't wear our fraternity insignia [only the fraternity's nickname can be displayed]. They have to know certain times that they are not allowed around the house, like during sorority socials.

The chairman served as police officer and judge in resolving disputes that involved women who were little sisters. He mediated conflicts among the women and between the women and men. . . . Without due process, or right to appeal, the chairman had considerable influence in the decision of whether a woman went or stayed.

Women as Little Sister Officers

Some fraternities allowed the women who were little sisters to elect their own officers, although this seldom happened in smaller fraternities. A member of a small fraternity said, "We don't have little sister officers. . . . Generally we have one person [a woman who is a little sister] that would just take command and let everyone know if the little sisters were going to do anything for the brothers." Larger fraternities allowed the women to hold elections for officers; they usually had a president, and some, a vice president, treasurer, secretary, chaplain, as well as positions such as social chairwoman. Elections were usually held at an organizational meeting early in the year (or term), soon after the newest women had been selected as little sisters. The candidates gave speeches and the women voted on their choice among themselves (although in some cases the brothers could vote as well, if they liked).

The women officers performed various duties such as helping to plan parties, outings, and banquets or doing administrative work such as organizing telephone lists, collecting dues, collecting money for kegs, planning community service, and notifying the women about upcoming events. The president presided over the little sister meeting that was held weekly at the fraternity house—in the living, dining, or chapter room. In some houses, the women who were little sisters met for an hour once a week and stayed afterward or arrived early to dine with the men. The women officers' duties varied at the discretion of the men. In some fraternities, the brothers ran the program and allowed the women minimal input. The brothers decided how much power women officers had and whether the organization would exist at all. . . .

Issues of Control

Little sister groups situated women as organizationally subservient to men. Fraternity norms discouraged women from sticking up for themselves and acting collectively or individually on their own behalf. If the women who were little sisters tried to assert themselves, the men resisted. . . . Some women complied with the men's expectations and viewed whatever was asked of them as legitimate; they served the fraternity in exchange for the men's approval and companionship. Caroline, a woman with fond memories of her little sister program who nonetheless quit because of her feelings of powerlessness, echoed this acceptance of male dominance, claiming that women who were little sisters "didn't deserve any rights whatsoever." Others resented the fraternity's demands and their lack of rights but felt powerless to oppose them. Through participating in activities that required subservience and dependence, little sisters helped to reconstitute gender inequality on campus, referred to by Chafetz (1990) as the "system of female disadvantage."

Discussion

Fraternity little sister organizations provide a formal structure on campus in which the system of female disadvantage (Chafetz 1990) is institutionalized. These organizations encourage women's subordination, exploitation, and dependence (Martin and Hummer 1989). Not only does the structure and organization of the little sister program create a hierarchy in which men rule and women serve, but the structure also stimulates and codifies the student "culture of romance" (Holland and Eisenhart 1990) in which women's value as persons is defined by their attractiveness to men. The fraternity little sister program provides an environment that organizationally structures the high-pressure heterosexual peer group that pushes women toward romance and dependence on men. The peer culture on campus defines gender relations, traditionally, where a male partner becomes a woman's symbol of self-identity, affirming the woman's existence and value (Cowie and Lees 1981; Holland and Eisenhart 1990; Lees 1986). How can gender inequality be challenged if it is maintained and created within peer groups? One way is to limit opportunities for high-pressure heterosexual peer groups to flourish within a formal campus structure. The fraternity little sister organization provides such a structure.

Little sister organizations foster the social and material interests of fraternities and individual fraternity men in numerous ways (Martin and Hummer 1989). They allow men to surround themselves with beautiful, sociable, charming women who will do their bidding and work on their behalf. Fraternity men enjoy nearly total control over the form and activities of these women's organizations, no doubt a heady experience for 18- to 20-year-old men. By advertising the fraternity, little sisters attract desirable pledges, thereby enhancing the fraternity's popularity, reputation, institutional reproduction, and financial success. Yet men's conceptions of women, the norms and values they attach to women, and their relationships with women may harm the women. Little sister organizations are, our findings suggest, far less benign than their defenders claim. . . .

Holland and Eisenhart (1990) have attributed much of women's lowered scholastic and career motivation and attainment, compared to men's, to the peer "culture of romance." The fraternity little sister organization formally embodies such a culture of romance, making it particularly effective in its promotion of gender inequality. By intensifying the informal traditional peer culture through formal rushing and initiation procedures and participation in the fraternity, the little sister organization structures gender inequality. Our research leaves little room for doubt that fraternity men have substantial power over women whom they select as little sisters. They select the women based on appearance—beauty and shapeliness; they allow the women to govern themselves only so long as they do what the men desire. Fraternity men prevent the women from pursuing their own agendas, they exclude them from most (if not all) decision-making processes in the fraternity, and they sometimes expel them from membership with no notice, explanation, or recourse (see Martin and Stombler 1993). In other words, the structure of fraternity little sister organizations fosters the belief that women have fewer rights and less value than do men and that women's worth depends on their attractiveness to, service to, and acceptance by men (Handler 1993; Risman 1982).

. . . At issue is not what individual women or men gain from little sister membership but whether little sister organizations foster positive transformational outcomes for women and men—or the reverse. Our data suggest the latter, that this element of campus culture devalues women. Although individual women who are little sisters cite a litany of benefits, we conclude that the program fails to enhance, and does much to harm, undergraduate women's lives when viewed through the critical lens of a gender perspective.

NOTE

1. Research on African American fraternity little sister organizations reports that women are less likely to be selected on this basis. Rather, African American men look for "strong Black women" who will put a

lot of hard work into the organization. For an analysis of the differences between African and Euro-American little sisters, see Stombler and Padavic 1994.

REFERENCES

Boeringer, Scot B., Constance L. Shehan, and Ronald L. Akers. 1991. Social contexts and social learning in sexual coercion and aggression: Assessing the contribution of fraternity membership. *Family Relations* 40:58–64.

Boswell, Ayres A., and Joan Z. Spade. 1993. Fraternities, gender relations, and rape culture on college campuses. Department of Sociology and Anthropology, Lehigh University. Unpublished manuscript.

Bryan, William A. 1987. Contemporary fraternity and sorority issues. In *Fraternities and Sororities on the Contemporary College Campus*. New Directions for Student Services, no. 40., edited by R. B. Winston, Jr., W. R. Nettles III, and J. H. Opper, Jr., 37–56. San Francisco: Jossey-Bass (Winter).

Chafetz, Janet. 1990. *Gender equity: An integrated theory or stability and change*. Newbury Park, CA: Sage.

Council abolishes all little sisters. 1991. *Gainesville Sun*, 4 April, 6B.

Cowie, C., and Sue Lees. 1981. Slags or drags. *Feminist Review* 9:17–31.

Curry, Timothy Jon. 1991. Fraternal bonding in the locker room: A profeminist analysis of talk about competition and women. *Sociology of Sport Journal* 8:119–35.

Ehrhardt, Julie K., and Bernice R. Sandler. 1985. *Campus gang rape: Party games?* Washington, DC: Association for American Colleges.

Fraternities phase out "little sister groups." 1989. *New York Times*, 17 September, p. 59.

Gabriel, Susan L., and Isaiah Smithson, eds. 1990. *Gender in the classroom: Power and pedagogy*. Urbana: University of Illinois Press.

Garrett-Gooding, J., and Robert Senter, Jr. 1987. Attitudes and acts of aggression on a university campus. *Sociological Inquiry* 57:348–72.

Georgia Tech Greeks ban all opposite sex auxiliary groups. 1991. *The Technique*, 8 January, pp. 1, 4.

A Greek tragedy. 1988. *St. Petersburg Times*, 29 May, pp. 1F–6F.

Gwartney-Gibbs, Patricia, and Jean Stockard. 1989. Courtship aggression and mixed-sex peer groups. In *Violence in dating relationships: Emerging social issues*, edited by Maureen A. Pirog-Good and Jan E. Stets, 185–204. New York: Praeger.

Hall, Roberta, and Bernice Sandler. 1982. *The classroom climate: A chilly one for women*. Project on the status and education of women. Washington, DC: Association of American Colleges.

Handler, Lisa. 1993. In the fraternal sisterhood: Sororities as gender strategy. Paper presented at the Annual Meetings, American Sociological Association, Miami Beach, Florida.

Holland, Dorothy C., and Margaret A. Eisenhart. 1990. *Educated in romance: Women, achievement, and college culture*. Chicago: University of Chicago Press.

Kalof, Linda, and Timothy Cargill. 1991. Fraternity and sorority membership and gender dominance attitudes. *Sex Roles* 25:417–23.

Lees, Sue. 1986. *Losing out: Sexuality and adolescent girls*. London: Hutchinson.

Lil' sister programs wait for IFC vote. 1991. *The Alligator*, 26 March, p.1.

Martin, Patricia Yancey, and Robert A. Hummer. 1989. Fraternities and rape on campus. *Gender & Society 3(4)*: 457–73.

Martin, Patricia Yancey, and Mindy Stombler. 1993. Gender politics in fraternity little sister groups: How men take power away from women. Department of Sociology, Florida Slate University. Unpublished manuscript.

McKee, C. William. 1987. Understanding the diversity of the Greek world. In *Fraternities and Sororities on the Contemporary College Campus*. New Directions for Student Services, no. 40., edited by R. B. Winston, Jr., W. R. Nettles III, J. H. Opper, Jr., 21–35. San Francisco, CA: Jossey-Bass (Winter).

Messner, M. A. 1992. Masculinities and athletics careers. In *Race, class and gender: An anthology*, edited by Margaret L. Andersen and Patricia Hill Collins, 147–62. Belmont, CA: Wadsworth.

Riker, Hal C.1983. Programming for personal development. In *The eighties: Challenges for fraternities and sororities*, edited by William A. Bryan and Robert A. Schwartz, 49–72. Carbondale: Southern Illinois University Press.

Risman, Barbara. 1982. College women and sororities: The social construction and reaffirmation of gender roles. *Urban Life* 11(2): 231–52.

Sadker, Myra. 1984. Sex bias in colleges and universities. *The report card.* no. 2. Washington, DC: Mid-Atlantic Center for Sex Equity and Project EFFECT, American University.

Sadker, Myra, and David Sadker. 1994. *Failing at fairness: How schools cheat girls.* New York: Scribner's.

Sanday, Peggy Reeves. 1990. *Fraternity gang rape: Sex, brotherhood, and privilege on campus.* New York: New York University Press.

Scary frat boys. 1993. Aired on *Jane Pratt.* 17 April. Lifetime Television.

Stombler, Mindy. 1994. "Buddies" or "slutties": The collective sexual reputation of fraternity little sisters. *Gender & Society* 8(3): 293–296.

Stombler, Mindy, and Irene Padavic. 1994. Getting a man or getting ahead. Paper presented at the meeting of the American Sociological Association.

PORTRAIT

Gatekeepers and Homeseekers: Institutional Patterns in Racial Steering

Diana M. Pearce

The segregated housing patterns documented by the Taeubers (1965) from 1940 to 1960 have remained basically unchanged, and seem to show no signs of substantial alteration toward desegregation in the seventies (Hermalin and Farley, 1973; Van Valey et al., 1977; Sorenson et al., 1975; deLeeuw et al., 1976). Although more whites may be exposed to token integration (as maintained by Bradburn et al., 1971), the predominant residential experience of Americans today remains that of the monoracial neighborhood. During this same time period, however, the legal supports for discrimination in housing have been largely destroyed. The Supreme Court outlawed racially restrictive covenants in 1948, and twenty years later it declared that all aspects of property transactions must be colorblind (Jones versus Mayer), thus broadening the already comprehensive Fair Housing Act of 1968 just passed by Congress. . . .

Three theoretical approaches have been used to explain the paradox of continued segregation and housing inequality within an "open" social and legal context. The first set of theories asserts that the phenomenon is really self-segregation, the result of preferences of blacks, as with other ethnics, to live in segregated neighborhoods. The second suggests that poverty, aided by the inertia of history, has perpetuated segregation. The third suggests that the decline of blatant discrimination of the past has revealed pervasive institutional racism. . . .

We shall approach the problem of whether a model of institutional racism helps explain the paradox of continued housing segregation by focusing on the actual behavior of [the] key actors in the housing market, real estate agents. In particular, we will address two questions. First, do real estate agents exercise their discretion and use their expertise in ways that result in treatment that is racially unequal? Second, can the racial practices described here be characterized as institutional racism?

From "Gatekeepers and Homeseekers: Institutional Patterns in Racial Steering" by D. M. Pearce, 1979, *Social Problems 26:* 325–343.

Design of the Study

. . . In order to answer the first question posed above—whether agent discretion is used to provide racially unequal services—the study was designed to "sample," in as unobtrusive a manner as possible (Webb, 1972), each agent's behavior towards two homeseeker couples who were basically alike except for race. The couples were all in their late twenties, had two children, and needed a house with at least three bedrooms. The woman was not working. The man had a job that required a college education, such as engineer, teacher or office manager, and had a steady work history. Each couple indicated that they were new to homebuying, as well as to the area or community. Each pair of couples visiting a particular agent had roughly the same stated income and savings. (The black couple's income was slightly higher to avoid suspicion.) The incomes were set at approximately ten percent above the 1970 median income (as reported in the census) of the community in which the particular agent was located. Basically, then, each agent was faced with two homeseeker couples, one white couple and one black couple, who presented the same housing needs and preferences, the same financial abilities, and the same geographic preferences.

The "couples" were actually trained and paid interviewer/participant observers.[1] They did not take notes, except to make "back of the envelope" calculations or jot down addresses, as would be natural for real homeseekers. They quickly acquired good memories, however, and the accuracy of recall was enhanced by the use of an exhaustive Recording Form. Immediately after the visit to the broker, they completed the form, which can be described as a self-administered interview schedule that "debriefed" them on their experience. The form was seven pages long, with an added page for each house seen, and took twenty to thirty minutes to complete. It covered numerous details of the interview and its setting, as well as the agent's words and actions—from their entrance to their exit from the office.[2] Use of this form resulted in finely graded measures of discriminatory behavior by the agents in several areas without creating an artificial and rigid set of stimuli. While the lack of "controls" on the process of the interview resulted in some unique and noncomparable data, it also resulted in a degree of naturalness frequently missing in field experiments. To the extent that we have been successful in creating genuine-appearing homeseekers, the experiences reported here *directly,* not by analogy or extrapolation or reinterpretation, reflect the real-life differences in treatment of black and white couples who seek to buy homes through a real estate agent.

Ninety-seven real estate agents, from the approximately ten thousand in the Detroit metropolitan area (Detroit and its suburbs), were randomly chosen.[3] The interviews were conducted between May 1974 and March 1975. Each agent was visited first by a black couple, and then several weeks later by a white couple. In order to obtain the same agent, the white couple asked by name for the agent seen by the black couple, but used a vague referral rather than the black couple's name such as, "Somebody at the office got your name from a neighbor who just moved from __________ City."[4] . . .

Findings

Frequently the first part of the interview ended with a look at the listings book, which lists all houses currently for sale, arranged by price and geographical area, and including for each house a brief description and a picture. At this point, if the agent did not offer to show homes, the couple requested to see some homes with the salesperson; such requests resulted in ten more *white* couples seeing homes than would have otherwise, while it did not change the number of black couples who were actually shown homes. Overall, the chances of seeing a house on the first visit to a real estate agent are

1 out of 4 if you are black, but almost 3 out of 4 if you are white, other things being equal. Even when homes were shown to blacks, fewer were shown per couple, so that overall only one-fifth of the homes shown were seen by the black couples.[5]

Note that there is no mention of the homeowner. In fact few of the couples met homeowners, and if they did, the contact was minimal. This was not accidental, for real estate agents consider themselves to be skilled professional salespeople, and do not wish to have the amateur homeowner sabotage the sale through a well-meaning but disastrous confession about the house's history or faults, or through personally offending the potential buyer. The same was true of the negotiations over purchase price, for again both the buyer's and the seller's agent will emphasize that they are more adequately prepared to bargain effectively than are their inexperienced clients. The end result is that homeseekers may see the homeowner when they are shown the house, but they are unlikely to meet the owner(s) until the closing of the sale. It is not surprising, then, that there were no slammed doors or hurled epithets by homeowners.[6] While the real estate agents may claim that they are acting on behalf of the homeowner, it is rare that anyone but the agent has the opportunity to refuse to show a home or homes to black homeseekers.

The efforts of black homeseekers to be shown homes by the agents were not met with strong or dramatic refusals. Instead, their requests were frequently met with reasonable sounding at excuses, such as "no key" [or] "need to make an appointment ahead of time," or with offers to show homes at some later date. In contrast, the same request to see homes, when it came from white homeseekers, was more often honored. Thus, the racially differentiated treatment of homeseekers in the showing of homes by real estate agents is gross in magnitude, but benign in execution. The lack of insult or apparent mistreatment of black couples becomes, upon comparison with the white couples' treatment, a cover that masks unequal treatment.

Comparisons of Homes Shown

We defined discrimination as actions that "limit or exclude financially equal blacks from full and equal access to housing." Many blacks are clearly excluded; but were those who were shown homes also discriminated against? In the latter cases, our real test of discrimination is whether blacks are shown homes that are in the same condition, and in the same areas, as those shown whites. On the assumption that a major cause of residential segregation is black exclusion from white areas, and not the reverse, our primary empirical question is whether blacks have access to predominantly white areas. Not only have very few whites expressed preferences for moving into all-black neighborhoods, but in the recent instances where whites have attempted to move into central city black neighborhoods, a process sometimes called "gentrification," they have met with little effective black resistance.

Given that being shown homes at all is problematic for the black couples, when they *are* shown homes, how do these homes compare with those shown white couples? Specifically, are the homes shown to blacks and the homes shown to whites characterized by (a) the same prices, (b) the same quality and (c) the same locations? While clearly different, these three characteristics are not independent, for house price is usually seen as the dependent characteristic. That is:

House Price = F(House Location, House Quality)

Thus, the first question is whether there is any variation, by race, in the average house price. . . . The homes shown the blacks are systematically less expensive, averaging $3300 less than the homes shown whites ($t = 2.69$, $p < .01$).[7] Using the house price equation, there are a number of logical explanations of this difference in prices of homes shown:

1. The *same houses* were shown, but the blacks were quoted lower prices.
2. Houses in the *same location* or neighborhood were shown, but blacks were shown houses of lesser quality (i.e., smaller size, older or poorer condition).
3. Houses of the *same quality* were shown, but in different locations such that the houses shown to blacks were in neighborhoods with generally less expensive homes.

Since the homeseekers did not request to see a specific home, the first explanation seems implausible: in fact only three homes were seen by both black and white couples. Let us examine first the possibility of house quality as the reason for lower house prices of houses shown blacks; note that by quality we are referring to strictly physical characteristics, such as size and condition of the home. Thus we will use location to refer to all other aspects of a house, such as the neighborhood, quality of schools, crime rate, pollution, and level of amenities and services that might contribute to the selling price of that house.

The homeseekers were asked to record basic descriptive characteristics of each house shown (e.g., number of bedrooms) and then compare the house with others in the neighborhood. . . . Both in terms of characteristics and in relative comparison to the neighborhood there was no significant difference in the average quality of homes shown blacks and whites. It seems, then, that almost none of the difference in the average price of homes shown is attributable to the poorer quality of houses shown black homeseekers.

In order to determine the importance of location as a determinant of house price differences, the average housing value of the city or suburb where the house was located, the average housing value of the community where the real estate firm was located, and the distance from black population areas were compared by race. First, the cities and suburbs where the real estate firms were located were rank-ordered by mean value of owner-occupied housing units using the 1970 census figures, and the sample was divided into thirds. That is, a third of the salespersons visited were in offices located in higher-priced housing communities, a third were in medium-priced communities, and a third were in lower-priced communities. The expected distribution of houses shown, then, would be that roughly a third of the houses shown would fall in each housing value group. Although *all* the homeseekers were shown housing lower in value than would be expected from the communities' housing values, compared to whites, blacks were shown disproportionately more houses in lower-priced communities.

It is apparent, then, that some of the difference in the prices of houses shown stems from the location of the houses, for the mean housing value in the communities where blacks were shown housing is about $700 lower . . . than the mean housing value of the communities where whites were shown homes. Nevertheless, much of the house price difference of $3300 remains unexplained. An anomalous finding that also remains unexplained is the high percentage of homes shown to blacks in *higher* priced areas; we will return to this later.

Some of the effect of house location may be due to racial composition, both of the immediate neighborhood and of those nearby. To examine this possibility, each of the homes shown was located on a census map and the 1970 racial composition of the tract and the block was recorded. . . . The likelihood of a white couple seeing a home in a block or tract with black families was quite low (less than ten percent for either block or tract). Similarly, two out of three of the black couples were also shown homes in all-white census tracts, and almost all of the remaining one-third were shown homes in areas with quite small percentages of blacks (1 to

15%). A similar pattern for the block data may be discerned. Clearly, most of the homes shown to both blacks and whites were in areas that were all white in 1970.

It is not unlikely that some of these areas that were all white in 1970 became racially mixed between 1970 and 1975, or were likely to become so in the near future. To assess this possibility, three measurements were made from each house to the nearest black population area.[8] These were: distance from the house to the nearest census tract that was five to forty-nine percent black; distance to the nearest tract that was fifty to eighty-nine percent black; and distance to the nearest tract that was ninety to one hundred percent black. Clearly there was not a random distribution of the homes shown to blacks and whites. Well over half the homes shown to blacks were within one mile of areas with five to forty-nine percent black population, and only a quarter of the homes shown whites were within a mile of such areas. The same difference in patterns is apparent for each measure—with striking regularity. Almost half the black couples' houses were within two miles of ghetto areas (90 to 100% black tracts). In sum, houses shown to blacks were nearly a mile closer to black areas, on the average, than the houses shown to whites.[9]

To assess the importance of distance from black population areas on the difference in prices of houses shown, distance from black areas[10] was correlated with house price for both races. For both blacks and whites, the correlation between house price and distance from ghetto areas is less than might be expected, but it is much greater for blacks than whites (.39 and .16 respectively). This suggests that distance from black population areas is only important relatively close to those areas. Because the houses shown to whites average over a mile further out from these areas, other things being equal, a house that is very close to or in racially mixed or black areas may have a *lower* price, but as one gets further out, it is not likely to have a *higher* price.

In contrast to the low explanatory power of distance from black areas (especially for houses shown to whites), when house prices are regressed on the mean housing values of the communities where they are located, there is a strong relationship for both races. That is, the average housing value of the community explains much more of the variance in the price of the house than does distance from black housing areas. In fact, when both variables are included in the equation, the R^2 is not appreciably increased for either blacks or whites. This suggests that the two variables are redundant; that is, housing values already reflect distance from the ghetto. . . . In fact, housing values may incorporate nonlinear, social distance between black and white neighborhoods, as well as physical distance. Thus the high housing values of some white communities that are very close to black neighborhoods reflect not physical distance between black and white communities, but the perception that black families are highly unlikely to cross that line.

The evidence of the strong effect of housing values on prices, together with the data on location and distance from the ghetto, suggests that much of the racial difference in the prices of the houses shown comes from there being a racial difference in their location. It seems reasonable to conclude that further measures of physical quality (e.g., age of the furnace) will not reveal differences that will in turn increase the explanation of racial differences in house prices. On the other hand, it is likely that other measures of *distance* (incorporating a factor reflecting discontinuity, or social distance), or finer measures of *housing values* (such as at the tract or even the block level) would increase the amount of difference explained. Let us turn now to an examination of some of these latter aspects of the location of houses shown to each racial group that are not captured by the measures used above.

Location and Racial Steering

In the discussion above, we used measures of distance from black population areas on the assumption that linear distance may measure meaningful social distance. City boundaries and intra-city neighborhood boundaries create much more distance than is shown in the hundred-foot width of a street. Put another way, the likelihood of black families moving from a mixed neighborhood on one side of the street to a previously all-white neighborhood on the other side of the street is much higher in parts of northwest Detroit than it is from southwest Detroit into all-white Dearborn. For example, a BBC reporter doing a documentary on race relations in the United States was told that Eight Mile Road (the northern boundary of Detroit) was the Mason-Dixon line of Detroit. Not only the major thoroughfares, but different land uses, transportation patterns and chance factors create and divide the metropolitan area into somewhat discontinuous communities (see Suttles, 1972). To the extent that the city racial composition is a series of communities that "shade" into each other gradually, physical distance is an accurate reflection of social distance. To the extent that there are impermeable boundaries instead, which at the extreme divide a 100 percent black population on one side from a 100 percent white population on the other, a physical distance of one block does *not* reflect the social distance.

This phenomenon of social distance is reflected in the patterns of racial steering found here in two ways. First, blacks more often than whites were shown houses *not* located in the city where the sales agent's office was located; that is, they were steered "out of town." Second, where and whether houses were shown to black couples depended upon the location of the sales office within the suburban ring. . . . The chances were significantly greater for whites to be shown houses in the same city as the real estate office's location (56% vs. 33%, $p < .05$). Moreover, when whites were "steered out," about four-fifths of the cities where they were shown houses were nearby white suburbs. In contrast, when blacks were "steered out," two-thirds of the houses shown were in the racially mixed cities of Inkster and Detroit. Detroit alone accounted for almost a third of the homes shown to blacks, although only 13 percent of the firms were located in the central city. . . .

. . . Not only did black couples see a disproportionate number of houses in Inkster and Detroit, they were "steered" there disproportionately by firms located in the western, southern and eastern shore suburbs. The map reveals this pattern most strikingly: the only houses shown to black homeseekers in the western and southern suburbs of Detroit (from the Detroit River clockwise to Eight Mile Road) were the six houses in Inkster. In contrast, north (and east) of Eight Mile Road, the houses were much more scattered: six were in Oak Park, but the other seven were in five different suburbs, ranging from Farmington in the West to East Detroit. The houses shown to whites, on the other hand, were more or less randomly distributed in both areas, although there was, as noted, a tendency toward lower priced areas.

. . . The geographic subareas fall into groups, indicated . . . as Pattern A (Discriminatory) and Pattern B (Nondiscriminatory) suburbs. By comparing the percentage of firms located in each area with the geographic distribution of homes shown these patterns become clear. While the Pattern A suburbs, in which fifty percent of the firms visited were located, accounted for approximately fifty percent of the homes shown to whites, these suburbs accounted for only about one-fifth of the homes shown to blacks; moreover, the homes shown were almost all in areas that were predominantly black. In contrast, while only a third of the firms visited were in Pattern B suburbs, forty-five percent of the homes shown to blacks were in Pattern B suburbs, and their locations were scattered throughout the area.[11]

Racial Steering: Wealth, History and Ecology

The fact that black couples were more often shown homes and urged to buy homes in areas that are racially mixed is not surprising, but the distinctive geographical concentration both in the showing of homes and the steering of people "out" is an unexpected finding. Why were blacks more often shown homes in the suburbs north and northwest of Detroit (Pattern B suburbs) than elsewhere? We will consider three possible explanations here: wealth, historical patterns and an ecological argument.[12]

First, if one calculates the mean housing values for each of the geographic groupings,[13] their rank order is as follows: Detroit ($16,100), Southern ($19,950), Western ($24,658), North Central ($24,736), Eastern Shore ($29,790), Northwestern ($31,858). Except for the Eastern Shore suburbs, it was the areas with somewhat more expensive housing in which disproportionately more homes were shown to blacks, in spite of the fact that more of the housing shown to blacks was less expensive. Thus, not only are relative housing values not an explanation of differential steering behavior between geographic areas, but the tendency of agents in the higher housing value suburbs (northern and northwestern) to show houses more often to blacks runs counter to the overall tendency for more expensive areas to be more discriminatory on measures of discrimination other than steering, such as the amount of time spent with the couple, and amount of advice given.

The paradox of blacks being shown homes that averaged lower prices (by about $3000) but were located in higher-priced housing areas (the north and the northwestern suburbs) does account for an anomaly noted earlier. That is, the housing shown blacks is located disproportionately not only in *more* expensive areas, but also disproportionately in *less* expensive areas; the moderately priced communities are underrepresented as places where houses were shown to blacks, and are concentrated geographically in areas west and south of Detroit.

A second explanation of this anomaly rests on historical patterns, both of racial succession and of metropolitan growth. There has been a century long pattern of the Detroit ghetto's expansion in a northwest direction (Deskins, 1965). Historically, black expansion (especially in the middle class) followed Jewish residential movement (Wolf, 1957). Wolf, Mayer (1960) and others have documented the transition in Detroit from Jewish-dominated neighborhoods to majority black neighborhoods in the 1950's and 1960's. It may be that the pattern will repeat itself (on the same geographic axis) in the northwestern suburbs and that this is the very beginning of the pattern.

Third, as can be seen on the map, there is only one large concentration of black population outside the Detroit ghetto, and that is the suburb of Inkster to the west of Detroit.[14] In many ways that city may be seen not as a smaller version of the Detroit ghetto, but rather as a suburb that "happens" to have a large black population.[15] Home ownership is high (72%), housing values (in 1970, $17,800) are above those of Detroit, and most of the housing is single family. Presented with would-be black suburbanites, then, it is possible for the real estate agent in the western or southern suburbs "legitimately" to show housing in Inkster, for it is suburban in character and location as well as racially mixed. North of Eight Mile Road (the northern boundary of Detroit), on the other hand, there is no concentration of black suburban population. Without an obvious place to steer would-be black suburbanites, they were shown homes in a variety of communities, although many were close to the edge of the city.

Summary and Conclusions

The patterns of racial steering examined here begin and end with the fact that most blacks did not experience racial steering simply because the majority of blacks were not shown homes on the first visit to the real estate office;

the majority of whites, however, were. Not only were black homeseeker couples seldom shown homes at all, but also the manner and method used in such refusals made the detection of discrimination very difficult. The first type of gatekeeping, then, was to keep the gate closed for all but a minority of black homeseekers. Needless to say, it is difficult to purchase a home if one is not shown any.

If black couples were shown homes, they were likely to be:

1. Less expensive, averaging $3300 less than the average house shown to whites. This was apparently not because the houses shown were of relatively poorer quality, but rather due to their location in cities with overall lower housing values and/or their location closer to black population areas.
2. Located, paradoxically, in the (more expensive) suburbs to the north and the northwest of Detroit, as well as in the (less expensive) suburb of Inkster and the city of Detroit.

Clearly, then, we have found a consistent pattern of racially differentiated treatment of homeseekers, both in the showing/not showing of homes, and in the price and location of homes shown.

But is this treatment, clearly differentiated by race, aptly characterized as "institutional racism"? First of all, the data show that these are not isolated instances of individual racism. Although there are differences between communities, there is a high level of consistency across the entire metropolitan area: the clear existence of practices that exclude three-fourths of black couples from ever seeing homes, and "steer out" many of the few that do see homes, strongly suggests a strong consensus among real estate agents about the desirable demographic character that Detroit communities should assume.

Next, most real estate agents belong to real estate boards, and many belong to NAREB, the National Association of Real Estate Boards. Whether or not one is formally a member of NAREB, it exerts a powerful influence over the real estate profession as a whole, and far beyond it as well. NAREB now supports Open Housing Laws, but that support has been somewhat circumscribed (see Yinger, 1975); and it vigorously opposed such laws at the local as well as national level until about 1968. While one can only guess what NAREB's role is in the discrimination documented here, both directly and indirectly NAREB has supported policies and practices that more often than not have been discriminatory in effect.

Finally, these data do document discrimination that took place during personal interviews, whereas institutional racism is often seen as "no fault" discrimination. That is, the unequal outcomes are portrayed as the accidental byproducts of actions taken for purposes other than racial exclusion. Certainly one cannot attribute intention solely on the basis of the sort of data we obtained on the real estate agents' actions (and inactions); but their actions are far from random and it is highly unlikely that they are done blindly or unwittingly.

I would argue, therefore, that a clearer answer to the question of whether the manifest differences in treatment afforded black and white homeseekers is institutional racism, requires reconceptualization of institutional racism. As a start, I think we must first reject the image of an automaton heedlessly and helplessly grinding out differential treatment. We also should not attribute discrimination to a handful of people, anomalous individuals whose discrimination against blacks contrasts with the behavior (and perhaps norms and values) of the majority of their peers. In fact, it is precisely because the individual real estate agents are typical, both in their communities and their professions, that these practices can be characterized as institutional racism (see Pearce, 1976).[16] . . .

NOTES

1. The homeseekers were forty people whose real backgrounds reflected a great deal of diversity. About half were graduate students in sociology, social work, political science, and psychology; the rest included a librarian, a trumpet player, an actor, a dental student, and a marriage counselor. Some were real couples, and some were not. Neither student status nor being a real couple explained variation in treatment (see Pearce, 1976).
2. Although each individual filled out a form separately, for simplicity's sake we report here a combined black and a combined white observation. For a discussion of differences by sex and race, which are systematically apparent only on the subjective evaluations of the interview *in toto*, see Pearce (1976).
3. Because it would have been unrealistic *and highly artificial* for a white couple to have sought housing in areas that were all or nearly all-black in racial composition, real estate agents located in these areas were eliminated from the sample (N = 7). Some were eliminated because the dealt only in commercial real estate (N = 8), or because the *pair* of interviews was not successfully completed because the agent became ill [or] left the business or the office closed (N = 14). The total of ninety-seven interviews thus represents agents in white or racially mixed areas who saw a black couple and a white couple.
4. Referrals are a source of about a third of a real estate agent's customers according to Hempel (1969), so homeseekers' explanations were not seriously questioned by the agents.
5. While it is possible that black homeseekers might have been shown homes on subsequent visits to the agent, it should be emphasized that the gatekeeping being exercised in the first visit is intrinsically important, for it is likely to discourage any but the most persistent black homeseeker from every trying again. Also, while subsequent visits may result in seeing homes, it is likely that the homeseeker will experience steering of the kind described above.
6. Only two instances of homeowner–homeseeker contact were at all negative—one white couple and one black couple met owners who did not want to sell to them.
7. More blacks than whites were told that the price was negotiable. . . . This is puzzling, as it implies that the blacks were being offered the possibility of a better deal; given that only a quarter of the real estate agents even showed homes to the black couples, some may have sincerely wished to enhance the likelihood that the black homeseekers buy a house. Or it may also be true, since blacks were shown homes in areas that were closer to black neighborhoods (see below), that the sales agent believed that whites would "panic" and sell at less than the stated price (believing that this black household would be followed by others). Apparently that belief has led real estate agents to encourage whites to sell at lower prices, making a belief into a self-fulfilling prophecy (see Helper, 1969; Wolf, 1957). A less sanguine approach is that the real estate agent would be able to later use the lack of the seller's price reduction as a means to prevent a sale, by suggesting that the black couple would be paying too much if they paid the stated price. Finally, it may just be a random difference; that is, the group of homes shown to blacks by chance included a few more sellers who were willing to bargain.
8. The underlying assumption in making these measurements is that racial succession between 1970 and 1975 occurred at roughly the same rate all along the edge of black population areas.
9. Note that the racial composition data is that of 1970 while the houses were seen in 1974 and 1975. To the extent that the racial composition of Detroit neighborhoods has not changed "regularly" between 1970 and 1975 (i.e., racial change has not occurred at the same rate at all edges of the ghetto), the distance figures will be inaccurate. Since more of the houses seen by blacks were in census tracts close to or contiguous to census tracts with some black population in 1970, it is probable that more of these areas have experienced an increase in the percent black between 1970 and 1975. This suggests that the percent black of the census tracts is underestimated to a greater extent for the houses shown to blacks than for the houses shown to whites.
10. Since "distance to nearest census tract with 90 to 100% black" showed both the greatest

difference by race and the widest variation, it was used here.

11. Compared to ten white couples, 21 black couples were "steered out," frequently to racially mixed communities.

12. The reader should be reminded that it is the *showing* of homes, not their *purchase,* that is being discussed. Strictly speaking, it is possible that blacks may be shown housing in these areas more than other areas precisely because the real estate agent is confident that it will not result in a purchase. That is, the agent assumes that the blacks would not be able to obtain a mortgage (because of mortgage discrimination, or lack of money, or both), or the homeowner would refuse to sell, or the couple would find it undesirable or too expensive to move to that area. On the other hand, while institutional racism in the mortgage market and other institutional barriers to black homeownership are important in the total picture of racism in the housing market, it is risky for an agent to count on such factors in any one particular situation. In addition, such an explanation is somewhat in conflict with the evidence presented above that blacks were, on the average, shown homes closer to black areas and in less expensive areas, and homes that were priced lower—all of which would enhance the chances of a black couple obtaining a mortgage.

13. These means are weighted by the number of firms in the community in the sample which in turn approximates the relative size of the suburbs (particularly their relative portion of the housing market).

14. There is a small unincorporated area on the northern edge of Detroit, contiguous with the ghetto, that is 100% black (Royal Oak Township). It seems to be an extension of the ghetto, rather than a suburb like Inkster.

15. Inkster was created to house black autoworkers separately from the white autoworkers; the latter lived, and still live, in Dearborn, an all-white suburb of Detroit.

16. The real estate agents studied were "liberal" in their racial attitudes, but tended to be the most discriminatory. Also, those who were the most business-like in orientation, and to some extent the more successful, tended to be more discriminatory. In other words, it is not the marginal members of the profession, but rather those who are well integrated into the institution, who account for more of the discrimination. For further discussion of this aspect of the study, as well as other measures of discrimination used, see Pearce, 1976.

REFERENCES

Bradburn, Norman B., Seymour Sudman and Galen L. Gockel with the assistance of Joseph R. Noel
1971 Side by Side: Integrated Neighborhoods in America. Chicago: Quadrangle Books.

deLeeuw, Frank, A. B. Schnare and R. J. Struyk
1976 "Housing." Pp. 119–178 in William Gorham and Nathan Glazer (eds.), The Urban Predicament. Washington, D.C.: The Urban Institute.

Deskins, Donald R., Jr.
1967 Residential Mobility of Negroes in Detroit, 1837–1965. Ann Arbor, Michigan: Department of Geography, University of Michigan.

Helper, Rose
1969 Racial Politics and Practices of Real Estate Brokers. Minneapolis: University of Minnesota Press.

Hempel, Donald
1969 The Role of the Real Estate Broker in the Home Buying Process. Storr, Connecticut: University of Connecticut.

Hermalin, Albert I. and Reynolds Farley
1973 "The potential for residential integration in cities and suburbs: Implications for the busing controversy." American Sociological Review 38:595–610.

Mayer, Albert J.
1960 "Russet Woods: Change without conflict: A case study of racial transition in Detroit." Pp. 52–86 in Nathan Glazer and Davis McEntire (eds.), Studies in Housing and Minority Groups. Berkeley: University of California Press.

Pearce, Diana
1976 "Black, white, and many shades of gray: Real estate brokers and their racial practices." Unpublished doctoral dissertation, University of Michigan.

Sorenson, Annemette, K. E. Taueber and L. J. Hollingsworth, Jr.
1975 "Indexes of racial segregation for 109 cities in the United States, 1940 to 1970." Sociological Focus 8 (April) 125–152.

Suttles, Gerald
1972 The Social Construction of Communities. Chicago: University of Chicago Press.

Taeuber, Karl and Alma F. Taeuber
1965 Negroes in Cities: Residential Segregation and Neighborhood Change. Chicago. Aldine

Van Valey, Thomas, W. C. Roof and J. E. Wilcox
1977 "Trends in residential segregation: 1960–1970". American Journal of Sociology 82 (January): 826–844.

Webb, Eugene J., Donald T. Campbell, Richard O. Schwartz and Lee Sechrist
1972 Unobtrusive Measures: Nonreactive Research in the Social Sciences. Chicago: Rand McNally.

Wolf, Eleanor P.
1967 "The invasion-succession sequence as a self-fulfilling prophecy." Journal of Social Issues 13:31–39.

Yinger, John
1975 An Analysis of Discrimination by Real Estate Brokers. Madison, Wisconsin: University of Wisconsin.

DEVELOPING YOUR OWN SNAPSHOTS *About Social Inequality*

1. *Research topic:* Make a list of 20 occupations representing the sorts of jobs that you and your classmates are likely to be doing after graduation. Give this list to several friends and ask them to rank all 20 occupations from 1 (most prestigious) to 20 (least prestigious). How much agreement is there regarding the prestige rankings of these jobs? What do your results indicate about the structured aspect of stratification?
2. *Writing topic:* Write a short essay in which you compare the everyday lives of two fictitious characters: a 25-year-old man or woman who possesses extraordinary wealth versus a 25-year-old man or woman who experiences extreme poverty. Specifically, compare them on such things as (a) what they are likely to do at leisure, (b) where they are likely to live, (c) their family lives, (d) health care, and (e) their jobs. Explain how each man or woman got that way and what the poverty-stricken individual might do to improve his or her social position.
3. *Research topic:* Popular culture often expresses our stereotyped images. Analyze any 10 birthday cards that you select from your local card shop or drug store. Choose only cards that make a direct reference to age. Are their messages positive or negative? How many refer, even if only in a joking reference, to lack of sexual activity, lack of attractiveness, lack of intelligence, or lack of physical ability? How many joke about age concealment?

How many make special mention of women's problems with aging? Does any card suggest that you might get better as you get older?

4. *Writing topic:* Herbert Gans ("Positive Functions of the Undeserving Poor: Uses of the Underclass in America") argued that middle-class people benefit from accepting the stereotype that poor people are dangerous and in need of intervention. Keeping Gans's study in mind, make a list of all the tasks that poor people do for society—tasks that might otherwise not get done or might have to be done by the middle class. For example, poor people buy day-old bread from thrift stores that might otherwise never be sold. Can you suggest other ways to get these tasks accomplished without relying on poor people to do them?
5. *Research topic:* Among the methods that sociologists use to assess social status is the subjective approach, whereby respondents are asked to place themselves in the stratification hierarchy. In 1949 Richard Centers asked a national sample of white adults, "If you were asked to use one of these four names for your social class, which would you say you belonged in: the middle class, the lower class, the working class, or the upper class?" Like many other sociologists, Centers found that most of his sample saw themselves as belonging to the middle class. Using the same question as Centers, ask a sample of 20 people you know fairly well how they see their social class membership. With which class does the majority identify? Explain your results.
6. *Research topic:* Every year, the U.S. Bureau of the Census produces a volume, easily accessible at most libraries or through the U.S. Government Printing Office, called *Statistical Abstract of the United States.* To determine how inequality may have increased or decreased over time, compare at least two years (say, one year from the 1990s versus one year from the 1970s) on several indicators of economic well-being such as unemployment rate, total personal income, families below the poverty level, and average annual pay. You can find these indicators in the table of contents of the book in sections on "Labor Force, Employment and Earnings" and "Income, Expenditures, and Wealth." You may also decide to look in the section on "Business Enterprise" for business failure rate and employment growth by major industry.
7. *Writing topic:* In "Fraternity Little Sister Organizations: Structures of Opportunity or Exploitation?" Mindy Stombler and Patricia Yancey Martin suggest that fraternities' little sister connections

actually help to reinforce the subservient position of women in society. Write a brief essay in which you speculate about other ways in which structural conditions in our nation's colleges and universities contribute to gender inequalities.

8. *Writing topic:* The photo essay for this section asked, "Rags to riches: myth or reality?" What do you think might help or prevent you from improving your own lot in life? In a short essay, identify and discuss the characteristics—for example, your gender, race, and ethnic background—that might affect your chances for upward mobility. Considering everything, is your own likelihood of gaining great wealth mostly a myth or more a reality?

CHAPTER 7

Social Change and Collective Behavior

USA

SNAPSHOT

Highway to Hell?

Fear and Loathing on the Road

Travel any highway into a major city during rush hour. While waiting to move, you are bound to observe at least a half-dozen drivers talking to themselves or singing along with a tune on the radio or scratching themselves.

Automobiles give an illusion of privacy. As long as drivers remain behind the wheel, they travel in isolation. Enclosed by steel and glass, they are physically independent of the thousands of other motorists with whom they share the road. No matter how jammed the highway is with vehicles, drivers feel alone, and in a social-psychological sense, they are. As a result, they may engage in bizarre, even deviant, behavior.

Having been associated with deviance ever since the advent of mass motoring, automobiles have long contributed to the direction of social and cultural change. In the 1920s many Americans for the first time owned a family car. And it was the automobile that critics blamed for what they saw as a precipitous decline in national morality. Newly freed from the rigid restrictions of previous generations, the flaming youth of the decade regarded the family's "tin lizzie" as their apartment on wheels—a place where they could kiss, neck, and pet. Sex researcher Alfred Kinsey reported that young women of the twenties were far more likely to have premarital intercourse than were those who had reached sexual maturity before the First World War. Not surprisingly, the automobile was blamed . . . and with cause. In Robert and Helen Lynd's classic 1929 community study, *Middletown,* the overwhelming majority of teenagers in Muncie, Indiana, reported that the automobile was the most common place to pet.

In a more extreme version of immorality, the automobile of the 1920s also became a brothel on wheels, providing prostitutes around the country a secure and secluded place where they might escape police oversight and ply their trade. The use of the automobile for these purposes posed a serious setback to the vigorous anti-vice campaigns during the First World War. The police were not yet equipped to patrol city streets and country highways.

By the 1950s teenagers around the country were holding their "submarine races" in lovers' lanes and drive-in theaters. The game of chicken became a deadly contest between males who sought to impress their dates. During subsequent decades young people relied on their automobiles as a safe haven in which to drink beer, have sex, and smoke dope.

Teenagers aren't the only drivers who play chicken. Every year some 46,000 Americans from all age groups are killed in motor vehicle accidents. Another 1.8 million are disabled. Among the leading causes of such fatal crashes are drinking and speeding—two human factors that could be totally controlled. In some single-victim automobile accidents the lack of control is deliberate: The driver purposely veers his or her vehicle into a tree or off a bridge to commit suicide. The victim chooses an automobile as an instrument of death to save his or her family the embarrassment that accompanies more obvious forms of suicide.

But most deaths and injuries are avoidable. Such accidents happen because the automobile offers power, especially to the powerless. The automobile satisfies the desire to be in charge. Even the most timid and passive individuals (or, perhaps, *especially* the most timid and passive individuals) may become fearless bullies and criminals just as soon as they get behind the 3,000 pounds of steel that separate them from the rest of humanity. Not only do they feel anonymous; they also feel invulnerable because they are caught up in an illusion of their own omnipotence.

At the extreme, unbridled power turns nasty, and arguments between drivers erupt into violence. The freeways of California have been particularly violent for the past decade, as small provocations have sent some frustrated motorists into a state of frenzy. In Sacramento a passenger inflamed by a freeway lane change lifted a rifle from a rack in the back window of his pickup truck and fatally shot the driver of the other vehicle. One passenger was shot in the head after a minor sideswiping incident. A tow truck operator was fired upon by a driver whose entry onto the Golden State Freeway was blocked. In Claremont the windshields of 10 vehicles were smashed, and a police officer was fired upon as he prepared to write a traffic ticket. During a single two-week period (August 1987) there were 18 different acts of violence on the highways of the Silicon Valley, not to mention the rest of California. What is more, shooting episodes quickly spread cross-country to trigger-happy drivers in Detroit, Boston, and New York.

For commuters, the experience of driving in rush-hour traffic is intensely frustrating. In most major cities parking places have become as rare as pollution-free air; and traffic jams at 5 P.M. are beginning to resemble never-ending parking lots. For visitors, the problems associated with negotiating traffic are exacerbated by a lack of street signs and the presence of one-way streets without pattern or logic.

Some drivers are already frustrated before they get behind the wheel of their vehicles. They decide to go for a drive to cool off after arguing with their boss, their spouse, or their friends. According to University of California psychologist Joseph Tupin, people with aggressive impulses frequently take their cars out for a spin as a release from the tensions of the day. They get into a minor confrontation on the highway and explode.

Of course, the most pervasive effects of the automobile are at the level of social change. As we have seen, the presence of the family car, beginning in the 1920s, significantly altered the ability of young people to achieve independence from their families. At the same time, the opportunities for deviant behavior became much more difficult to challenge. Moreover, the pattern of commuting traffic in most major cities has determined, for the most part, the clustering of skyscrapers, the placement of sports arenas and convention centers, work schedules, the direction of suburban sprawl, and the general aesthetics of urban life. In a few cities (for example, Los Angeles), the urban landscape is virtually dominated by the presence of interconnected networks of freeways.

Americans continue their love affair with their cars. No matter how efficient, public transportation will probably never quite take the place of the beloved automobile. After all, the gargantuan automobile industry (not to mention all of the peripheral industries that it has spawned) literally cannot afford for that to happen and so continues to spend incredibly large amounts of money for advertisements and commercials in which the virtues of driving are extolled. It is perhaps no exaggeration to suggest that the automobile is now as American as apple pie. Of course, so is violence.

SNAPSHOT

The Boomerang Effect in Planning Social Change

In the Social Arena, Good Intentions Sometimes Go Wrong

Social policies and programs usually are a mixed bag; they have multiple effects. We should have learned this lesson from our experience with "hard scientists" who have long recognized the need to weigh costs against benefits in evaluating outcomes. Thalidomide probably eased the suffering of numerous pregnant women; unfortunately, it also produced serious birth deformities. Urea formaldehyde made an effective form of home insulation; it also made some people sick.

Antipsychotic drugs improve everyday psychological functioning, but when prescribed without caution, they can also produce an irreversible nervous disorder.

In the social arena, affirmative action legislation has opened doors for women and minorities who would otherwise have been excluded from many decent jobs. It has also stigmatized its beneficiaries by giving the impression that African Americans, Hispanics, and women enjoy an unfair advantage and are not qualified for the jobs that they hold. Similarly, social security is, for many older people, the difference between survival and starvation; it also leads millions of young people to believe that they have no choice but to retire by the age of 65 or 70.

Aside from government intervention, multiple effects often confound those who give the rest of us advice. Marriage counselors who encourage troubled couples to "air their differences" may make their clients feel more comfortable with themselves; they may also inadvertently precipitate a divorce by escalating conflicts between husbands and wives. Nursing homes frequently provide humane care; they also foster dependence. And the voluntary rating system used by the motion picture industry provides guidance in the selection of movies appropriate for children; it also stimulates countless cinematic scenes of gratuitous sex and violence in order to justify a PG-13 or R rating (the G rating is the kiss of death for the commercial success of a film) and is a guide for children seeking plenty of sex and violence.

The same principle applies to the influence of the generations. To their credit, people who grew up in the 1960s worked hard for civil rights and equality of the sexes. But they must also take the blame for having weakened our resolve to teach basic skills to our youngsters. The demolition of the open classroom later marked our realization that we were producing a generation of well-adjusted functional illiterates.

In some cases, intelligent people implementing intelligent policies produce a boomerang effect: They actually create more of whatever it is they seek to reduce in the first place.

The boomerang effect has been achieved many times in recent years by people of good will. State legislatures around the nation have recently raised the drinking age to 21 in an effort to reduce the prevalence of violent deaths among our young people. But such policies seem instead to have created the conditions for even more campus violence. Some college students who previously drank in bars and lounges under the watchful supervision of bouncers (not to mention owners eager to keep their liquor licenses) now retreat to the sanctuary of their fraternity houses and apartments, where they no longer control either their behavior or their drinking.

The boomerang effect has also played a role in attempts to reduce the availability of illicit drugs. During recent years the federal government has been successful in reducing the supply of (but not the demand for) street drugs like marijuana. As fields are burned and contraband confiscated, the price of marijuana has skyrocketed to a point where cheap alternatives (such as crack) have begun to compete in the marketplace. Unfortunately, the cheap alternatives are even more harmful than the illicit drugs they replace.

Lest those who argue for a hands-off policy get too smug, we suggest that the failure to act also has its unanticipated side effects. Ronald Reagan's neglect of poverty in America may have helped cut double-digit inflation; it also reduced the size of the middle class and increased permanent poverty in our cities to an unprecedented level. Also, in what was called "deinstitutionalization," we emptied our nation's mental hospitals in the 1970s without providing adequate services or supervision for the mentally ill individuals released into the community. Some of them joined the growing ranks of the homeless; many stopped taking the medications that had made possible their release from institutions.

Of course, not all policies are as well intentioned as they may appear to be. How do we ascertain another person's motives, let alone those of an organization? Was the ratings system initiated to help parents or to get government off the back of the movie industry? Did all those who supported emptying our mental hospitals really desire more humane treatment of the mentally ill, or were they merely trying to cut costs? Motivation is often a mixed bag.

If a spokesperson for the cigarette industry claims that the link between smoking and lung cancer has not been established, we are suspicious. We may perceive a self-serving, biased assessment. Exactly the same skeptical mind-set is valuable in evaluating the effectiveness of social services and policies—skepticism without cynicism.

SNAPSHOT

Riding the Rumor Mill

Our Basic Anxieties Are Projected in Various Tall Tales

Rumors frequently touch on our important fears and anxieties. Where food shortages exist, individuals circulate stories about the supply and distribution of provisions; where access to economic resources depends on tracing descent through uncertain genealogies, they gossip about one another's ancestors; where witchcraft is a cultural belief, they spread tales about who is and is not a witch; and when economic times are bad, workers depend on the office grapevine to forecast management changes.

Temple University's Ralph Rosnow suggests that rumors on a national level prey on our basic anxieties about death, disaster, and illness. Thus, a number of celebrities have reportedly died in the face of overwhelming evidence to the contrary (including their personal denials)—Paul McCartney, Jerry Mathers of "Leave It to Beaver" fame, and Life Cereal's "Mikey," to mention a few. Some who have by all credible accounts actually died—Elvis, Jim Morrison, J.F.K., and Hitler—have been seen alive! In addition, many recent rumors have incorrectly reported the contamination of popular food; for example, spider eggs in bubble gum, candy that explodes when eaten with a carbonated beverage, worms in hamburgers, mice in Coke bottles, rats in fried chicken, and cats in Chinese food.

According to Tulane sociologist Fredrick Koenig, author of *Rumor in the Marketplace: The Social Psychology of Commercial Hearsay,* rumors do not necessarily reduce anxiety; instead, they often confirm our worst suspicions. But in one sense such doomsday stories can also be comforting; at the very least, they confirm the validity of our perception of the world, especially if we see that world as dangerous.

The anxiety multiplies when the danger is seen as encroaching on our personal safety. Take living in the suburbs, for example. For decades, young families scrimped and sacrificed, denying themselves all but the barest necessities, in order to accumulate the down payment on their dream house in East Norwich, New York, Longmeadow, Massachusetts, or Glencoe, Illinois. By moving to the suburbs, they hoped to escape the poverty, crime, and congestion associated with city living.

But during the past decade the suburban version of the American Dream slipped away as real estate values and property taxes skyrocketed, the quality of local services declined, pollution increased, energy costs remained high, and crime invaded the outer reaches of suburbia. Local newspapers daily reported increasing incidents of the very crimes that anxious suburbanites had left the city to escape—rape, aggravated assault, and automobile theft. Facing severe local tax restrictions, suburban school systems and governments began laying off teachers, firefighters, and police. Public roads and buildings were left in a state of disrepair. And in the process, the suburbs increasingly began to resemble the pathologies associated with urban decay.

In 1979 tension surrounding an invader of the suburbs—the Reverend Sun Myung Moon's Unification Church, the so-called Moonies, which purchased real estate in Gloucester, Massachusetts—was manifested in a classic rumor. Hearing stories of teenagers coerced into the Moonie cause, people began believing that the regionally powerful Entenmann's Bakery was owned by the Unification Church and that its products were tainted.

Although Entenmann's was then actually owned by the Warner-Lambert Corporation, that detail didn't stop hundreds of customers from complaining to store managers who carried Entenmann's products. Moreover, church bulletins, letters to the editor, and callers to radio talk shows all warned about Moonie ownership of the bakery and urged everyone to boycott Entenmann's products. As they attempted to deliver their goods, Entenmann's drivers were physically assaulted by angry customers. The bakery's sales declined. So long as public anxiety remained at a high level, Entenmann's continued to serve as a convenient but innocent target of hostility.

Eventually the anxieties fueling the Entenmann's rumors faded into the distance. In its place, rumormongering about the deterioration of suburbia coalesced around images of the shopping mall as dangerous and threatening, as a place where the most pernicious influences of the inner city had altered suburban life. After all, the mall had previously represented the heart and soul of the suburban lifestyle, being inaccessible except by automobile, protected from crime by security guards, sheltered by its physical isolation, and attractive to a largely homogenous segment of the middle-class customers who spent their days leisurely strolling through the corridors spending money. If crime and poverty invaded the tranquil, secure confines of the suburban shopping mall, then nobody was safe.

In 1983, in western Massachusetts, there surfaced a story about a "woman" shopping at a local mall who asked various customers for a ride home. It was said that when authorities finally apprehended her, she turned out to be an ax-wielding man wearing makeup and a wig to protect his true identity. Similarly, in the early 1980s Connecticut residents heard various stories about a young girl who suddenly disappeared while walking with her mother in a mall. According to this tale, worried security guards later found her in a restroom, where she had been given a short haircut and dressed in boy's clothing. By 1985 some version of these mall stories had spread across the country from New York to Texas to California. Only the name of the shopping center and some of the details of the crime varied from location to location.

The rumors of abduction and crime in suburban shopping malls, although not completely gone, have receded somewhat. But in their place there are new reports around the country that newly constructed shopping malls are in imminent danger of being transformed into underground shopping centers; they are, it is said, structurally unsound and literally sinking.

In the most recent episode the mammoth, three-story Emerald Square Mall in North Attleboro, Massachusetts, has been the target of unfounded rumors since it opened in August 1989. Among the most widely told tales are those contending that the mall has already sunk six inches, that its third floor has been closed, that the top floor of the adjoining parking garage has been closed, that the garage has separated from the main building, that many of the windows have shattered, that the mall will soon close, and that the mall will be torn down and rebuilt. Although there is no truth to any of this, that hasn't prevented customers from calling the mall's building inspector with wild stories, excitedly discussing the rumors in shops and restaurants, and, in some cases, taking their business elsewhere.

Those who attempt to explain such rumors of sinking shopping malls might point to some off-handed, ill-informed remark made by an engineer or the presence of a neighboring shopping center that really did have structural problems. People sometimes get confused by the facts. But for those who take a long-term view, the sinking mall rumors are merely a new variation of an old theme, beginning with the stories of children allegedly being abducted from mall restrooms and continuing with the ax-wielding "woman." You don't have to be a genius to figure it out: It really isn't the shopping mall sinking we worry about—it is our whole way of life.

SNAPSHOT Fads

Is Goldfish Gobbling Next?

With the all-purpose response "I know, Mom, but everyone's doing it," millions of teenagers have sought to explain to their parents why they experiment with drugs or alcohol, color their hair purple, or wear multiple pierced earrings. Their desire to conform to fashions of their fellows is more than an excuse. Adolescents often do what everyone else is doing; they go along with a fad or fashion simply because they don't want to look different or to be seen as out of step with their peers. Given their other-directedness, teenagers are especially sensitive to what is current versus passé, what is "in" versus "out."

It should come as no surprise, therefore, that many fads and fashions originate in what is called adolescent subculture. By conforming to the latest crazes in haircuts, dress, music, and gadgetry, many teenagers hope to gain approval from their friends.

But peer approval is not the only appeal of such fads. While they hope to impress their friends with their compliance, teenagers also seek to distance themselves from their parents. As a result, behavior that appears to adults to be irrational and even dysfunctional may be valued by the young for exactly that reason: Such behavior is outrageous enough to the older generation. If their parents drank beer when they were young, then teenagers will try marijuana; if parents wore long hair and peace beads, their offspring will shave their initials into their hair or don spiked jewelry or join the Young Republicans; if parents wore their designer labels under their garments, then their offspring will insist on wearing their labels outside.

Ironically, and of course unwittingly, even the most outrageous teenage fads touchingly reflect the tenor of their times. During the Roaring Twenties, for example, Charles Lindbergh and Amelia Earhart were busy setting records with their derring-do across the Atlantic. Rapid industrial growth and expanding capitalism generated intense competition for scarce economic resources. How did the flaming youth of the decade respond? With contests of skill and endurance: flagpole sitting, rocking chair derbies, cross-country races, pea-eating contests, kissing and dancing marathons, and gum-chewing and peanut-pushing contests.

During the Sputnik era of the late 1950s, competition was once again intense. The United States and the Soviet Union vied for supremacy in science and technology, and American schools responded by attempting to raise their standards. Teenagers once more designed contests to set and break records. Throughout the decade, young people crammed themselves into hearses, Volkswagen Beetles, and telephone booths. They stacked dozens of students on a single bed and stuffed their rooms with paper.

Teenage fashion has also been affected by the culture of its period. During the 1920s, when American women were first allowed to vote, youthful flappers literally threw off the bras and corsets of their mother's generation in favor of knee-length skirts, low-cut gowns, and bobbed hair. Some 40 years later, motivated by the women's movement of the sixties, teenage girls wore miniskirts, cut their hair short, and took to the streets.

Conventional values influence adolescent fads in yet another way. They set the limits as to just how far those fads are permitted to go before they are condemned by adult society. In 1974 undergraduates began to engage in "streaking": dashing nude through public places.

Society's tolerance for streaking was a result of the sexual revolution of the 1960s. The same act would undoubtedly have received quite a different reception if it had occurred during the 1950s. Any student who dared run naked through a college campus then would in all likelihood have been quickly locked away as a sexual pervert and a menace to society. In 1954 streaking could not have gained fad popularity.

Even the most absurd practices can become the basis for an adolescent fad, given the right social climate. During the Great Depression of the 1930s, at a time when many Americans were having trouble putting food on the table, parents lost their appetites because of a fad that hit college campuses. From Massachusetts to Missouri, students had taken to swallowing goldfish.

A Harvard freshman was the first to swallow a single live fish while fellow students at the Freshman Union looked on in disgust. Three weeks later, an undergraduate at Franklin and Marshall in Lancaster, Pennsylvania, ate three goldfish. New records for goldfish consumption were then set almost daily. At the University of Pennsylvania, one intrepid soul swallowed 25; at the University of Michigan, 28; at Boston College, 29; at Northeastern University, 38; at MIT, 42; and at Clark University, 89 were devoured at one sitting. One college student gained fame by coming up with the first recipe for a goldfish sugar cookie; the chef at the Hotel Statler put the dish on the menu as a special. But a pathologist with the U.S. Public Health Service cautioned that goldfish can contain tapeworms that lodge in the intestines and cause anemia; and by the spring of 1939 the goldfish-gobbling craze had gone the way of the dance marathon.

Teenagers in 1990 tripped over their own feet by wearing their sneakers unlaced. To this day they continue to increase their susceptibility to illness by refusing to wear winter hats or raincoats and ruin their feet with pointed-toe shoes, all because these are in fashion. In general, they are seen as doing things that aren't very good for them. Teenagers aren't swallowing goldfish yet . . . but for those who are too young to remember, that could very well be next.

SNAPSHOT

Enquiring Times

The Tabloidization of Hard News

I confess to having thumbed through a copy or two of the *National Enquirer* and the *Star,* usually while waiting in line at the supermarket checkout counter. It takes little more than a cursory reading to discover that the two-headed baby stories—the gory items for which they are notorious—have all but disappeared. According to a recent article in *Journalism Quarterly,* the tabloids now print profiles; 61 percent of their articles focus on celebrities (singer Michael Jackson's obsession with cleanliness, Dolly Parton's diet, Johnny Carson's latest divorce) and 37 percent on the accomplishments of ordinary people who do extraordinary things (the man who lost 350 pounds by stapling his stomach, the 87-year-old woman who gave up her social security check to feed the homeless, the man who swam for four days in shark-infested waters).

For those who prefer the gore, there are still a few relatively obscure tabloids that specialize in it. The *Sun* and the *Weekly World News* can be counted on for a story featuring a human pregnant with animal or an animal pregnant with human. But the most popular supermarket tabloids—the *National Enquirer,* the *Star,* the *Globe,* and the *National Examiner*—have removed most of the grisly pieces, and they still attract some 10 million readers.

These tabloids continue to run into thorny ethical problems, however, mainly concerning their aggressive methods of reporting and reliance on hearsay rather than hard news. Hollywood celebrities often claim that *Enquirer* reporters invade their privacy, rely on unreliable informants, and fabricate information about their personal lives. As a result, tabloids continue to have only marginal status among print journalists.

Yet mainstream journalists must be aware, perhaps even envious, of the tremendous popularity of supermarket tabloids. At a time when newspapers around the country are shutting down, publishers are looking for new models that might keep them in business.

Because of their vast appeal, supermarket tabloids have provided such a model. Many mainstream papers have become tabloidized; that is, they have imitated not only the tabloid's size and shape but its sensational headlines. Some have begun to rely more on hearsay and ethically questionable investigative techniques. The *National Enquirer* continues to be the butt of criticism from Hollywood celebrity types, television talk-show hosts, and the public. It remains a whipping boy of mainstream journalists even as they imitate its content and format.

Before we blame the messenger for sending a message we detest, let us recognize that the tabloidization of news reflects a large-scale social change: Gossip about powerful people has assumed an important place in the American psyche. During the 1960s we treated our rich and famous like royalty. They could do no wrong; and if they did, we would look the other way. John F. Kennedy's acts of infidelity in the White House were summarily ignored by the press. Whatever their faults and frailties, the rich and powerful were still regarded as paragons of virtue and exemplars for the ethical and intellectual standards we hoped to impart to our children.

In the wake of Watergate, Chappaquiddick, Abscam, Irangate, Jim and Tammy Bakker, Leona Helmsley, Ivan Boesky, Whitewater, Bob Packwood, and the savings and loan scandal, however, public naïveté has given way to widespread skepticism, if not outright cynicism. We no longer trust the people who run things—the national politicians, Hollywood celebrities, and New York business tycoons. They have been caught too often literally with their pants down.

In response to an apparently insatiable appetite for gossip, information about the private lives of public figures has become part of mainstream news, just as it has long been the backbone of tabloid journalism. It was not the *Star* or the *National Examiner* but the legitimate *Las Vegas Sun* that first revealed that Liberace was dying of AIDS. It was not the *National Examiner* but the *Miami Herald* that snooped on Gary Hart to expose his affair with Donna Rice. Gossip about the lives of such celebrities as Bill Clinton, Kitty Dukakis, Nancy Reagan, Barney Frank, Ted Kennedy, Martin Luther King, Jr., and Gerry Studds has been featured in front-page stories not only in the *Star* but in local newspapers around the country.

Some people still remember Carol Burnett's successful mid-1970s lawsuit against the *National Enquirer*. She was able to show that the tabloid had acted with reckless disregard for the truth when it published defamatory information about her. According to University of Arkansas Law Professor Rodney Smolla, the establishment press tried, in the wake of a verdict favorable to Burnett, to disassociate itself from such tabloids as the *Enquirer*.

Tabloid journalism uses hearsay—the anonymous source—as a method for collecting information about celebrities' private lives. Establishment newspapers are known for their reliance on eyewitness accounts and interviews with participants. But legitimate print and broadcast journalists have made mistakes of their own, some of which rival the *Enquirer's* shoddy treatment of Burnett. Libel cases have been successfully aimed at mainstream news ranging from "60 Minutes" to *Time* magazine.

Arnold Arluke and I tried to determine the prevalence of hearsay in legitimate journalism. To this end we examined the front page of *The New York Times* Sunday edition from October 1985 to September 1986. We found that as many as 70 percent of these front-page stories were unattributable. Many were so vague that they could have referred to almost anyone: sources close to the investigation, officials, intelligence sources, a key official, critics, campaign strategists, and the like. Some reporters even admitted to using third-hand sources or obtaining information over the phone from an unknown person.

The reliable source has always been an important and legitimate technique of investigative journalism. (Without "Deep Throat," we might never have learned of the Watergate cover-up.) In the 1970s unadulterated hearsay could be found in only 35 percent of the front-page articles published in *The New York Times*. But in the 1990s the anonymous source has become common in front-page reportage.

When *Enquirer* reporters use an anonymous source to get some dirt on Carol Burnett, they harm one individual. When a daily newspaper uncritically accepts the word of an anonymous source concerning an international event, it may damage the reputation of an entire country or the relationship between nations. When the *Star* bases a story about Michael Jackson on a source close to the celebrity, we are skeptical. When *The New York Times* or the *Washington Post* relies on an off-the-record comment to develop a front-page story, we think of it as hard news. In the era of the tabloidization of news, the distinction between supermarket tabloids and legitimate daily newspapers has blurred in fact, if not yet in the public mind.

SEEING SOCIAL CHANGE AND COLLECTIVE BEHAVIOR THROUGH SNAPSHOTS AND PORTRAITS

I've been on a diet for the past three months. As of this date, I have lost 24 pounds and hope to lose another 10 or so. Twenty years ago, it would have been relatively easy for me to lose 34 pounds over a short period. I would simply have cut down a little on sweets and also reduced the quantity of what I ate at meals. Now that I have reached middle age, however, losing weight seems to require more than just a minor adjustment in my diet. It's not that I lack the will; it's that my metabolism has changed over the years. As a result, only a severe drop in calorie intake along with some kind of exercise regimen seems to make any difference. I understand now why so many Americans suffer from "middle-age spread." If you ask me, the more you age, the more you must reduce your intake of calories to maintain the same weight. Medical research supports my belief.

Just as the structure and functioning of the human body are modified with age, so too the structure of our social lives is capable of profound change. In a sense, the metabolism of our society changes over time. More and more women have entered the labor force, 25 percent of all college students are now over 30, and the juvenile crime rate is once again dramatically on the rise. Just a few years ago it was inconceivable that the Berlin Wall would come down or that the Soviet Union would crumble; and yet all of these changes are now realities.

Social change, then, refers to modifications in either culture or social structure. Interestingly enough, much social change is orderly. Just as structure has discernible characteristics, so change often has patterns. Sociologists try to identify those patterns of social change in the hope of eventually predicting and possibly even determining its direction.

Theorists disagree as to precisely what that social change looks like. In the 19th century theorists such as Herbert Spencer argued that societies inevitably *evolve* from the simple to the complex and always toward greater progress. Karl Marx suggested instead that societies develop through a series of definite stages—from primitive communism, to feudalism, to capitalism, to socialism—depending on the organization of their economic institutions. Marx believed that all history is the history of class conflict. Finally, some sociologists saw a cyclical pattern in social change. They asserted that history repeats itself in an orderly fashion. Pitirim Sorokin, for example, identified three cultural themes—ideational, sensate, and idealistic—through which the pendulum of change repeatedly swings back and forth.

This brief summary of social change theory is meant only to indicate its diversity. Most modern-day sociologists would agree that the earlier theories of social change were too simple. Spencer's views need to be modified: Not all change is for the better, and some is for the worse. Thus, progress is far from inevitable. Marx's views need to be modified: Not all conflict is class-based. In modern life we see conflicts between political alliances, age groups, countries, religions, racial groups, and so on. Many of these conflicts generate social change. Sorokin's views need to be modified: The pendulum of change doesn't necessary swing on the course that he predicted.

Still, the idea of evolution continues to play an important role in our thinking about social change. There seems to be a strong tendency for culture and social structure to become more complex over time. Societies tend to move from small-scale and simple to large and complex forms. America is an apt example. Over the centuries we have moved from 13 colonies to 50 states; from an economy dominated by agriculture to a diverse economic system in which manufacturing, service, and farming all play an integral part; from a nation of family farms, small towns, and a few cities to a nation of connecting metropolitan areas. Unlike living organisms, however, the evolution cannot be characterized as inevitable. Moreover, the direction and speed of change are not the same in all societies. Societies seem to evolve on their own terms. Some third world countries look very much as they did three or four centuries earlier.

One thing that I learned the hard way about dieting is that timing is everything. If you're not ready to make the commitment, don't bother trying. If you can't dedicate yourself to an exercise regimen, don't make the effort. You will only fail.

In "Fads: Is Goldfish Gobbling Next?" we observed that popular fads and fashions since the 1920s have depended on the timing of changes in the larger culture. Indeed, many fads are made possible by large-scale cultural change. For example, our shared ideas regarding sexuality had been modified so much during the 1960s that streaking became fairly widespread on college campuses and was usually considered a harmless prank or minor annoyance. Ten years earlier, however, the same act of public nudity would probably have been regarded as a major sexual perversion, and offenders would have been immediately shuffled off to serve time in prison or in a mental hospital.

The aging of the human body is a mixed bag of developmental changes. For many people, aging brings about an increase in verbal ability, a more mellow temperament, and more of a tendency to vote. But aging can also engender problems such as a worsening of both memory and hearing.

A major theme in "Riding the Rumor Mill" was that longstanding rumors about crime and disaster in suburban shopping malls actually mirror a trend in the aging of our society that many

Americans view with alarm. The social problems once associated with the inner city are now spreading to the suburbs, formerly regarded as bastions of middle-class respectability. Suburbanites often express anxiety about maintaining their lifestyle by contributing to unfounded rumors of the demise of the shopping mall. Though focusing on the safety of the mall, these rumors actually express anxiety about more basic changes in suburban life.

Just as the human body is a system of interrelated parts, so too do the parts of our society affect one another. A change in one area has implications for other areas as well. Thus, a healthy diet and sensible exercise program will likely strengthen the functioning of the heart, kidneys, and lungs. On a societal basis, what happens in the area of illness or disease changes not only the physical health of a population but its social relationships as well. This becomes frighteningly clear in the case of concern about contracting human immunodeficiency virus (HIV) and AIDS. Leo Carroll's study, "Concern with AIDS and the Sexual Behavior of College Students," examines changes in the dating behavior of college students in 1986, shortly after evidence began to mount that the virus may be transmitted heterosexually. Over half of the sexually active students claimed to have modified their behavior because of a concern about contracting AIDS. These claims had not, however, yet shown up in the actual behavior of the students in question.

Another dangerous social change has had ramifications throughout the fabric of society. "Highway to Hell?" examined the effect of the automobile on everyday behavior. Anyone who routinely commutes in rush-hour traffic knows the meaning of the phrase "hot under the collar." Unfortunately, the presence of thousands of pounds of steel in the control of angry and frustrated commuters helps to create the conditions necessary for violent outbursts. Even worse, some motorists who are already angry before they get on the highway decide to go for a drive to cool off. This creates an explosive mix. "Highway to Hell?" focuses our attention not on the personality characteristics of drivers but directly on a social situation—the act of driving on our roadways—as it influences differing conceptions of deviant behavior over the decades. But there are other important sociological issues to address: Exactly why did the automobile have such a profound influence on the shape of American cities? And why didn't Americans maximize the use of public transportation?

It's not just the automobile that represents systematic social change over time. Change the structure of the American family (for example, by increasing the number of dual-career families) and you change the economy as well. Change our political institutions and you change the character of mass communication. Thus, "Enquiring Times" wasn't only about newspapers and books: Celebrity gossip has become an important force in politics and mass entertainment. In the presidential campaign of 1988, for example, Gary Hart was a target; in 1992 it was Bill Clinton. Gossip was very much involved in the televised Senate hearings to confirm Justice Clarence Thomas and in the televised rape trial of William Kennedy Smith. Millions of Americans eavesdropped on an entire cast of characters—Thomas, Hill, and Smith—as they divulged the intimate details of their private lives. More recently, O. J. Simpson and the murders of Nicole Brown and Ron Goldman have provided the focal point for small talk during prime time. Some cultures will cut off your lips for gossiping. Here, we put the gossip on national TV!

"Highway to Hell?" focused attention on the impact of technology (in this case the automobile) in determining the direction and quality of social change. Many theorists have emphasized the role of technological innovation, beginning with William Ogburn's classic treatment *Social Change,* originally published in 1922. To illustrate the power of technology in the process of social change, Ogburn suggested that slavery in the United States was greatly encouraged by the invention of the cotton gin in 1795. By increasing productivity and therefore profits, this single technological innovation—the gin—required large numbers of laborers to work the cotton fields. The plantation economy quickly dominated the southern landscape, where it remained in full force for more than a hundred years.

Ogburn also developed the notion of *cultural lag,* according to which different parts of a culture may change at different rates. During periods of technological innovation, cultural lag may become especially problematic as society struggles to adapt to changing material conditions. The rapid introduction of new technological inventions—from bombs and firearms to automobiles and computers—has tended to outpace our ability to govern them in any constructive, orderly way. Before developing effective cultural rules or norms for the proper usage of automobiles, for example, we had already polluted the environment of our major cities, destroyed viable neighborhoods for the sake of highway construction, and increased vehicular homicide to an unacceptable level.

On an individual level, there are literally millions of people who go on diets and take up exercise programs to influence the course of biological change. Many avoid fatty foods, cut down on sugar, or give up red meat. Others buy treadmills and exercise bicycles or jog daily. Such efforts don't always work as well as we would like. In fact, some dieting plans have an incredibly high 90 percent failure rate over the long term.

Human beings have similarly sought to help social change along in one or another area of concern. Since 1960, for example, we have seen numerous programs and policies directed toward improving public education, reducing racial, age, and gender discrimination, combatting violent crime, improving the economy, and aiding the mentally ill. As suggested in "The Boomerang Effect in Planning Social Change," not all of these efforts have succeeded. In fact, some of them have backfired by creating even more social problems for us to solve. The failure rate of programs and policies may not approach 90 percent, but our effectiveness could be much better.

In the 1940s sociologist Robert Merton recognized that unanticipated and anomalous results—perhaps even the boomerang effect—are rather commonplace in sociological research. Such unexpected, even surprising findings may not always generate the most effective proposals for change at the time, but they frequently have a positive consequence as well. In being forced to deal with inconsistencies and contradictions, sociologists must rethink their work, extend their inadequate theories, or create new theories that better explain the phenomena they seek to understand. In the long run, their serendipitous findings may become the basis for more powerful theories of social behavior and perhaps more effective social policies and planning as well.

Whatever the extent of the boomerang effect, many Americans aren't happy with the idea of planned change. Our political leaders have never tried to convince us of the wisdom of following a 3-year plan, a 5-year plan, or a 10-year plan—the likes of which were a mainstay of life under communism in the Soviet Union until its collapse.

As close as we Americans came in the 20th century to adopting a long-term, comprehensive economic strategy were President Franklin D. Roosevelt's efforts in response to the Great Depression. During the 1930s, as the national unemployment rate soared to 25 percent, Roosevelt enacted a number of economic measures including social security and large work programs designed to stimulate economic growth and reduce unemployment.

Overall, however, the notion of planned change is anathema to most Americans. If anything, we have recently decided to cut back on federal programs and policies with long-range goals, instead letting the chips fall where they may. At the global level, recent changes have been dramatic, but increasingly haphazard. The character of American society has been greatly affected both by the worldwide migration of unprecedented numbers of refugees who have fled from political and economic hardship and by global economic competition.

In the absence of long-term planning, social change is frequently facilitated by the fact that not all social behavior comes entirely under the control of conventional norms and values. In episodes of what sociologists refer to as *collective behavior*—crowds, riots, social movements, and rumors—individuals come together in a relatively spontaneous or impromptu manner.

Sociologists haven't always appreciated the role of collective behavior as a source of change. Indeed, early writers such as Gustave Le Bon, in his 1895 book *The Crowd,* emphasized the irrational and expressive components of collective behavior. He argued that individuals who gather together in a crowd lose their individual identities so that they feel anonymous. As a result, the experience of being in a crowd and acting in concert with many other anonymous people caught together in an unstructured situation actually reduces the controls that normally restrain irrational or deviant behavior. Members of a crowd feel they can get away with much that they simply wouldn't attempt under ordinary conditions.

Recent research in the area of collective behavior supports the view that crowds can be more instrumental or purposeful in provoking change than even Le Bon might have suspected. Norris Johnson's "Panic at 'The Who Concert Stampede': An Empirical Assessment" concludes that mob psychology does not always rule the behavior of individuals caught in dangerous crowd situations. In a 1979 Who concert stampede, those caught in the mob actually had the presence of mind, as well as the composure, to try to rescue those who were crushed by the weight of the crowd.

Komanduri Murty, Julian Roebuck, and Gloria Armstrong's study of "The Black Community's Reactions to the 1992 Los Angeles Riot" suggests that riots or civil disturbances—though viewed by outsiders as chaotic or purposeless—are regarded by participants as a force for change. In their study, these researchers found that many rioters opposed rioting in principle but believed that collective violence would pay off. They saw themselves as worthy protestors and as freedom fighters.

When civil disturbances gain momentum and continuity, they may become a more permanent source of change. What begins as a connected series of riots, demonstrations, or protests may turn out to be part of a more structured *social movement.* In recent American history we have seen a number of social movements develop including the civil rights movement, the women's movement, and the environmentalist movement. When a social movement seeks, in a violent manner, to totally restructure most of society's institutions, it can contribute to a *revolution.* In the Russian revolution of 1917, for example, widespread discontent in czarist Russia led to the dissolution of feudal society and the imposition of communist rule. Thus, collective behavior can actually become an integral part of the most profound sorts of social change, even those that overturn conventional institutions.

PORTRAIT

Panic at "The Who Concert Stampede": An Empirical Assessment

Norris R. Johnson

On December 3, 1979, eleven young people were killed in a crush entering Riverfront Coliseum in Cincinnati, Ohio, for a concert by the British rock group, The Who. The incident was immediately labeled as a "stampede" by the local media, and commentators were quick to condemn the "mob psychology" which precipitated the seemingly selfish, ruthless behavior of participants. Crowd members were thought to have stormed over others in their rush for good seats within the arena, leading a national columnist (Royko, 1979) to refer to the crowd of young people as barbarians who "stomped 11 persons to death [after] having numbed their brains on weeds, chemicals, and Southern Comfort . . . ," and a local editor to write of the "uncaring tread of the surging crowd" (Burleigh, 1979). . . .

Those who interpreted the incident in this way and labeled it as a "stampede" recognized that other factors contributed, such as the unreserved seating and the late opening of an inadequate number of doors. The unreserved or "festival" seating prompted many in the crowd to arrive several hours early to compete for the choicest locations within the building. During the hours before the doors were opened, the large crowd became so tightly packed outside the arena doors that some people who wanted to withdraw could not do so, and policemen patrolling the area could not see the problems that were developing near the doors. In addition, the densely packed crowd was swaying to and fro creating a "wave" effect—people at the edge of the crowd were observed shoving on its fringes just to see the effect begin. . . . This resulted in some people being pushed to the concrete floor of the concourse before the surge for entry began. Nevertheless, police described the crowd at this point as "normal" for a rock concert. Soon after the doors opened, as many as 25 people were pushed down into a pile. Eleven died lying on the concourse just a few feet from the entrances, eight others were hospitalized, and several were treated and released at the first aid station. Although the people were not trampled as more dramatic accounts reported, the event did appear to fit the image of panic held by the public and many scholars.

Previous Research and Theories of Panic

Many social scientists would categorize the crowd behavior described above as a special form of panic—usually termed an "acquisitive panic" (Brown, 1965) or "craze" (Smelser, 1963). Smelser distinguishes it from the classic panics of escape, e.g., flight from a burning building, in that the latter is a "headlong rush *away* from something" while the craze is a rush "toward something [the participants] believe to be gratifying . . . " (1963:170; also see Brown, 1965). In this form, the competition that arises is not to escape possible entrapment, but to acquire some valued commodity. The special group investigating the event for the city preferred the term "craze" to the "stampede" label affixed by the media (City of Cincinnati, 1980). . . .

Although many collective behavior theorists discuss the phenomenon, systematic studies of panic are uncommon. Research conducting such studies generally conclude that panic is a rare form of crowd behavior. Quarantelli and Dynes (1972) report that they have found few instances of panic after years of disaster research. They indicate that even within the famous Cocoanut Grove fire most people did not panic. Smith (1976), a participant observer in a flight from the Tower of London after a 1976 bomb explosion, reported that panic responses were few, and that primary group bonds and roles were crucial in maintaining order in the situation. In fact, primary group ties were important in the minimal panic that did occur. . . .

The core of my analysis is an examination of the Cincinnati Police Division's file on The Who Concert incident. First, I describe the data source and then present a description of the surge based on that evidence. I then use material from the taped transcriptions of interviews with people present at the concert to assess the extent of unregulated competition, breakdown of group ties, and other behaviors characteristic of panic. . . .

Data and Methods

My analysis is based on data contained in a file created and kept by the Cincinnati Police Division, supplemented by accounts in daily newspapers. The police file includes 46 statements taken by officers investigating the event—22 from patrons, 13 from police officers present, and 11 from Coliseum employees or private security guards. The file also includes 10 statements presented by patrons at hearings conducted by a committee of the Cincinnati City Council. My primary data source is transcribed patron interviews and statements that I coded for analysis. I also coded and analyzed six interviews or statements from patrons which appeared in news articles reporting the incident.

I analyzed these materials by developing a questionnaire with which to "interview" each transcript. The questionnaire called for information relevant to theories of panic, particularly evidence of unregulated competition. For example, one question asked whether the "respondent" observed crowd members showing a "lack of concern for others," and another specifically asked, "Did the person report receiving help from others?" Coded responses to the latter question indicated whether, and from whom, help was received. A similar question concerned giving help to others. Other questions pertained to potential control variables such as age and sex of respondent, size and type of group with which the person arrived, time of arrival, and physical location relative to the doors.

I base most of my interpretations on vivid descriptions of the event by those present, particularly those most directly involved, and on the interviews with policemen, security guards, and Coliseum employees. In addition, I present quantitative results from the 38 questionnaires I coded. Of course, these data represent only those persons selected by others for interview (often because they were injured or had accompanied an injured person) or who came forward to write to newspapers or appear before a public hearing.

Analysis

I will focus mainly on the issue of whether the observed behavior involved unregulated competition. I assume that competition in crowds awaiting entry into a concert is regulated by appropriate situational norms. I also assume that such crowd members are characterized by a rudimentary social structure, reflecting at least the ties of crowd members to others with whom they arrived. Aveni (1977) has shown that crowd members typically arrive in small, primary groups. Accordingly, all of the persons whose transcripts contain relevant information reported that they arrived at the Coliseum with at least one other person, most often primary group members such as their spouse or other family member. An important research question, then, is whether these elements of social organization constrained behavior. A second question, which emerged during the research, is whether the conventional distinction between panics of escape and of acquisition (i.e., crazes) is a useful one. . . .

Helping Behavior

Since most theoretical explanations of panic focus on unregulated competition, the first research question is whether such competition existed in this case. That many people were killed and injured in a crowd of pushing people is not in dispute; the key issue is whether this was the result of callous competition for a seat at the concert at the expense of the lives of others.

However, evidence from the transcripts does not provide support for the theoretical models of panic and is in clear conflict with interpretations reported in the newspapers. One witness before the City Council committee specifically objected to newspaper accounts of the people as animals or barbarians and asserted:

> [T]he people in our area were the most helpful people that I've ever known. . . . Everybody I saw was helping everybody else. At some point in the crowd people could not help them. It's not that they didn't want to. They were physically unable to (Police Division, I, YZ).

The coded interview data support this claim. Approximately 40 percent of those interviewed reported helping behavior in each of three coded categories—giving, receiving, and observing help. Of the 38 people interviewed, 17 reported that they had received some help from others, 16 reported that they had given help to others, and 16 reported observing helping behavior by others. Some reported more than one of the categories of helping activities, and when indicators are combined, more than three-fourths of those interviewed (29) reported at least one form of pro-social activity.

Helping behavior possibly was even more common than indicated by those results. It is likely that additional respondents observed, but did not report, helping activity since interviewers did not ask a direct question concerning helping. In fact, only seven respondents reported action by others that was coded as showing a lack of concern for others, and six of these also reported helping behavior. Thus, just one of the 38 respondents reported *only* self-interested, competitive behavior. Although we cannot infer from this selective sample that a comparably large proportion of the entire crowd continued to behave in a cooperative manner, this evidence does suggest that many of those centrally located within the crowd, at just the location where persons were in most danger, demonstrated concern for others.

Helping behavior began during the early crush, long before the surge, and continued throughout the episode. People first simply tried to get people to step back and relieve the pressure, but others around them either could not hear or could not move. One young man noticed that the girl next to him could not breathe and "turned to ask people to back up, but soon realized that the only people who could hear me shouting couldn't move either." (Police Division, III, M). A small 17-year-old girl near the doors away from the worst crush . . . reported having problems nearly an hour before the "stampede." She pleaded with people to let her out, but neither she nor they could move. She told the police detective interviewing her:

> I lost my footing an' slowly but surely began going down. People behind me could do nothing to stop the pushing. I was saying "No. No. Please help me . . . " Some of the people around didn't even hear me. . . . So then I grabbed someone's leg an' whoever that was told three other guys about me. They all pushed me up, pulled me up, but it was hard. . . . At about 7 o'clock I passed out. The four guys who pulled me off the ground helped me to stay up until we got through the door (Police Division, II, V).

. . . A few were successful in extricating themselves and helping others out of the crush. One man reported that he and friends picked up and carried from the crowd two nearly unconscious girls who had fallen (Police Division, III, M). These particular young men knew the girls they helped, but many helped others with whom they had no social ties. Thirteen of the 17 mentioned above as having received help were aided by others they did not know, and 12 of the 16 giving help gave it to strangers. As one person reported in a letter to a newspaper, "Total strangers probably saved my life" (*Cincinnati Enquirer*, 1979). . . .

Although most of the evidence leads to a conclusion that acts of ruthless competition were rare, there *were* such reports. For instance, one patron, who from a position just inside the arena doors was pulling people inside to safety, reported being angry with the mob:

> People were climbin' over people ta get in . . . an' at one point I almost started hittin' 'em, because I could not believe the animal, animalistic ways the people, you know, nobody cared (Police Division, II, A).

But both the analysis of the coded transcripts and the impressionistic accounts indicate that even in the face of the throng, most persons tried to help others as long as possible. If a total disregard for others developed—and their is hardly any evidence that it did—it was only after cooperation was no longer possible.

Sex Differences in Helping Behavior

Normative expectations dictate generally that the stronger should help the weaker; specifically, men are expected to help women. The evidence indicates that such sex-role expectations continued to be an important influence on behavior during the event. Nine of the 13 females received help while only one reported giving help. On the other hand, almost twice as many men gave as received help. A few (three) reported helping their wives or members of their group, but, as noted above, most gave help to those around them, either friends or strangers. Thus, the sex-role norms of men helping women did not collapse when confronted with a threat.

Altruistic behavior, either generally or specifically toward women, was not universal; there *was* selfish competition. For instance, a young woman, interviewed in her hospital room late on the evening of the concert with the horror still fresh in her memory, complained that no one would move back:

> They just kept pushin' forward and they would just walk right on top of you, just trample over ya like you were a piece of the ground. They wouldn't even help ya; people were just screamin' "help me" and nobody cared (Police Division, II, Mc). . . .

Conclusion

We cannot conclude from one study that there are *no* situations in which competition for some valued commodity occurs without regard for social obligations. Perhaps there are situations such as a fire in a crowded theater in which people totally ignore others as they try to escape from danger. However, documented cases of either form of panic are surprisingly scarce in the literature.

One possible reason for the lack of evidence of unregulated competition in The Who concert incident is that the appropriate conditions did not exist. Perhaps the people in this situation did not place such a high value on a preferred location for the concert that they would do harm to others in order to get inside; perhaps those trying to escape the crush did not actually perceive a serious threat to their lives. Kelley et al. (1965) have noted that panic-like responses are less likely when there is variation in perception of the danger; those who define the situation as less urgent are more willing to wait their turns. In this case, those who placed less value on their concert location would be less likely to compete with others. Many did try to leave the crush, giving up their valued locations nearer the entrance. Mann et al. (1976) reached a similar conclusion in their study of the bank run.

But the repeated failure of researchers to find examples of ruthless competition suggests another conclusion. Most crowds are comprised not of unattached individuals but of small, often primary, groups (Aveni, 1977; Smith, 1976). Group bonds constrain totally selfish behavior, even when the situation seems life threatening; thus, the type of unregulated competition generally labeled as panic occurs very infrequently. More case studies of such infrequent and irregularly occurring social forms must accumulate before general conclusions can be drawn with confidence. However, the evidence from this study is more than sufficient to discount popular interpretations of "The Who Concert Stampede" which focus on the hedonistic attributes of young people and the hypnotic effects of rock music.

REFERENCES

Aveni, Adrian
1977 "The not-so-lonely crowd: Friendship groups in collective behavior." Sociometry 49:96–99.

Brown, Roger
1965 Social Psychology. New York: Free Press.

Burleigh, William R.
1979 "Editors notebook: At death's door." Cincinnati Post (December 8).

Enquirer (Cincinnati)
1979 "Readers' views: A dear price has been paid to learn an obvious lesson." December 10:A14.

Kelley, Harold H., J. Condry, Jr., A. Dahlke, and A. Hill
1965 "Collective behavior in a simulated panic situation." Journal of Experimental and Social Psychology 1:20–54.

Mann, Leon, Trevor Nagel, and Peter Dowling
1976 "A study of an economic panic: The 'run' on the Hindmarsh Building Society." Sociometry 39:223–35.

Police Division, City of Cincinnati
No date Final Report Concerning the Eleven Deaths Which Preceded the "Who" Rock Concert Held at Riverfront Coliseum. Cincinnati: City of Cincinnati.

Quarentelli, Enrico and Russell R. Dynes
1972 "When disaster strikes." Psychology Today 5:66–70.

Royko, Mike
1979 "The new barbarians: a glimpse of the future." Cincinnati Post (December 4).

Smelser, Neil J.
1963 Theory of Collective Behavior. New York: The Free Press.

Smith, Don
1976 "Primary group interaction in panic behavior: A test of theories." Paper presented at the annual meeting of Southern Sociological Society, Miami Beach.

PORTRAIT

The Black Community's Reaction to the 1992 Los Angeles Riot

Komanduri S. Murty, Julian B. Roebuck, and Gloria R. Armstrong

. . . Several crucial precipitating events preceded the Los Angeles disorders. The battery of Rodney Glenn King, a black, 25-year-old male motorist by four white Los Angeles male police officers on March 3, 1991 (recorded on a camcorder and videotaped by an amateur photographer, a bystander to the beating); the change in venue of these four defendants' court cases from Los Angeles to Simi Valley[1]; and the not guilty verdict of these four policemen handed down by a jury of 10 whites, one Asian, and one Hispanic on April 29, 1992. The beating of Reginald Denny, a white truck driver, by four black males on April 29, 1992, has also been factored in by many reporters as an explanatory element in the civil disruptions (Assembly Special Committee 1992; Webster Commission 1992). The South Central Los Angeles (SCLA) inner-city disturbances encompassing the riot covered a period from April 29 through May 4, 1992, leaving more than 50 people dead, thousands injured, 5,000 adults arrested, more than 700 businesses burned, and 1 billion dollars in property damages. . . . During the first 72 hours, the most intense and destructive period of the riot, looting, burnings, brutal beatings, trashings, and acts of vandalism transpired throughout the city. The unrest touched the lives of all classes and ethnic groups, spanning the areas of Long Beach, Compton, SCLA, Korea Town, Wilshire, Westwood, and Beverly Hills. The most concentrated area of pillaging and violence was SCLA, a heavily populated black and Hispanic-American community. As well as blacks, Hispanics and Orientals participated in the riot (Assembly Special Committee 1992; Cooper 1992; Lieberman 1992).

. . . Generally speaking, the press has been sympathetic toward Rodney King and the black community, and issues concerning the fairness of the criminal justice system and the use of force by police in the black community have resurfaced. Although important, these secondary accounts do not disclose the feelings and reactions of the natural actors on the scene of the riot, the black SCLA community members in situ during the riot. What did the riot mean to them in their everyday lives? To this end this study for the first time (1) examines the general reactions and feelings of the SCLA black community members to the riot; and (2) compares the black riot participants in SCLA with black nonparticipants in that area on selected demographic and personal characteristics, as well as on perceptions of the riot.

Materials and Methods

Data

An interview schedule (available from first author upon request) was used to collect the data for this study, which was specifically designed to: (1) ascertain the reactions and feelings of SCLA black community members to the riot; and (2) compare a sample of SCLA black participants in the riot (that is, those who claimed to have actively participated in the riot) to black nonparticipants. Initially, two screening questions were posed to all potential subjects: "Do you live or work in SCLA?" and "Were you on the scene or in the proximity of the riot?" Those who answered "yes" to these two questions were asked to participate in the interview. The interview instrument consisted of eight questions on demographic and personal characteristics; two perceptual questions about the LAPD police; three questions about reactions and feelings to the events leading to the riot; five questions about reactions and feelings to the riot; and two questions about participation in the riot.

The third author, a black American female and former resident of SCLA, conducted 30- to 40-minute long street interviews (from January 15, 1993 to February 10, 1993) with 227 black Americans who responded "yes" to the two screening questions. Seven other subjects who answered "yes" to these two questions declined to participate because, they said, they "were too busy." The interviewer introduced herself to prospective interviewees as a graduate student at a predominantly black university. She told them she was a former resident of SCLA and that she was conducting research on the riot. She explained to those solicited on a face-to-face basis that their views were essential to the study; that they were free to express themselves in any way; that the anonymity of their responses would be maintained; that they knew more about the riot than outsiders, including the press; and that, hopefully their responses would eventually be of some use in rebuilding SCLA, improving the economic conditions of its citizens, and restructuring the LAPD.

Sample

Although a scientific sampling could not be drawn from any existing population frames to address the issues at hand, we targeted people (who were expected to be found on the street) in the following categories: SCLA residents; shop owners and employees; other business owners, managers, and employees; cafe and restaurant workers; street vendors; city employees other than police; street idlers; high school and college students; members of black community organizations; church members; well-known community leaders; shoppers and business patrons; and other assortments of people on the street. Areawise, we covered the central locale where most of the riot disturbances transpired: Crenshaw Boulevard, Florence Avenue, Vernon Avenue, and adjoining streets. The study sample consists of 227 black Americans, including both male and female respondents who were selected from the black SCLA community on the basis of a convenience sample procedure.

Data Analysis

Analysis of Total Sample

Of the 227 respondents, 118 (52%) were males and 109 (48%) were females. The younger age group (15 to 30 years) made up 70.5% of the respondents and 29.5% were in the older age group (31 years or above). At the time of the interviews, 39.2% were employed full time, 34.8% part time, and 26% were unemployed. The personal income level of 71% was less than $20,000; 29% earned $20,000 or more. Of the sample, 37% had a level of education at high school graduate or above and 63% had less than a high school education. Twenty-four percent had lived in the community where the riots occurred for 10 years or less (median = 5.5 years) and 74% of all respondents had worked in the community for approximately the same length of time (median = 6.0 years). Seventy-six percent had lived in the community for more than a decade (median = 13.2 years) and 26% had worked there for approximately the same length of time (median = 13.4 years). Twenty-two percent had been arrested prior to the riot. Sixty percent perceived the LAPD as a negative force, whereas 40% perceived it to be a positive force. Fifty-five percent believed that the use of unnecessary force by the LAPD was increasing, 37% believed it to be about the same, and the remaining 8% believed it to be decreasing.

The reaction of many respondents to the Rodney King beating was, "It could just as well have been us taking the beating." All were outraged and angered by this event, and 36% reported additional feelings of sadness and fearfulness about it. All defined the Rodney King beating as police brutality and as an exaggerated example of routing police violence against blacks in SCLA. They hoped that all police officers who had participated in this beating, all police spectators to the beating, and the police chief would be fired. Most (75%) were upset, angered, and disappointed by the change in trial venue of the four white policemen charged with the beating of Rodney King. They believed this action was a deliberate attempt on the part of the criminal justice system to ensure a not guilty verdict. The remainder (25%) said they were suspicious of this action. All claimed to have been outraged, disappointed, angered, and emotionally shocked in the Simi Valley not guilty verdict, and viewed it as a failure of the criminal justice system to mete out equitable justice. Additionally, more than 40% reported the feeling that the criminal justice system in this verdict had failed them once again, and that the black race had no value to those in authority. Twenty percent said the not guilty verdict granted the police freedom to mistreat all "black folks" at will. In one way or another 90% expressed the dire and immediate need for a total revampment of the police department, the firing of all police officers connected in any way to the King beating, the hiring of more black police officers, and a change in criminal court proceedings. No one made any specific suggestions as to how the criminal court proceedings were to be changed in order to meet their satisfaction.

Of the respondents 12% were outraged and angered by the Reginald Denny beating, 41% were saddened, and 46% were indifferent. Some (30%) expressed the view that "one beating did not deserve another." Ten percent felt that the four black men accused of beating Denny should be punished despite the inequalities of the criminal justice system that favored whites over blacks. Those who were indifferent to the Denny beating stated that he was simply "at the wrong place at the wrong time," and that the four black men who assaulted him should receive the same criminal justice treatment as that meted out to the white officers who beat Rodney King—a verdict of not guilty.

Three-fourths of the respondents said they did not participate in the riot because of the violence and property damage involved and the casualties among innocent citizens. Eighty percent expressed feelings of sadness and fearfulness about the riot. Though they were aware of the criminal justice system's weaknesses and discriminatory practices, 65% expressed the view that riots were not an appropriate or moral means to effect social change. Despite moral proscriptions against the riot by many, 90% perceived it as a clarion call for the improvement of SCLA's economic and social conditions—ranging from the elimination of racial discrimination to an increase in employment opportunities to far drastic changes in the criminal justice system (particularly the police department). None had any specific programmatic suggestions except increasing the number of black police officers and firing some white officers.

Despite the violence in their midst, the large majority did not choose to participate. However most (90%) did not condemn or chastise those who did. Seventy-five percent thought that participants acted on good faith for what they thought to be a worthy cause. Only 10% reported that the rioters should be punished. Eighty-five percent asserted that "changes for the better" would come about as a consequence of the protests. Twenty-five percent stated they would like to have engaged in the riot in some way, but were afraid to do so. These respondents fully embraced the riot as a "good and timely thing." They justified the participants' actions, viewed the participants as freedom fighters, thoroughly condemned the criminal justice system including the police, deplored the relative economic deprivations of the black community, thought the riot might bring changes, and volunteered themselves as future riot participants should things not change and should they be provoked by further instances of police brutality.

In summary, most respondents expressed mixed, ambivalent, and contradictory feelings and reactions to the riot. On the other hand, the 25% who fully embraced the riot, "the militants," were much more consistent and assured in their answers.

Comparison of Riot Participants and Nonparticipants

. . . [There are] five significant differences between riot participants and nonparticipants.

1. Nearly 89% of the riot participants and a significantly lower percent of nonparticipants (68%) were between the ages of 15 and 30 years.
2. Nearly 73% of the riot participants and a significantly lower percent of nonparticipants (49.5%) were males.
3. Nearly 42% of the riot participants and a significantly higher percent (72.5%) of nonparticipants had a high educational level (high school or above).
4. Nearly 81% of the riot participants and a significantly lower percent of nonparticipants (60.7%) were with a low level of income (less than $20,000).
5. Nearly 46% of the riot participants and a significantly lower percent of nonparticipants (19.1%) had been arrested prior to the instant riot.

Thus, there is a higher probability of riot participation by young males with low levels of education and income as well as prior arrest records than those without these characteristics. No significant differences were found between these two groups by employment, duration of living or working in SCLA, or perception of police force.

One interesting set of findings in this study involves a further comparison of the nonparticipant and participant groups. The nonparticipant group did not accept rioting as either a proper or moral means to effect social change. In fact 25% of these nonparticipants feared that the present or subsequent riots could result in a white backlash. Yet, in a contradictory fashion, 75% of the nonparticipants reported that the rioters were justified in their actions. A large proportion understood the rioters' degree of frustration, hostility, and violence; understood why they rioted; and did not blame them for rioting and looting. Furthermore, most thought the riot would bring about positive change for the city.

The participants, on the other hand, fully embraced the riot and stated (in different ways) that they had been suffering and struggling under unequal and unjust social, economic, living, and criminal justice conditions (including police brutality) for too long—and without any noticeable improvement in their situations. They asserted that they had decided their views must be heard through and by force because other alternatives had failed. They claimed that the anger and dismay following the King beating and the ensuing not guilty verdict of the four white policemen triggered them to violent action. According to them, the time had come to change things, and their actions might make things better for themselves and other blacks in the future—"no justice no peace." In brief, they presented themselves as freedom fighters.

Conclusion

We found that the preriot structural facilitators in South Central Los Angeles were similar to those found in other communities preceding such disturbances: poverty, relative deprivation, unemployment, police brutality, racial discrimination, and negative police–community relations. As in other studies, the disorders were triggered by an instance of police brutality and were centered in an ethnic community. The general feelings and reactions of community members to the riot also approximate those disclosed in the studies elsewhere. Though these reactions were mixed and contradictory, both participants and nonparticipants generally understood the functions of riot in promoting social change, even though rioting may not be seen by respondents as the best way to bring about change. Differentials in reactions were in degree rather than in kind. Justification of the riot as based on the failure of the criminal justice system to punish the men who beat Rodney King, thereby demonstrating racial injustice and the power structure's lack of concern for blacks in Los Angeles. Most, as good citizens, objected to riot in principle but concluded that collective violence "pays off." Neither unpopular or faulty jury decision nor adverse social conditions give any ethnic group the right to riot. Furthermore, any overt or covert threat to riot by any group weakens the legal and social order and escalates reciprocal group violence. Regardless of the sensitivity of the cases involved, jury decisions must not be thwarted by the fear of riot.

The remarks of most respondents about the Reginald Denny beating indicate justification of an illegal terrorist-type act on the basis of blind ethnic retribution. This beating also served as a symbolic message meant to intimidate a targeted institution, the criminal justice system, rather than the immediate victim. To the participants and their supporters, the Denny attack was a political act, not a crime—a "rational" response to the injustice of the criminal justice system. The same tactics were used in Denny's case as those employed against Rodney King. (A similar beating of a white male took place in Miami on May 28, 1993, following the not guilty verdict of police officer William Lozano in Orlando, Florida. The verdict was the second for Lozano, who on June 11, 1989, was convicted by a Miami jury of manslaughter in the deaths of two black motorcyclists. Subsequently, an appeals court granted Lozano a retrial in another city because it ruled that the Miami jurors in the first trial may have feared a riot if they acquitted Lozano. See Williams 1993.)

Many respondents' reactions to the "parallel beatings" of King and Denny (as they perceived them) denote an attempt to "balance injustice in the absence of a balance of justice." This so-called "balancing act" indicates the willingness of some blacks to induce change in the criminal justice system by and through force. Actually this balancing metaphor is specious. Though the beatings of King and Denny were both illegal and reprehensible, King was an offender resisting arrest, whereas Denny was an innocent motorist. Furthermore, under the rule of law, the commission of a crime to rectify another is flagrantly illegal. Such action often leads to backlash and further escalation of violence.

Some of the participants' reasons for engaging in the riot may be recapitulated rationalizations for what they wanted to do anyway, for whatever reason. No matter, these participants now present themselves, to themselves and to others (including the interviewer), as worthy protesters and fighters for justice. Therefore, their message should be heeded and acted upon. Unless social change is effected in order to alleviate or ameliorate the social and economic problems of the group under study (and other similarly placed ethnic minorities) and the communities from whence they come, other similar riots are likely (see the literature above). Democracies are riot-prone and are not very effective in representing public disorders because police restraint (against the populace) is a built-in component of all democracies. Finally, the police must maintain a good image in the community in order to minimize the risk that their actions will become a focal point or a precipitating event for riot (Murty et al. 1990).

NOTE

1. The trial began on February 3, 1992, in a Ventura County courtroom following a change in venue from Los Angeles to Simi Valley, a predominantly white community and the home of an estimated 4,000 active and retired law enforcement officers (Wall 1992).

REFERENCES

Assembly Special Committee. 1992. *To Rebuild Is Not Enough: Final Report and Recommendations of the Assembly Special Committee on the Los Angeles Crisis.* California Legislature, Sacramento, CA. 1992.

Cooper, Marc. 1992. "L.A.'s State of Siege." Pp. 12–19 in *Inside The L.A. Riots,* edited by Don Hazen. New York, NY: Institute for Alternative Journalism.

Lieberman, Paul, 1992, June 18. "51% of Riot Arrests were Latino, Study Says." *Los Angeles Times* E8–10.

Murty, Komanduri S., Julian B. Roebuck, and Joann D. Smith. 1990. "The Image of Police in Black Atlanta Communities," *The Journal of Police Science and Administration* 17:250–257.

Webster Commission. 1992, October 21. *The City in Crisis. A Report by the Special Advisor to the Board of Police Commissions on the Civil Disorder in Los Angeles.* Los Angeles, CA: Institute of Government and Public Affairs, UCLA.

Williams, Mike. 1993, May 29. "Miami Officer Lozano Acquitted." *The Atlantic Journal: The Atlantic Constitution,* pp. A1, A6.

PORTRAIT

Concern with AIDS and the Sexual Behavior of College Students

Leo Carroll

Not since the polio epidemic of the 1950s has such widespread and intensive media attention been given to a public health problem as has been given to AIDS over the past several years. This is true especially . . . as evidence has mounted that the virus may be transmitted heterosexually.[1] To date, however, little is known about the impact of concern over AIDS on sexual behavior. Careful studies of gay men demonstrate the possibility of dramatic behavioral change in certain high-risk groups, but past research in public health suggests that behavioral changes are unlikely in the absence of such demonstrated high risk (Leishman, 1987: 40–41). This expectation of no change appears to be confirmed by a[n] . . . *NBC/Wall Street Journal* survey, which finds that concern over AIDS has had no effect on the way in which 92% of the population lead their lives (Smilgis, 1987: 52).

College students, in particular, are portrayed in journalistic accounts as being quite

From *Journal of Marriage and the Family, 50,* pp. 405–411.

unconcerned about AIDS. Although the risk would seem to be higher among this population than the population at large, the impression conveyed is that students do not believe themselves susceptible and continue to engage in impulsive and indiscriminate sexual behavior (e.g., Smilgis, 1987: 52). However, there are reasons to believe that college students may be more receptive to the publicity given AIDS. More educated than the general public, more likely to be single and highly concerned with sex, they are quite possibly more attuned to the issue. Moreover, while the majority are sexually active, for most it is a recent experience and, for many, not yet fully integrated into their lives. Caught between the perceived standards of their peers and more traditional standards espoused by parents, church, and other groups in which they may be involved, a good number may have considerable ambivalence about their sexual behavior and thus be more likely to change it in the face of a serious threat.

The purposes of this analysis are twofold: (*a*) to determine the extent and distribution of concern about AIDS among a sample of college students and (*b*) to assess the relation of reported behavior changes to independent measures of the behavior.

Data and Methods

In October 1986 a questionnaire was distributed to a sample of undergraduate students enrolled at the University of Rhode Island. The questionnaires were distributed in classes but students were asked to complete the questionnaire, which as lengthy, at home and return it at the next class. In all, 673 questionnaires were distributed. Out of this number 447 usable questionnaires were returned (66.4%).

While it was not a random sample, care was taken to select classes in such a way as to ensure the sample would be broadly representative of the undergraduate population. Comparisons of the sample on the basis of sex, college year, and SAT scores indicate that this goal was substantially achieved although the sample somewhat overrepresents females (56% vs. 49%) and underrepresents juniors and seniors (36% vs. 46%). In the current analysis, responses of juniors and seniors are weighted by 1.3.[2]

The 23-page questionnaire was designed to replicate a number of studies employing student samples that were conducted in the 1950s. In a section on dating, in the middle of the questionnaire, students were asked a number of questions regarding their sexual behavior and attitudes, including an estimate of the average frequency of intercourse per month in the past year. The question regarding the effect of concern over AIDS was included near the end of the questionnaire in a section on social and political issues. It is thus unlikely that responses to the attitude and behavioral questions were biased by responses to the question regarding AIDS. Possible responses to the question on AIDS ranged from "no effect" through "caused me to be more selective in my choice of partners" and "to engage in sex less frequently" to "prevented me from becoming sexually active" and "caused me to stop having sex."

Also included in the analysis are measures of variables found to be related to premarital sex: sex, age, father's education, religious affiliation, attendance at religious services, perceptions of parental happiness, parents' marital status, SAT scores, attitudes toward premarital sex, frequency of dating, and whether the student is currently involved in a relationship or not. Unfortunately, given the purpose of this inquiry, no question regarding sexual preference was asked. . . .

Results

Concern with AIDS

Over 40% of the students, as can be seen in Table 1, report that a concern over AIDS has affected their sexual behavior in some way. As one would expect, concern is strongly related to whether or not the student is sexually active. The vast majority of those who are not active

Table 1. Effect of Concern over AIDS for Unmarried Students, by Sexual Activity

Reported Effect	*Sexual Activity*		
	Not Active	*Active*	*Total*
None	84.7%	45.9%	56.3%
Less frequent	—	1.2	1.1
More selective	—	30.0	21.8
More selective and less frequent	—	20.0	14.5
Stopped or prevented	15.3	2.9	6.3
Total	100.0%	100.0%	100.0%
(*n*)	(121)	(321)	(442)

report no effect, while over half of those who are sexually active claim to have been affected. Among the nonactive students, some 15% say they have been prevented from engaging in sexual intercourse by their concern over AIDS, and 3% of the sexually active students report a cessation of sexual activity as a result of their concern. The most common responses of sexually-active students who report an effect, however, are that they have become more selective in their choice of partners with no decrease in coital frequency (30%) and that they have become more selective with some decrease in frequency (20%).

. . . Only one variable, SAT scores, emerged as a significant predictor of non-sexually active students reporting they have been prevented from engaging in sexual activity. The direction of this relationship is negative. Among those whose scores are 1100 or more, only 9% claim to have been prevented, compared to 12% of those with scores between 900 and 1099 and 26% of those with scores under 900.

Responses of the sexually active students were grouped into three categories—"no effect," "more selective," and "more selective and less frequent." The last-named category also includes those who report having stopped engaging in sex and is referred to simply as "less frequent" in Table 2.[3] . . .

To clarify the differences among the three response groups even further, each group was profiled in terms of the significant discriminators. These data are presented in Table 2.

Table 2. Profile of Groups Defined by Response to AIDS (unmarried, sexually active students)

	Response to AIDS						
Discriminating Variable	*Total*	*No Effect*	*More Selective*	*Less Frequent*	*n*	*p*	*Cramer's V*
Female	54.4%	59.6%	38.0%	63.6%	289	.002	.21
Father a college graduate	42.5	45.6	43.6	34.7	287	.327	.09
Catholic or Jewish[a]	62.2	67.8	48.0	68.0	289	.007	.18
Date 1 per week +	49.6	58.3	52.0	28.6	288	.000	.24
Involved	53.4	65.9	40.3	43.3	289	.000	.24
Parents happy	58.2	53.7	63.6	61.2	285	.301	.09

[a]Catholic and Jewish are combined because of the small number of Jewish students ($n = 13$). The distribution of the responses of Jewish students was quite similar to that of Catholic students.

Consistent with the analysis above, response to AIDS is most strongly associated with involvement, dating frequency, sex, and religion. Those who claim no effect are disproportionate only in terms of the percentage who are currently involved, and this variable clearly sets them off from each of the other two groups. Students who claim to have become more selective are disproportionately males, Protestants or of no religious affiliation, and uninvolved. They are distinct from the other two groups both in sex and religion. Finally, those who report both greater selectivity and less frequency are disproportionately female, infrequent daters, and uninvolved. They are distinguished from the other students primarily in terms of their low dating frequency.

Involvement

As we have seen, students who report that AIDS has affected their behavior are less likely than others to be currently involved in a relationship. But they also differ from these other students in other ways (e.g., sex, religion, and attitudes toward sex) that may influence involvement. As a result of their greater selectivity, a larger percentage of them may now be involved than would otherwise be the case. . . .

If concern over AIDS were causing students to alter their behavior significantly, we might expect that a larger percentage of those who report becoming more selective should be currently involved in a relationship than is predicted on the basis of their background characteristics. In fact, however, it is those who claim no effect on their behavior who are more likely to be involved than is to be expected, while those who claim to have become selective, with and without a decrease in coital frequency, are involved just about as much as predicted from their sexual behavior and background characteristics. Thus, while these students may be becoming more selective in their choice of partners, it does not appear that a significant number of them have entered exclusive dating relationships as a result of their concerns.

Coital Frequency

Students who report a decrease in the frequency of intercourse as a result of concern over AIDS also reported significantly lower levels of coital frequency over the past year. . . .

Students who date more frequently, those who are involved in a relationship, who have been sexually active for a longer period of time, who hold permissive attitudes, who perceive their parents as unhappy, and who are female have higher levels of coital frequency.[4] With these factors taken into account, the reported decrease in frequency of intercourse as a result of fear of AIDS is not significantly related to the level of coital frequency in the past year. . . .

Conclusion

Contrary to popular accounts, the students in this sample express widespread concern about AIDS. Over half of the sexually active students claim they have altered their behavior in some way as a result of this concern, and 15% of the nonactive students report that their concern has prevented them from becoming sexually active. However, there is no relationship, net of other factors, between the changes reported by sexually active students and independent measures of their behavior. Those who claim to have become more selective in their choice of partners are not any more involved in relationships than is predicted on the basis of their background characteristics, and there is no relationship between a reported decrease in the frequency of sex and reported coital frequency over the past year.

Two explanations for these inconsistencies seem plausible. On the one hand, in the face of the publicity given AIDS, students may be reporting what they think they should be doing rather than what they are doing. On the other hand, the survey as administered so soon after the publicity began that students may have been in the process of altering their behavior and the changes they are making were not as yet so great as to be captured by the questions asked.

While the former explanation cannot be ruled out, the latter seems more consistent with the data. The expressed concerns of students are strongly related to factors indicative of both risk and behavioral predispositions. Those claiming an effect, for example, are clearly distinct from those claiming no effect by virtue of the lower percentage of them who are involved in exclusive relationships. Those claiming to be more selective are distinct only in being disproportionately male and of no religious affiliation. These students are much more widely active than others and may thus perceive greater risk, but the risk, as yet undefined, is perhaps not seen as sufficiently great to cause them to behave in ways radically at odds with the extremely permissive attitudes. And those who claim not only to be more selective but to engage in sex less frequently are disproportionately female and distinct from others in dating significantly less. This finding suggests the possibility that these students, who are more restrictive in their attitudes, while not establishing exclusive relationships, are in fact becoming more selective by dating less.

Finally, the finding that students who say they have been prevented from becoming sexually active have significantly lower SAT scores than others who are not active is an intriguing one. As they are indistinct from other virgins in terms of their religiousness and sexual attitudes, they do not appear to be like the potential nonvirgins identified by Herold and Goodwin (1981). Moreover, their SAT scores are also significantly lower than those of the sexually active students. Lacking sexual experience of nonvirgins and being of less ability and perhaps intellectual curiosity than others, these students perhaps have less information about AIDS. Dramatic media portrayals may thus cause them to overexaggerate the risk, thereby reinforcing their existing inhibitions with the perception of an all-pervasive, immediate threat.

This study has a number of limitations. Among them are the absence of information on questions such as sexual orientation, the number of people with whom a student had been sexually involved in the previous year, and the adoption of "safe sex" practices. The findings must therefore be seen as tentative. Nonetheless, it clearly shows that college students are more concerned with AIDS than previously believed and suggests they may have begun to alter their behavior in response to that concern.

NOTES

1. The National Center for Disease Control estimates that about 500,000 heterosexuals carry the virus, and in 1.8% of documented cases of AIDS the infection was transmitted heterosexually (Stone, 1987). There is considerable disagreement among medical researchers about how rapidly, and even if, AIDS will spread among the heterosexual population. Some experts note that virtually all known cases of heterosexual transmission involve sex with members of a high-risk group, primarily IV-drug users and bisexuals. Others point to the experience of Africa and predict that it is only a matter of time before a similar pattern develops here unless there are radical changes in behavior.
2. Percentages reported in the following tables are based on the weighted number of cases. There are in some instances slight discrepancies between the number of cases reported and the number that would be calculated with the reported percentages. These discrepancies are due to rounding errors involved in the weighting procedure.
3. Four students who reported only engaging in sex less frequently were dropped from the analysis so as not to confuse interpretations about the process by which a decrease in frequency occurs, if, in fact, it does.

4. Given popular stereotypes, the finding that unmarried female college students engage in sex more frequently than males may be surprising to some. It is, however, consistent with previous research (DeLamater and MacCorquodale, 1979: 68; Katz and Cronin, 1980).

REFERENCES

DeLamater, John, and Patricia MacCorquodale. 1979. Premarital Sexuality. Madison: University of Wisconsin Press.

Herold, Edward S., and Marilyn S. Goodwin. 1981. "Adamant virgins, potential nonvirgins, and nonvirgins." *Journal of Sex Research* 17: 97–113.

Katz, Joseph, and Denise M. Cronin. 1980. "Sexuality and college life." *Change* 12: 44–48.

Leishman, Katie. 1987. "Heterosexuals and AIDS." *Atlantic Monthly,* February, pp. 39–58.

Smilgis, Martha. 1987. "The big chill: Fear of AIDS." *Time,* February 16: pp. 50–53.

Stone, Michael. 1987. "Q. and A. on AIDS." *New York Magazine,* March 23, pp. 34–43.

DEVELOPING YOUR OWN SNAPSHOTS *About Social Change and Collective Behavior*

1. *Research topic:* This task requires some library work. Find a best-selling magazine that has been around for several decades and contains advertisement photos featuring men and women. Select at least a couple of different time periods—for example, war versus peace, prosperity versus recession. Examine each ad photo to determine how changes in the larger society may have influenced fashions of the day. Be sure to keep a written record of important information such as the year, magazine title, whether the model in an ad was a man or a woman, and so on.
2. *Research topic:* Construct a sociological "family tree" of social changes over the generations. For example, go back in your own family at least two generations, comparing yourself with your parents and grandparents. Compare the generations on such variables as (a) last year of school completed, (b) jobs held, (c)place of birth, (d) favorite music, (e) the racial composition of the block on which they grew up, (f) attitudes toward family life, and (g) cost of a single-family home or monthly rent.
3. *Writing topic:* After conducting research in question 2, write a short essay in which you discuss social changes over three generations, using your own family to illustrate your discussion.
4. *Research topic:* Investigate changes in the importance of gossip in election campaigns by locating library files of a daily newspaper that has been around for a few decades. Compare the front-page newspaper coverage of any presidential election campaign before 1970 versus the 1992 campaign coverage. You might want

to read just the front page of Sunday papers beginning with the Iowa caucus or the New Hampshire primary and ending with election day. How many references do you find concerning the personal lives of the candidates? How many references do you find regarding their moral character? How have the "issues" changed? Finally, how many of these reports are based on unidentified or "reliable" sources?

5. *Writing topic:* The role of the automobile—as an item of material culture—in social change has been discussed. Unlike Canada and many European countries, America never developed its system of public transportation to its maximum potential. In a short essay, develop the argument that the automobile industry is largely responsible for maintaining our love affair (or should I say, marriage) with the automobile to the exclusion of alternatives like public buses, trains, and subways.
6. *Research topic:* According to Murty, Roebuck, and Armstrong's study of the 1992 Los Angeles riots, rioters often see themselves as freedom fighters rather than criminals. How effective are such civil disturbances at provoking social change? To find out, examine newspaper accounts following the 1992 Los Angeles riots. In particular, look for any public or private policies—for example, welfare expenditures or assistance to minority business—that were initiated or enhanced in response to the rioting.
7. *Research topic:* Using Leo Carroll's ("Concern with AIDS and the Sexual Behavior of College Students") questions as a guide, prepare a one-page questionnaire to determine how fear of contracting AIDS may have altered the dating behavior of students on your campus. Photocopy your questionnaire and give it to a small sample of students (say, 30 or 40). Then, after your data have been collected, calculate the percentage of students giving each response. How do your results differ from those obtained by Carroll?
8. *Writing topic:* The photo essay for this section asks whether college students are part of a distinct and separate "Generation X." Using your own experiences and those of your friends and classmates as a guide, explain how your generation is different from those before you. How do you anticipate the generation following yours will be different? Why do such generational differences occur?

Into the Future

One of the most important goals of sociology as a social science is to make accurate predictions. As far as the major problems of American society are concerned, William J. Wilson's *The Truly Disadvantaged* (Chicago: University of Chicago Press, 1987) has focused squarely on the state of the black underclass. If Wilson is correct, the ranks of the permanently unemployed may continue to swell. However, the future of poverty in America was at least vaguely discernible decades ago. In 1973 Daniel Bell was already speculating about the characteristics of postindustrial America in *The Coming of the Postindustrial Society: A Venture in Social Forecasting* (New York: Basic Books).

In *Forecasting Crime Data* (Lexington, Massachusetts: Lexington Books, 1978), my colleague James A. Fox shows how sociologists can successfully project the future based on demographic data. He correctly predicted the soaring crime rate we are presently experiencing. Unfortunately, he sees more of the same in the years ahead.

But sociologists aren't psychics; we don't pretend to have perfectly clear snapshots of the future. (We are doing well to come up with clear pictures of the present.) Like economists and political scientists, we may be willing to occasionally take an educated guess about the direction of society, admitting that there are too many variables to make precise predictions about almost anything. Sure, X will grow, unless, of course, Y suddenly declines. A will improve, assuming, of course, B isn't modified first. We don't always know Y and B, so our projections about X and A are less than perfect. And we haven't even mentioned the assumptions we make about the many other important variables that influence changes in social structure and culture.

It's not just sociologists, of course, who are imperfect prognosticators. Few economists were able to predict the energy shortage that began in 1973; even fewer political scientists forecast the crumbling of the Berlin Wall or the toppling of the Soviet Union. And our 1991 Persian Gulf war seemed to come out of nowhere, as far as the literature of social science is concerned.

By the year 2000, the leading edge of the baby boomer generation will be well into the late 50s, and their children will be approaching young adulthood. Like every other generation, the baby boomers will make plans to retire from the labor force. However, they won't feel pressured to do so. Instead, they are likely to be offered incentives to remain in what is likely to become an ever-shrinking labor force. At this point you can expect the typical retirement age to move from 65 to 70 or even older. Early retirement will all but disappear as an option.

Also by the turn of the century, the children of the baby boomers will be deeply entrenched in the crime-prone age group—the late teens through early twenties (there will be a 17 percent increase in teenagers over the next decade)—and the rate of violent crime is likely to soar, even by today's horrific standards. For the same reason, college admissions requirements are likely to become increasingly competitive. Academically marginal and older students (those often called "nontraditional" by college administrators) will have to compete against growing numbers of traditionally defined college-aged students—the children of the baby boomers between the ages of 18 and 22. Academic late bloomers are likely to lose out as they are no longer wooed by formerly eager admissions committees.

If they are like every generation to precede them, the aging baby boomers will reduce their spending and stop using credit cards. As they actually begin to retire from the labor force, the boomers will, as a result, finally forfeit their cultural clout as well. Just as members of the twenty-something generation presently feel they are playing second fiddle to the boomers, so many young Americans in the future will resent the presence of huge numbers of retired elders who draw social security benefits and require expensive health care.

By the year 2000 multiculturalism will become a focal point of social change. Growing numbers of immigrants and minorities—African, Asian, and Latin Americans—will ensure that white Anglo-Saxons are no longer the majority. In our postindustrial society there will be growing conflict between groups for scarce economic resources.

In their recent effort, *The Good Society* (New York: Knopf, 1991), Robert Bellah, Richard Madsen, William Sullivan, Ann Swidler, and Steven Tipton argue that we can solve our growing social problems by transforming our institutions—our schools, families, corporations, churches, and state. As they so eloquently did in *Habits of the*

Heart, Bellah et al. decry the rise of raw individualism in American society. Calling for public debate concerning our social ills, they propose a blueprint for the future of American society. In *The Good Society* they assert that we are fully capable of changing our values and taking responsibility for our economic and political institutions.

The technological outlook may be even rosier, according to Gene Bylinski. In an article in *Fortune* (July 18, 1988) titled "Technology in the Year 2000," he is sanguine about our ability to employ future technological discoveries in order to heal the human body and help us to live fuller lives.

Sociology has often been regarded as subversive. In a sense, it is. That is, sociologists often challenge our taken-for-granted assumptions, the status quo, and, more precisely, the people in charge of things. No wonder totalitarian societies rarely permit their college students to study the field of sociology; or, when they do, they keep it under rigid controls. For the same reason, even in societies that permit greater freedom of choice, sociologists aren't always welcome or appreciated. They might rock the political boat. They might advocate expensive programs and policies. Their research might be useful to reformists who agitate for social change.

The importance of the field of sociology—or, more precisely, the collective respect for it—varies according to the urgency of our social problems and the extent of our prosperity as a society. In popular cultural terms, we have to believe that we *need* sociologists, but we also have to feel we can *afford* them. The "hip generation" of the 1960s and early 1970s, for example, saw a heyday for the field. By 1973 the number of college students earning bachelor's degrees in sociology had reached a record high of 35,996. Inflation was relatively low, the economy was growing, and there were several important social issues to inspire interest. Civil rights, feminism, and war were on almost everybody's mind. Our inner cities were burning while thousands marched through the streets to protest, demonstrate, or riot. As a result, millions looked to social scientists for advice about how to run society, how to solve the urgent problems of the day. Not that anyone in charge implemented the answers that sociologists provided, but at least we were asked.

In the February 3, 1992, issue of *Newsweek,* reporter Barbara Kantrowitz, in her article "Sociology's Lonely Crowd," summarizes some of the problems and prospects of the discipline. She reports that by 1989 the number of students receiving bachelor's degrees in sociology had dwindled to only 14,393. Long holding a reputation as being among the more liberal of the arts and sciences, sociology apparently did not fit very well into the cultural milieu of the 1980s. Students turned to majors such as business and engineering—majors they considered to be more practical. Many undergraduates enrolled in specialized professional programs—criminal justice, social work, urban studies, and market research—that began in and are actually offshoots of sociology.

In the last few years, however, we have seen a reversal of this trend. Enrollment in sociology courses is again on the rise. We are just beginning to recognize the need to address growing social problems like homelessness, crime, and poverty. The black underclass is perhaps four times larger today than it was in the 1960s when civil disorder enveloped our major cities in flames. Kids are murdering one another at ever-younger ages. If present trends continue unabated, it is safe to predict that sociologists will gain prominence in the next century. Our nation continues to struggle with long-standing problems that reduce our quality of life and frustrate our collective aspirations. Finding effective solutions will require that we put aside our differences and pull together as a society. It is to be hoped that Americans will rise to the challenge.

References

Allport, Gordon, & Postman, Leo (1952). The basic psychology of rumor. In G. E. Swanson, T. M. Newcomb, & E. L. Hartley (Eds.), *Readings in social psychology.* New York: Holt.

Anastos, Ernie (1983). *Twixt: Teens yesterday and today.* New York: Franklin Watts.

Anti-Defamation League (1988, October). "JAP baiting": When sexism and anti-Semitism meet. *ADL Periodic Update* (New York).

Archer, Dane, & Gartner, Rosemary (1984). *Violence and crime in cross-national perspective.* New Haven, CT: Yale University Press.

Arms, Robert, et al. (1979, September). Effects of viewing aggressive sports on the hostility of spectators. *Social Psychology Quarterly.*

Asch, Solomon (1952). Effects of group pressure upon the modifcation and distortion of judgment. In G. E. Swanson (Ed.), *Readings in social psychology.* New York: Rinehart & Winston.

Ball-Rokeach, Sandra, & Cantor, Muriel (1986). *Media, audience, and social structure.* Newbury Park, CA: Sage.

Barcus, F. Earle (1983). *Images of life on chidren's television: Sex roles, minorities, and families.* New York: Praeger.

Bateson, Mary Catherine (1990). *Composing a life.* New York: Plume.

Becker, Howard S. (1967, Winter). Whose side are we on? *Social Problems.*

Bell, Daniel (1973). *The coming of the postindustrial society: A venture in social forecasting.* New York: Basic Books.

Bellah, Robert, Madsen, Richard, Sullivan, William, Swidler, Ann, & Tipton, Steven (1985). *Habits of the heart: Individualism and commitment in American life.* Berkeley: University of California Press

Bellah, Robert, Madsen, Richard, Sullivan, William, Swidler, Ann, & Tipton, Steven (1991). *The good society.* New York: Knopf.

Bowers, William J. (1974). *Executions in America.* Lexington, MA: Lexington.

Breines, Winifred (1992). *Young, white, and miserable: Growing up female in the fifties.* Boston: Beacon.

Butler, Robert (1975). *Why survive? Being old in America.* New York: Harper & Row.

Bylinski, Gene (1988, July 18). Technology in the year 2000. *Fortune.*

Cantor, Muriel, & Pingree, Suzanne (1983). *The soap opera.* Newbury Park, CA: Sage.

Centers, Richard (1949). *The psychology of social classes* (Princeton: Princeton University Press).

Chernin, Kim (1981). *The obsession: Reflections on the tyranny of slenderness.* New York: Harper & Row.

Chudacoff, Howard (1989). *How old are you?* Princeton, NJ: Princeton University Press.

Cooley, Charles H. (1909). *Social organization.* New York: Free Press.

Coser, Lewis (1956). *The functions of social conflict.* New York: Free Press.

Davis, Kingsley, & Moore, Wilbert (1945, April). Some principles of stratification. *American Sociological Review.*

Donnerstein, Edward, Linz, Daniel, & Penrod, Steven (1987). *The question of pornography.* New York: Free Press.

Durkheim, Emile (1933). *The division of labor in society.* New York: Free Press.

Durkheim, Emile (1951). *Suicide: A study in sociology.* New York: Free Press.

Durkheim, Emile (1964; originally published 1897). *Suicide.* Glencoe, IL: Free Press.

Durkheim, Emile (1965). *The elementary forms of religious life.* New York: Free Press.

Durkheim, Emile (1966). *The rules of sociological method.* New York: Free Press.

Ehrlich, Howard V. (1990). *Campus ethnoviolence and the policy options.* Baltimore: National Institute Against Prejudice and Violence.

Faludi, Susan (1991). *Backlash: The undeclared war against American women.* New York: Crown.

Fox, James A. (1978). *Forecasting crime data.* Lexington, MA: Lexington.

Gans, Herbert J. (1972, September). The positive functions of poverty. *American Journal of Sociology.*

Gerbner, George, Gross, Larry, Morgan, Michael, & Signorielli, Nancy (1982). Charting the mainstream: Television's contributions to political orientations. *Journal of Communication, 32.*

Gerth, H. H., & Mills, C. Wright (Eds.) (1946). *Max Weber: Essays in sociology.* New York: Oxford University Press.

Glazer, Myron Peretz, & Glazer, Penina Migdal (1989). *The whistleblowers: Exposing corruption in government and industry.* New York: Basic Books.

Goffman, Erving (1961). *Asylums: Essays on the social situation of mental patients and other inmates.* Chicago: Aldine.

Goffman, Erving (1963). *Stigma: Notes on the management of spoiled identity.* Englewood Cliffs, NJ: Prentice-Hall.

Goldstein, Jeffrey (1986). *Aggression and crimes of violence.* New York: Oxford University Press.

Goode, Erich (1984). *Deviant behavior.* New York: Prentice Hall.

Gottfredson, Michael, & Hirschi, Travis (1990). *A general theory of crime.* Stanford, CA: Stanford University Press.

Harris, Marvin (1979). *Cultural materialism.* New York: Random House.

Hughes, Everett (1962, Summer). Good people and dirty work. *Social Problems.*

Jensen, Arthur R. (1969, Winter). How much can we boost I.Q. and scholastic achievement? *Harvard Education Review.*

Johnson, Richard (1985). *American fads.* New York: Beech Tree.

Jones, Landon Y. (1980). *Great expectations: America and the baby boom generation.* New York: Ballantine.

Kanter, Rosabeth M. (1977). *Men and women of the corporation.* New York: Basic Books.

Kantrowitz, Barbara (1992, February 3). Sociology's lonely crowd. *Newsweek.*

Katz, Jack (1988). *Seductions of crime: Moral and sensual attractions of doing evil.* New York: Basic Books.

Kaufman, Debra Renee (1991). *Rachel's daughters.* New Brunswick, NJ: Rutgers University Press.

Keen, Sam (1986). *Faces of the enemy: Reflections of the hostile imagination.* San Francisco: Harper & Row.

Kennedy, Daniel, & Kerber, August (1973). *Resocialization: An American experiment.* New York: Behavioral Publications.

Koenig, Fredrick (1985). *Rumor in the marketplace: The social psychology of commercial hearsay.* Dover, MA: Auburn House.

Kohn, Alfie (1990). *The brighter side of human nature.* New York: Basic Books.

Largey, Gale, & Watson, David (1972). The sociology of odors. *American Journal of Sociology, 77.*

Le Bon, Gustave (1960; originally published 1895). *The crowd.* New York: Viking.

Leinberger, Paul, & Tucker, Bruce (1991). *The new individualists: The generation after the organization man.* New York: HarperCollins.

Levin, Jack, & Arluke, Arnold (1987). *Gossip: The inside scoop.* New York: Plenum.

Levin, Jack, Arluke, Arnold, & Levin, William C. (1992). *Powerful elders.* Paper presented at the annual meeting of the American Sociological Association.

Levin, Jack, & Fox, James A. (1991). *Mass murder: America's growing menace.* New York: Berkeley.

Levin, Jack, & Levin, William C. (1980). *Ageism: Prejudice and discrimination against the elderly.* Belmont, CA: Wadsworth.

Levin, Jack, & Levin, William C. (1982). *The functions of discrimination and prejudice.* New York: Harper & Row.

Levin, Jack, & Levin, William C. (1991, December). Sociology of educational late-blooming. *Sociological Forum.*

Levin, Jack, & McDevitt, Jack (1993). *Hate crimes: The rising tide of bigotry and bloodshed.* New York: Plenum.

Leyton, Elliott (1986). *Compulsive killers.* New York: Washington News.

Linton, Ralph (1936). *The study of man.* New York: Appleton.

Lurie, Alison (1981). *The language of clothing.* New York: Random House.

Lynd, Robert S., & Lynd, Helen M. (1929). *Middletown.* New York: Harcourt Brace.

Mark, Vernon H., & Ervin, Frank R. (1970). *Violence and the Brain.* New York: Harper & Row.

Marx, Karl (1967; originally published 1895). *Das kapital.* New York: International Publishers.

Marx, Karl, & Engels, Frederick (1964). *On religion.* New York: Schocken.

Mead, George H. (1934). *Mind, self and society.* Chicago: University of Chicago Press.

Mecca, Andrew, Smelser, Neil, & Vasconcellos, John (Eds.) (1989). *The social importance of self-esteem.* Berkeley: University of California Press.

Merry, Sally E. (1984). Rethinking gossip and scandal. In Donald Black (Ed.), *Toward a general theory of social control.* Orlando, FL: Academic Press.

Merton, Robert K. (1957). *Social theory and social structure.* Glencoe, IL: Free Press.

Millman, Marcia (1980). *Such a pretty face.* New York: Simon & Schuster.

Mirowsky, John, & Ross, Catherine (1989). *Social causes of psychological distress.* New York: Aldine de Gruyter.

Murdock, George P. (1949). *Social structure.* New York: Macmillan.

Murray, Charles, & Herrnstein, Richard J. (1994). *The bell curve.* New York: The Free Press.

Newman, Katherine (1988). *Falling from grace: The experience of downward mobility in the American middle class.* New York: Free Press.

Ogburn, William F. (1922). *Social change.* New York: Viking.

Oliner, Samuel, & Oliner, Pearl (1988). *The altruistic personality.* New York: Free Press.

Orbach, Susie (1978). *Fat is a feminist issue.* New York: Paddington.

Parsons, Talcott (1937). *The structure of social action.* New York: McGraw–Hill.

Phillips, David (1983, August). The impact of mass media violence on U.S. homicides. *American Sociological Review.*

Phillips, Kevin (1990). *The politics of the rich and the poor.* New York: Random House.

Portes, Alejandro, & Rumbaut, Ruben G. (1990). *Immigrant America: A portrait.* Berkeley: University of California Press.

Reiman, Jeffrey (1986). *The rich get richer and the poor get prison.* New York: John Wiley.

Riesman, David, et al. (1950). *The lonely crowd.* New Haven, CT: Yale University Press.

Rosenhan, David (1973). On being sane in insane places. *Science.*

Rosenthal, Robert, & Jacobson, Lenore (1968). *Pygmalion in the classroom.* New York: Holt.

Rosnow, Ralph, & Fine, Gary (1976). *Rumor and gossip: The social psychology of hearsay.* New York: Elsevier.

Shibutani, Tamotsu (1966). *Improvised news.* Indianapolis: Bobbs-Merrill

Sieber, Samuel (1981). *Fatal remedies.* New York: Plenum.

Sipes, Richard G. (1973). War, sports, and aggression. *American Anthropologist, 75.*

Sorokin, Pitirim A. (1937). *Social and cultural dynamics.* New York: American Books.

Spiro, Melvin E. (1956). *Kibbutz: Venture in utopia.* Cambridge, MA: Harvard University Press.

Stipp, David (1992, March 4). The insanity defense in violent-crime cases gets high-tech help. *Wall Street Journal.*

Sumner, William Graham (1906). *Folkways.* Boston: Ginn.

Tumin, Melvin (1953, August). Some principles of stratification: A critical analysis. *American Sociological Review, 18.*

Weber, Max (1946). *From Max Weber: Essays in sociology.* New York: Oxford University.

Weber, Max (1958). *The Protestant ethic and the spirit of capitalism.* New York: Scribner's.

Whyte, William H. (1956). *The organization man.* New York Simon & Schuster.

Wilson, William J. (1987). *The truly disadvantaged.* Chicago: University of Chicago Press.

Wolf, Naomi (1992). *Beauty myth.* New York: Doubleday.

Wright, Charles R. (1986). *Mass communication: A sociological perspective* New York: Random House.

Wrong, Dennis H. (1961). The oversocialized conception of man in modern sociology. *American Sociological Review, 26.*

Zimbardo, Philip C., Haney, Craig, & Banks, William C. (1973, April 8). A Pirandellian prison. *New York Times Magazine.*

Zurubavel, Eviatar (1981). *Hidden rhythms: Schedules and calendars in social life.* Chicago: University of Chicago Press.

INDEX

C

D

E

L

M

N

T

U

V

W

X

Y

Z